CHARITIE

An Industry Accou

Auditing Gui

GW01048568

CHARITIES

An Industry Accounting and Auditing Guide

Third edition

David Chitty
Nick Morgan
Chantrey Vellacott DFK

abg
professional
information

40 Bernard Street
London
WC1N 1QP
Tel: 020 7920 8991
Fax: 020 7920 8992
Website: www.abgweb.com

© 2001 The Institute of Chartered Accountants in England and Wales.

ISBN 1-84140-157-9

First edition 1995
Reprinted 1995
Second edition 1997

British Library Cataloguing-in-Publication Data
A catalogue record for this book is available from the British Library.

Throughout this book the male pronoun has been used to cover references to both the male and female.

Typeset by Mac Style Ltd, Scarborough, North Yorkshire
Printed and bound in Great Britain by Clays, Bungay, Suffolk

Foreword by David Taylor

The new edition of this Guide comes out just over a year after the publication of the revised SORP 'Accounting and Reporting by Charities'. This SORP is really only just getting into its stride, with accounts commencing on or after 1 January 2001 required to comply but with early adoption encouraged by the Charity Commission. This publication should help all users to achieve high standards in reporting to and relating with the public and other stakeholders.

The Guide is not just about accounting and auditing. There is plenty to interest those concerned with the wider charity environment as well as those who need to know 'how to run things'. An example is the extensive treatment of the regulatory framework. I am delighted that there is extensive cross-referencing to and extensive quotation from Charity Commission publications.

While much water has flowed under the bridge since early 1997, when the previous edition of the Guide was published, much remains the same. Charity accountability is still a major issue, but now even more so. The study of the voluntary sector by the Government's Policy and Innovation Unit has also identified and confirmed many areas where change could be made.

At a time when some trustees perceive that their task is becoming more of a challenge, chapters on their responsibilities and liabilities are particularly helpful.

Fundraising has not been forgotten. This is just as well, with this aspect of charitable activity attracting so much attention from all sides. Tax measures to promote giving have not been forgotten. This information is supplemented with help on business and trading income, an aspect of charity management that creates some headaches for management and which is a frequent cause of concern to the Commission.

The Guide provides very comprehensive coverage of SORP 2000, not just what the SORP requires for the Accounts and Trustees' Report, but helpful chapters detailing many of the individual requirements. There is help not only with the basic framework of the statement of financial activities, the balance sheet, cash flow statement and consolidated accounts, but also with reserves, fund accounting and risk management. Even accounting policies and the notes to the accounts receive a healthy airing! SORP 1995 raised the temperature on recognition and consolidation of branches; those affected will find this aspect extensively covered.

For those of a technical persuasion, there is also full treatment of relevant Accounting Standards and many of the angles to be considered in deciding whether to incorporate or not. Other general management issues are catered for, with extensive help on VAT issues and employment law.

An understanding of the role and responsibilities of those who carry out the statutory review of accounts is helpful, not only for existing and potential reviewers, but also for those reviewed. The Guide appropriately offers detailed coverage of the statutory audit and independent examination.

The importance of small charities is recognised, with coverage of the different and softer approach to regulation ... they are, after all, in the majority.

So, there is a great amount of detail on many aspects of charity governance, accounting and auditing. This is a book to be dipped into as a work of reference and is a welcome assembly of information for many who work in the sector.

David Taylor
Charity Commissioner
November 2001

Preface and acknowledgements

In April 1997 Richard Derwent noted in the Preface to the second edition of this publication that 'it would be very useful if in, say, two years the SORP is revisited and its recommendations reviewed in the light of its initial implementation and any changes to other statutes'. It was in fact in September 1998 that a consultation exercise was launched in order to carry out that review and, following an exposure draft of the revised SORP in December 1999, the final version was issued in October 2000.

Although a full overview of the revised SORP is given in chapter 5, most people consider that the areas which will affect charities are the additional reporting requirements in respect of risk and reserves and, where applicable, investments and grants, together with the changes in the presentation of the statement of financial activities.

The format of the revised SORP is an enormous improvement on its predecessor and the new special sections are particularly welcome as is the concept of certain paragraphs being marked **AA**, indicating that these paragraphs must be addressed by all charities. The third edition of this publication therefore concentrates on the revised SORP whilst much of the general and background information has been retained from the earlier edition. There are however some new chapters and in particular those on fundraising, reserves, incorporated charities and risk management.

The new (2000) Regulations and SORP do not have to be implemented until accounting periods beginning on or after 1 January 2001 and therefore at the time of publication of this book there are limited practical examples of the new SORP to draw upon as most charities have chosen not to make the changes earlier than necessary. The examples in the book therefore draw extensively from the book of examples (CC66) produced by the Charity Commission as we feel that these very adequately reflect not only the provisions, but also the spirit, of the revised SORP.

We are indebted to a number of people within Chantrey Vellacott DFK for their contributions to this book and in particular to Alan Thomson and Peter Ladanyi, who wrote the revised chapters dealing with taxation, Sally Kirby for her contribution to chapter 20 together with a number of secretarial staff who greatly assisted in the preparation of the draft text. We are also grateful to the Charity Commissioners for allowing us to reproduce extensively from their various publications.

David Chitty and Nick Morgan
November 2001

Contents

Contents

Contents

Abbreviations

Unless stated otherwise, the following abbreviations are used in this book:

Professional and regulatory bodies:

AAPA	Association of Authorised Public Accountants
ACCA	Association of Chartered Certified Accountants
APB	Auditing Practices Board
ASB	Accounting Standards Board
ASC	Accounting Standards Committee
CCAB	Consultative Committee of Accountancy Bodies
CIPFA	Chartered Institute of Public Finance and Accountancy
Commissioners	Charity Commissioners
DTI	Department of Trade and Industry
ICAEW	Institute of Chartered Accountants in England and Wales
ICAI	Institute of Chartered Accountants in Ireland
ICAS	Institute of Chartered Accountants in Ireland
NCVO	National Council for Voluntary Organisations
Registrar	Registrar of Companies
UITF	Urgent Issues Task Force

Accounting and statutory terms:

1960 Act	Charities Act 1960
1985 Act	Companies Act 1985
1989 Act	Companies Act 1989
1992 Act	Charities Act 1992
1993 Act	Charities Act 1993
AG	Auditing Guideline
ED	Exposure Draft
FA	Finance Act
FRAG	Financial Reporting and Auditing Group
FRS	Financial Reporting Standard
ICTA	Income and Corporation Taxes Act
IHTA	Inheritance Tax Act
para	Paragraph
Pt	Part
reg	regulation

s	section
SAS	Statement of Auditing Standards
Sch	Schedule
SI	Statutory Instrument
SOFA	Statement of Financial Activities
SORP	Statement of Recommended Practice 'Accounting by charities'
SSAP	Statement of Standard Accounting Practice
SSRA	Statement of Standards for Reporting Accountants
TCGA	Taxation of Chargeable Gains Act
The Regulations	The Charities (Accounts and Reports) Regulations 1995
TR	Technical Release

Unless otherwise stated paragraph references are to the SORP.

Chapter 1 – Definitions, registration, status and names

1.1 Introduction

The 1960 Act introduced a requirement for a register of charities to be established and maintained by the Commissioners and for all charities, generally unless exempt or excepted, to be registered. The register remains at the heart of the Commissioners' work.

The register provides both potential donors and other interested members of the public with access to basic information on the existence of registered charities, their purposes and administrative structure. It is, also, an important resource to the Commissioners in their monitoring and supervision. In addition, the process of registration allows the Commissioners to:

'ensure that an organisation's objects are charitable in law and to try to secure that its constitution is appropriate. The point of registration thus provides a key opportunity for the development of the law on charitable status in the light of changing needs and of public perceptions of the proper scope of charity' (see 1994 Annual Report of the Commissioners, p. 6).

To be effective, the register must be both accurate and up to date. In accordance with the recommendations of the Woodfield Report (*Efficiency scrutiny of the supervision of charities*), published in 1987, the register has now been computerised. The completion and submission of an annual return to the Commissioners should ensure systematic updating.

Some changes have been made as regards the arrangements for exemptions and exceptions from registration. Larger registered charities are now required to state the fact that they are registered on certain business documents and provisions, similar to those in the 1985 Act, have been introduced regarding the acceptability of charity names.

1.2 Definition of a charity

Section 96(1) of the 1993 Act states that, unless the context otherwise requires, 'charity' means:

'... Any institution, corporate or not, which is established for charitable purposes and is subject to the control of the High Court in the exercise of the court's jurisdiction with respect to charities.'

However, s96(2) states that the expression 'charity' is not, in that Act, applicable:

'(a) to any ecclesiastical corporation (that is to say, any corporation in the Church of England, whether sole or aggregate, which is established for spiritual purposes) in respect of the corporate property of the corporation, except to a corporation aggregate, having some purposes which are not ecclesiastical in respect of its corporate property held for those purposes;

(b) to any Diocesan Board of Finance within the meaning of the Endowments and Glebe Measure 1976 for any diocese in respect of the diocesan glebe land of that diocese within the meaning of that Measure; or

(c) to any trust of property for purposes for which the property has been consecrated.'

As regards subsection 2(a), as a Dean and Chapter (or a Provost and Chapter) is an ecclesiastical corporation aggregate established for charitable purposes, the corporate property of cathedrals would, for example, fall outside the scope of the Commissioners' jurisdiction. It can, therefore, be concluded that cathedrals are not obliged to comply with the new accounting requirements prescribed by the 1993 Act, except to the extent that they may hold corporate property for non-ecclesiastical purposes or trust property other than in respect of consecrated land and buildings. Cathedrals are, however, required to produce annual audited accounts to the Church Commissioners, under the provisions of the Cathedrals Measure 1963.

The definition provided by para 3 of Appendix 1 to the revised charity SORP is wider:

'A "charity" is any institution established for purposes which are exclusively charitable. Where the institution is involved in more than one activity, operates more than one fund, or is not centralised into one unit of operation, the term is used in this statement to include all those activities, units and funds which fall within the scope of a single governing instrument (or instruments supplemental to the main instrument) or for which the trustees are otherwise legally liable to account (e.g., branches ...).'

The aim has been to embrace all activities which fall within the charity trustees' responsibility. This should, *inter alia*, help trustees identify which activities should be accounted for within the accounts of the main charity.

Whilst not charities for the limited purposes of the 1993 Act, cathedrals are nonetheless established for exclusively charitable purposes. (That was made clear in the debates on the Charities Bill of 1960, the Lord Chancellor emphasising that ecclesiastical corporations would continue to enjoy the income tax and rating reliefs they had enjoyed, as charities, previously, see House of Lords debates 1 March 1960, col. 647.) Accordingly, unless a more specialised SORP applies, cathedrals will need to comply with the revised charity SORP.

1.2.1 'Any institution, corporate or not'

A charity is a legal entity that may be created in a number of different ways. For example, by declaration of trust, whereby a person declares that he holds certain property on trust or for a specific permitted object or purpose, or by conveyance to a trustee, whereby a person transfers property to another person in order for him to hold it on trust.

Another form of legal structure is the unincorporated association (although not partnerships, as trading with a view to making a profit would not be consistent with the charitable purpose). Many smaller local charities, such as parent/teacher associations, are set up in this way and produce a rule book to act as their governing document.

Charities incorporated under the Companies Acts are usually formed as companies limited by guarantee. They are subject, generally without dispensation, to the same accounting and disclosure provisions as companies limited by shares. Many larger charities are constituted as such.

Some charities are incorporated under the Industrial and Provident Societies Act 1965. This category includes the majority of housing associations which are subject to the complex accounting and disclosure requirements of the Housing Corporation, under the Housing Acts and statutory accounting requirements (Determinations).

Several charities, for example Nightingale House (The Home for Aged Jews), whose original trusts have become out of date, may be governed by a 'scheme' made by the Commissioners under, what are now, ss16 and 17 of the 1993 Act.

Some are incorporated by Royal Charter, including the Royal National Lifeboat Institution, the Royal Society for the Protection of Birds and the British Red Cross Society. Others are formed under their own special Act of Parliament, such as The National Trust and the Royal Society for the Prevention of Cruelty to Animals. In these circumstances, their constitutions are governed by their own charter, or Act.

Paragraph 30(b) of the revised SORP recommends that an indication of the nature of the governing document and how the charity is, or its trustees are, constituted are given in, or appended to, the trustees' annual report.

Rather than on its constitutional form, however, whether or not an institution is a charity will depend on what it has been established to do.

1.2.2 'Established for charitable purposes'

As chapter 2 of the White Paper *Charities: A framework for the future* (Cm 694) said:

'The starting point for the modern law of England and Wales is found in the preamble to the Statute of Elizabeth I (the Charitable Uses Act, 1601). Guidance on what was to be considered charitable was found there in a list of objects which included:

"Relief of aged impotent and poor people ... the maintenance of sick and maimed soldiers and mariners, schools of learning, free schools and scholars in universities ... the repair of bridges, ports, havens, causeways, churches and others."

'For all practical purposes the courts have, for many years, accepted the classification which was made by Lord Macnaghten in 1891 in what has now become well-known as the "Pemsel" case (Income Tax Special Commissioners v Pemsel). This classification (which does not constitute a definition) reads as follows:

"Charity in its legal sense comprises four principal divisions-trusts for the relief of poverty, trusts for the advancement of education, trusts for the advancement of religion, and trusts for other purposes beneficial to the community, not falling under any of the previous heads."

'Lord Macnaghten's classification has largely superseded the 1601 preamble, though in doubtful cases which arise under the head of "purposes beneficial to the community" the courts still refer to the preamble for guidance. The loose framework, which was set by the 1601 preamble and clarified by Lord Macnaghten, has enabled the courts over the years to develop the law in a way which has been sensitive to changing needs whilst maintaining the fundamental principles on which the concept of charity rests.'

From time to time there have been proposals that a definition of charity be formulated and given statutory effect. The White Paper suggested that by:

'(i)   listing the purposes which are deemed to be charitable;
 (ii) enacting a definition of charity based on Lord Macnaghten's classification; or
 (iii) defining "charitable purposes" as "purposes beneficial to the community".'

However, the White Paper reported that:

'The Government consider that an attempt to define charity by any of these means would be fraught with difficulty, and might put at risk the flexibility of the present law which is both its greatest strength and its most valuable feature.

In particular, they consider that there would be great dangers in attempting to specify in statute those objects which are to be regarded as charitable.

'Even if it was possible to draw up a list which could command a reasonable measure of agreement it might well lead to the exclusion of trusts which have long been treated as charitable, depriving them of any means of enforcement. A list might be inflexible and quickly outdated by changing public opinion. Listing the details in statute would not evade for long the problems which are inherent in any system of case law. Disputes would undoubtedly quickly arise on which the courts would be asked to adjudicate. There is no reason to believe that a new body of case law would be any less complex than the old.

'... Unless it were proposed to preserve the present case law, the incorporation of Lord Macnaghten's classification into statute would throw the law into confusion and uncertainty by depriving the courts of recourse to previous decisions when they were asked to interpret the new statutory provisions. On the other hand, if some form of words were to be found which would successfully preserve the present valuable case law, it is hard to see what the new definition would achieve.

...There would appear, therefore, to be few advantages in attempting a wholesale redefinition of charitable status-and many real dangers in doing so.'

1.3 Registration

A system of registration was introduced by the 1960 Act, continued, with amendments, by the 1992 Act and, through consolidation, by the 1993 Act. As the White Paper stated:

'Contrary to popular understanding, registration does not confer charitable status; this is inherent in an organisation's purposes and trust instrument. Registration does, however, provide conclusive evidence-subject only to correction by the High Court-than an organisation is charitable in law'

Under s3 of the 1993 Act, a duty is placed on all charity trustees to apply for registration unless the charity is:

(a) exempt;
(b) excepted;
(c) small; or
(d) a place of worship.

1.3.1 Exempt charities

Section 3(5)(a) of the 1993 Act excludes 'exempt charities' from the requirement to register. These institutions generally have some other form of supervision approved by Parliament and insofar as they are charities include:

- the universities of Oxford, Cambridge, Durham and London, including the colleges and halls of the first three, and any higher education corporation or its successor company;
- the trustees of the British Museum and the British Library and also various other specified museums and galleries;
- the Church Commissioners and any institution which is administered by them;
- any registered friendly or industrial and provident society or branch.

Since the 1960 Act, the list of charities exempt from registration has been extended by numerous Acts. A complete list of exempt charities is provided by Sch 2 to the 1993 Act.

Under s4(2) of the 1960 Act, exempt charities were permitted to register voluntarily. This is no longer possible. Section 2(3) and (8) of the 1992 Act effected two changes: firstly, the possibility of registering on a voluntary basis was removed; and, secondly, registration of any exempt charity ceased, automatically, to have effect. These changes were brought into force on 1 September 1992 by The Charities Act 1992 (Commencement No. 1 and Transitional Provisions) Order 1992 (SI 1992 No 1900).

Exempt charities which have previously registered voluntarily might have been somewhat concerned about their loss of registered status and number. But there appears to be no reason why business documents could not contain a statement such as 'We are an exempt charity under Sch 2 to the Charities Act 1993'.

1.3.2 Excepted charities

Section 3(5)(b) excludes from the registration requirement certain charities excepted by regulation or order.

The following charities have been excepted by regulation:

(a) by The Charities (Exception of Voluntary Schools from Registration) Regulations 1960 (SI 1960 No 2366), all voluntary schools which have no permanent endowment other than the premises of, or connected with, the school;
(b) by The Charities (Exception of Certain Boy Scouts and Girl Guides from Registration) Regulations 1961 (SI 1961 No 1044), funds, not permanent endowments, accumulated for the purpose of local units of the Boy Scouts Association or the Girl Guides Association and which produce an income of more than £15 a year;
(c) by The Charities (Exception from Registration) Regulations 1996 (SI 1996 No 180), certain religious charities connected with certain bodies

(this exception is temporary and expires on 1 March 2001) and trusts conditional upon the upkeep of graves. (Note: The Charities (Exception from Registration and Accounts) Regulations 1963 (SI 1963 No 2074) and The Charities (Exception from Registration and Accounts) Regulations 1964 (SI 1964 No 1825) are revoked);

(d) by The Charities (Exemption from Registration and Accounts) Regulations 1965 (SI 1965 No 1056), charities generally concerned with the promotion of the efficiency of any of the armed forces of the Crown; and

(e) by The Charities (Exception of Universities from Registration) Regulations 1966 (SI 1966 No 965), every university which is not an exempt charity.

In the case of the Roman Catholic Church and the Church of Wales, the Commissioners have dealt with the charities vested in diocesan trustees by order, excepting the charities individually (see the 1960 Annual Report of the Commissioners).

1.3.3 Small charities

Section 4(4)(c) of the 1960 Act excluded from registration any charity which had neither a permanent endowment nor the use or occupation of any land and whose income from property did not amount to more than £15 a year.

Section 2(5) of the 1992 Act (now s3(5)(c) of the 1993 Act) amended the last proviso to that subsection, such that charities 'whose income from all sources does not in aggregate amount to more than £1,000 a year' will not be required to register. This amendment was effected so that charities with a small investment income but a large income from other sources (e.g., fundraising or individual benefactors) would be brought into the supervisory net.

This change resulted in a large increase in the registration of small charities. The 1993 Annual Report of the Commissioners reported that 12,559 charities were registered in that year. Many of the increased applications were from parent/teacher and home/school associations, pre-school playgroups and women's institutes. The 1994 Annual Report reported the continued high level of new registrations, 'undoubtedly accounted for by the number of applications still coming in from bodies with an annual income of over £1,000 which are now required to register under section 3(5) ...', as did the 1995 Annual Report.

What is 'income' in the phrase 'whose income from all sources does not in aggregate amount to more than £1,000 a year'? Section 96(4)(a) of the

1993 Act provides that such a reference shall be interpreted by reference to the '*gross revenues* of the charity' and s96(4)(b) empowers the Commissioners to determine the amount, and their decision is final. And s96(5) provides that 'the Commissioners may direct that for all or any of the purposes of this Act an institution established for any special purposes of or in connection with a charity (being charitable purposes) shall be treated as forming part of that charity or as forming a distinct charity'. If such a direction were made to unite the two charities for, for example, registration and accounting purposes, then both their incomes, as well as any income from special trusts, would need to be aggregated in determining whether the £1,000 threshold has been exceeded. If so, registration will be compulsory.

Elsewhere in the 1993 Act the term 'gross income' is used. For the meaning of 'gross income' see chapter **3**, at **3.4.2**. While 'income' is assessed according to the 'gross revenues of a charity', 'gross income' is assessed by reference to its 'gross recorded income from all sources, including special trusts'.

Other than the automatic inclusion in 'gross income' of income from special trusts, it is not clear if there is any other substantial difference between these terms.

Charities with an annual income of less than £1,000 will still be subject to registration if they have a permanent endowment or use, or occupy, land.

While 'land' includes buildings (this is in s5 of, and Sch 1 to, the Interpretation Act 1978, not in the Charities Acts), there is no definition, nor any guidance notes, of the phrase 'use or occupation of land'. There is some merit, however, in the maxim 'the law does not concern itself with trivialities'. Thus, were a charity to hire a hall for one night of the year (and does not otherwise have the use or occupation of any land), then it is highly unlikely that this situation would be caught by the legislation and require the charity to register as it would not have continuous occupation. As stated at **1.3.2**, s3(5)(b) excepts certain scout associations from registration. If they are not excepted, however, and they have the 'use or occupation of any land', for example a scout hut, they will be required to register, regardless of their level of income. This is because they will not be excepted by s3(5)(c).

Section 3(2) of the 1993 Act continues to allow charities excepted from registration to register voluntarily. Any advantage of registration, however, may be counterbalanced by certain disadvantages. For example, charities excepted by virtue of s3(5)(c) will, *inter alia*, have to submit their accounts (which may be subject to independent examination), annual report and annual return to the Commissioners. There are provisions allowing existing charities which now fall below the registration threshold to deregister. The Commissioners are required to comply with the request.

Section 3(12) allows the Secretary of State to amend the limit of £1,000 either so as to keep pace with inflation or with a view to extending the scope of the exception provided for.

1.3.4 Places of worship

Provided that places of worship are registered under the Places of Worship Registration Act 1855, they are excepted from registration.

1.4 Declaration of status

Under s5(2) of the 1993 Act (previously s3 of the 1992 Act), registered charities with a *gross income* in their last financial year greater than £10,000 are required to state the fact that they are registered on certain specified business documents. (Note: the limit of £10,000 was raised, from £5,000, by The Charities Act 1993 (Substitution of Sums) Order 1995 (SI 1995 No 2696) as a result of a recommendation of the eighth Deregulation Task Force and took effect on 1 December 1995.)

Section 5(2) applies to the following documents:

(a) notices, advertisements and other documents issued by or on behalf of the charity and soliciting money or other property for the benefit of the charity;

(b) bills of exchange, promissory notes, endorsements, cheques and orders for money or goods purporting to be signed on behalf of the charity; and

(c) bills rendered by it and invoices, receipts and letters of credit.

It is regarded as good practice to include the statement on letterheads as well.

The purpose of the provision is to alert the public to the fact that they are dealing with a registered charity (which is subject to the Commissioners' jurisdiction and about which information and accounts may be obtained) and not with a private individual or commercial organisation.

Excepted charities which have registered voluntarily will have to comply with these requirements.

The statement may be in a language as well as, but not instead of, English. It must be clear and easy to read, but otherwise may be printed, rubber stamped or handwritten. In their booklet *A trustees' guide to the Charities Act 1992*, the Commissioners suggested that the following examples would satisfy the requirement: 'A Registered Charity'; 'Registered Charity No.', followed by the number; 'Registered as a Charity'; or 'Registered with the Charity Commissioners'.

There is no requirement to give the charity registered number, although charities may do so if they wish.

While s68 of the 1993 Act is similar to s5, it is not identical. Section 68 requires that where a company is a charity and its name does not include the word 'charity', or the word 'charitable', the fact that the company is a charity must be stated in English (in legible characters) on certain documents. The documents are very similar to those in s5 but, unlike that section include, for example, business letters. It applies to all charitable companies, whether or not registered. And, because it is concerned with charitable status, rather than registered charity status, it seems charitable companies will need to ensure that their documents comply with both sections.

Under s5(4), trustees and staff of charities who are involved in the issue of any document falling within (a) or (c) above without this statement will be committing an offence and liable, on summary conviction, to a fine. Section 5(5) imposes a similar penalty on any person who signs a document, falling within (b) above, without the necessary statement.

Section 5(6) confers powers on the Secretary of State to amend the limit, now of £10,000.

1.5 Charity names

Prior to the 1992 Act, the Commissioners could not refuse registration on the grounds that the charity had a name similar to, or even the same as, an existing charity.

With effect from 1 September 1992, ss4 and 5 of the 1992 Act (now ss6 and 7 of the 1993 Act) give powers to the Commissioners to give directions requiring a charity to change its name in certain specified circumstances. These are if:

(a) at the time when the name is entered in the register, the registered name is the same as, or is too like that of, another charity (whether or not registered);

(b) the name of the charity is likely to mislead the public as to the true nature of the purposes or activities of the charity;

(c) the name of the charity includes any word or expression specified in regulations made by the Secretary of State which is likely to mislead the public as to its status;

10

(d) the name of the charity is likely to give the impression that it is connected in some way with the government, or any local authority, or with any body of persons or any individual, when it is not so connected; or

(e) the name of the charity is offensive.

While any direction in respect of (a) must be given within 12 months of registration, there are no time limits for (b) to (e) inclusive. The powers apply to all charities, whether or not registered (although (a) is specifically concerned with changing the registered name of a registered charity), except for exempt charities which are excluded by s6(9).

Chapter 2 – Trustees, responsibilities, liabilities and insurance

2.1 Introduction

The 1992 Act was a response to the growth of the charity sector and the need for increased accountability. The requirements for charity accounts, increased controls over fundraising and the strengthened powers of the Commissioners are part of a general initiative to upgrade the regulatory framework within which charities operate. That Act apart, other aspects of the law to which charities may generally be subject are constantly evolving, as a result of which trustees may be unsure whether or not they are acting within the law.

2.2 Who is a 'charity trustee'?

Section 97(1) of the 1993 Act defines 'charity trustees' as 'the persons having the general control and management of the administration of a charity'. Paragraph 4 of Appendix 1 of the SORP states that 'the status of a charity trustee is defined in terms of the function to be performed, and not by reference to the title given to any office, or membership of any committee or committees'. Thus, regardless of the constitutional form of a charity, the group of individuals who have responsibility for the overall management and administration, e.g., members of the board of directors, or management or executive committee or similar description, will be the charity trustees. Where a non-charitable body corporate acts as a trustee of the charity, as in the case of the NHS charities, it and not its directors will be the charity trustee. Persons elected to manage a branch, where it is an integral part of the whole charity, may not be charity trustees. Conversely, some national charities have a structure where their local groups are constituted as independent registered charities. Those in charge will be charity trustees in these circumstances. 'Custodian' (or 'holding') trustees would not fall to be included within either of the above definitions, as they do not actively involve themselves in the management and administration. Rather, their responsibilities are limited to holding the assets of the charity for safe-keeping and in carrying out the instructions of the charity trustees.

2.3 Who may not be a charity trustee?

Sections 72 and 73 of the 1993 Act implemented the recommendation of the earlier Woodfield Report but widened the grounds for disqualification.

Under s72(1), a person is disqualified from acting as a charity trustee if he:

(a) has been convicted of any offence involving dishonesty or deception (including theft, forgery or fraud);
(b) has been adjudged bankrupt or sequestration of his estate has been awarded and (in either case) he has not been discharged;
(c) has made a composition or arrangement with, or granted a trust deed for, his creditors and has not been discharged in respect of it;
(d) has been removed from the office of charity trustee by order of the Commissioners or by the High Court on the grounds of any misconduct or mismanagement in the charity's administration for which he was responsible or to which he was privy, or which he by his conduct contributed or facilitated;
(e) has been removed under s7 of the Law Reform (Miscellaneous Provisions) (Scotland) Act 1990 (powers of Court of Sessions to deal with management of charities), from being concerned in the management or control of any body; or
(f) is subject to a disqualification order under the Company Directors Disqualification Act 1986 or to an order made under s429(2)(b) of the Insolvency Act 1986 (failure to pay under county court administration order).

Disqualification is, generally, automatic. Disqualified trustees, who may have been appointed lawfully, do not have to take steps to resign or be removed from trusteeship. They should immediately cease to take any further part in the charity's affairs. Under s73(4), the Commissioners may even require the return to the charity of the value of any benefits trustees may have received from the charity while disqualified. However, acts done for a charity while disqualified will not be invalid by reason only of the disqualification (s73(3)).

Section 72(4) allows the Commissioners to waive disqualification either generally or in respect of a particular charity or a particular class of charities, for example in the case of charities working with ex-offenders. However, a waiver may not be granted in relation to any charitable company if the person is disqualified under the Company Directors Disqualification Act 1986 and has not been granted permission under that Act to act as director of any other company.

Section 73 imposes penalties (either a term of imprisonment or a fine, or both) for acting as a trustee while disqualified. This does not apply to a trustee disqualified on the grounds of (b) or (f) above, as those offences will be dealt with under company law.

Section 72(7) requires the Commissioners to keep a register, which is open to the public, of all persons removed from office by them.

2.4 What are the trustees' responsibilities?

It is important that trustees not only know that they are trustees but, also, have an awareness of their responsibilities in order that they may effectively discharge them.

The Commissioners have published a leaflet (CC3) *Responsibilities of charity trustees* and, for ease of reference, the most recent edition is reproduced as the Annex to this chapter. Some other specific responsibilities are covered in the sections that follow.

2.5 Responsibility for preparing the report and accounts

The accounts should include an adequate description of the trustees' relevant responsibilities. (Where such a description is not provided, Auditing Standard 600.3 in SAS 600 *Auditors' reports on financial statements* requires the auditors' report to include one.) The matters to be included will reflect the specific requirements of the reporting entity. The APB Practice Note No. 11 *The audit of charities* gives an illustrative wording of a description which may be included in a charity's accounts and the examples in CC66 include such statements in connection with these particular responsibilities. Two of these are reproduced below dealing respectively with incorporated and unincorporated charities.

Example A   *Arts Theatre Trust Limited*

Trustees' responsibilities in relation to the financial statements
Company law requires the trustees to prepare financial statements that give a true and fair view of the state of affairs of the charity at the end of the financial year and of its surplus or deficit for the financial year. In doing so the trustees are required to:

- select suitable accounting policies and then apply them consistently;
- make judgements and estimates that are reasonable and prudent; and
- prepare the financial statements on the going concern basis unless it is inappropriate to presume that the charity will continue in business.

The trustees are responsible for maintaining proper accounting records which disclose with reasonable accuracy at any time the financial position of the charity

14

and enables them to ensure that the financial statements comply with the Companies Act 1985. The trustees are also responsible for safeguarding the assets of the charity and hence for taking reasonable steps for the prevention and detection of fraud and other irregularities.

Example C   *The Rosanna Grant Trust*

Trustees' responsibilities in relation to the financial statements
Law applicable to charities in England and Wales requires the trustees to prepare financial statements for each financial year which give a true and fair view of the charity's financial activities during the year and of its financial position at the end of the year. In preparing those financial statements, the trustees are required to:

- select suitable accounting policies and then apply them consistently;
- make judgements and estimates that are reasonable and prudent;
- state whether applicable accounting standards and statements of recommended practice have been followed subject to any departures disclosed and explained in the financial statements; and
- prepare the financial statements on the going concern basis unless it is inappropriate to presume that the charity will continue in business.

The trustees are responsible for keeping accounting records which disclose with reasonable accuracy at any time the financial position of the charity and enable them to ensure that the financial statements comply with the Charities Act 1993. They are also responsible for safeguarding the assets of the charity and hence for taking reasonable steps for the prevention and detection of fraud and other irregularities.

The trustees are responsible for the preparation of the annual report and accounts. Paragraph 28 of the SORP recommends that both documents are approved by the trustees as a body in accordance with their usual procedures (e.g., at a quorate trustees' meeting). The system and details of approval are covered more fully in Chapter **6** (at **6.4**).

2.6   Other financial responsibilities

The financial responsibilities of trustees are neatly summarised in CC3:

> 'Trustees are accountable for the solvency and continuing effectiveness of the charity and the preservation of its endowments. They must exercise overall control over its financial affairs. They should ensure that the way in which the charity is administered is not open to abuse by unscrupulous associates or employees, and that their systems of control are rigorous and constantly maintained'.

In practice, this statement can be broken down into a number of areas.

2.6.1 Internal controls

Should trustees fail to act prudently, lawfully and in accordance with their governing document they may be in breach of trust and personally liable to meet any resulting call on the charity's property or to make good any loss to the charity. Furthermore, since trustees must act jointly in administering a charity, they will be responsible jointly for any liability incurred by them or on their behalf.

It follows that while trustees should exercise appropriate care when entering into transactions or contracts on behalf of the charity, their responsibilities extend to careful oversight of the activities of others. Key to this is the establishment, monitoring and updating of appropriate internal controls. As emphasised time and time again in Charity Commission inquiry reports, delegation of these duties to a chief executive or senior management team is not appropriate unless the trustees then exercise appropriate scrutiny in respect of the activities of that chief executive or team.

2.6.2 Investment of surplus funds

Whatever the agreed level of reserves maintained by a charity, it is good practice to invest any funds not needed for immediate expenditure.

Trustees are responsible for taking appropriate advice and ensuring that any investment is suitable in terms of its duration, risk and rate of return. They are responsible also for constant monitoring of the performance and continuing suitability of the investments chosen. From the point of view of internal controls, it is advisable that no single trustee should be in a position to control a particular investment or policy generally.

2.6.3 Budgeting

It is essential that trustees make proper estimates about expected income and expenditure in order to plan ahead effectively.

Budgeting, cashflow forecasts and financial planning generally should form a central part of a charity's financial controls and this area should be subject to regular reporting to and monitoring by the trustees as a body. The charity should have in place effective mechanisms to obtain the necessary level of information at an appropriate frequency. Variances against budget should be questioned and, if deemed necessary, the underlying causes addressed.

2.6.4 Borrowing

Before borrowing any sum, trustees should consider whether appropriate powers are present in their governing document (if there is any doubt, the

Charity Commission should be consulted). If suitable powers exist, the trustees should obtain advice from a person of appropriate experience who has no interest in the proposed loan. This advice should cover whether the loan is necessary, whether the terms are reasonable and whether the charity will be able to repay the loan on those terms.

2.6.5 Fundraising

Trustees are responsible for ensuring that any fundraising activity is properly undertaken and that all funds raised are properly accounted for.

Where trustees allow others to undertake fundraising on their behalf, they should ensure that all sums are paid into a bank account in the charity's name before deduction of expenses. Trustees should ensure that all fundraising methods are subject to their approval and, where external fundraisers are employed, should arrange for a proper contract to be drawn up.

Finally, it should be noted that trustees should not benefit financially (or otherwise) from the charity either directly or indirectly. In the absence of an express provision in the governing document or specific authority from the Charity Commission, trustees are not entitled to receive any payment out of the charity's property beyond the reimbursement of reasonable expenses (and these should only be paid when supported by appropriate documentation). Any other payments, borrowing, contracts or other business with the charity may constitute a breach of trust. In such cases, the trustee may be required to make good to the charity any loss that results or to account for any profit made.

2.7 Risk

Under SORP 2000 the trustees are now required to include a statement in their annual report confirming the major risks to which the charity is exposed, as identified by the trustees, have been reviewed and systems have been established to mitigate those risks. This is covered more fully in chapter **6** (at **6.3.2**) and in chapter **20** dealing with risk management.

2.8 Investment of charitable funds

Following the Trustee Act 2000, which came into effect on 1 February 2001, the Charity Commission produced guidance dealing with its effects and much of this will be incorporated in an updated CC14 (*Investment of Charitable Funds: Basic Principles*).

The guidance (which does not apply to the corporate property of charitable companies and of other charities incorporated by or under legislation or to trustees of common investment funds (other than pooling schemes) or common deposit funds), should be followed when investments are being made. In particular it refers to:

- the statutory duty of care;
- trustees' investment powers;
- employing agents and delegating functions;
- appointing nominees and custodians;
- trustee responsibility for review;
- effects of trustees exceeding their powers; and
- investing in land.

Further guidance is also available in other Commission leaflets and in particular in connection with the disposal and acquisition of land (CC28 and CC33).

2.9 Liabilities and insurance

In the case of liability to third parties in contract, an incorporated charity will enter into contracts, sue and be sued in its own name. In contrast, if unincorporated, creditors contract with the trustees and it will be them from whom they may seek redress.

Whether or not a charity is incorporated, however, all charity trustees will be personally liable for all acts and omissions where a duty of care is owed to third parties. This will be so where there has been a breach of trust, for example where the charity has purchased investments not authorised by its constitution or under the Trustee Act 2000, where funds have been spent on unauthorised activities, or where the trustees have acted outside of the objects of the charity. Thus, the sometimes-held perception that charity trustees of an incorporated charity are protected from personal liability is something of a myth.

Section 727 of the 1985 Act affords a measure of protection for officers in cases where they may be liable in respect of negligence, default, breach of trust or breach of duty, but have acted honestly and reasonably and where, having regard to all the circumstances of the case, they ought fairly to be excused. Section 61 of the Trustee Act 1925 offers similar protection.

Prior to the 1989 Act, s310 of the 1985 Act provided that certain provisions indemnifying directors were void. The void provisions were generally those for exempting any officer of the company from default, or indemnifying him against default, breach of duty or breach of trust in relation to the company. And, it did not matter whether the provisions were contained in a company's Articles or in any contract with the company, or otherwise. This section was amended by s137 of the 1989 Act, such that a company may now take out insurance against those liabilities without that insurance being void. It is understood, however, that this relaxation does not of *itself* permit a charitable company to provide indemnity insurance for its directors. Provision and maintenance of such insurance would confer a personal benefit to trustees. Thus, directors of a charitable company would, generally, be precluded by its Memorandum of Association from securing any such benefit. An amendment would, therefore, normally be required to the Memorandum and Articles in order fully to take advantage of this relaxation.

For a charitable company, s64(2) of the 1993 Act requires the Commissioners' consent to any amendment of:

(a)   the objects clause in the Memorandum; or
(b)   any other provision in either the Memorandum or Articles which directs, or restricts, the manner in which property is used, or applied.

For an unincorporated entity, the provision of indemnity insurance could only be given if there were an express power in its constitution. If there were no such power, the provision of that insurance would need to be authorised by the Commissioners. An amendment to the governing document to permit the trustees to provide for indemnity insurance from the charity's funds cannot be made without the Commissioners' consent, even if that document contains a power of amendment. Once again, this is because the trustees cannot use a power to confer a personal benefit.

The Commissioners have indicated that they would raise no objection to such an amendment provided that it was limited to covering trustees from personal liability only for acts properly undertaken in the administration of the charity or undertaken in breach of trust but under an honest mistake.

In their 1990 Annual Report, the Commissioners noted that there was a growing public concern about the extent to which trustees could be held personally liable for the financial consequences of their actions, and whether they could properly insure themselves at the charity's expense against such liabilities. They recognised that potential trustees may be deterred from trusteeship because their personal assets may be at risk due to misjudgement rather than malicious intent. Therefore, the Commissioners agreed, in principle, that, where trustees' liability insurance is in the interests of the charity, the premiums may, in some cases, be paid from charity funds. The Commissioners are anxious to avoid giving the impression that approval for insurance to be taken out will be granted automatically. The range of circumstances in

19

which they are likely to agree to such an amendment will, in practice, be quite small. Trustees will need to demonstrate that:

(a) the insurance is in the interests of the charity, and not those of the trustees;

(b) the insurance will be for the benefit of the charity and not to the trustees, even in their capacity as trustees; and

(c) there is a reasonable risk of liability falling on the trustees.

The Commissioners require the insurance policy to contain the following exclusion clause:

> 'The insurers shall not be liable for loss arising from any act or omission which the trustee knew to be a breach of trust or breach of duty or which was committed by the trustee in reckless disregard of whether it was a breach of trust or breach of duty or not.'

The Commissioners will not object to a charitable company purchasing insurance which indemnifies the charity trustees against liability arising from wrongful trading: This is subject to the policy containing a prescribed exclusion clause.

There is no objection, in principle, to a charity insuring against loss to its funds resulting from the acts and defaults of the trustees.

For further information refer to the Commissioners' leaflet (CC49) *Charities and insurance.*

Annex – Responsibilities of charity trustees

CC3— Responsibilities of Charity Trustees

Contents

What is this publication about?

1. We are often asked to explain what is expected of someone who is appointed to act as a charity trustee. Trusteeship carries legal responsibilities and duties. To be a charity trustee is not a position of honour without responsibility: it requires time, understanding and effort. This leaflet answers some of the more common questions and sets out briefly and simply the duties of charity trustees. It covers such aspects as:

- what is a charity trustee, who can be one, and what personal qualities are needed;
- appointment, length of service and retirement of trustees;
- general principles of trusteeship;
- trustees' duties in relation to charity investments and property;
- trustees' duties in relation to registration, fundraising and accounting;
- liability of trustees, and delegation.

Meanings of words and expressions used in this publication

2. It may help to explain some of the expressions used in this publication. In most cases the rules for running the charity will be set out in a trust deed, a will, a constitution or the memorandum and articles of association of a company. They may sometimes (though not often) be found in a Royal Charter or an Act of Parliament. In any of these cases, except that of a company, there may also be one or more Schemes made by the Charity Commission or by the High Court. Whatever form the documents take in any particular case, they are called '**the governing document**' in this publication.

3. '**Permanent endowment**' means property belonging to the charity which can not be expended for the purposes of the charity: usually it is only the income of the property which may be expended for those purposes. A '**permanently endowed**' charity is one which has permanent endowment.

4. **Should** or **must** are used to refer to actions that trustees, or their agents or employees, are obliged to take by law.

5. **Recommend** or **advise** are used where we are suggesting to the trustees actions which we consider to be good practise but which do not represent a legal requirement.

Who are the 'charity trustees' of a charity?

6. The charity trustees are the people responsible under the charity's governing document for controlling the management and administration of the charity, regardless of what they are called. For instance, in the case of an unincorporated association the executive or management committee are its charity trustees, and in the case of a charitable company it is the directors who are the charity trustees.

7. Some charities have **custodian** or **holding trustees**, whose function is simply to hold the legal title to the charity's property or investments. Custodian or holding trustees have no role as such in the charity's management. They must act on the instructions of the charity trustees, unless they are told to do something which is in breach of trust.

Can anyone act as a trustee?

8. No-one under the age of 18 can be appointed as a trustee, and some people are disqualified by law from acting as charity trustees, including anyone described in section 72(1) of the Charities Act 1993. Broadly that covers –
   - anyone who has been convicted of an offence involving deception or dishonesty, unless the conviction is spent;
   - anyone who is an undischarged bankrupt;
   - anyone who has previously been removed from trusteeship of a charity by the court or the Commissioners;
   - anyone who is under a disqualification order under the Company Directors Disqualification Act 1986.

It is an offence to act as a charity trustee while disqualified unless we have given a waiver under section 72(4) of the Charities Act 1993.

What are the qualities needed to be a trustee?

9. We recommend that trustees be selected for what they can contribute to the charity. They ought not be appointed for their status or position in the community alone: this is the function of patrons. Trustees need to be able – and willing – to give time to the efficient administration of the charity and the fulfilment of its trusts. We recommend they be selected on the basis of their relevant experience and skills and must be prepared to take an active part in the running of the charity.

What are the first steps that newly appointed trustees need to take?

10. Trustees can be effective only if they have a sound knowledge of the purposes of the charity, the trusts and procedures which govern the trustees' actions and the nature and condition of the property and resources of the charity. So every trustee (or person asked to be a trustee) should study the governing document or documents of the charity.

11. If there is any difficulty in obtaining a copy of the governing document, we may be able to help.

12. We advise trustees to take the first opportunity to meet their fellow trustees and anyone else concerned with the administration of the charity and ask about its activities, its funding and the nature and condition of its property.

13. They need also to ensure, where the property of the charity is held in the names of individual trustees (and not in the Official Custodian for Charities or a corporate body), that all the property of the charity is transferred into the names of the people who are the charity trustees at the time.

14. In addition, we recommend that they study the latest annual report and accounts of the charity and, where necessary, ask for an explanation of their content and layout.

15. People who are invited or appointed to be trustees also need to be aware of their duties and responsibilities under trust and charity law. We recommend that every trustee read this leaflet carefully when they are appointed.

16. Finally, where necessary, new trustees (particularly *ex officio* trustees) should show that they accept their responsibilities and duties by signing the minute book.

How often do the trustees need to meet?

17. A charity cannot be administered properly unless the trustees meet regularly. How often that needs to be will depend on the size and nature of the charity but may sometimes be set out in the charity's governing document.

18. If the governing document requires the charity to have a certain number of trustees, or specifies a minimum number of trustees who must be present if a meeting of the trustees is to be properly constituted (a quorum), the trustees must ensure that their strength does not fall or, if it does, does not stay below that number. If no such requirements are made in the governing document of the charity, then the number of trustees must be kept up to an effective working strength, having regard to the administrative requirements of the charity and

the legal rule (if the governing document does not specify otherwise) that no decision can be taken except by all or a majority of the trustees.

How long does the appointment of a trustee last?

19. If the governing document does not specify the length of service of a trustee, the appointment continues until the trustee dies or resigns or is removed from office. However, in many cases the governing document says that trustees are to serve for a given period (usually a number of years, or, if the trustee is appointed to fill a vacancy, until the trustee who is replaced would have retired).

20. Trustees appointed to a local charity by a local authority under section 79 of the Charities Act 1993 are usually appointed for a term of four years.

Can a trustee resign?

21. Yes, if the governing document says so. The resignation is then handled in the way set out in the governing document. Normally, however, a trustee cannot resign unless there will be at least two trustees left after the resignation. If the trustee was appointed by deed there will usually have to be a deed of retirement which may appoint a new trustee or trustees in place of the retiring trustee. A trustee who resigns should ensure that there is someone else willing to be appointed in his place.

Who appoints new trustees?

22. In many cases the governing document says who is to appoint new trustees. In some cases it says that some people are to be trustees because of an office which they hold (i.e., ex-officio trustees). This is often the Vicar of a parish or the Vicar and churchwardens. Sometimes a named person is given the right to say who shall be new trustees. Sometimes different organisations are given the right to appoint representatives. If the governing document does not say anything about this, the law allows the trustees themselves to appoint new trustees **if** there are enough of them left to take proper decisions (i.e., there is a quorum). A retiring trustee can usually be appointed for a further term of office, but the governing document may in some cases not allow it. This should be checked before a new appointment is made.

23. If there is any difficulty about appointing new trustees, either because there is no person who has the right to appoint new trustees or because there is not a quorum who can appoint them, we should be told as we have the power to appoint new trustees in those circumstances.

Can trustees be paid for their duties?

24. Generally, no. Trustees are not entitled to receive any payment out of the charity's property other than reasonable and necessary out-of-pocket expenses which can be met from the charity's income. Furthermore they cannot directly or indirectly benefit personally from the charity by, for instance:
    - taking a lease of the charity property;
    - borrowing its money; or
    - making contracts to do business with the charity.

25. This is a legal rule and breaking it may constitute a breach of trust. A person who commits a breach of trust may have to make good any loss which results to

the charity out of their own money. Even if there is no loss, a trustee who makes a profit from dealing with the charity or its property when that is not allowed by the governing document or by one of the rules mentioned in this paragraph, will have to account to the charity for the profit made (i.e., they will have to pay the amount of any such profit to the charity).

26. There is an exception to this rule where there is an express provision in the governing document but even then any personal benefit must be strictly confined within the terms of the exception. In very special circumstances we may authorise a transaction between the trustees and a trustee personally. If you are in any doubt about this, ask us for advice.

What principles are needed to guide trustees when administering their charity?

27. The income and property of the charity must be applied for the purposes set out in the governing document and for no other purpose. It must be applied with complete fairness between persons who are properly qualified to benefit from it. The trustees should not allow the charity's income to accumulate unless they have a specific future use for it in mind. If the trustees are allowed a discretion about the use of the charity property, but are in some doubt about the proper exercise of that discretion, they should ask us for advice.

28. Trustees are required to act reasonably and prudently in all matters relating to the charity and need always to bear in mind the interests of the charity. They cannot let their personal views or prejudices affect their conduct as trustees. They need to exercise the same degree of care in dealing with the administration of their charity as a prudent businessman would exercise in managing his own affairs or those of someone else for whom he was responsible.

29. Where trustees are required to make a decision which affects the personal interests of one of their number, that person should not be present at any discussion or vote on the matter.

What else do charity trustees think about?

30. We recommend that trustees should find out what work is being done by similar charities and voluntary organisations operating in the same area. In some cases this can be done by joining an umbrella charitable association co-ordinating work in a particular field. Trustees should co-operate with other charities and exchange information with them so as to avoid overlapping or duplicating their efforts. They should also work with local authorities and other statutory bodies which provide services similar or complementary to those of the charity.

31. Charities should not, however, use their resources (unless the governing document clearly permits) to do what is already being done by statutory services financed out of rates or taxes; but they may supplement those services by providing additional benefits beyond the actual statutory provision.

Can the trustees delegate their responsibilities?

32. It is important and a general rule that trustees must act in person and decisions concerning the charity must be taken by the trustees acting together. They can always invite some of their number to look into particular matters connected with the charity and to make recommendations, but the decision whether or not to act on the recommendations is for the trustees to take together. No single

trustee should be allocated a part of the income of a charity or manage any particular aspect alone. In some cases the governing document of a charity may permit the trustees to set up committees with limited powers to carry out particular functions.

33. A provision in the governing document allowing the employment of a clerk or other officers does not, in itself, authorise the trustees to delegate the administration of the charity to those officers. The trustees of some charities, because of the scale or nature of the work of the charity may, of necessity, have to delegate to employees decisions on day-to-day management matters. But the scope of the delegated authority must be clearly laid down in writing and instructions given for decisions on important matters to be reported to the trustees. The trustees remain legally responsible and must supervise and control the work of the officers.

34. We strongly recommend that a person acting as delegate of the trustees should always make clear in dealings with third parties that they are acting in that capacity, and should always record in writing what was agreed in conversation.

Can trustees employ agents?

35. Yes. Trustees may seek the assistance of professional advisers on technical matters and employ agents or servants to give effect to their decisions. But it is important that where they do so they both retain and exercise overall control of the management of the charity and lay down in writing clear guidelines within which their agents and servants must act. Employees must be engaged under a formal contract of employment and should be issued with a written job description.

What are the liabilities of trustees?

36. If trustees act prudently, lawfully and in accordance with their governing document then any liabilities they incur as trustees can be met out of the charity's resources. But if they act otherwise they may be in breach of trust and personally liable to meet any call on the charity's property arising from their actions, or to make good any loss to the charity. Since trustees must act jointly in administering a charity, they will also be responsible jointly to meet any liability incurred by them or on their behalf.

37. We are able to take proceedings in court for the recovery, from trustees personally, of funds lost to a charity as a result of a breach of trust by the trustees.

38. We recommend that trustees should be particularly careful when entering into substantial contracts or borrowings to ensure that the charity has the means to meet its obligations. If trustees incur liabilities or debts which amount in total to more than the value of the charity's assets they may be sued personally for the difference by the charity's creditors.

Can trustees use the charity's funds to insure themselves against personal liability?

39. Trustees can, on condition, insure themselves out of the funds of the charity against personal liability arising from acts properly undertaken in the administration of the charity or acts undertaken in breach of trust but under an honest mistake. The conditions are that the governing document must empower them to do this, and that

it must be justified in the interests of the charity (not in the interests of the trustees personally). When deciding whether insurance is justified, trustees should consider the nature of the charity's activities, the degree of risk of personal liability to which the trustees are exposed, the number of trustees, the value of indemnity required, and the cost to the charity of paying the premiums demanded.

40. Trustees may use the charity's funds to insure the charity against loss to its own funds resulting from the acts and defaults of the trustees.

41. More information about charities and insurance is contained in our leaflet *CC49*.

42. Trustees have the general duty of protecting all the charity's property. *Property not only means land but includes books and financial records belonging to the charity. This underlines the importance to ensure that all documents and records which includes the minute book are held in a safe manner. We are not allowed to hold documents on behalf of charities this is the trustees' responsibility.*

What duties do trustees have in respect of charity property?

43. Trustees are accountable for the solvency and continuing effectiveness of the charity and the preservation of its endowments. They must exercise overall control over its financial affairs. They should ensure that the way in which the charity is administered is not open to abuse by unscrupulous associates or employees; and that their systems of control are rigorous and constantly maintained.

44. If the charity owns land, trustees need to know on a continuing basis what condition it is in, if its boundaries are being encroached upon, what can be done with it and how it is or should be used. They should ensure that the land, including any buildings on it, has appropriate and adequate insurance cover.

45. It is good practise that money not needed for immediate expenditure should be invested. We recommend that if expenditure is expected in the near future, it be deposited to earn interest. Investments need to be reviewed periodically to ensure that they remain suitable for the charity's needs. Wherever possible, we suggest that funds be placed in a range of investments so as to avoid substantial losses caused by the failure of a single investment or institution. We recommend that bank accounts be controlled by at least two of the trustees. It is unadvisable for one trustee to be allowed to operate a bank account alone. It is unacceptable for the second signatory to pre-sign blank cheques for countersigning by another.

46. In particular, trustees need to ensure that property which is permanent endowment is preserved and invested in such a way as to produce a good income while at the same time safeguarding the real value of the capital.

47. Trustees are obliged to ensure that all income due to the charity is received and that all tax and rating relief due is claimed.

What powers do trustees have when investing funds?

48. The governing documents of some charities make special reference to the trustees' powers of investment. Otherwise these powers will principally be found in the Trustee Investments Act 1961 (as amended).

49. The trustees are under a duty to decide what form of investment will be most suitable for the needs of their charity and obtain skilled advice for this purpose. They need to bear in mind the long-term future of the charity as well as the short-term,

and try to counteract the effects of inflation on their capital and income. Also they ought to constantly monitor the performance of the investments chosen.

50. Publications *CC32*, explaining the 1961 Act and *CC14*, offering guidance to trustees in selecting and managing the charity's investments, are available from any of our offices.

Common investment funds and common deposit funds

51. The duties of charity trustees may be simplified by contributing money, on proper advice, to a common investment fund. These funds are established specifically to meet the needs of charities and operate on lines similar to a unit trust by providing a wide spread of investments and specialised investment management which smaller charities individually cannot afford. Trustees may wish to look into the advantages that investment in any of these funds may offer.

52. There are a number of such funds each of which has different objectives. They can take investments only from charities and may have different requirements about minimum investments.

53. The Charities Act 1993 also allows for the establishment of common deposit funds. These funds are designed to provide charities with the opportunity to deposit their money along with sums belonging to many other charities and so secure a more favourable rate of interest than if they were investing alone. These funds will also be managed by specialised investment managers.

What are trustees' duties in relation to fundraising?

54. Trustees are responsible for ensuring that any fundraising activity carried out by or on behalf of their charity is properly undertaken, and that all funds collected are properly accounted for. Where trustees allow or employ people to undertake fund-raising on their behalf, they should ensure that all funds raised are paid into a bank account in the charity's name before deduction of the fundraiser's expenses.

55. We would advise that trustees always:
   - insist on approving both the fund-raising methods which will be adopted, and any appeal literature which will be used on their behalf;
   - make sure that any appeal properly describes what donations from the public will be used for;
   - be prepared to be open and honest about the costs of such an appeal if asked; and
   - ensure that where professional fundraisers are employed as agents for the charity, a proper contract is drawn up.

   Our publication *Charities and Fund-raising (CC20)* explains this in more detail.

Can trustees dispose of land belonging to the charity?

56. Generally, yes; but before trustees may sell, lease or otherwise dispose of land or buildings, they will either have to follow a statutory procedure or obtain an Order from us consenting to the disposal. Our publication *Disposing of Charity Land (CC28)* giving guidance to trustees who are considering selling charity property gives further details.

57. Briefly, trustees must instruct a qualified surveyor who acts for them alone to report to them in writing and must follow his advice on the marketing of the

property. Trustees may not sell land for less than the best price reasonably obtainable, and their surveyor must confirm that any offer they propose to accept meets this requirement.

58. Trustees wishing to lease their land for more than seven years must follow the statutory procedure for sales, but there is a simpler procedure for leases for seven years or less.

59. If in either case trustees are unable to follow the statutory procedure, or they wish to sell land to a person connected with themselves they **must** seek our consent.

60. When the property being sold or leased is subject to trusts requiring it to be used for specific purposes of the charity (as an almshouse, for example) the trustees must give public notice of the disposal. They may also need to apply to us for a Scheme to give them power to sell such property, and this should be done before the property is put on the market.

Can the charity borrow money on the security of its property?

61. Generally, yes. However, before they mortgage the charity's property, trustees must obtain advice from a person with ability in, and experience of, financial matters who has no personal interest in the proposed loan. This person can be a trustee or employee of the charity, and must advise on whether the loan is necessary for the charity, whether the terms are reasonable, and whether the charity will be able to repay the loan on those terms.

62. Trustees should seek advice in the same way even where the borrowing, such as a temporary overdraft, is unsecured. Trustees who do not seek advice on matters on which they are not themselves experts could be regarded as having acted imprudently and may be personally liable for the consequences.

Is there any requirement for charities to be registered?

63. Generally, yes. The Charities Act 1993, requires trustees to register charities in England and Wales with us and to give any information needed for the purposes of registration. Any charity which has permanent endowment, or an income from all sources exceeding £1,000 a year, or which uses or occupies land for its own purposes is required to register, though some special classes of charity are excepted or exempted. Further information on the requirements for registration can be found in our publication *Registering as a Charity (CC21)*.

64. Once a charity has been registered, we must be told about any changes in the registered particulars or if it ceases to exist or to operate.

65. While a charity is registered there can be no question about whether or not it is a charity (except for settling the question of whether it should be on the Register). This may well help in obtaining tax and rating relief or in obtaining grants from other charities which can make grants only for charitable purposes.

66. Every registered charity with an annual income over £10,000 is required to state that it is a registered charity on any appeal documents and on many of its financial documents, such as cheques, invoices and receipts.

Are the trustees required to keep accounts?

67. Yes. New legal requirements for the:
- maintenance of accounting records;
- preparation of charity accounts and annual reports;

- audit or independent examination of accounts;
- submission of accounts, annual reports and annual returns to us; and
- availability of accounts to the public, came into force on 1 March 1996.

68. These requirements are contained in Part VI of the Charities Act 1993 (as amended) and Regulations made under that Act. The extent to which you your charity will have to comply with these requirements depends upon its level of gross income or income and/or expenditure. Trustees must familiarise themselves with the appropriate requirements. In addition, a revised **Statement of Recommended Practice (SORP), Accounting by Charities** was issued in October 1995. This is usually referred to as the Charities SORP and may be obtained from the Policy Division at our London address. It is priced at £5 per copy, the first copy free to registered charities. Telephone orders, 0870 3330123.

69. We expect all charities to follow the Charities SORP or to provide a clear explanation of the reasons for any departure from it.

70. The books of account and statements of account prepared in accordance with these requirements must be preserved for at least six years. Registered charities should submit their accounts to us each year.

71. Preparing accounts is, however, only part of proper financial planning and control. It is also essential to make proper estimates about expected income and expenditure in order to plan ahead effectively.

Do charity accounts need to be audited?

72. Deciding whether, and, if so, how the accounts need to be externally scrutinised is not necessarily straightforward, particularly if the governing document makes provision for this. We strongly recommend you read our publication *CC51 Charity Accounts: The framework* for guidance on external accounts scrutiny requirements. However in general, the *statutory* requirements mean that all registered with an income over £10,000 must have their accounts scrutinised by an 'independent person'. This can be by independent examination or by audit by a registered auditor. To be 'independent' the person concerned should not be:
   - a trustee;
   - involved in the administration of the charity;
   - a major donor or beneficiary; or
   - a close relative, business partner or employee of any of the above.

73. However, if the charity's income or expenditure exceeds £250,000 in the current or preceding two years, the accounts **must** be audited by a registered auditor.

74. A governing document of a charity can impose external accounts scrutiny requirements which are more stringent that the statutory ones, but it cannot detract from the statutory requirements.

75. If you have any questions about your charity's accounts please contact us for advice (the helpline telephone number is 0870 3330123; minicom 0870 3330125).

If the objects no longer serve a useful purpose can the trustees change them?

76. We strongly advise trustees of charities to regularly review the effectiveness of the trusts of their charity. Sometimes a charity can be made more effective by changes which do not affect the existing trusts but in other cases a change in the trusts themselves may be needed.

77. The governing documents of some unincorporated charities may contain a power enabling the trustees or members to amend the purposes. In such instances, the required amendment may be made without our intervention, subject to the requirements of the governing document and the general law. But in redrawing the objects of the charity, the new objects should be kept close to the original intention of the charity and the purposes of the charity must remain legally charitable.

78. Any trustees intending to make or propose to the members an alteration are strongly advised to seek our views before they proceed.

79. Section 64 of the Charities Act 1993, requires a charitable company to seek our prior consent to any amendment of the company's objects or provisions relating to the way the company's property must be used. Amendments made without consent will be ineffective.

80. Sections 74 and 75 of the Charities Act 1993, replace the Charities Act 1985. Trustees of most charities with an income under £5,000 and whose trusts are no longer effective, are able to modify the purposes or administrative provisions of their charity, or to transfer their charity's property to another charity having similar purposes. Trustees of most permanently endowed charities with an income under £1,000 are allowed to expend the permanent endowment if they believe the income is not large enough to be useful.

81. Further details can be found in our leaflet *Small Charities (CC44)*.

Can a charity be wound up or its assets transferred to another charity?

82. A charity can only be brought to an end if:
    - all its property is expendable and has been disposed of; or
    - if the governing document contains a dissolution or winding up provision; or
    - if sections 74 and 75 of the Charities Act 1993 apply.

83. A provision in the governing document will normally require the assets remaining on dissolution to be passed to a similar charity. The trustees should follow the procedure contained in the dissolution provision closely and send copies of all relevant resolutions to us.

84. Whenever a registered charity is wound up or ceases to operate because all its property has been spent, the trustees are required to send a copy of the final accounts to us, with a request to have the charity removed from the Register of charities.

What can be done if a charity is permanently endowed and the governing document contains no winding-up powers?

85. If a charity is permanently endowed and the governing document contains no power of dissolution the charity cannot usually be wound up. However, if the trustees are satisfied that:
    - their charity no longer serves a useful purpose; or
    - the purpose for which it was originally established has been fulfilled by other means,

    we have the power under the Charities Act 1993 to make a Scheme to amalgamate the charity with others. In these circumstances the trustees are under a duty to apply to us for a Scheme to change the purposes of the charity.

(Version – September 1999)

Chapter 3 – The regulatory framework

3.1 Introduction

Sections 41 to 49 of the 1993 Act, and the Regulations made thereunder, heralded a new statutory regime for charities. Revised regulations were issued in 2000 as The Charities (Accounts and Reports) Regulations 2000 (SI 2000 No 2868). The general principles of the Regulations were not changed by the revisions, although there was an extension of the definition of 'smaller' charity to enable more charities to take advantage of reporting concessions.

The requirements apply in different ways to charities which are registered, those which are exempt and those which are excepted from registration. In general, charities have to maintain proper accounting records and submit, annually, to the Commissioners, accounts, a report and return. The 1993 Act introduced for the first time in charity law a requirement for most accounts to show a true and fair view and to be audited or subject to some degree of independent scrutiny.

The regime represented the culmination of many years' debate, which has run parallel to the increasingly visible profile which charities have enjoyed. The regime is, thus, no more than commensurate with the important role which charities play in the UK today.

3.2 The 1960 Act

Section 32 required trustees of all charities, whether or not registered, to:

(a) keep proper books of account;
(b) prepare consecutive statements of account, consisting of an income and expenditure account, relating to a period of not more than 15 months' duration, and a balance sheet relating to the end of that period; and
(c) preserve books and statements of account for at least seven years.

There was no general requirement to submit statements of account to the Commissioners. Trustees were required to submit statements of account to the Commissioners on request, however, and trustees of permanently endowed charities, unless excepted, were required to send a statement of account relating to the permanent endowment without any request.

Although the Act contained no general requirement for the accounts of charities to be audited, some trustees were under an obligation, imposed by the governing document, to have the accounts audited. Under s8, the Commissioners were entitled to order an audit of a charity's accounts (other than those of an exempt charity), but the costs thereof were to be borne by them.

3.3 The impetus for reform

Both the Woodfield Report and that of the Public Accounts Committee (*Monitoring and control of charities*), published in 1988, highlighted charity accounts as a key area of weakness. These reports found that, in spite of the importance of good financial information for supervision and accountability, the requirements for submitting annual accounts to the Commissioners were being 'widely ignored'; only a limited number of accounts were examined each year, and only a small proportion of accounts was professionally audited.

Both the government and the Commissioners fully accepted that the arrangements for submitting and examining accounts needed to be considerably strengthened. Accordingly, the White Paper, published in May 1989, identified, *inter alia*, the regular provision of good-quality financial information by charities as an essential element in their public accountability and an important means for their supervision.

Among the White Paper's proposals were:

(a) a requirement that, in future, all registered charities should submit, annually, statements of account to the Commissioners. Such charities would be required to supplement their statement of account with a trustees' report, and to provide legal and administrative details of the kind recommended by that SORP;

(b) the introduction of graduated requirements governing the content and audit of accounts; and

(c) a requirement for trustees to make copies of their charity's accounts available to the public on request.

The White Paper was followed by the Charities Bill, which was introduced by the government in 1991. This received the Royal Assent on 16 March 1992.

3.4 The 1993 Act

3.4.1 Overview

What is the regulatory framework?

The following diagram summarises the regulatory framework under the 1993 Act.

Up to £1,000 aggregate income per year; no use or occupation of land	Over £1,000 aggregate income per year; no use or occupation of land	Over £10,000 gross income or total expenditure per year	Over £100,000 gross income per year	Over £250,000 gross income or total expenditure in current or either of two preceding fin. years
Below registration threshold	'Light touch' regime	Independent examination and receipts & payments accounts	Independent examination and accruals accounts	Audit and accruals accounts
Proper accounting records must be kept				
Receipts and payments (R & P) basis of accounts may be chosen		Must prepare accounts on accruals basis		
Charity Commission may request annual report and accounts		Annual report and accounts must go to the Charity Commission		
No external scrutiny automatically required		Independent examination may be chosen		Must be audited
–	Annual return will be requested by CC	Annual return must go to the Charity Commission		

To which charities does the regulatory framework apply?

The framework applies to different charities in different ways. The following identifies the principal categories of charity, but does not address every possible situation:

(A) NHS charitable trusts

NHS charitable trusts are subject to the 1993 Act, as well as to NHS legislation governing the activities of the Health Service bodies administering them. A detailed manual, *NHS Charitable Funds: A Guide* has been produced.

(B) Friendly and industrial and provident societies

Friendly and Industrial and Provident Societies which are charities and registered with the Registrar of Friendly Societies are exempt charities (Sch 2 to the 1993 Act). The exemption does not extend to a charity administered by such a registered industrial and provident or friendly society, nor to a charity simply because it has a subsidiary which is an exempt society

(C) Registered social landlords (RSL's)

RSL's which are charities and registered with the Housing Corporation (and which are not registered industrial and provident societies and, therefore, exempt) are subject to Reg 5 of the 2001 Regulations.

(D) Higher/further education institutions

Most universities and higher education colleges are exempt. For the few which are not, the accounts they prepare for the relevant funding council will satisfy the requirements of Reg 5 of the 2001 Regulations, which makes special provision for them.

(E) Charitable companies

Charities which are companies are subject to the 1985 Act. They are, however, also subject to charity law. Unless they are excepted from registration with the Commissioners and have chosen not to register, they must file an annual report and their own statutory accounts with the Commissioners if their income or expenditure exceeds £10,000, or they are requested to do so by the Commissioners in other cases.

(F) Exempt charities

Charities listed in Sch 2 to the 1993 Act are exempt from registration with the Commissioners. They are required to keep proper accounting records and prepare statements of account under s46(1) and (2), unless they are subject to an alternative statutory regime, e.g., industrial and provident societies. Section 47(2) of the 1993 Act provides that members of the public may have access to these charities' accounts on request.

(G) Excepted charities

Certain charities are excepted from registration with the Commissioners. Such charities may choose to register, but, if they do, are treated like any other registered charity.

3.4.2 Accounting

Accounting records

Section 41 of the 1993 Act requires charity trustees to ensure that accounting records are maintained which are sufficient to:

(a) show and explain all the charity's transactions;
(b) disclose, at any time, with reasonable accuracy, the financial position of the charity at that time;
(c) enable the trustees to ensure that any statements of account required by section 42(1) comply with the requirements of the Regulations made thereunder;

and, in particular, contain:

(d) entries showing, from day to day, all sums of money received and expended by the charity, and the matters in respect of which the receipt and expenditure takes place; and
(e) a record of the assets and liabilities of the charity.

In March 1992 the Council of the ICAEW updated its guidance for members on the interpretation of the obligations of companies to keep accounting records under s221 of the 1985 Act and this is given, for ease of reference, as the Annex to this chapter. In view of the fact that the requirements of that section echo those in the 1993 Act, this guidance should, also, prove useful for charities which are not charitable companies.

Accounting records are to be preserved for a minimum of six years from the end of the financial year to which they relate, although s41(4) permits the Commissioners to agree, in writing, to the records being destroyed or otherwise disposed of should a charity cease to exist. Interestingly, the requirement to keep accounting records for a charity which is not a charitable company appears onerous. Under s221 of the 1985 Act, while a public company must retain its accounting records for six years, a private company, which would include charitable companies, needs only to preserve them for three years. Although s41 does not apply to charitable companies, by virtue of their being required to comply with the requirements in the 1985 Act, such companies would be well advised to retain their accounting records for the longer period.

The section does not apply to exempt charities. Such charities must comply with s46(1) and (2), which requires the charity trustees to keep proper books of account with respect to the charity's affairs and to retain them, together with statements of account, for a minimum period of six years unless the charity ceases to exist and the Commissioners consent, in writing, to their being destroyed or otherwise disposed of.

This section does, however, apply to all excepted charities, whether or not registered.

Duty to prepare accounts

Section 42 introduced new provisions relating to the preparation of annual accounts.

Trustees of charities with a gross income which, in any financial year, does not exceed £100,000 may elect to prepare a simpler form of accounts on the receipts and payments basis comprising a receipts and payments account and a statement of assets and liabilities.

The trustees of charities whose gross income in any financial year exceeds £100,000 must prepare a 'statement of accounts', the detailed requirements relating to which are laid down in the Regulations. In circumstances where a charity is trading, committed to substantial capital expenditure or has significant investment assets, the trustees are advised to prepare their accounts on the accruals basis.

Section 42 does not apply to charitable companies, by virtue of their being required to comply with the requirements in the 1985 Act.

Exempt charities are excluded from this provision (s46(1)) but, if not required by another statutory regime (e.g., industrial and provident societies are bound to comply with the Friendly and Industrial and Provident Societies Act 1968 to prepare periodical statements of account), are required to prepare consecutive statements of account consisting of an income and expenditure account of not more than 15 months' duration, and a balance sheet relating to the end of that period.

The section does, however, apply to all excepted charities, whether or not registered.

Statements of accounts – Introduction

Section 42(1) and (2) requires statements of accounts to comply with such requirements as to their form and content as prescribed by the Regulations made by the Secretary of State.

The Regulations make provision as to the form and content of the statements of accounts, including the methods and principles to be used, and information to be provided by way of notes. They also make provision with respect to the financial years of charities, the requirements relating to audit, or examination, of their accounts and the annual reports of charity trustees.

The Regulations prescribe the form and content of statements of accounts prepared by charity trustees under s42(1), including the information to be provided by way of notes to the accounts and the methods and principles applicable.

The statement of accounts must comprise:

(a) a SOFA, which satisfies the requirements of reg 3(4)(a);
(b) a balance sheet, which satisfies the requirements of 3(4)(b); and
(c) by way of notes to the accounts, the information specified in the schedule to the 2000 Regulations.

Statements of accounts – Methods and principles

Regulation 3(6)(a) requires the statement of accounts to be prepared in accordance with the methods and principles specified in the SORP.

Regulation 3(5) requires the SOFA and the balance sheet to give a true and fair view of, respectively, the incoming resources and application of those resources of the charity in, and the state of affairs of the charity at the end of, the financial year in respect of which the statement of accounts is prepared.

Where compliance with the Regulations would not be sufficient for the statement of accounts to give a true and fair view, para 3(5)(c) requires the necessary additional information to be given either in the accounts or in a note to them. If, in special circumstances, compliance with any of those provisions would be inconsistent with the requirement to give a true and fair view, para 3(5)(d) requires the charity trustees to depart from that provision to the extent necessary to give a true and fair view, and to give particulars of the departure, the reasons for it and its effect in a note to the accounts. The provisions regarding use of, and disclosures relating to, the true and fair override for charity trustees are the same as those for directors of companies, as set out in s226(4) and (5) of the 1985 Act. (Note: The interpretation of those disclosure requirements by FRS 18 applies.)

The comparative total figure must be given for each heading in the SOFA, but there is no requirement to show comparatives for each of the principal funds. Comparatives are required for all balance sheet headings (para 3(6)(b)).

If not comparable, the corresponding figure must be adjusted and particulars of the adjustment (but not the reasons for it as required by para 4(2) of Sch 4 to the 1985 Act) disclosed in the notes to the accounts (para 7).

For charities preparing accounts on the accruals basis and whose gross income in any financial year exceeds £250,000, para 1(w) of the Schedule to the Regulations requires the notes to the accounts to give a statement as to whether or not the accounts have been prepared in accordance with applicable accounting standards and statements of recommended practice and particulars of any material departure from those standards and practices and the reasons for such departure. Compliance with the SORP is, thus, not mandatory, but charity trustees will be expected to follow its recommendations, which are consistent with accounting and reporting standards.

Headings for which there are no figures to be shown both for the current and previous years, should be omitted (para 3(8)).

As regards measurement, para 3(6)(a) requires the values of the assets and liabilities of the charity to be determined in accordance with the methods and principles for their inclusion in the balance sheet set out in the SORP.

Statements of accounts – Special cases
Regulation 4(1) to (6) and Sch 2 of the 1995 Regulations prescribe the form and content of statements of accounts of common investment funds and common deposit funds and reg 4(7) prescribes the form and content of statements of account of registered housing associations and charities conducting higher and further education institutions. The regulatory framework relating to these charities is not dealt with further in this book.

Financial years – How are these determined?
Section 42(2) allows the Secretary of State to make provisions with respect to the determination of a charity's financial year. (Note: These will not apply to charitable companies, as they are subject to s223 of the 1985 Act.) Regulation 5 of the 1995 Regulations sets out these provisions.

Financial years are determined by reference to periods, which are calendar-based, and end on the charity's accounting reference date. In order to allow for the use of 52/53 week years, the period can vary by up to seven days either side of that date.

For a charity established before 1 March 1996, its first financial year, for the purposes of the Regulations, will begin immediately after the accounting period for which a statement of accounts was required to be prepared under any statutory provision applicable to it before that date and will end on its accounting reference date (reg 5(2)(a)). Thus, for a charity with an accounting reference date of 31 March, its first financial year will begin on 1 April 1996 and, assuming it is of 12 months' duration, end on 31 March 1997.

For a charity established after 1 March 1996, its financial year will begin on the day established and end with its accounting reference date (reg 5(2)(b)).

Subsequent financial years run from the previous financial year end to the next accounting reference date, plus or minus seven days (reg 5(3)).

Accounting reference dates are determined as follows:

(a) in the first financial year of a charity established before 1 March 1996, such date, not less than six, nor more than 18, months after the date on which that financial year began;
(b) in the first financial year of a charity established on or after 1 March 1996, such date, not less than six, nor more than 18, months after the date on which the charity was established; and
(c) in any subsequent financial year, the date which is 12 months after the previous accounting reference date or such other date, not less than six, nor more than 18, months after the previous accounting reference date.

As regards (c), there are provisions to restrict the frequency with which accounting reference dates may be changed. Such dates cannot be changed unless the immediately preceding two financial years were each of 12 months' duration. And, as regards (a) or (c), reg 5(4)(ii) permits trustees to change the accounting reference date only where satisfied that there are exceptional reasons (which are not defined), which must be disclosed in the notes to the accounts (reg 5(4)(ii) and para 1(s) of Pt IV of Sch 1).

What is 'gross income' and 'total expenditure'?

'Gross income' is defined in s97(1) as 'gross recorded income from all sources, including special trusts'. (This definition is similar, but not identical to that in respect of 'income', as used in s3(5)(c)). The Home Office Voluntary Services Unit's publication *Charity accounts and reports: Core guide* states that all incoming resources of a charity are income unless they are permanent or expendable endowment (permanent endowment is capital which may not be expended as income; expendable endowment may be so expended, at the trustees' discretion). Trading income, donated income, transfers from capital to income, income from investments including property, and asset disposal gains are to be included, but revaluation gains are to be excluded. Total expenditure includes depreciation of fixed assets for use by the charity and asset disposal losses.

Appendix 3 of the Commissioners' publication *Independent Examination of Charity Accounts 2001: Directions and Guidance Notes* states that gross income 'is the total recorded income of the charity in all unrestricted and restricted funds, but not resources received as capital (endowment) funds'. Therefore donations made to permanent endowment (including property to be retained as endowment) do not count as gross income.

Income, which should be calculated before deduction of any costs or expenses, includes:

- donations (including covenanted donations), grants, gifts, legacies, covenants and subscriptions;
- tax refunds;
- investment income (including interest receivable, dividends and rents);
- money received from the sale of goods or services in furtherance of the charity's objectives;
- gross proceeds from fundraising; and other income. When trustees decide to spend expendable capital, they should include the amount spent as 'other income'. This is because capital receipts are not included as income when they first come into the charity,

and excludes:

- the receipt of a loan by, and loan repayments to, the charity;
- the proceeds of sale of investment assets and tangible assets for use by the charity;
- gains or profits on disposal of investment assets and tangible assets for use by the charity; and
- donations etc., which the donor expects will, or may, be retained for investment by the charity and other capital donations, e.g., gifts of land and buildings to be retained and used for a particular charitable purpose.

Expenditure will include:

- expenditure relating to the objects of the charity including grants, donations, cost of services provided and support costs;
- management and administration costs of the charity;
- fundraising and publicity costs;
- interest payable; and
- when the accounts are prepared on an accruals basis, depreciation or amortisation of the assets,

and exclude:

- the granting or repayment of a loan;
- the purchase of investment assets and tangible assets for use by the charity;
- losses on disposal of investment assets and tangible assets for use by the charity.

Where accruals accounts are prepared, gross income will be the total of the figures entered in the SOFA under para 59 of SORP 2000 (excluding any amount included under para 118 which represents gains on the disposal of tangible assets for use by the charity). Total expenditure will be that entered under para 60 of SORP 2000 after omitting any amount relating to losses on disposal of tangible assets for use by the charity.

While the interpretations in the documents mentioned above are similar, they are not identical. For example, while the Home Office's interpretation of the composition of gross income and total expenditure includes profits and losses on the disposal of assets, the Commissioners' interpretation excludes them. Clearly, this may have a significant effect on which of the thresholds a charity falls under. It should be noted that s96(4) of the 1993 Act empowers the Commissioners to determine the amount of a charity's income from all sources and makes their decision final and binding If any unrecorded income is discovered, it is advised that it should be taken into account in determining gross income.

3.4.3 Auditing

Audit or independent examination?
Section 43 requires the annual accounts of a charity generally to be audited or independently examined.

If the gross income, or total expenditure, exceeds £250,000 in the year for which the accounts are being prepared, or in the immediately preceding two years, the accounts must be audited by a person who is:

(a) eligible to act as a company auditor under s25 of the 1989 Act (i.e., a registered auditor); or
(b) a member of a body specified under regulations made by the Secretary of State and, under the rules of that body, is eligible for appointment as auditor of the charity.

(Note: Sections 43(2)(b) and 44(1)(a) enable other auditors to be specified in regulations. At the time of writing, the Regulations do not extend the definition of charity auditor beyond those who are registered auditors. It is understood, however, that the DTI is always willing to consider applications from professional bodies wishing to become recognised qualifying bodies under the 1989 Act. The Regulations do, however, give the Commissioners the power to disapply the audit, and independent examination, provisions in circumstances where an adequate scrutiny of the accounts is otherwise carried out.)

If gross income or total expenditure are not more than £250,000 (but over £10,000 gross income or expenditure) in both the year for which the accounts are being prepared and in the immediately preceding two financial years, the charity trustees must elect to have the accounts either examined, or audited.

Where a charity's governing document requires an audit to be carried out, consideration should be given to the intention at the time it was drawn up. The governing document may contain more rigorous provisions than the Regulations. For example, if a charity's governing document requires the accounts to be audited, but the charity trustees wish to elect (assuming that they are able so to do) for an independent examination to be carried out, they may have the power to vary the governing document themselves or they may be able to make the change, under the 1993 Act's small charities' provisions. If not, the trustees are advised to obtain the Commissioners' approval to an amendment to the document.

It has been suggested by some commentators that if a charity's governing document imposes higher requirements than those in the 1993 Act, the charity need only comply with the latter's requirements. This is not, however, an interpretation which is generally held.

A lack of clarity of the provisions of the governing document may highlight other practical problems, e.g., not only in relation to the level of scrutiny required, but by whom that scrutiny should be carried out. It is often the case that governing documents were drawn up many years ago, when the term 'audit' had a different interpretation, given the then regulatory framework. Accordingly, if an audit is required, governing documents may not state by whom that audit should be carried out, e.g., by a registered auditor. It is recommended that all governing documents (and, for that matter, letters of engagement) are revisited and, where necessary, amended to reflect actual requirements, given the new regulatory frameworks which are in place.

A further issue which may raise practical problems is the threshold of £250,000 and its attendant provisions, particularly for any charity which receives large or unexpected donations late in its accounting year or for a charity which is undertaking a major project likely to generate substantial funds and expenditure, possibly over a limited period of time. It may well be that such charities will be caught by this provision in one year, but then revert to having gross income and total expenditure less than £250,000. The accounts will continue to require to be audited for a further two years, which might prove to be expensive.

Section 43 has been amended by s28 of the Deregulation and Contracting Out Act 1994. If a charity's gross income and total expenditure do not exceed £10,000 in a financial year, then, subject to s43(4), the accounts will need neither to be audited, unless required by the Commissioners (s43(4)(b)), nor independently examined. The effect of this amendment has been to introduce a 'light touch' regulatory band and was made as a result of one of the recommendations of the eighth

Deregulation Task Force. As a consequence of this, s43(8) has been amended so that the threshold of £10,000 (like that of £250,000), can be altered at any time by the Secretary of State. Section 43(8) uses the word 'different' rather than 'higher'. Thus, were there to be abuse (e.g., fraud), on a large scale, of the light touch regime, the option is open for the Secretary of State to remove the relief for smaller charities of this right conferred on them.

What are the duties of an auditor?

Section 44(1)(b) allows for the Secretary of State to make provisions with respect to the duties of an auditor, including provisions with respect to the form of report (either on the statement of accounts or the account and statement). These duties are provided in reg 6 of the 1995 Regulations.

(A) The auditors' report – Statement of accounts

Where a statement of accounts has been prepared for a financial year, the auditor must make a report on that statement to the charity trustees. The report must:

(a) state:
  (i) the name of the charity; and
  (ii) his name and address;
  (reg 6(2)(a));
(b) be signed by him and state that he is a registered auditor (reg 6(2)(b));
(c) be dated and specify the financial year in respect of which the accounts to which the report relates have been prepared (reg 6(2)(c));
(d) specify that it is a report in respect of an audit carried out under s43 and in accordance with the Regulations (reg 6(2)(d)); and
(e) state whether, in his opinion, the statement of accounts complies with the requirements of reg 3 (or, as the case may be, reg 4) and, in particular, gives a true and fair view of the state of affairs of the charity at the end of the financial year and of the incoming resources and application of the resources of the charity in that year (reg 6(2)(e)).

If the auditor is of the opinion that:

(a) accounting records have not been kept in accordance with s41;
(b) the statement of accounts is not in agreement with those records;
(c) any information contained in the statement of accounts is inconsistent in any material respect with the annual report for the financial year; or
(d) any information or explanation to which he is entitled under reg 8 has not been afforded to him;

reg 6(2)(f) requires his report to contain a statement of, and of his grounds for forming, that opinion.

There are some noticeable differences between the responsibilities in reg 6(2)(f) of the 1995 Regulations and those of auditors under ss235 and 237 of the 1985 Act. Firstly, under the 1985 Act, and where applicable, auditors are required to form an opinion as to whether proper returns adequate for their audit have been received from branches not visited by them. There is no such obligation under the 1993 Act for an auditor of a charity with branches. Secondly, unlike the 1993 Act, the 1985 Act does not require the auditors to give their grounds for forming their opinion (under (i) to (iv) of reg 6(2)(f)). And, thirdly, reg 6(2)(f)(iii) requires any material inconsistency between the statement of accounts and the annual report to be expressed with reference to *the accounts* as this relates to the relevant power in the 1993 Act; the equivalent provision in the 1985 Act is with reference to the *directors' report*.

(B) The auditors' report – Receipts and payments account

Where a receipts and payments account and statement of assets and liabilities have been prepared under s42(3) for a financial year, the auditors shall make a report on that account and statement to the charity trustees which must:

(a) state:
   (i) the name of the charity; and
   (ii) his name and address,
   (reg 6(3)(a));
(b) be signed by him and state that he is a registered auditor (reg 6(3)(b));
(c) be dated and specify the financial year in respect of which the accounts to which it relates have been prepared (reg 6(3)(c));
(d) specify that it is a report in respect of an audit carried out under s43 and in accordance with the Regulations (reg 6(3)(d)); and
(e) state whether, in his opinion:
   (i) the account and statement properly present the receipts and payments account of the charity for the financial year and its assets and liabilities at the end of that year; and
   (ii) the account and statement adequately distinguish any material special trust, or other restricted fund of the charity.
   (reg 6(3)(e)).

If the auditor is of the opinion that:

(a) accounting records have not been kept in accordance with s41;
(b) the account and statement is not in agreement with those records;

or

(c) any information or explanation to which he is entitled under reg 8 has not been afforded to him, reg 6(3)(f) requires his report to contain a statement of, and of the grounds for forming, that opinion.

SAS 600 applies to the report on the audit of accounts prepared on the receipts and payments basis as it does to those prepared on the accruals basis.

(C) Carrying out investigations for the purposes of the report
Regulation 6(4) requires the auditor to carry out such investigations as will enable him to form an opinion as to the matters specified in paras (e) and (f) of paras (2) or (3) of the Regulations.

(D) 'Whistleblowing'
In keeping with similar arrangements for other regulated bodies (e.g., friendly societies), reg 6(5) places a duty on the auditor to inform the Commissioners, in writing, of any matter which he becomes aware of in his capacity as auditor which relates to the activities or affairs of the charity which he has reasonable cause to believe is, or is likely to be, of material significance to the Commissioners' functions under s8 (general power to institute inquiries) or s18 (power to act for protection of charities) of the 1993 Act. This might include the discovery of material breaches of trust, or serious deficiencies in the charity's administration which expose its assets to the risk of loss and would also include circumstances making it impossible for the auditor to give an opinion.

Such matters may relate not only to the activities or affairs of the charity, but, also, to any institution or body corporate which is a connected person of the charity.

This obligation is essential to strengthen accountability and public confidence in charities. It is understood that the Commissioners will respond in a practical and constructive way to information disclosed in this way, and would welcome enquiries from auditors or charities about matters they wish to clarify.

(E) Ceasing to hold office
Where an auditor ceases for any reason to hold office, reg 6(6) requires him to send to the charity trustees a statement of any circumstances connected with that cessation which he considers should be brought to their attention or, if he considers there are no such circumstances, a statement to that effect. Except where there are no such circumstances, a copy of any statement must, also, be sent to the Commissioners and, in the case of an incorporated charity, to the Registrar of companies.

What form does an independent examiner's report take?
Section 44(1)(c) enables the Secretary of State to make provision with respect to the form of report of the independent examiner. This is set out in reg 7 of the Regulations.

An independent examiner who has carried out an examination of the accounts in accordance with s43 must make a report to the charity trustees. The report must:

(a) state:
    (i) the name of the charity; and
    (ii) his name and address;
    (reg 7(a));
(b) be signed by him and specify any relevant professional qualifications or professional body of which he is a member (reg 7(b));
(c) be dated and specify the financial year in respect of which the accounts to which it relates have been prepared (reg 7(c));
(d) specify that it is a report in respect of an examination carried out under s43 and in accordance with any directions given by the Commissioners under s43(7)(b) which are applicable (reg 7(d));
(e) state whether or not any matter has come to his attention in connection with the examination which gives him reasonable cause to believe that in any material respect:
    (i) accounting records have not been kept in accordance with s41;
    (ii) the accounts are not in agreement with those records; or
    (iii) in the case of an examination of a statement of accounts, that statement does not comply with any of the requirements of reg 3 of the 2000 Regulations; and
(f) state whether or not any matter has come to his attention in connection with the examination to which, in his opinion, attention should be drawn in order for a proper understanding of the accounts to be given (reg 7(f)).

Where:

(a) any material expenditure or action appears not to be in accordance with the trusts of the charity;
(b) any information or explanation to which he is entitled under reg 8 has not been afforded to him; or
(c) in the case of an examination of a statement of accounts prepared under s42(1), any information contained in that statement is inconsistent in any material respect with the annual report of the charity trustees, reg 7(g) requires his report to contain a statement to that effect.

What are the auditors' and independent examiner's rights?
Section 44(1)(d) and (e) enable the Secretary of State to make provision conferring on the auditor, or independent examiner, a right of access to books, documents and other records (however kept) which relate to the charity. These provisions are set out in reg 8.

Regulation 8(1) provides that an auditor or independent examiner has a right of access to any books, documents and other records (however kept) which relate to the charity concerned and which the auditor, or examiner, considers necessary to inspect for the purposes of carrying out the audit, or examination.

Regulation 8(2) provides that the auditor, or independent examiner, is entitled to require such information and explanations from past or present charity trustees or trustees for the charity, or from past or present officers or employees of the charity, as he considers necessary for the purposes of carrying out the audit, or examination.

Commissioners' powers to require an audit

Where the statutory requirements for the accounts to be audited, or independently examined, have not been complied with within 10 months of the end of the relevant financial year, s43(4)(a) confers upon the Commissioners a power to require an audit of the accounts. In these circumstances, the auditor will be appointed by the Commissioners and the trustees will be personally liable, jointly and severally, for his costs. Only if it appears to the Commissioners that it would not be practical to seek recovery of the costs of the audit from the trustees, will the costs be met from the funds of the charity.

Section 43(4)(b) confers on the Commissioners a power to require an audit of the accounts of any charity to which the section applies in circumstances where, although the requirement for an audit does not apply, it appears to them that one would be desirable. In these circumstances, the trustees may appoint the auditors and, provided the trustees comply with the Commissioners' order, the costs of the audit will be met from the charity's funds.

Dispensation from audit or independent examination requirements in certain circumstances

Section 44(1)(f) allows the Secretary of State to make provision enabling the Commissioners to dispense, in certain circumstances, with an audit, or independent examination, for a particular charity or any particular financial year of a charity where an adequate scrutiny of the accounts is otherwise carried out. Those circumstances, which are set out in reg 9, are where the Commissioners:

(a) are satisfied that the accounts of the charity are required to be audited in accordance with any statutory provision contained in or having effect under an Act of Parliament which, in their opinion, imposes requirements which are sufficiently similar to the requirements of s43(2) for those requirements to be dispensed with;

(b) are satisfied that the accounts of the charity have been audited by the Comptroller and Auditor General;

(c) are satisfied that the accounts of the charity for the financial year have been audited or examined in accordance with requirements or arrangements which, in their opinion, are sufficiently similar to the relevant requirements of s43 applicable to that financial year for those requirements to be dispensed with;

(d) are satisfied that, in the financial year in question, there has been no transaction which would be required to be shown and explained in the accounting records; or

(e) consider that, although the financial year of a charity is one to which s43(2) applies, there are exceptional circumstances which justify the examination of the accounts by an independent examiner rather than an audit in accordance with that subsection and the accounts have been so examined, and where the charity trustees have supplied to the Commissioners any report made to them with respect to the accounts of that charity for the financial year which the Commissioners have requested.

Exclusions

These provisions do not apply to:

(a) charitable companies, although s69 retains the powers of the Commissioners, under what was s8(5) and (6) of the 1960 Act, to require the accounts of such a charity to be investigated and audited, but at the cost to the Commissioners;

(b) exempt charities; and

(c) excepted charities which have neither a permanent endowment nor the use or occupation of any land and whose income is not greater than £1,000 a year and which are not registered (s46(3)). If they register voluntarily, the provisions apply. The provisions do, however, apply to other excepted charities.

3.4.4 Annual reports

Section 45 requires charity trustees to prepare an annual report for each financial year. This is an important document in its own right and will contain a report on the activities of the charity during the year and such other information relating to the charity, or to its trustees or officers, as is prescribed by the Regulations.

Unless a charity's gross income and total expenditure do not exceed £10,000 in a financial year, trustees must submit the annual report, together with the statement of accounts, or account and statement, together with the auditors', or independent examiner's, report within 10 months of the year end. The Commissioners may grant a longer period where there are special reasons (s45(3)(b)).

Exempt charities and excepted charities which have neither a permanent endowment nor the use or occupation of any land and whose income is not greater than £1,000 a year and which are not registered on a voluntary basis are excluded from this provision (s46(1) and (3)). Other excepted charities which are not registered on a voluntary basis are also excluded, unless the Commissioners specifically request them to prepare and submit an annual report (s46(5) and (6)). In these circumstances, the annual accounts and the report of the auditors, or independent examiner, should be attached.

3.4.5 Public inspection of accounts

Section 47 provides for all annual reports kept by the Commissioners to be open to public inspection at all reasonable times. This will ensure that the public have access to information about registered charities.

Where a person requests, in writing, the trustees of any charity to provide them with a copy of that charity's accounts and pays them a reasonable fee in order to comply with the request, the trustees must comply with the request within two months of receiving it. This provision applies to all charities, including exempt charities. Thus, the accounts of any charity may be obtained by a member of the public which, hitherto, may have been difficult to obtain.

3.4.6 Annual return

The 1993 Act provides for more active supervision of the charity sector by the Commissioners through the process of annual monitoring.

Subject to below, s48(1) requires the trustees of all registered charities to complete an annual return in the form prescribed by regulations made by the Commissioners and submit it to them within 10 months of the year end.

Section 48(1A), as inserted by s30(3) of the Deregulation and Contracting Out Act 1994, states that these requirements do not apply to registered charities whose gross income and total expenditure do not exceed £10,000 in a financial year. This implemented a further recommendation of the eighth Deregulation Task Force.

Section 48(3) provides for the Commissioners to dispense with the need to prepare an annual return in the case of a particular charity or particular class of charities, or in the case of a particular financial year of a charity or of any class of charities.

The Secretary of State may, again, amend the figure of £10,000 by substituting a different amount, at any time (s48(4), as inserted by s30(4) of the Deregulation and Contracting Out Act 1994.)

The 1995 Annual Report of the Commissioners cast more light on the monitoring process:

'In advance of the full implementation of the new accounting framework a significant number of charities were asked to assist with monitoring developments by completing pilot questionnaires. Even at the developmental stage we are beginning to get some productive information from the monitoring procedures. We are confident that the arrangements, when fully in place, will encourage greater accountability, and give the public more confidence about the health of the charity sector. Eventually the various facets of monitoring will enable us to:

(a) get in touch with charities where there are problems identified through the information they return;
(b) give advice and assistance to trustees;
(c) investigate possible causes for concern; and
(d) identify trends among types of charities or across the whole sector, highlighting examples of good practice or areas of difficulty.

The annual return will be divided into three parts, and completion of each part will be determined by the income or expenditure band of the charity. In keeping with the "light touch" regime for smaller charities (i.e., where income or expenditure is less than £10,000 a year), the information required from those charities will be only what is needed to update the basic registration details on the charity database. Our active supervision of the charity sector will concentrate largely on registered charities whose gross income or total expenditure exceeds £10,000 a year. It is estimated that only about 40,000 of the 150,000 main registered charities will be asked to complete the annual return with responses to more detailed monitoring questions.

Our questionnaire-based approach to monitoring will be supplemented by scrutiny of the trustees' annual report and the annual accounts which the larger charities will have to send in with their annual return. It will only be in rare cases that charities below the £10,000 a year level will be asked to send in their report and accounts, although we shall conduct a random sampling check to ensure that the limits are being observed.'

3.4.7 Penalties for non-compliance

Under s49, charity trustees will commit an offence if persistently in default, without reasonable excuse, in:

(a) preparing and submitting annual reports and accounts to the Commissioners;
(b) making available accounts to the public; or
(c) preparing and submitting an annual return.

Such a person will be liable, on summary conviction, to a fine. Persistent failure to supply this information would be evidence of mismanagement and the Commissioners could then institute enquiries.

3.5 Charitable companies

Unless stated otherwise, charitable companies are excluded from the accounting and auditing requirements, but must comply with the accounting and disclosure provisions in the 1985 Act. Disapplying these provisions to such companies, however, means that they do not have to comply with the Regulations made thereunder with which other charities would have to comply.

There are some important differences between the regimes under the 1985 and 1993 Acts. For example, for charities not subject to an audit, the level of scrutiny and the qualifications required to carry out that scrutiny differ. And, the requirement to report to the Commissioners in certain circumstances (i.e., 'whistleblow') in the 1993 Act does not apply to auditors of charitable companies.

Charitable companies may still be subject to scrutiny by the Commission as ss8 to 11 of the 1993 Act confer general powers on the Commissioners to institute enquiries into any charity (other than an exempt charity) and to call for documents and to search records. They may direct any person to attend to give evidence or produce documents and are entitled to obtain and seek explanations of that documentary evidence. It is an offence for a person knowingly or recklessly to provide information to the Commissioners which is false or misleading in a material particular.

3.6 Current developments

Currently, the Government's Performance and Innovation Unit is undertaking a broad-ranging review of the legal and regulatory framework for charities and the voluntary sector. The aims are to enable existing and new not-for-profit organisations to thrive and grow; to encourage the development of new types of organisation; and to ensure public confidence in the sector. Its findings are likely to be made known early in 2002.

During 2001 the final report of the Company Law Review Steering Group was also published. Included in the report is the recommendation that there should be a separate form of incorporation designed specifically for charities.

It is therefore likely that the regulatory framework for charities will undergo considerable changes within the foreseeable future.

Annex – Guidance on accounting records

Statement issued in March 1992 by the Council of the Institute of Chartered Accountants in England and Wales for the guidance of members on the obligations of companies to keep accounting records under the Companies Act 1985.

This statement has been settled in consultation with counsel.

References are to the Companies Act 1985 as amended by section 2 of the Companies Act 1989.

1 Section 221 of the Companies Act 1985 obliges all companies to have accounting records satisfying the requirements set out in that section. The term 'accounting records' was introduced by the Companies Act 1976 in recognition of the fact that the term 'books of account' (used in earlier Acts) was no longer apt in the age of computers. Current concern about the incidence of fraud and negligence has directed attention to the need for guidance on the interpretation of this section. No account is taken in this paper of specific requirements of other legislation (e.g., VAT legislation) in respect of accounting records.

The legal requirements

2 The Act's requirements are as follows:

Duty to keep accounting records

Disclose with reasonable accuracy, at any time, the 221(1) Every company shall keep accounting records which are sufficient to show and explain the company's transactions and are such to

a) financial position of the company at that time, and
b) enable the directors to ensure that any balance sheet and profit and loss account prepared under this Part complies with the requirements of this Act.
(2) The accounting records shall in particular contain
    a) entries from day to day of all sums of money received and expended by the company, and the matters in respect of which the receipt and expenditure takes place, and
    b) a record of the assets and liabilities of the company.
(3) If the company's business involves dealing in goods, the accounting records shall contain
    a) statements of stock held by the company at the end of each financial year of the company,

b) all statements of stocktakings from which any such statement of stock as is mentioned in paragraph (a) has been or is to be prepared, and

c) except in the case of goods sold by way of ordinary retail trade, statements of all goods sold and purchased, showing the goods and the buyers and sellers in sufficient detail to enable all these to be identified.

The key requirement is in section 221(1). Subsections (2) and (3) supplement this.

3 Subsection (4) of section 221 obliges a parent company which has a subsidiary undertaking to which the requirements of subsections (1), (2) and (3) do not apply to take reasonable steps to secure that the undertaking keeps such accounting records as to enable the directors of the parent company to ensure that any balance sheet and profit and loss account prepared under Part VII of the Act complies with the requirements of the Act. Subsections (5) and (6) of section 221 contain penalty provisions.

Contents, form and organisation of accounting records

4 The accounting records should comprise an orderly, classified collection of information capable of timely retrieval, containing details of the company's transactions, assets and liabilities. An unorganised collection of vouchers and documents will not suffice: whatever the physical form of the records, the information should be so organised as to enable a trial balance to be constructed. If, for example, the information is held in a computer database as a subset of a set of wider information, the software should be capable of retrieving the appropriate data.

Preservation of the accounting records

5 Section 222(5) of the Act requires that accounting records, once made, must be preserved for at least 6 years (public companies) or 3 years (private companies). It follows that where programmed instructions and any supporting documentation are needed for retrieval of information in usable form, for example from a computer database, they must be available for the same period, as must any necessary hardware.

Disclosure of the financial position at any time

6 The Act requires that accounting records should be such as to disclose with reasonable accuracy, at any time, the financial position of the company at that time. The words 'at any time' emphasise the obligation to keep accounting records up to date and do not impose an obligation to keep accounting records capable of disclosing the financial position as at any time in the past. The requirement to keep accounting records up to date does not mean that transactions and events must be recorded instantaneously. It is sufficient if they are recorded within a reasonable time. What is a reasonable time depends upon the nature of the business and other circumstances. What, for example, is urgent for a bank, calling for immediate action, may be less so for another business. Records made to disclose the current financial position (including any stock records or memoranda, such as are referred to in paragraphs 10 and 11 below) must be retained for the statutory period.

7 In requiring that the accounting records be sufficient to disclose with reasonable accuracy, at any time, the financial position of the company at that time, the Act recognises that it is not practicable to keep accounting records in such a way as to enable accounts to be prepared giving a true and fair view at every moment during the year. The concept of 'true and fair' is extremely wide and embraces information not necessarily contained within the accounting records themselves.

8 Whether a company is keeping the right kind of accounting records to meet the requirements of the Act is a question of fact to be decided in any particular case. Regard will be had, among other things, to prevailing practice of the time in businesses of the type in question although this consideration will not itself be conclusive.

9 The accounting records should be such as would enable the directors at any time to prepare a reasonably accurate statement of the company's financial position. The accounting records should therefore contain the primary material on which a set of accounts would be based. However, they need not contain whatever additional items of information it would be necessary to know in order to make those accounts true and fair (see paragraph 7 above). The financial position is not limited to the cash position. It comprises the assets and liabilities including items such as those referred to in paragraph 11 below.

10 What is a sufficient record of stocks within the total picture will depend on the circumstances. The materiality of stock and the extent of stock movements are relevant factors. Continuous stock records can provide adequate information when supported by systematic physical checks. The information may, however, require to be supplemented by judgements with respect to realisable value including times of potential realisation and this may require accounting entries to be made, for example by way of memorandum, as indicated in paragraph 11 below. Continuous records are not essential if the stock position can be assessed with sufficient reliability from other accounting records, including in appropriate cases any interim stocktakings. Express requirements with respect to stocks held at the end of financial years are contained in section 221(3), and are discussed in paragraph 16 below.

11 Provisions for such matters as depreciation, bad debts and other losses are often made only at the end of an accounting year. The requirement to disclose the financial position with reasonable accuracy at any time during a financial year will normally be satisfied if a procedure exists to ensure that an adequate record is made and retained – for example by way of memorandum – of any expected loss, liability or contingency material to the assessment of the current position. Such a memorandum would constitute part of the accounting records.

Annual accounts

12 The records must also be such as to enable the directors to satisfy the requirements of the Act with regard to annual accounts, including the notes to the accounts (section 221(1)(b) and section 221(4)).

Cash records to be kept

13 Section 221(2)(a) requires the accounting records to contain entries from day to day of all sums of money received and expended. Accordingly, the accounting records must contain:

(1)   the date of transactions;
(2)   the sums received and expended;
(3)   the matters in respect of which the receipt and expenditure took place.

As noted above, it is not necessary in all cases for entries to be made instantaneously, although they must be made within a reasonable time.

14   It will sometimes be appropriate to record groups of transactions rather than individual transactions (e.g., in the records of the daily cash takings of a shop where a record of individual receipts is not necessary to explain the transactions). Paragraph 17 below sets out the position as regards records of goods sold and purchased.

Assets and liabilities

15   Assets and liabilities must be recorded (section 221(2)(b)). Details must therefore be included of all the company's assets and liabilities such as debtors, creditors, properties and plant. The accounting records must show the dates of transactions.

Stocks

16   Section 221(3)(a) requires that where the company's business involves dealing in goods, statements of stock held at each financial year-end are to be part of the accounting records. 'Statements of stock' is taken to mean a summary supporting the amount included in the annual accounts in respect of stock. It is further required, by section 221(3)(b), that any statements of stocktakings supporting the year-end stock summary are to form part of the accounting records. Any continuous stock records used for that purpose, or if stock is taken physically the original stock sheets, are therefore to be treated as part of the accounting records.

Purchases and sales of goods

17   Where the company's business involves dealing in goods, section 221(3)(c) requires details of goods sold and purchased, and of individual buyers and sellers, to be recorded. This does not, however, apply to sales by way of ordinary retail trade.

Penalties and disqualification orders

18   Under the penalty provisions in section 221(5) and (6) non-compliance with section 221 is a criminal offence. In addition, by virtue of section 9 of, and paragraph 4(a) of Schedule 1 to, the Company Directors Disqualification Act 1986, the extent of the director's responsibility for any failure by the company to comply with section 221 is one of the matters to which the court must have regard on an application for disqualification of a director.

Chapter 4 – Fundraising regulations

The Charitable Institutions (Fund-Raising) Regulations 1994, SI 1994 No 3024 brought controls on fundraising for charities into force on 1 March 1995. They implemented Part II of the Charities Act 1992.

4.1 Summary

Professional fundraisers are required to give an indication of the institutions benefiting and arrangements for remuneration. Charities have a right to prevent unauthorised fundraising and there is a new crime – the coupling of solicitation of money with a false representation that the institution concerned is a registered charity, although there is a defence of belief on reasonable grounds that the institution was so registered. There is a right for donors to request the repayment of donations made by credit or debit card following radio or TV appeals by fundraisers acting for reward and to request repayment or cool off where there has been a telephone appeal, provided at least £50 is involved.

Professional fundraisers may not solicit money or property for a charity and no person engaged in a promotional venture for reward may represent that contributions are to be given or applied for the benefit of the charity except in accordance with an agreement with the charity which satisfies prescribed requirements.

If these rules are contravened, the charity can apply to the High Court or a County Court for an injunction and offending agreements are only enforceable to the extent allowed by court order.

4.2 Definitions

Section 58 of the Act defines two distinct categories of commercial organisation:

- *The professional fundraiser* – a person who carries on a fundraising business or who, for reward, solicits money or other property for the benefit of a charity otherwise than in the course of carrying on a fundraising business as such. There are a number of exclusions in s58, e.g., a charity itself or a company connected with it (an associate trading company, celebrities fronting a radio or television appeal, and so on). Collectors are also excluded unless they can be regarded as promoters of the collection. Commercial participators are excluded too, but are controlled under their own definition (see below).

- *The commercial participator* – a person who carries on, for gain, a business other than a fundraising business, but in the course of that business engages in promotional ventures in the course of which it is represented that charitable contributions are to be given to or applied for the benefit of a charitable institution. This could be a bank or building society that issues a credit card on the basis that a percentage of the customer's monthly debits will be donated to a particular charity or charities.

4.3 Agreements with fundraisers and participators

Section 59 of the Act prohibits fundraisers or participators from soliciting money or other property for a charity, or representing that charitable contributions will be made except in accordance with an agreement. Regulations 2 and 3 prescribe the requirements and state that agreements must specify:

- the names and addresses of the parties;
- the date of signature by the parties;
- the duration of the agreement;
- any provision relating to earlier termination;
- any terms relating to variation;
- the principal objectives and methods to be used to achieve them;
- the charitable institutions to benefit and their shares;
- the method of determining the proportion of consideration, proceeds or donations; and
- what they will receive from participators, or the remuneration payable to fundraisers.

4.4 Availability of books, documents and other records

Under reg 5, fundraisers and participators must, on request and at all reasonable times, make available to any charity that is party to a relevant agreement any books, documents or other records (however kept) that relate to the charity and are kept for the purposes of the agreement.

4.5 Transmission of money or property

Under reg 6, any monies or other property due to a charity are to be transmitted by the fundraiser or participator to the charity as soon as is practicable, and in any case not later than 28 days from receipt or such other period as may be agreed.

4.6 Indications of benefits and remuneration

Section 60 of the Act provides that a fundraiser soliciting money or other property for a charity must draw up an accompanying statement that identifies the benefiting charity or charities and indicates, in general terms, the methods of calculating the fundraiser's remuneration. The section also covers participators who represent that 'charitable contributions' will be given to or applied for a charity or charities. They must identify the benefiting charity or charities and, in general terms, the method of determining:

- what proportion of the consideration given for goods sold or for services the participator supplies, or of any proceeds of promotional ventures he or she has undertaken, will be given to or applied for the charity or charities concerned; and
- what sums by way of the participator's donations as a result of the sale or supply of any goods or services are to be given or applied, as the case may require. Failure to comply with s60 is a criminal offence punishable by a fine not exceeding £5,000.

Regulation 7 contains similar provisions where funds are raised for charitable purposes otherwise than by professional fundraisers or commercial participators. Persons involved are those who carry on, for gain, a business other than a fundraising business, and are not participators, but who on occasion carry out promotional ventures for charities. There is no requirement of reward.

4.7 Cancellation of payments

Section 61 of the Act provides a right of repayment for charitable donations made by credit or debit card in response to a television or radio broadcast or a telephone appeal. Because of the need to balance the interests of donors and charities, repayment is restricted to payments over £50. Notice must be served on the relevant fundraiser within seven days of the solicitation, and the charity may deduct administrative expenses. Relevant donors must be given notice of these repayment rights.

4.8 Unauthorised fundraising and false statements

Sections 62 and 63 introduce powerful safeguards under which a charity may obtain an injunction against any person raising funds for it if the charity objects to the method being used or does not wish to be associated with a promotional venture. In addition, persons making false representations that an institution is a registered charity when it is not are guilty of a criminal offence punishable by a fine of up to £5,000. Section 26 of the Deregulation and Contracting-Out Act 1994 adds a defence of belief on reasonable grounds that the institution concerned was a registered charity.

Failure to comply with the requirements could lead to difficulty in enforcing agreements with charities and a criminal prosecution leading to a fine.

Fundraisers and participators will need to review their arrangements with charities since the provisions described above apply from 1 March 1995 to both new and existing arrangements.

4.9 Street collections

Raising money or selling goods for charity in streets or public places usually requires a permit or licence from either the appropriate local authority or if the collection takes place in London, the police or the Common Council of the City of London.

Legislation allows local regulations to be made. These deal with such matters as the obstruction and hindrance caused to traffic by events, and the conditions under which, persons may collect money or sell articles for charitable and other purposes.

4.10 House-to-house collections

House-to-house collections must have a licence or an exemption from a licence. Licences are issued by local authorities or in London by the police of the Common Council of the City of London. Exemptions may be granted by the Home Office for collections covering a wide area or the police for a local collection being held over a short period of time.

Regulations exist governing the conduct of collections on door steps, in public houses and at places of work. The regulations cover collections of both money and other property.

4.11 Lotteries

Charities may run lotteries in order to raise funds for their charitable purposes as defined in ss3 and 5 of the Lotteries and Amusements Act 1976. The profits of such lotteries, that are promoted by charities or by subsidiary companies on their behalf, are exempt from tax provided the lottery is conducted within the requirements of this Act and the lottery profits are applied solely to the purposes of the charity. Where a subsidiary company, rather than the charity, is registered as the society under s5 of the Lotteries and Amusements Act 1976 the lottery profits will belong to the company and not to the charity for tax purposes. The exemption will not apply and the company will need to pass the profits to the charity under Gift Aid to obtain relief from tax.

There are two main types of lotteries of interest to charities both regulated by the Lotteries and Amusements Act 1976 as amended by the National Lottery etc Act 1993:

- small lotteries; and
- society lotteries.

4.11.1 Small lotteries

Small lotteries do not need to be registered but they have to be incidental to an exempt entertainment. Exempt entertainments are defined by the 1976 Act and include fetes, bazaars and dinner dances. Certain conditions have to be met which include no cash prizes, the sale and issue of tickets and announcement of the results must be carried out during the entertainment and on the premises where it is held and no more than £250 can be spent on buying prizes.

Trustees are advised to seek professional advice if they are in any doubt.

4.11.2 Society lotteries

Where a charity is promoting the sale of lottery tickets which will exceed £20,000 in value (or if taken together with sales from previous lotteries in the same year will exceed £250,000) it will be necessary to register with the Gaming Board. Charities conducting lotteries below these thresholds are required to register with the local authority.

There are detailed statutory regulations about the conduct of lotteries covering accounts, age restrictions, the maximum price of tickets and the amounts which may be paid out in prizes and deducted for expenses. Trustees are advised to consult the appropriate local authority or the Gaming Board for further advice. The address of the Gaming Board is:

Lotteries Section
Berkshire House
168/173 High Holborn
London
WC1V 7AA
(tel: 020 7306 6200)

Further detailed guidance on the above and other matters is given in the Charity Commission publication *CC20: Charities and Fund-raising*.

Chapter 5 – SORP 2000

5.1 Introduction

It was as long ago as 1981 that *Financial reporting by charities*, a report of a research study by Peter Bird and Peter Morgan-Jones, highlighted the need for greater consistency and clarity in accounting by charities. The study surveyed and evaluated the accounting and reporting practices of charities and found substantial room for improving reporting standards and enhancing comparability of information.

In 1982 the then ASC set up a working party to consider financial reporting by charities. In particular, the working party was asked to explore ways of enhancing the usefulness of charities' annual reports and to examine the possibility of reducing the number of diverse practices of financial accounting and reporting then adopted.

The result was *Accounting by charities: a discussion paper*, published in February 1984. It was a wide-ranging paper which dealt not only with the accounts of a charity, but, also, with the information which should accompany the accounts in the annual report. As Denis Peach, the then Chief Commissioner, explained in the Foreword:

> 'Quite apart from their duty to be accountable for the funds they hold and use, charity trustees will want to work in the light of day and to provide as much information as is practicable, and useful to the public they serve and indeed to public at large. Informative and easily-understood accounts – and indeed annual reports – will serve the purpose of averting suspicion and overcoming ignorance and should positively encourage support, not just for individual charities but for charity at large.'

The response to the paper indicated that guidance on how charities should account for the funds they held and use would be welcomed and a proposed SORP, ED 38, was published in late 1985, the recommendations of which were based largely on the conclusions of the discussion paper. This was followed by SORP 2 *Accounting by charities*, in May 1988, the purpose of which was to improve the quality of reporting by charities, to reduce the number of diverse accounting practices adopted and to provide assistance to those responsible for the preparation of charities' annual reports. The recommendations were intended to apply to all charities (except universities), regardless of their constitution, size or complexity and regardless of the reporting requirements, if any, imposed on them.

Why a SORP? The ASC considered that, although many charities were required by law to prepare accounts, only a small minority were subject to detailed requirements on the form and content of accounts or were required to prepare an annual report. The ASC did not seek to impose inflexible accounting practices and standardise formats of presentation on charities. Rather, it believed that, at that time, it was more appropriate to issue guidance which:

(a) left discretion to trustees of each charity to apply the provisions of the SORP according to the character of the charity and the significance of the figures concerned; and
(b) was helpful to the majority of charities in the evolution of their accounting methodology.

For five years SORP 2 represented the benchmark for accounting by charities, providing general guidance embodying best practice. But it offered alternative treatment in a number of instances. Experience of working with the SORP had shown that many of the alternatives needed to be eliminated for, as the ED to the revised SORP described, 'the sake of simplicity and consistency'.

Accordingly, in March 1993, the Charity Accounting Review Committee, set up under the auspices of the Commissioners, published an ED of a revised SORP. In framing its proposals, the Committee was mindful not only of a new statutory regime but, also, of developments internationally, particularly in the United States.

There followed a period of over two and a half years, during which time comments on the ED were taken into account and protracted discussions between the Committee and the ASB took place. Finally on 16 October 1995, the revised SORP was issued and this, together with the 1995 Regulations, represented modern charity accounting as we now know it.

There were many new requirements which affected most charities, which had to reflect them for accounting periods beginning on or after 1 March 1996. For example:

- the concept of a Statement of Financial Activites (SOFA) was introduced;
- there were minimum requirements for the Trustees' Report;
- investments had to be stated at a market value with unrealised gains or losses being shown within the SOFA;
- there were specific and detailed requirements regarding the notes to the accounts; and

- incorporated charities had to reflect the requirements of the SORP (but not the Regulations) into the already strict regime regarding company accounts.

5.2 The revised charity SORP issued in October 2000 (SORP 2000)

5.2.1 Background

The 1995 SORP introduced major changes to the reporting and accounting requirements of charities and at long last the format of charity accounts became more standardised. At the same time there was a commitment to review that SORP and a consultation exercise was launched in September 1998 followed by the publication of the Exposure Draft of a revised SORP in December 1999.

Following comments made on the Exposure Draft, SORP 2000 was issued on 17 October 2000. Generally, there were few changes from the Exposure Draft; possibly the main one was the requirement in the Trustees' Annual Report to confirm that major risks facing the charity be identified and systems established to mitigate them, which replaced the reference to internal controls in the Exposure Draft.

SORP 2000 is a comprehensive statement supported by the new Regulations made by the Home Office in a Statutory Instrument (SI 2000 No 2868). Thus the Regulations are the legal requirements conferred by the Charities Act; the SORP states how those requirements and other matters should be reflected in charity reports and accounts.

5.2.2 Effective date

SORP 2000 applies to accounting periods beginning on or after 1 January 2001 (i.e., normally those ending on 31 December 2001 or later). However, charities are encouraged to adopt the SORP earlier and may do so provided that their accounts were not approved before 15 November 2000 (e.g., accounts to 31 December 2000 may be prepared either under the 1995 or the revised SORP).

5.2.3 Overview

Although the SORP has been rewritten and the sequence of paragraphs changed in order to eliminate inconsistencies, reduce repetitions and make the requirements clearer, there are no major changes to the structure of the accounts and no new requirements that the Charity Commission regard as onerous.

The SORP has been updated for new accounting standards and, in particular, Financial Reporting Standards 8-16 that have been issued since the 1995 SORP. Charities will need to ensure that they comply with subsequent relevant accounting pronouncements. SORP 2000 has also clarified many of the accounting requirements such as those dealing with legacies, gifts in kind and grants paid.

The requirements for the Trustees' Annual Report are more flexible and require additional reporting of matters such as reserves and risk management. The increased emphasis on reporting is reflected in the title of the SORP which is *Accounting and Reporting by Charities*; the 1995 SORP did not include the words 'and Reporting'.

The SORP also introduces the concept of certain paragraphs being marked as **AA** which are considered as being applicable to all charities and should be included in the accounts or Trustees' Annual Report as required. They are summarised in an Appendix to the SORP, which has been reproduced at the end of this chapter.

There are now special sections in the SORP dealing with the following:

- Consolidation of Subsidiary Undertakings;
- Associates, Joint Ventures and Joint Arrangements;
- The SORP in Relation to Charitable Companies in the UK; and
- Accounting for Smaller Charities.

In addition to an Introduction and the above special sections, the other main sections in the SORP deal with:

- Trustees' Annual Report;
- General Principles;
- Statement of Financial Activities;
- Balance Sheet;
- Cash-flow Statement;
- Disclosure of Accounting Policies;
- Summary Financial Information and Statements;
- Appendices :
  - Glossary;
  - Application of Accounting Standards;
  - The Funds of a Charity;
  - A List of Disclosure Paragraphs Marked as **AA** (Applicable to All);
  - Thresholds;
  - The Charity Accounting Review Committee (1999/2000);
- Index.

5.2.4 Objective

The main objective of the SORP (para 2)

'is to improve the quality of financial reporting by charities and to assist those who are responsible for the preparation of the Charity's Annual Report and Accounts. The intention is that these recommendations will reduce diversity in accounting practice and presentation. In all but exceptional circumstances charities preparing accruals accounts should follow this SORP in order for their accounts to give a true and fair view'.

However

'each recommendation should be considered in the context of what is material to the particular charity' (para 13).

5.2.5 Obligation

Paragraph 9 states that

'the main obligation of the trustees in preparing accruals accounts (but not receipts and payments accounts) is to give a true and fair view of the charity's incoming resources and application of resources during the year and of its state of affairs at the end of the year. To achieve this, the trustees' judgement may dictate the disclosure of more information than specifically recommended in this SORP. Similarly trustees may occasionally find that following a recommendation is incompatible with the obligation to give a true and fair view. They should then use the alternative accounting treatment which gives a true and fair view and provide particulars (in accordance with paragraph 280) of any material departure from the recommendations in this SORP, in the Annual Report and the notes to the accounts. A departure is not justified simply because it gives the reader a more appealing picture of the financial position or results of the charity'.

In addition the introductory statement in the SORP made by the Charity Commissioners states:

'The Trustees of all charities are under a duty to keep proper accounting records for their charity which are sufficient to show and explain all the charity's transactions. The revised Statement of Recommended Practice (SORP) sets out how a charity should report annually on resources entrusted to it and the activities it undertakes.

This SORP applies to all charities regardless of their size, constitution or complexity – except where a more specialised SORP applies (eg Higher Educational Institutions, Registered Social Landlords). The impact of the SORP will, however, depend upon the size and complexity of a charity's operation. To help smaller charities in particular, the Charity Commission produces a range of simplified guidance.

The Commission expects charities to comply fully with this or any other applicable SORP. In so far as a charity diverges from the SORP in material respects, the charity's accounts should identify any divergence clearly and provide a full explanation. If no explanation is given or the explanation is unsatisfactory, the Commission may raise the matter with the charity and, if circumstances warrant it, institute an inquiry.

Where the Commission finds that difficulties have arisen as a result of any divergence from this or any other applicable SORP, the Commission will take such divergence and any explanation the Trustees have given into account. The failure of Trustees without good reason to apply the appropriate SORP principles may be relevant to their responsibility for the difficulties arising.'

The principle which holds, therefore, is that, unless the presumption in favour of the SORP can be justifiably rebutted, which is clearly and fully explained in the notes, charity trustees of all charities, regardless of status, when preparing accounts which are required to show a true and fair view, should comply with the SORP's recommendations.

5.2.6 Scope

To which charities does the revised SORP apply? Paragraph 12 states that

'this SORP is intended to apply to all charities in the United Kingdom and the Republic of Ireland regardless of their size, constitution or complexity. It provides the basis for the preparation of accruals accounts to give a true and fair view and also provides recommendations in other cases eg on the preparation of receipts and payments accounts. However, where a separate SORP exists for a particular class of charities, the trustees of charities in that class should adhere to that Statement of Recommended Practice'.

At the time of writing other SORP's are in existence for:

(a) registered social landlords;
(b) common investment funds; and
(c) the higher education sector.

Further, a number of 'special interest groups' have been set up, supported by the Commissioners. Two such groups have produced guidance for independent schools and parochial church councils.

In addition, guidance has been provided for cathedrals.

Furthermore, The Scout Association has produced guidance on the new accounting and auditing requirements for groups and districts and the Department of Culture, Media and Sport have published a specialised SORP guide for museums and galleries.

Much debate has taken place regarding the position of charitable companies. Although this is set to continue, SORP 2000 hopefully clarifies a number of issues by way of including a separate section entitled 'the SORP in Relation to Charitable Companies in the UK' (paras 331 to 343). These matters are covered in more detail in chapter **16**.

5.2.7 The main changes from the 1995 SORP

At a glance
The main changes may be summarised as follows:

- Fewer detailed requirements in the Trustees' Annual Report but more narrative information on corporate governance and certain policies adopted by the charity, particularly those relating to investments, grants, reserves and areas of risk.
- Changes to the presentation of some headings in the SOFA. However, the gross income threshold for charities that may wish to disregard the prescribed expenditure headings is increased from £100,000 to £250,000.
- Resources expended now consist of two categories of expenditure.
- Fundraising costs are now included in a new heading 'Costs of generating funds' which may optionally be deducted from the total of incoming resources to give a sub-total entitled 'Net incoming resources available for charitable application'.
- Management and administration expenses are now included as part of charitable expenditure.
- Changed disclosures relating to staff costs.
- Realised and unrealised investment gains or losses may be combined on one line (but not for incorporated charities unless they prepare a separate income and expenditure account).
- Consolidation of subsidiaries is now on a line-by-line basis as set out in FRS 2.
- The rules for capitalising inalienable and historic fixed assets have been brought into line with FRS 15.
- There are restated rules regarding the recognition of incoming resources and, specifically, legacies. 'Entitlement, certainty and measurement' are now key factors.
- Recognition of liabilities must now be in line with FRS 12. This may particularly affect the treatment of grants payable.
- The requirements for the detailed disclosures of grants payable and rules for non-disclosure have been tightened.

The above changes, together with some other relevant matters which are likely to affect most charities, are summarised below in the order of the SORP. The detailed requirements are given in subsequent chapters.

Trustees' Annual Report

This report should consist of legal and administrative information, which is essentially the same as that required by the 1995 SORP, together with narrative information.

Paragraph 31 requires the Trustees' Annual Report to

'explain what the charity is trying to do and how it is going about it. It should show whether the charity has achieved its objectives during the year and explain its plans for the future. It should also help the reader of the report and accounts understand how the numerical part of the accounts relates to the organisational structure and activities of the charity'.

The following narrative information should be included in the report of the charity:

- An explanation of its objects by reference to its governing document and, if appropriate, its mission statement.
- The organisational and decision-making structure.
- Relationships with related parties and other charities and organisations with which it co-operates.
- A review of the activities of the charity (or group if applicable) in the context of its strategy, including significant changes, developments and achievements in the past year, post-balance sheet events and future plans. If applicable, comments should be made on the contribution of volunteers and the effectiveness of fundraising activities.
- An explanation of any funds in deficit and what action is to be taken.
- A statement confirming that the major risks facing the charity have been identified and reviewed and that systems have been established to mitigate them.
- A statement of policies, and in particular those relating to:
  - reserves (further information is available in CC19);
  - investment policy and performance against policy;
  - grant-making.

General principles

These remain largely unchanged although the position regarding permanent endowment fund expenses has been clarified. The key principles are summarised below.

Fundamental accounting concepts
- Other than Receipts and Payments Accounts, accounts should be prepared on the going concern assumption and the accruals concept and provide information that is relevant, reliable, comparable and understandable. They should also follow accounting standards.

Fund accounting

The main funds are normally:
- unrestricted income funds
  - general
  - designated
- restricted funds/special trusts
  - income
  - endowment/capital
    - expendable
    - permanent
- The notes to the accounts should include:
  - split of assets and liabilities between each type of fund;
  - brief description of each fund;
  - separate disclosure of funds in deficit, together with an explanation in the Trustees' Annual Report;
  - summary of material movements in the funds, including an explanation of transfers between funds;
- Expenses incurred in the management, administration or protection of a permanent endowment fund should be charged against the capital in the fund.
- A reasonable allocation of overhead expenses can normally be set against restricted funds.

Branches

- There are no major changes but charities with branches should be familiar with paras 51 to 55.
- The definition of branches is clearly stated in the Glossary to the SORP.

Statement of Financial Activities (SOFA)

The presentation of both incoming and outgoing resources **has been altered to provide a more logical layout and individual charities should expand the SOFA where necessary** 'in order to present a true and fair view and convey a proper understanding of the nature of all their activities. It is recommended that the charity's aim is to have a clear link between the incoming and outgoing resources and in particular the functional split of activities' **(para 70). Paragraph 70 also shows how incoming and outgoing resources can be linked together by using similar or identical headings within the SOFA.**

Charities with a gross income not exceeding £250,000 do not have to use the standard expenditure headings and sub-headings but can choose expenditure classifications to suit their circumstances.

The format still requires, for the current year, a columnar split between unrestricted, restricted and endowment funds with a total column, together with a total column for the previous year.

The structure and format is covered in paras 57 to 74.

Other presentation matters (including disclosure requirements in the notes to the accounts) are covered in paras 75 to 180, of which the following are the most relevant or represent changes from the 1995 SORP.

Recognition of incoming resources

- Incoming resources should not be recognised until the conditions for receipt have been met and there is reasonable assurance of receipt. There is greater emphasis on three key factors, being entitlement, certainty and measurement.
- There are detailed paragraphs dealing with reporting incoming resources gross, deferral of income, the treatment of income which does not belong to the charity and incoming resources subject to restrictions.

Donations, legacies and similar incoming resources

- The material components should be separated either in the SOFA or in the notes to the accounts.
- There are clearer guidelines relating to legacies and in particular:
  - a legacy should only be treated as receivable if it has been received or otherwise the three above factors (entitlement, certainty and measurement) are satisfied;
  - it should also be clear that the personal representatives had agreed the legacy before the year end;
  - otherwise the notes to the accounts should refer to material legacies notified to the charity, including an estimate, where possible, of the amounts involved.

Intangible income

- This should only be included in the SOFA when it is provided at a cost to a third party and the benefit to the charity is quantifiable and measurable (e.g., staff on secondment to the charity or costs of rent-free accommodation borne by the landlord). There should be an analysis of this income in the notes to the accounts.
- The contribution made by volunteers is normally excluded from this requirement but there should be an appropriate comment in the Trustees' Annual Report.

Incoming resources from operating activities

- These should be split between those in furtherance of the charity's objects (e.g., sales of goods and services including government or local authority grants towards those objects) and those for generating funds (e.g., fundraising events, selling donated goods and certain sponsorship income). Further details are given in paras 101 to 107.
- An analysis should be given in the notes to the accounts to supplement the information given in the SOFA.

Subsidiary undertakings
- The charity's own SOFA should show separately, and appropriately describe, all receipts from its subsidiaries.

Investment income
- The notes to the accounts should continue to show gross investment income arising from each category of investment. Where applicable, FRS 16 requires transitional relief included therein to be disclosed.

Recognition of liabilities
- The SORP now specifically refers to FRS's 5 and 12 and requires a liability (whether legal or constructive) to be recognised in full when the obligation arises.
- If the commitment is conditional there may not be a liability. However, there is likely to be a contingent liability in such cases.

Costs of generating funds
- Dealt with in paras 132 to 135, this is a wider category than before and specifically includes investment management costs for both income generation and capital maintenance.
- Where material the different categories of these costs should be shown in the SOFA or in the notes to the accounts.

Grants payable in furtherance of the charity's objects
- The disclosure requirements have been considerably tightened where grant making is material. Grant-making charities are strongly advised to read paras 138 to 146 in detail.
- Grant-making is material if a charity makes grants totalling at least 5 per cent of its total resources expended.
- An analysis is required differentiating between individual and institutional grants (as defined in para 141) and it should disclose the total number and value given for different charitable purposes.
- A sufficient number of institutional grants should also include the name of the recipient institution and the number and total value of the grants made to that institution in the accounting year to convey a proper understanding of the charity's grant-making activities. To be 'sufficient' this information will normally relate to the 50 largest grants (or all grants if less than 50) but those below £1,000 in total may be excluded.
- However, and exceptionally, if the above information could seriously prejudice either the recipient institution or the charity itself then details of each grant may be withheld. In such cases the notes to the accounts should show the total number, value and general purpose of the non-disclosed grants. Reasons for their non-disclosure, together with full details should be sent in writing to the Charity Commission and the Trustees' Annual Report should confirm that this has been done.

Support costs in furtherance of the objects of the charity
- Where applicable and material these should be shown separately in the SOFA and further analysed in the notes to the accounts.

Management and administration
- These expenses must continue to be shown separately but are now part of 'charitable expenditure'. They include both direct costs (e.g., audit and legal fees, costs of trustee meetings and preparing statutory accounts) and indirect costs (i.e., apportionment of certain overheads).
- The main items should be analysed in the notes to the accounts.

Other related SOFA matters to be shown in the notes to the accounts
Related party transactions

- Following the issue of FRS 8, this rewritten section of the SORP replaces the previous one on transactions with trustees and connected persons. Any charity involved in such transactions should read paras 157 to 165 in detail. Basically, these transactions are those 'where the charity has a relationship with another party or parties (the related party) which might inhibit it from pursuing its own separate interests' (para 157).
- Related parties include a charity trustee, or other person related to the charity, or somebody who is connected to them. There are further definitions in the Glossary to the SORP.

Trustee remuneration and expenses
- These sections remain largely unchanged but it should be noted that:
  - the legal authority under which any remuneration is paid, and the reason it is paid, should be disclosed;
  - trustee expenses met by direct payment to a third party must now also be disclosed.

Staff costs and emoluments
- The analysis must now include costs in respect of seconded and agency staff and those employed by connected companies.
- There are changes to the disclosures relating to higher paid employees:
  - the number of employees with emoluments of £50,000 (previously £40,000) or more must be shown in bands of £10,000;
  - pension details must also be disclosed in total for higher paid employees showing:
    (i) contributions to money purchase schemes; and
    (ii) the number of staff to whom retirement benefits are accruing under money purchase and defined benefit schemes respectively;
  - it should now be stated if there are no employees with emoluments above £50,000.

External examination costs
- In addition to the costs of audit or external examination the disclosures now include amounts payable to the reporting accountant (i.e., for incorporated charities not requiring an audit) and branch audit costs.

Indemnity insurance and ex-gratia payments
- These are covered in paras 170 and 178 to 179 respectively. However, there may be limitations on when these expenses may be borne by the charity.

Balance sheet
Generally, the form and content of the balance sheet remains unchanged and in particular, investments must continue to be shown at market value. However, the following should be noted.

Inalienable and historic fixed assets
- These are defined in the Glossary to the SORP and include such assets as ancient monuments, historic buildings and art and museum collections. The rules for capitalising these assets reflect the requirements of FRS 15.
- These assets may be excluded from the balance sheet if reliable cost information is not available or significant costs are involved in obtaining the extra information compared with the benefits gained by users of the accounts.
- Information on such assets (whether or not they have been capitalised) should be given in the notes to the accounts or in a separate, publicly available publication to which reference is made in the notes to the accounts.
- Charities which have such assets are strongly advised to read in full paras 208 to 217.

Impairment of fixed assets
- Impairment occurs if the net book value of the asset is higher than its recoverable amount. In these cases, the requirements of FRS 11 must be applied.
- Examples of the possible occurrence of impairment are shown in para 226. The methods used in the impairment review must be disclosed in the notes to the accounts.

Provisions for commitments
These are covered in paras 250 to 259 and include both liabilities on the balance sheet and those that are 'intentions'. In particular:

- Where provisions are to be paid over several years it may be necessary to discount the future outflow of resources to their present value.

- If expressions of financial support do not constitute a constructive obligation but there is still an 'intention' to settle out of existing unrestricted funds then an appropriate designated fund should be created.

Cash-flow statement
- There are no changes in the requirements to prepare a cash-flow statement and this must therefore continue to be prepared in accordance with FRS 1 if the statement is required.
- The starting point for a cash-flow statement will normally be the figure on the SOFA against 'Net incoming resources before revaluations and investment asset disposals'.

Movements in endowments should not be included in cashflows from 'operating activities' but should be treated as increases or decreases in the 'financing' section. Details of how this is achieved and other information on the cash-flow statement is shown in paras 272 to 276.

Disclosure of accounting policies
Paragraph 277 states 'charity accounts should include notes on the accounting policies chosen which should be the most appropriate in the particular circumstances of each charity for the purpose of giving a true and fair view. The policies should be consistent with this SORP, Accounting Standards and relevant legislation'.

This section of the SORP continues to para 291 and includes guidance on policies relating to:

- Basis of the preparation of the accounts
- Departures from the SORP and Accounting Standards
- Split of direct and indirect expenditure within the SOFA and methods of apportionment
- Fixed assets (including depreciation)
- Omissions of branches from the accounts
- Investments (including gains and losses)
- Legacies

- Gifts and intangible income
- Funds structure
- Pension contributions
- Grants receivable
- Foreign exchange transactions
- Deferred income
- Exceptional items
- Life membership subscriptions
- Finance and operating leases
- Endowment funds
- Irrecoverable VAT
- Recognition of liabilities

Summary Financial Information and Statements
- The information which must accompany summarised accounts remains unchanged.

- If summarised information, in whatever form, does not include information on the SOFA and balance sheet, then it must be accompanied by a statement signed on behalf of the trustees as to:
  - the purpose of the information;
  - whether or not it is from the full accounts;
  - whether or not the full accounts have been externally examined;
  - details as to how copies of the full accounts can be obtained.
- If branch accounts are produced it must be stated that the summary is for the branch only and has been extracted from the main charity accounts (showing also the name of that charity).

The new special sections of the SORP

As mentioned earlier in this chapter there are new sections dealing with four specific matters. Where these apply to a charity it is recommended that the sections are read in detail. Some of the more fundamental matters are summarised below.

Consolidation of subsidiary undertakings

- Consolidation is brought into line with FRS 2 which now requires consolidation on a line-by-line basis.
- If the gross income of the group is no more than £250,000 then it may not be necessary to consolidate.
- Although technically there should be a SOFA for both the group and the parent, that for the parent is often omitted. The Charity Commission is prepared to accept such accounts provided that the assets and liabilities of the charity can be distinguished from those of its subsidiaries and that the turnover and results of the subsidiaries are clearly stated. However, the Commission retains the power to require a charity SOFA and the public have a legal right to request it.
- Funds or reserves of subsidiaries, other than those used for carrying out the charity's objects, should be shown separately on the consolidated balance sheet.

Associates, joint ventures and joint arrangements

- In accordance with FRS 9 associates should be included in the accounts based on the net equity method and joint ventures on the gross equity method.
- There are detailed disclosure requirements contained in paras 329 and 330.

The SORP in relation to charitable companies in the UK

- Charitable companies must comply with the Companies Act 1985 with respect to the form and content of their accounts. In practice, most of the reporting requirements will be met by following the SORP.

- The Charity Commission will normally accept the Directors' Report as also fulfilling the purpose of the Trustees' Annual Report provided that it contains all of the necessary additional information required. In practice it is recommended that this is made clear in the report.
- Company law requires an income and expenditure account to be prepared. However, this may not always be necessary for charitable companies provided that:
  - the title makes it clear that the SOFA includes the income and expenditure account; and
  - there are no movements on endowment (capital) funds;
  - there are no unrealised gains or losses or if there are, then these are below a line entitled 'Net income/(expenditure) for the year', which replaces or is in addition to 'Net incoming resources before revaluations and investment asset disposals'. However, realised gains/(losses) will need to be included before arriving at the above sub-total (i.e., realised and unrealised gains/losses will need to be separately shown for charitable companies).
- If a separate (summary) income and expenditure account is prepared it should be derived from and cross-referenced to the corresponding figures in the SOFA.
- Where there is an upward revaluation of fixed assets, a revaluation reserve will arise and this should be separately shown on the balance sheet of charitable companies probably by way of a prominent inset.

Accounting for smaller charities

A smaller charity is defined in para 344 as **'one which due to its size does not have to adopt all the requirements of this SORP'**.

- Charities below a certain threshold can follow the Financial Reporting Standard for Smaller Entities (FRSSE) except where it conflicts with the SORP in which case the SORP must be followed. This does not apply to consolidated accounts. The current thresholds, of which at least two of three conditions must be met, are:
  - Annual Gross Income – not exceeding £2,800,000
  - Balance Sheet Total – not exceeding £1,400,000
  - Average number of employees – not exceeding 50.
- Charities with gross income not exceeding £250,000:
  - may elect not to have an audit subject to any other regulatory or constitutional requirements. In such cases (subject to the above gross income threshold):
    - unincorporated charities with gross income or total expenditure over £10,000 require an independent examination;
    - incorporated charities with gross income over £90,000 require an audit exemption report,

- may choose expenditure classifications in the SOFA to suit their circumstances;
- the section of the Trustees' Annual Report dealing with activities may be a brief summary of the main activities and achievements during the year. The Regulations also exclude the requirement to report on areas of risk although the Charity Commission would still prefer to see this included;
- the Regulations permit the exclusion of references to compliance with, or departures from, accounting standards and SORPs and details of professional indemnity insurance.
- Charities with gross income not exceeding £100,000:
  - accounts may be prepared on the Receipts and Payments basis, the format of which remains unchanged. This does not apply to charitable companies, others which may be subject to another regulatory framework or those with another specific requirement in their governing document.

Annex – List of SORP disclosure paragraphs marked as AA (applicable to all)

Requirement	Paragraph
Duty to Prepare Annual Report and Accounts	**26-29**
Legal and Administrative Information	**30**
Charity name	30(a)
Governing document	30(b)
Trustee details	30(c)(i)-(iv)
	(v) for companies
Address of principal office	30(d)
Address of others	30(e)
Investment powers	30(g)
Narrative Information	**31**
Objects	31(a)
Organisational Structure	31(b)
Connected Parties	31(c)
Review of activities	31(d)
Policies (reserves and others as applicable)	31(e)
Funds in deficit	31(f)
Risk	31(g)
Particulars of individual funds and notes to the accounts	
Assets and liabilities by fund	49(a)
Nature and purpose of each fund	49(b)
Funds in deficit	49(c)
Material movements and transfers	49(d)
Recognition of Liabilities	
Accounting policies recognising different liabilities	128/284(a)
Costs of Generating Funds	
Categories and major items of expenditure	135
Costs of Activities in Furtherance of the charity's objects and Support Costs	
Major items in support costs	150

Management and Administration	
Major items in management and administration	152
Allocations of Costs	
Accounting policies, basis and principles	154/284(c)
Trustee Remuneration	
If there is remuneration	**166(b) & (c)**
If there is not remuneration	166(d)
Trustee Expenses	
If there are expenses	167 & 168
If there are not expenses	169
Staff Costs and Emoluments	
If there are higher paid staff	173 & 174
If there are not any higher paid staff	175
Costs of Audit, Independent Examination or Reporting Accountant Services and other Financial Services	
Costs of external scrutiny and advice	176
The Basis of the Preparation of the Accounts	
Basis of preparation	279
Departures from this SORP and accounting standards	280
Incoming Resources Policy Notes	
Policies for material incoming resources	283
Resources Expended Policy Notes	
The policy for the recognition of liabilities including constructive obligations	284(a)
The policy for including items within types of resources expended	284(b)
The methods and principles for the allocation and apportionment of all costs	284(c)
Fund Structure Policy Notes	
Description of different types of funds	289

Chapter 6 – Trustees' annual report

6.1 Introduction

Like directors' reports of commercial organisations, the trustees' annual report forms the main narrative section accompanying the accounts. Unlike commercial organisations, however, many features of a charity's operations, particularly those in respect of voluntary help, donations-in-kind and other intangible income, can be difficult to measure in financial terms. Accordingly, both in terms of accountability and in order to complement the remainder of the accounts, the trustees' annual report should measure the achievement of the charity's objectives not only in quantitative, but also in qualitative, terms, as imaginatively and openly as possible.

The report's completeness and transparency are, thus, prerequisites if the charity's operations and accounts are to be properly understood and appreciated.

The Charity Commission now attach greater importance to the report than before and this increased emphasis on reporting is reflected in the title of the SORP which is *Accounting and Reporting by Charities*; the 1995 SORP did not include the words 'and Reporting'. The Commission have been quoted as stating

> 'Annual Reports provide charities with a wonderful opportunity to tell their story, but they can often be presented in dull and outdated prose and be unimaginatively structured. We would like to see every charity's report become a key document, explaining why and how the charity does its work and adding to the stock of accountability by charities'.

6.2 Preparing the trustees' annual report

The charity trustees of all charities, including small charities, must prepare an annual report. The report should describe what the charity is trying to do and how it is going about it and, as part of the report or attached to it, there should also be a statement containing the legal and administrative details of the charity. Whilst the report is legally a separate document from the accounts, they are normally presented together in the same publication (para 26).

Where required, or requested to, charitable companies must send the annual report to the Commissioners, together with annual accounts prepared under the 1985 Act and an auditors' report, or one made for the purposes of s249(2) of that Act. The directors' report, as prepared under s234 of that Act, will not simply suffice as the trustees' annual report. To be valid as a trustees' annual report, and to avoid the preparation of two separate documents, the directors' report could be expanded to incorporate the additional information recommended by the SORP and the Regulations. In cases where the two reports (re Trustees' and Directors') are combined as one document it is recommended that this be made clear either at the beginning of the report and/or in the heading to the report.

6.3 Structure and components

Paragraph 4 of the SORP states that the report and accounts should:

(a) provide timely and regular information on the charity and its funds;
(b) enable the reader to understand the charity's objectives, structure, activities and achievements; and
(c) enable the reader to gain a full and proper appreciation of the charity's financial transactions during the year and of the position of its funds at the end of the year.

Therefore a properly structured annual report plays a major role in fulfilling the above requirements.

Paragraph 27 recommends that the trustees should include any additional information which they are required by law to report and to confirm that the accounts comply with current statutory requirements, the requirements of the charity's governing document and the requirements of this SORP.

6.3.1 Legal and administrative information

Paragraph 30 of the SORP recommends that the following legal and administrative disclosures are provided within the trustees' report although in practice much of this information is appended to the report.

(a) The full name of the charity (as registered) including any other name by which it is known, together with its registration number and if applicable, the company registration number.
(b) An indication of the nature of the governing document and how the charity is constituted.
(c) The names of all of the charity's trustees on the date the report was approved or the names of at least 50 trustees (including all the officers of the charity: e.g., Chair, Treasurer, etc. and Custodian Trustees)

where there are more than 50 trustees; where the charity trustees are incorporated this should include the name of the corporate body.

In addition, the name of any other persons who served as charity trustees of custodian trustees during the financial year in question should be given.

The method of appointment or election of trustees should be given, as should the name of any body or persons entitled to nominate or appoint one, or more, of the trustees. If a corporate trustee is acting as sole trustee, the names of its directors, or other persons managing it, should be given.

Where disclosure of the names of any charity trustees and persons with power of appointment – and likewise the charity's principal address (see (d) below) – could lead to that person being placed in personal danger (e.g., in the case of a women's refuge) the trustees may dispense with the disclosure provided that the Charity Commission has given the trustees the authority to do so. It is recommended that the reasons for such non-disclosure should be given in the report. The directors of charitable companies should note that there is no corresponding dispensation in relation to the disclosure requirements for the statutory directors' report.

(d) The address of the charity's principal or registered office; however, this may be omitted as described in (c) above unless it is also the registered office of a charitable company, which must always be given.

(e) The names and addresses of the charity's main agents and advisers. This would include bankers, solicitors, auditors, reporting accountants or independent examiners, investment managers etc.

(f) Details of any specific restrictions imposed by the governing document concerning the way in which the charity can operate, e.g., whether there are any borrowing limits, whether any property is permanent endowment etc.

(g) A summary of any specific investment powers and their authority (e.g., governing document, Charity Commission Order etc.).

Section 234(2) of the 1985 Act requires disclosure of the names of the persons who were directors at any time during the year; and, s706(2)(a) requires the accounts (among other documents delivered to the Registrar) to show prominently the company's registered number.

6.3.2 Narrative information

It is difficult to be too prescriptive about this part of the annual report as the narrative information will vary from charity to charity. Indeed, there is conflict between para 7 of the Regulations and the SORP itself. The conflict is between smaller charities (i.e., those with a gross income not exceeding £250,000) where less information is required by the Regulations as compared to the SORP. However, in order to observe best practice, the SORP should always be followed.

All charities should specify the financial year to which the report relates but, in the case of the activities of smaller charities, the Regulations say only that the report should 'be a brief summary of the main activities and achievements of the charity during the year in relation to its objects'. The Regulations prescribe in more detail the disclosure requirements regarding the activities of charities whose gross income exceeds £250,000 and specifically mention a statement regarding risks.

The SORP (para 31) states that the report should explain what the charity is trying to do and how it is going about it and should show whether the charity has achieved it objectives during the year and explain its plans for the future. It should also help the reader of the report and accounts to understand how the numerical part of the accounts relates to the organisational structure and activities of the charity. Each charity should adapt the narrative according to its own particular circumstances but should cover all of the matters below.

Objects
There should be an explanation of the objects of the charity by reference to its governing documents including, if appropriate, the mission statement of the charity.

Organisational structure
There should be a description of the organisational structure of the charity and how decisions are made. Where the charity is part of a wider network, then the relationship involved should be explained. (Note: the Regulations do not require details of the organisational structure to be given for smaller charities.)

Related parties
There should be a statement regarding the relationship between the charity and related parties and with any other charities and organisations with which it co-operates in the pursuit of its charitable objectives. The disclosures relating to related parties are included in FRS8 and in some detail in paras 157–165 of the SORP. Further reference is made in chapter **13**.

It is therefore likely that this section of the report can usefully describe in some detail the nature of any such relationships with a cross-reference to the relevant note within the accounts themselves.

Example A includes the following paragraph regarding related parties.

Example A   *Arts Theatre Trust Limited*

The charity has a very close relationship with N Arts, which is a charity, BF Borough Council and B Town Council, all of which nominate trustees and provide funding to enable the charity to carry out its charitable objectives. A summary of transactions with those parties is set out in note 20 to the financial statements.

Review of activities

This review should be given in the context of the charity's strategy, including significant changes, developments and achievements in the past year, events affecting those activities since the year end and plans for the future.

The book of *Example Reports and Accounts* contains many examples of the relevant disclosures, often under a variety of different headings.

Example D   *Aid Overseas*

Financial results and future activities

During the year, the charity raised almost £16 million net of costs from the general public, governments and other agencies and through its shops to carry out the programmes mentioned above. Of this, almost £14 million was used in the current year.

As shown in the restricted funds column in the Statement of Financial Activities, £8.5 million of income was for particular projects and we still hold £2.8 million which will be used as these projects progress. We have secured an additional £4 million funding for particular ongoing projects for the ensuing year and there are applications under consideration by a variety of bodies for a further £12 million.

£5.5 million was raised with no restrictions through fund-raising activities and grants, and £2 million through trading activities. This money was used to supplement and extend programmes and was particularly invaluable in developing our information campaign.

We are particularly pleased with the trading results for the year ended 30 September 2001, part of which is carried out through our wholly owned trading subsidiary Aid Overseas Trading Limited. This area of operation was reviewed in 1999 and a new business plan was formulated, the benefits of which have flowed through in the current year. This concentrated on better systems for sorting and displaying second hand clothes and a greater emphasis on volunteer training.

For the forthcoming year, we are launching a major fund-raising campaign in 2002 which emphasises the need for higher standards of education in developing countries, particularly regarding sexual health because AIDS is fast becoming the biggest killer in many developing nations. We are planning a major newspaper campaign supported by advertisements in the cinema and on television. We have secured for free the services of Advertising International, the world's largest advertising agency, who have kindly offered their services. The campaign has a fund-raising target of £15 million against anticipated costs of £1.2 million and funds raised will be used exclusively for promotion of sexual health. We plan to lobby governments and other agencies on this particular issue which we hope will raise a further £6 million. It is intended that this will become a long term programme which helps to eliminate the unnecessary pain, suffering and death caused by lack of awareness of the disease.

A more detailed review is given in Example F:

Example F   *The Higher College Charity*

Review of activities and achievements

In the year, Higher College had 825 (1999/00: 793) pupils of whom 163 (1999/00: 152) were day pupils and Junior College had 230 (1999/00: 217) pupils 24 (1999/00: 26) of whom were day pupils. Waiting lists are full, and this gives us confidence that these numbers will continue in the foreseeable future. This is a result of our continued resolve to keep up the academic standards which for the 2001 results were the highest ever achieved. Higher College was placed in the top 20 schools in the country for the third year. Junior College is now regarded as one of the best preparatory schools in the country and accepted as a good start for all pupils even if they do not wish to go on to Higher College.

In addition, we were able to award £686,000 in scholarships, bursaries and grants to 113 pupils through our general and special trust funds, which as a percentage of our pupil total we believe to be one of the highest in the country. This gives us an opportunity to maintain our educational standards.

These academic achievements were attained without affecting our sporting activities. Our 1st XV Rugby Team were undefeated until their last game when they lost to Harrow and the 1st Cricket XI did not lose a game. Junior College's sporting record matched that of Higher College, and we are very proud of our coaching programme for 11 year olds set up five years ago in all the major sports.

Developments

The modernisation of the houses has been completed at an overall cost of £960,000 of which £490,000 was in this financial year. A new appeal has been launched for the building of a new Engineering and Science centre to meet the demands of the millennium. The appeal target is £2 million by the end of the year 2003. By the end of this year £320,000 had been received, with outstanding promises of another £200,000. A good start to the Appeal. Both schools will then have a range of facilities rivalling the best in the country.

Financial activities and results

The net incoming resources for the year amounted to £536,000 of which the operating surplus on school activities was £470,000. This was below our targeted percentage of fee income set out in our long term plans, but was after charging

£335,000 expenditure on refurbishment of the houses. This surplus has been achieved with a less-than-inflation increase in fees and against a background of strongly rising operating costs, so that in the circumstances we consider it a highly satisfactory achievement. Gross income for the year was up by some 10% on last year, reflecting the increase in pupil numbers throughout the school.

The schools are helped considerably each year by the support of the 'Crickets' charity, which provides £50,000 in grants for 11 pupils.

Our trading company continues to hire out Higher College facilities during vacations and school hours, and has contributed £225,000 to the schools' operating surplus.

Total funds increased by £875,000 for the year, including revaluations.

Where applicable, there should also be comments dealing with the contribution of volunteers and effectiveness of fundraising activities. Examples of these are given below:

Example D *Aid Overseas*

Voluntary help and gifts in kind
The trustees are very grateful to the thousands of volunteers who helped by staffing our shops, carrying out fund-raising on our behalf and in particular those who work overseas. The public has been very generous in providing gifts in kind, particularly donations of clothing for resale through our shops and blankets and clothing provided for disaster relief.

Example G *The ABG Charity*

Volunteers
The charity is grateful for the unstinting efforts of its volunteers who are involved in service provision, charity shops and fund-raising. It is estimated that over 120,000 volunteer hours were provided during the year. If this is conservatively valued at £6 an hour the volunteer effort amounts to over £720,000. The charity has recently appointed a volunteer coordinator to ensure that best value is derived from the sterling efforts of our volunteers.

Section 234(2) of the 1985 Act requires the principal activities of the company (and, where applicable, subsidiaries) to be stated, including significant changes during the year; Section 234(1)(a) requires a fair review of the development of the company/subsidiaries during the year; para 6(b) of Sch 7 requires an indication of the likely future developments in the business of the company/subsidiaries.

Policies
This is basically a new area of charity reporting and covers reserves, investments and grant-making.

(a) Reserves

Chapter 7 deals with reserves in detail but the SORP requires the trustees' annual report to state the charity's policy on reserves, stating the level of reserves held and why they are held. Responsibility for establishing an appropriate reserves policy lies with the trustees as does the responsibility for justifying and explaining the level of reserves held. This process should be an integral part of the charity's financial management.

The glossary to SORP 2000 clarifies the meaning of 'reserves'. The reserves policy should cover 'free' reserves so it should not include permanent or expendable endowments, or restricted or designated funds. The SORP does not prescribe what the policy should be, nor does it suggest what the actual level of reserves should be, or set down the process for devising the policy. These are matters for the trustees to address.

The trustees may wish to formally review what they consider the 'free' reserves to be in the charity, and decide what the optimum reserves level should be. This needs to be based on a realistic assessment, bearing in mind factors such as the income and expenditure forecasts, contingencies and future needs.

Although the reserves policy may be proposed by senior employees or a sub-committee of trustees, it should be formally ratified by the whole body of trustees and minuted. The policy should be periodically reviewed and compared to the actual reserve's position. If the optimum levels have not yet been achieved, the steps being taken to address this should be documented and disclosed.

The time spent formulating the policy and the extent of detail necessary will depend on the size and complexity of the charity. Further guidance on establishing a reserves policy can be found in CC19 (reproduced as an annex to Chapter **7**).

Examples of reserves policies can be found in the example reports and accounts and are reproduced in chapter **7**.

(b) Investments

The SORP requires a statement, where applicable, of the investment policy and the performance against policy although for smaller charities the Regulations only require a description of the policy for the actual selection of investments.

It may therefore be necessary to refer to discussions with, and reports from, the investment managers to ensure that a proper disclosure is given. Examples of disclosures are shown below:

Example B   *Dorsetshire Drugs Advice Centre*

Investment policy

The management committee has considered the most appropriate policy for investing funds and has found that specialised unit trusts, designed for the charity sector, meets their requirements to generate both income and capital growth. The management committee consider the return on investments, at over 8% in the year, to be satisfactory.

Example D   *Aid Overseas*

Investment policy

The trustees have the power to invest in such assets as they see fit.

The charity sometimes needs to react very quickly to particular emergencies and has a policy of keeping any surplus liquid funds in short-term deposits which can be accessed readily. The charity has an active treasury management department and is pleased to report that it has managed to obtain a return of 6% in interest on these deposits. The charity has some investment property which it acquired by virtue of vacating one of its premises and letting the remainder of the space to an existing tenant. It is not our policy to hold such properties and therefore we plan to sell the freehold in the forthcoming financial year.

Example F   *The Higher College Charity*

Investment powers, policy and performance

The trustees' investment powers are governed by the Trust Deed, which permits the Charity's funds to be invested in any security listed on the London Stock Exchange.

The Board's policy is to maintain income whilst preserving the real value of endowed investments, to maximise income on temporarily invested restricted funds, and to match the return on invested Advance Fees Scheme monies in line with the maturation profile of the related liability to provide schooling in future years.

The Charity's investments have continued to be managed in conformity with our policy and the Trust Deed, and their performance for the year has exceeded expectations, thanks to the expert advice of our investment managers.

(c) Grant making

The main grant-making policies should be disclosed and, in addition and where applicable, if the notes to the accounts do not contain the information required regarding grants given then the trustees' annual report should, in addition, include a statement as to whether or not the required details have been given to the regulatory body. Examples of grant-making policies are as follows:

Example C   *The Rosanna Grant Trust*

Grant-making policy
The charity invites applications for funding of projects through advertising in specialist medical media. Institutional applicants are invited to submit a summary of their proposals in a specific format. The applications are reviewed against specific criteria and research objectives which are set by the scientific panel. Most projects are funded for three years and are monitored on an annual basis.

The charity also invites individuals from any part of the world carrying out PhD or MD studies concerned with Alzheimer's Disease and related matters to apply for scholarships. These can amount to a maximum of £9,000 per annum. Applicants are asked to provide a summary of their proposed thesis and in certain cases are invited to interview by a scholarship panel. Progress towards a PhD is monitored every six months.

The charity requests a copy of the final reports on each piece of research which are made publicly available.

Example F   *The Higher College Charity*

Grant-making policy
This year the Charity awarded grants and bursaries in excess of £250,000, all from restricted funds. The Governors' policy, in line with that of other independent schools, is to award grants on the basis of educational ability, subject to the restrictions imposed by the original donor of the funds.

Funds in deficit
If any funds are in deficit then an explanation of why they are in deficit and what action is to be taken on them should be given be given in the trustees' annual report.

Risks
Although technically these disclosures are not required by smaller charities under the Regulations, the SORP does not exclude such charities and there should be a statement that the major risks to which the charity is exposed, as identified by the trustees, have been reviewed and systems have been established to mitigate those risks. This is one of the most significant changes in SORP 2000 and one which may fill some trustees with trepidation.

Charities are often, by their very existence, operating in inherently 'risky' areas and, experience shows that in many cases, charities already have in place mechanisms for identifying and managing risks. The key will be to identify these processes, collate them, formalise them and document them. There should also be a process for ensuring that there is ongoing monitoring and review. As the charity's activities evolve, and as the environment in which it is operating changes (for example, through legal or economic developments), so will the major risks to which the charity is exposed.

SORP 2000 makes it clear that the statement about risk has to be made by the trustees. This will need to be supported by evidence of the risk identification and management process. Trustees may want to include this as a regular item on their meeting agenda and when risk issues are discussed, they should be documented and the actions minuted.

Trustees should be in a good position to use their knowledge and wider experience to identify a variety of risks facing the charity, such as financial, operational, and regulatory risks, as well as, perhaps of most concern, risks in connection with damage to the charity's reputation. A practical way to capture this information is through the development of a high level 'risk register'. This could highlight the major risks, then document the controls, procedures or other factors which are in place to manage, mitigate or eliminate them. The register should be reviewed regularly by the trustees to ensure that it remains complete and up to date. Assurance on risk can be assisted by an effective external or internal audit process.

The risk-management process should become part of the charity's day-to-day activities, as opposed to an exercise which is divorced from what the charity is trying to achieve. It may enable the trustees to identify areas where more risk may be taken, or where opportunities are not being fully exploited. The risks facing the charity will exist, whether or not the trustees choose to recognise and address them – it is better to identify and manage them with confidence rather than be exposed to them unwittingly.

CC66 includes some examples of the types of disclosure which trustees may want to make about risk. As discussed previously, the Regulations exclude small charities from the requirement to report on areas of risk although the Charity Commission would still prefer to see this included.

Some examples are given below from a very simple statement to a more complex one. The subject of risk management is dealt with in detail in chapter **20** and in guidance issued by the Charity Commission in October 2001.

Example B   *Dorsetshire Drugs and Advice Centre*

Risk review
The management committee has conducted its own review of the major risks to which the charity is exposed and systems have been established to mitigate those risks. Significant external risks to funding have led to the development of a strategic plan which will allow for the diversification of funding and activities. Internal risks are minimised by the implementation of procedures for authorisation of all transactions and projects and to ensure consistent quality of delivery for all

operational aspects of the charitable company. These procedures are periodically reviewed to ensure that they still meet the needs of the charity.

Example C   *The Rosanna Grant Trust*

Risk management
The trustees have examined the major strategic, business and operational risks which the charity faces and confirm that systems have been established to enable regular reports to be produced so that the necessary steps can be taken to lessen these risks.

Example D   *Aid Overseas*

Risk management
The trustees actively review the major risks which the charity faces on a regular basis and believe that maintaining our free reserves at the levels stated above, combined with our annual review of the controls over key financial systems carried out through an internal audit programme, will provide sufficient resources in the event of adverse conditions. The trustees have also examined other operational and business risks which we face and confirm that they have established systems to mitigate the significant risks.

Example E   *The Edinburgh Educational Trust*

Risk management
The Trustees have assessed the major risks to which the charity is exposed, in particular those related to the operations and finances of the Trust, and are satisfied that systems are in place to mitigate our exposure to the major risks.

Example G   *The ABC Charity*

Governance and internal control
A panel comprising existing trustees selects members of the trustee board. Applications for trusteeship are sought by advertisement. Trustees serve for a three year period and may be re-elected for a further three year period. The trustees meet six times a year; this includes a weekend meeting to review the strategy and performance and to set the operating plans and budgets. The Finance and General Purposes Committee and the Fund-raising Committee are made up of trustees and other individuals. Both committees operate under specific terms of reference which delegate certain functions from the trustee board. Each committee has its decisions ratified by the full board.

During the year the trustees carried out an exercise to review their composition and effectiveness. This identified the need for a trustee with marketing and public relations experience. The trustees are actively seeking candidates who will meet the requirements.

Company and charity law requires the trustees to prepare financial statements for each financial year which give a true and fair view of the state of affairs of the charity and of the surplus or deficit of the charity for that period. In preparing those financial statements, the trustees have:

- selected suitable accounting policies and then applied them consistently;
- made judgements and estimates that are reasonable and prudent;
- stated whether applicable accounting standards have been followed, subject to any material departures disclosed and explained in the financial statements; and
- prepared the financial statements on the going concern basis.

The trustees have overall responsibility for ensuring that the charity has appropriate systems of controls, financial and otherwise. They are also responsible for keeping proper accounting records which disclose with reasonable accuracy at any time the financial position of the charity and enable them to ensure that the financial statements comply with the Companies Act 1985. They are also responsible for safeguarding the assets of the charity and hence for taking reasonable steps for the prevention and detection of fraud and other irregularities and to provide reasonable assurance that:

- the charity is operating efficiently and effectively;
- its assets are safeguarded against unauthorised use or disposition;
- proper records are maintained and financial information used within the charity or for publication is reliable;
- the charity complies with relevant laws and regulations.

The systems of internal control are designed to provide reasonable, but not absolute, assurance against material misstatement or loss. They include:

- A strategic plan and an annual budget approved by the trustees.
- Regular consideration by the trustees of financial results, variance from budgets, non-financial performance indicators and benchmarking reviews.
- Delegation of authority and segregation of duties.
- Identification and management of risks.

The trustees have, with advice from their auditors, introduced a formal risk management process to assess business risks and implement risk management strategies. This involved identifying the types of risks the charity faces, prioritising them in terms of potential impact and likelihood of occurrence, and identifying means of mitigating the risks. As part of this process the trustees have reviewed the adequacy of the charity's current internal controls. The trustees are pleased to report that the charity's internal financial controls, in particular, conform with guidelines issued by the Charity Commission.

In addition, the trustees have considered the guidance for directors of public listed companies contained within the Turnbull Report. They believe that although this is not mandatory for the charity it should, as a public interest body, adopt these guidelines as best practice. Accordingly they have:

- Set policies on internal controls which cover the following:
  - consideration of the type of risks the charity faces;
  - the level of risks which they regard as acceptable;

- – the likelihood of the risks concerned materialising;
- – the charity's ability to reduce the incidence and impact on the business of risks that do materialise; and
- – the costs of operating particular controls relative to the benefit obtained.
- Clarified the responsibility of management to implement the trustees' policies and identify and to evaluate risks for their consideration.
- Communicated that employees have responsibility for internal control as part of their accountability for achieving objectives.
- Embedded the control system in the charity's operations so that it becomes part of the culture of the charity.
- Developed systems to respond quickly to evolving risks arising from factors within the charity and to changes in the external environment.
- Included procedures for reporting failings immediately to appropriate levels of management and the trustees together with details of corrective action being undertaken.

The trustees have considered the need for a specific internal audit function and have decided not to appoint an internal auditor. However, head office staff visiting projects carry out internal audit reviews to a programme agreed with the finance committee and with the external auditors.

6.3.3 Funds held on behalf of others

Paragraph 32 of the revised SORP states that it is the responsibility of the charity trustees to prepare the annual report and accounts. Accordingly, custodian trustees should make available to the charity trustees copies of their records relating to the administration of the charity's funds.

Where a charity is, or its trustees are, acting as custodian trustees, para 32 recommends that the annual report should:

(a) give a description of the assets which they hold in that capacity;
(b) state the objects of the charity on whose behalf the assets are held and how this activity falls within their own objects; and
(c) give details of the arrangements for safe custody and segregation of such assets from the charity's own assets.

In requiring this disclosure, charity trustees not only need to make clear, *but be clear*, what funds do and do not pass through their hands. This disclosure might be interpreted as being restricted to money funds. Where trustees have taken over responsibility for other assets, e.g., chattels, this could be disclosed in the interests of completeness.

Unless a charity's gross income in a financial year does not exceed £250,000 reg 7(4)(n) requires to be disclosed a description of any assets held by the charity or by any charity trustee of, or trustee for, the charity, on behalf of another charity, and particulars of any special arrangements made with respect to the safe custody of such assets and their segregation from assets of the charity not so held and a description of the objects of the charity on whose behalf the assets are held. Unlike the Regulations, the SORP contains no equivalent exemption from disclosure.

6.3.4 Other disclosures

In addition to the above disclosures, charitable companies are required to provide further information prescribed by s234 of, and Sch 7 to, the 1985 Act.

Market value of land
Paragraph 1(2) requires the difference between the book amount and the market value of land and buildings to be stated, if it is of such significance that, in the opinion of the directors, the attention of members ought to be drawn to it.

Research and development
An indication of the activities (if any) of the company (and subsidiaries) in the field of research and development is required by para 6(a). The principal activities of some charities are in this field.

Disabled employees and employee involvement
Paragraph 9(3) requires disclosure of the policy concerning the employment of disabled persons in regard to:

(a) full and fair consideration of applications;
(b) continuing employment and training while employed; and
(c) generally their career development and promotion.

And, para 11(3) requires a description of the action taken during the year to introduce, maintain and develop arrangements aimed at:

(a) systematic provision of employee information;
(b) regular consultations so that views of employees can be taken into account;
(c) encouraging employees' involvement in the company's performance through share schemes or by other means; and
(d) achieving a common awareness of the financial and economic factors affecting the company's performance.

Neither of these disclosures needs to be provided where the number of employees (disregarding employment outside the UK) does not exceed 250.

Example G contains an example of these disclosures.

Example G   *The ABC Charity*

Employee involvement and employment of the disabled
Employees have been consulted on issues of concern to them by means of regular consultative committee and staff meetings and have been kept informed on specific matters directly by management. The charity carries out exit interviews for all staff leaving the organisation and has adopted a procedure of upward feedback for senior management and trustees.

The charity has implemented a number of detailed policies in relation to all aspects of personnel matters including:

• Equal Opportunities policy
• Volunteers' policy
• Health & Safety policy

In accordance with the charity's equal opportunities policy, the charity has long established fair employment practices in the recruitment, selection, retention and training of disabled staff.

Full details of these policies are available from the charity's offices.

6.4 Approving the report and accounts

Paragraph 28 of the SORP states that:

'the annual report and accounts should be approved by the trustees as a body in accordance with their usual procedures (drafts being given to the trustees a reasonable time in advance) and both documents should be signed on behalf of the trustees by one of their number authorised so to do. (Note: the Regulations state that "one or more" of the charity trustees can approve and sign the accounts). The date of approval should be stated. The usual procedure of charity trustees will not require the unanimous approval of the report and accounts, but any trustees who consider that the report and/or accounts should not be approved, or should not have been approved, should report to the Charity Commission (in the case of charities in England and Wales) or other regulator, any of their concerns which they are unable to resolve with their fellow trustees and/or with the auditors or examiners of the accounts.'

Once the report has been approved it should be attached to the accounts whenever a full set of accounts is distributed. Any audit, independent examination or other statutory report on the accounts should also be attached.

Section 233(1) of the 1995 Act requires the annual accounts of a company to be approved by the board of directors and signed on behalf of the board by one of them. Section 233(2) requires the signature to be on the balance sheet and s234(1) requires the directors' report to be similarly approved and signed, either by a director or by the secretary.

Chapter 7 – Reserves

7.1 Introduction

In the commercial world the term 'reserve' is used in a variety of ways and to describe many areas of business activities. The accounts of businesses normally include reserves in one form or another: for example, the accounts of trading companies are required to have a heading 'Capital and Reserves' on the face of the balance sheet and, at the very least, reserves will normally include the balance on the profit and loss account.' Indeed, the definition of reserves given in the appendix to the SORP begins by stating that such term 'has a variety of technical and ordinary meanings, depending on the context in which it is used'.

In contrast to trading companies, however, the balance sheet of a charity is required to disclose its 'funds', split, as a minimum, between income funds (whether unrestricted or restricted) and endowment funds. Indeed there is no reference to reserves within the SORP paragraphs dealing with the structure of the balance sheet. Although the public may often, in practice, consider the funds of a charity are its reserves, the term has no legal definition in relation to charities.

However, the Charity Commission quite clearly do regard a charity as having reserves and their guidance and requirements are extensive. This chapter deals with charity reserves as viewed by the Commission and therefore their booklet CC19 (*Charities Reserves*) is included as an appendix at the end of this chapter. In addition the Commission have produced operational guidance (OG) on charity income reserves, which is available on the Commission's website and in particular it describes why the issue is so important to them by, for example, discussing the question of reserves which may be either too large or too small.

7.2 Charity reserves

7.2.1 Funds of a charity

Before discussing the level of reserves within a charity it is important to understand the different funds that a charity may have and these are dealt with both in chapter **10** ('Accounting for separate funds') and in CC19. In summary, the funds of a charity may be divided as follows:

Unrestricted income funds:	General
	Designated
Restricted income funds	
Endowment funds:	Permanent
	Expendable

7.2.2 Reserves of a charity

In both the OG and CC19 the Commission use the term 'reserves' to describe that part of a charity's income funds that are freely available for its general purposes after it has met its commitments and covered its other planned expenditure. These are therefore normally referred to as 'free reserves'. The appendix to the SORP then goes on to say:

'More specifically this defines reserves as income which becomes available to the charity and is to be spent at the trustees' discretion in furtherance of any of the charity's objects (sometimes referred to as 'general purpose' income); but which is not yet spent, committed or designated (i.e., is 'free').

This definition of reserves therefore excludes:

- permanent endowment;
- expendable endowment;
- restricted funds;
- designated funds; and
- income funds which could only be realised by disposing of fixed assets held for charity use.

There is an argument for saying that expendable endowment and designated income funds ought to be counted as reserves. The argument is that in each case the trustees are free to regard the funds, if they so choose, as available for general purpose expenditure. There are no legal restrictions preventing trustees treating two types of funds as free, general purpose funds. But there are practical reasons, why the funds should not normally be regarded as free (though there are exceptions). A charity will not be justified in creating, or transferring resources to, a designated fund where the main purpose of doing this is to allow the charity to show a reduced level of reserves.

By contrast, restricted funds can never be regarded as general purposes funds. Restricted income funds do not fall within the scope of reserves as the term is used in this SORP. Nevertheless, the legal principles on the retention of income apply to restricted income funds, as do the principles of justifying and explaining any retention. For the purpose of applying the principles in this SORP it is suggested that trustees treat each restricted income fund as if it were a separate charity. Thus, each material restricted income fund could have its own 'reserve', which should be justified and (if practicable) explained in its own right.

7.2.3 Reserves policy

The Charity Commission first recommended that charities should have a formal reserves policy when CC19 was originally issued in May 1997 (reissued in June 1999). The SORP and 2000 Regulations now formalise that recommendation into a requirement. Reading and understanding CC19 is therefore fundamental and the reason why it has been reproduced in full at the end of this chapter.

In summary, however, the trustees should:

- justify the holding of reserves;
- formally discuss, agree and record in writing the reserves policy based on a realistic assessment of their reserves needs; and
- report on the reserves policy and level of reserves in the annual report (see chapter **6**).

In general, the reserves policy should cover, as a minimum:

- the reasons why the charity needs reserves;
- what level (or range) of reserves the trustees believe the charity needs;
- what steps the charity is going to take to establish or maintain reserves at the agreed level (or range); and
- arrangements for monitoring and reviewing the policy.

Examples of reserves policies are given below.

7.3 Examples of reserves policies

Each example report in CC66 (*Example Reports and Accounts*) contains a reserves policy and these are reproduced below, the first of which also incorporates information on risk management.

Example A   *Arts Theatre Trust Limited*

Reserves policy and risk management
In 1999 the trustees carried out a detailed review of the charity's activities and produced a comprehensive strategic plan setting out the major opportunities available to the charity and the risks to which it is exposed. The trustees monitor

progress against the strategic objectives set out in the plan at each quarterly meeting and a comprehensive review of the plan is carried out annually. As part of this process, the trustees have implemented a risk management strategy which comprises:

- an annual review of the risks which the charity may face;
- the establishment of systems and procedures to mitigate those risks identified in the plan; and
- the implementation of procedures designed to minimise any potential impact on the charity should any of those risks materialise.

The strategic plan focussed the trustees on the need to refurbish and develop our ATC Park site further, resulting in the applications for funding mentioned previously. A successful outcome is dependent on the charity meeting the challenges such a major project presents and managing our finances prudently.

The trustees have forecast the level of free reserves (that is those funds not tied up in fixed assets, and designated and restricted funds) the charity will require to sustain its operations over the period when it is anticipated that some of the income generating activities may be curtailed temporarily whilst the anticipated project will be carried out. The trustees consider that the most appropriate level of free reserves at 31 March 2001 would be £475,000 reducing to £325,000 at 31 March 2002. The actual free reserves at 31 March 2001 were £381,000 which is £94,000 short of our target figure. Whilst the current level of reserves may prove sufficient, it is the trustees' view that it is prudent to ensure that there are sufficient free reserves to provide financial flexibility over the course of the forthcoming challenges.

The trustees have therefore planned a new fund-raising strategy concentrating on raising funds from our existing audiences and customers of our wholly-owned trading subsidiary, HTC Limited, with a view to increasing our free reserves to the appropriate level. The trustees will closely monitor this initiative against the targets which have been set. As part of the feasibility study, we have shared our plans with our bankers, Cruffs Bank plc, which has indicated that it will provide support in order to see our planned developments come to fruition.

Example B   *Dorsetshire Drugs Advice Centre*

Reserves policy

The management committee have established a policy whereby the unrestricted funds not committed or invested in tangible fixed assets ('the free reserves') held by the charity should be between 3 and 6 months of the resources expended, which equates to £60,000 to £120,000 in general funds. At this level, the management committee feel that they would be able to continue activities of the charity in the event of a significant drop in funding. It would obviously be necessary to consider how the funding would be replaced or activities changed. At present the free reserves, which amount to £16,567, do not reach this target level and the management committee are considering ways in which additional unrestricted funds will be raised.

Example C   The Rosanna Grant Trust

Reserves policy
It is the policy of the charity to maintain unrestricted funds, which are the free reserves of the charity, at a level which equates to approximately six months unrestricted expenditure. This provides sufficient funds to cover management and administration and support costs and to respond to emergency applications for grants which arise from time to time. Unrestricted funds were maintained at this level throughout the year.

Example D   Aid Overseas

Reserves policy
As explained above the charity carries out a variety of both long term and short term projects. The trustees have examined the requirement for free reserves which are those unrestricted funds not invested in fixed assets, designated for specific purposes or otherwise committed. The trustees consider that, given the nature of our work, this should be approximately £3 million, which gives flexibility to cover temporary timing differences for grant claims, adequate working capital for our core costs, and will allow us to respond quickly to emergencies where immediate relief is needed. The free reserves at 30 September consist of the general reserves of £2.7 million less financial commitments not accrued in the financial statements amounting to approximately £0.9 million when secured funding is taken into account. The trustees plan to retain £0.5 million each year until the target for unrestricted free reserves is reached.

The East Asia Fund (note 22) was in deficit at 30 September 2001. This has been cleared subsequent to the year end by donations received specifically for projects in this region.

Example E   The Edinburgh Educational Trust

Reserves policy
The **Reserve Fund** represents the unrestricted funds arising from past operating results. It also represents the free reserves of the charity, as all fixed assets are included in endowment funds. The trustees are satisfied that the balance of the fund (£311,109) approximates to the equivalent of two months operating expenditure, which is satisfactory given the revenue funding secured with the Scottish Executive and local authorities, the contractual obligations to staff and the ongoing maintenance of those parts of the campus not affected by the current major building works. The trustees have examined the requirement to maintain free reserves and concluded that the most appropriate level is between 2 and 3 months of operational expenditure.

The **Millennium Appeal Fund**, which started last year, attracts legacies and donations for the purpose of providing modern sports facilities and a swimming pool for the children. As such it is a restricted fund and is utilised as and when the actual expenditure on these facilities is incurred. A transfer is made from the fund to Endowment funds when the expenditure enhances or improves assets which form part of that fund. At 31 March 2001, the fund was in deficit but the trustees are pleased to confirm that the continuation of the appeal has cleared the deficit since the year end.

The **Endowment Fund** is a restricted fund under the terms of the trust deed and part of it must be held permanently and part is expendable (as explained in note 14). Its purpose is to ensure a suitable income stream to finance the ongoing work of the charity and to provide facilities for the students. It is represented by a portfolio of investments, which are managed by investment managers who have been given discretionary power to acquire and dispose of investments within the policy set by the Trustees. The fund also holds the tangible fixed assets which consist of our two properties and which must be held in perpetuity.

Example F *The Higher College Charity*

Reserves

Note 14 to the financial statements shows the assets and liabilities attributable to the various funds by type, and also describes the various trusts of the Charity and summarises the year's movements on each fund. Unrestricted funds amounted to £9,261,000, but only £1,146,000 of this is freely available because the balance is invested in fixed assets or is designated for other purposes (see note 14). The Board has determined that the appropriate level of free reserves which are not invested in tangible fixed assets should be equivalent to 12 weeks expenditure, approximately £2,000,000.

Our policy is, therefore, to continue building up reserves to that level by means of annual operating surpluses and judicious management of our investment assets, supplemented by general-purpose appeals from time to time.

The board has continued to keep the secured overdraft facility under review to ensure that in the absence of free reserves, it remains adequate to cover the school's working capital requirements.

Tangible fixed assets are all held for use by the schools, but in the present uncertain property market the Governors are unable to estimate whether the current value of these assets is materially different from that shown in the financial statements.

Example G *The ABC Charity*

Reserves

The Trustees have reviewed the reserves of the charity. This review encompassed the nature of the income and expenditure streams, the need to match variable income with fixed commitments and the nature of the reserves. The review concluded that to allow the charity to be managed efficiently and to provide a buffer for uninterrupted services, a general reserve equivalent to £3,500,000 should be maintained. This equates to approximately seven months of unrestricted fund expenditure. During the year the charity's general reserve increased from £2,900,000 to £4,785,000 (see note 17). The budget for the next two years has forecast deficits to reduce the general fund to the level agreed by the trustees.

Restricted funds have decreased from £3,900,000 to £3,090,000. The Emergency services fund was in deficit by £145,000 at the year end and was temporarily funded from the general reserve. This was as a result of the need to incur expenditure in advance of anticipated income which has subsequently been received.

The charity has a number of other designated and restricted funds which are represented by investments and fixed assets. The purpose of these funds is detailed in note 17 in the financial statements.

7.4 Revaluation reserve

Where fixed assets (other than investments) are revalued (see chapter **9**) then, assuming the revaluing is upwards, a revaluation reserve will arise. However, since any such revaluation is reflected within the Statement of Financial Activities (SOFA) it will automatically form part of the funds in which the revalued asset is held and is therefore not necessarily shown separately. Nor will it form part of the charity's free reserves as these specifically exclude this class of fixed assets.

However, under the Companies Act 1985 there is a requirement to show separately the revaluation reserve. The SORP therefore recommends that charitable companies disclose revaluation reserves by way of a prominent inset on the face of the balance sheet.

Where there are impairment losses or downward reductions, then, in certain circumstances, these can be offset against the revaluation reserve.

Annex – CC19 – Charities' Reserves

Contents

Section 1: Introduction

1. Most charities are keenly aware of the need to secure their viability beyond the immediate future. To provide reliable services or funding over the longer term, charities must be able to absorb setbacks and to take advantage of change and opportunity. Many provide for this by putting aside, when they can afford it, some of their current income as a reserve against future uncertainties.

2. Underlying much public discussion of charity reserves is the belief that holding significant amounts of reserves is tantamount to hoarding. This belief is likely to persist unless charities justify and explain their reserves position. The giving public are not generally concerned with the legal and accounting technicalities. But they are entitled to be reassured that a charity with reserves has good reasons for keeping funds in reserve, and to know what those reasons are. Ideally, a charity would want to show donors and others that it would be irresponsible not to hold the level of reserves it holds.

3. The fact that a charity holds, or does not hold, reserves is not in itself, reason either to criticise or to commend the charity. In our view a charity should be judged on whether or not its level of reserves, whatever it is, is justified and clearly explained. *Justifying reserves – a central theme of this guidance - does not mean excusing or being defensive about reserves. It means being able to demonstrate, by reference to a charity's current position and future prospects, why holding a particular level of reserves is right for the charity at that time.*

4. We explain in this guidance what we think a charity should do to justify its reserves in that sense. Our aim is also to help trustees and senior staff make decisions about reserves levels in a way that is consistent with the legal requirements for the use of charity income, which are explained in *section 4*.

Charity Commission's rôle

5. Responsibility for establishing an appropriate reserves policy lies with the trustees of each charity. So too does the responsibility for justifying and explaining what the charity is doing in that respect. It is not for us to substitute our own judgments for those of reasonable trustees who know the business of their charity, who have taken care to plan properly and who have justified their plans.

6. It *is* our responsibility to concern ourselves with the way in which trustees are managing their resources. Our powers of intervention arise when resources are mishandled or put at risk. But we do not think it helpful to do nothing until things reach that point. Accordingly we believe it our duty to encourage trustees to apply the principles set out in this guidance.

7. If we come across a charity where the trustees have not done this, or where the level or use of reserves seems unjustifiable by any reasonable measure, we will begin by exploring the reasons with the trustees. We will continue to encourage them towards the principles of this guidance. Cases where we have to use any of our statutory powers to secure the necessary changes are likely to be those few in which mismanagement or misconduct persist, charity resources are at risk, or breaches of the law remain uncorrected.

Section 2: Meaning of terms used in this guidance

8. 'SORP' means the **Statement of Recommended Practice: Accounting by Charities** (October 1995). Copies of SORP have been sent to all larger charities. Further copies are available from our London office by telephoning 020 7674 2336. Every charity is entitled to one free copy of SORP, though extra copies cost £5 each.

9. The following terms are used in this guidance with the same meanings as they have in the SORP. Readers not familiar with SORP will need to study these meanings carefully to make the best use of this guidance. The meanings are given on page 15:
   - capital;
   - permanent endowment;
   - expendable endowment;
   - fixed assets for charity use;
   - income;
   - restricted funds;
   - unrestricted funds; and
   - designated funds.

Section 3: What are charity reserves?

10. The term 'reserves' has a variety of technical and ordinary meanings, depending on the context in which it is used. In this guidance we use the term 'reserves' to describe that part of a charity's income funds that is freely available for its general purposes. 'Reserves' are therefore the resources the charity has or can make available to spend, for any or all of the charity's purposes, once it has met its commitments and covered its other planned expenditure.

11. More specifically we define reserves as
    - income which becomes available to the charity and is to be expended at the trustees' discretion in furtherance of any of the charity's objects (sometimes referred to as 'general purpose' income); but which
    - is not yet spent, committed or designated (i.e., is 'free').

    Our definition of reserves therefore excludes:
    - permanent endowment;
    - expendable endowment;
    - restricted funds;
    - designated funds; and
    - income funds which could only be realised by disposing of fixed assets held for charity use.

12. There is an argument for saying that two of these types of funds – expendable endowment and designated (income) funds – ought to be counted as reserves. The argument is that in each case the trustees are free to regard the funds, if they so choose, as available for general purpose expenditure.

13. We acknowledge that there are no legal restrictions preventing trustees treating those two types of funds as free, general purpose funds. But there are practical reasons, explained below, why the funds should not *normally* be regarded as free (though there are exceptions).

14. By contrast, restricted funds can never be regarded as general purpose funds. Restricted income funds do not fall within the scope of reserves as we use the term in this guidance. Nevertheless, the legal principles on the retention of income (*Section 4 of the guidance*) apply to restricted income funds, as do the principles of justifying (*Section 5*) and explaining (*Section 6*) any retention. We suggest that, for the purpose of applying the principles in this guidance, trustees treat each restricted income fund as if it were a separate charity. Thus, each restricted income fund could have its own 'reserve', which should be justified and (if practicable) explained in its own right.

Expendable endowment

15. When invested an expendable endowment, like a permanent endowment, provides a relatively secure and predictable stream of income. The advantage of an expendable, over a permanent, endowment is that it also gives trustees the option of spending all, or part, of the endowment itself.

16. In reality many charities with an expendable endowment depend on the income it produces to fund core or continuing activities. Expending any of the endowment itself would reduce the income from it and might jeopardise some of those activities. The charity would then either have to increase its income from other sources – which, if that were readily feasible, the charity would surely

106

have tried to do anyway – or have to cut back its activities. The endowment cannot be regarded as free funds if a charity has that degree of dependence on income from it.

17. Trustees who make a regular practice of reinvesting some of their income with a view to building up the principal of the endowment will need to think very carefully about the justification for doing this, since the income should normally be spent.

18. Reinvesting income generated from capital funds does not have the effect, legally, of converting the income into extra capital. The reinvested funds remain income funds and must be treated as such: adding them to the principal does not overcome this obligation.

Designated funds

19. Designation is an administrative act by which trustees may earmark unrestricted funds for a particular project or use, without restricting or committing the funds legally. The designation may be cancelled by the trustees if they later decide that the charity should not proceed or continue with the use or project for which the funds were designated.

20. The act of designating particular funds neither:
    • allows those funds to be used for a purpose for which they could not previously be used; nor
    • by itself provides a justification of their use for the designated purpose.

21. SORP recommends (appendix 3, para 1) that 'the precise purpose of all designated funds should be stated in the notes to the accounts'. We expect charities to follow this recommendation and to ensure that the amount of any funds held as designated funds is appropriate to the purpose or use for which the funds have been designated.

22. A charity will not be justified in creating, or transferring resources to, a designated fund where the main purpose of doing that is to allow the charity to show a reduced level of reserves.

Section 4: Legal basis for holding reserves

23. There is no legal definition of 'reserves' in relation to charities and no specific legal rule about the amount or proportion of a charity's income funds which it is allowed to hold as a reserve.

24. Trustees are under a general legal duty to apply charity funds within a reasonable time of receiving them. With income funds 'apply' can, in practice, be taken to mean 'expend' unless the governing document specifies otherwise.

25. Before trustees can use income funds in a way which does not comply with this duty, they need to have a legal power which overrides this general duty. Holding income funds in reserve rather than expending them is one use that does not comply with the duty, since the trustees are delaying the application of the funds beyond what the law would normally accept as a reasonable time. Trustees therefore need a legal power to hold income funds in reserve.

26. A small number of trustees have an express legal power in their charities' governing document to hold income in reserve instead of expending it promptly. Much more often, trustees will not have an express power and will have to rely on their *implied* power – a power not written into the governing

document but one which the trustees possess in order to take actions which are necessary for the charity to function properly. As with all discretionary powers, trustees are justified in exercising their power to hold income reserves – whether express or implied – only if in their considered view it is necessary in the charity's best interests to do so.

27. If it is done without justification, the holding of income in reserve may amount to a breach of trust. In *Section 5* we give our view on what steps trustees should take to be sure that they have justified the holding of reserves.

28. Some trustees have in their governing document a power to convert income into capital, which is not the same as a power to hold income in reserve. Converting income into capital takes the converted resource outside the scope of reserves (since our definition of reserves does not include any capital funds).

29. Some charities have reinvested income regularly over a number of years by adding it to the principal of their expendable or (as the case may be) their permanent endowment. If they have not kept precise records they may now be unable to specify exactly what portion of the invested funds represents income and what portion represents capital. We would nevertheless expect a charity to be able to make an estimate of the size of the respective portions. We will not, as a general rule, require charities to draw up plans for spending the income portions immediately. But we may ask a charity to justify any plans it has for continued retention of those income funds. If in future the charity intends to reinvest income as it arises we may ask it to justify that too.

Charity with more resources than it needs

30. If a charity has more resources than it could reasonably need to fulfil all of its purposes, the trustees should contact us. The law requires that charitable resources are applied for charitable purposes, even if trustees cannot find a way of using those resources within their existing objects. We can help by making a Scheme altering the governing document to allow the charity to use its resources more widely than its existing objects permit. Trustees have a legal duty (s.13(5) Charities Act 1993) to apply for such a Scheme where it is appropriate. Our publication *Making a Scheme(CC36)* gives more information about Schemes.

Tax relief

31. Income is generally exempt from direct tax if it is both applicable, and actually applied, for charitable purposes only. The Inland Revenue's normal practice is to allow tax exemption on income which either has been expended for charitable purposes or has been invested for the benefit of the charity.

32. Tax exemption is **not** available if either:
    - the income has been invested in an investment which is not a 'qualifying investment' (within the meaning of schedule 20 to the Income and Corporation Taxes Act 1988) investments made for the benefit of a charity and not for the avoidance of tax are likely to count as qualifying investments, but trustees in any doubt whether or not an investment is a qualifying investment will need to take advice; or
    - the income is retained in the charity's hands without being placed on deposit or otherwise invested.

Donations and legacies: are they income or capital?

33. People who give or leave money to charities do not usually specify whether their donation or legacy should be treated as income or as expendable endowment. If any evidence exists, or can be inferred from the circumstances of the donation or legacy, that a donor or testator had a specific intention one way or the other, the charity must treat the gift or legacy accordingly. But if there is no such evidence the donation should be treated as income and the trustees should use it, consistently with the terms of the charity's governing document, in any way they think will benefit the charity.

Section 5: Justifying reserves

34. To justify their holding of reserves, trustees should have a **reserves policy** based on a **realistic assessment of their reserves needs**. Apart from providing justification for trustees to exercise their legal power to hold reserves, many charities believe this process to be an essential part of good financial management practice.

35. A charity which builds up reserves by retaining, as a matter of habit alone, any annual surpluses it makes will scarcely be able to justify holding those reserves.

Reserves policy

36. In some charities the policy will be proposed by senior employees or by a sub-committee of the trustee body, but it should be formally agreed by the trustees acting as a Board and recorded in writing.

37. The policy should cover as a minimum:
    - the reasons why the charity needs reserves;
    - what level (or range) of reserves the trustees believe the charity needs;
    - what steps the charity is going to take to establish or maintain reserves at the agreed level (or range); and
    - arrangements for monitoring and reviewing the policy.

38. We *stress that the amount of time spent preparing the policy, and the detail with which it is set down, should be in proportion to the scale and complexity of the charity's affairs.* A small charity with a simple, stable pattern of receipts and payments, few if any commitments, and little susceptibility to outside influences should be able to cover the matters above relatively quickly and to record briefly the trustees' conclusions.

39. Without a reserves policy trustees cannot be confident that their reserves level matches the charity's needs at the time. The charity could be holding reserves that are too high or too low for its needs. If a charity's reserves are too high, it is retaining income funds without justification. Those funds ought to be expended for charitable purposes. While the funds remain in the trustees' hands the charity's current users or beneficiaries – actual or potential – are not being as well-served as they could be.

40. If a charity's income is volatile or insecure, it has high commitments, and its state of affairs is highly susceptible to factors outside its own control, it may find that its reserves are too low to protect it from the risk of insolvency or serious disruption to its charitable work.

41. Some charities will be able to justify holding a certain level of reserves but will be unable to build up reserves to that, or perhaps to any, level at all. Many recently established charities, in particular, will be in that position. While we

accept that some charities will simply not have had the resources to establish any reserves, we would expect a charity to have given thought to a reserves policy even if it currently has no reserves.

Realistic assessment of reserves needs

42. A charity's reserves policy should be informed by:
    - its forecasts for levels of income in future years, taking into account the reliability of each source of income and the prospects for opening up new sources;
    - its forecasts for expenditure in future years on the basis of planned activity;
    - its analysis of any future needs, opportunities, contingencies or risks the effects of which are not likely to be able to be met out of income if and when they arise; and
    - its assessment, on the best evidence reasonably available, of the likelihood of each of those needs etc arising and the potential consequences for the charity of not being able to meet them.
43. Trustees who hold reserves without making any attempt to relate their need for reserves to factors such as these will probably have great difficulty explaining in any convincing way why they hold reserves.

Section 6: Explaining reserves

44. Any charity could find its reserves subject to scrutiny and comment in the public arena. Charities:
    - which operate in areas where there is clear evidence of immediate human need; or
    - which rely on a strong emotive appeal involving vulnerable groups or animals; or
    - which are running public appeals emphasising the urgency of their own need for donated funds,

    are likely to attract the most attention, especially if they hold sizeable sums as reserves. There is a risk that charities in that position could be seen as self-indulgent, because they are retaining funds which could be used with immediate effect to alleviate acute need. This risk can be greatly reduced by a clear and positive explanation of the reasons why reserves are held.
45. We believe that once a charity has taken the trouble to explain its reasons, the great majority of its donors, supporters and users/beneficiaries will be quite prepared to accept that it should hold appropriate reserves.
46. Charities applying to statutory or voluntary funders are also likely to have their reserve levels closely assessed.
47. Commentators, funders, charities and ourselves all have a part to play in promoting a better-informed treatment of the subject of reserves. This section of the guidance is concerned with charities' reporting of their reserves. We set out below what we regard as good practice and emphasise that we believe it to be in charities' own interests to adopt it.

Reporting of reserves

48. A charity's purpose in reporting on reserves is to disclose the level of its reserves and to explain convincingly why it needs that level of reserves.

49. Paragraph 28 of the SORP lists the narrative information which trustees should include in their annual report. Information about a charity's reserves should be included as part of the narrative prepared under paragraph 28. We believe that trustees should:
    - state whether or not they hold reserves;
    - explain why they hold or do not hold reserves and, if they do, in respect of what future needs, opportunities, contingencies or risks; and
    - give the level of reserves at the last day of the financial year to which the report relates.
50. Paragraph 5 of SORP says that 'a departure [from the recommendations of SORP] is not justified simply for the purpose of presenting to the reader a more appealing picture of the financial position or results of the charity.'

Fundraising

51. Every charity is responsible for ensuring that its appeals – whether for voluntary public donations, corporate donations, legacies, grants, or any other form of income, and whether they are made by advertising, direct mail, in person, or by any other method – do not misrepresent the charity's financial position.

52. If a charity is widely believed to have large reserves, appeals for further funds may provoke resentment against the charity for apparently seeking funds which it does not need. In wording its appeals, and in dealing with any reaction to the appeals, it should take care not to give anyone the wrong impression about the extent or urgency of its need for funds.

Meanings of terms used in this guidance

'Capital' and 'expendable endowment'

53. **Capital** means resources which become available to a charity and which the trustees are legally required to invest or retain and use for its purposes. Capital may be permanent endowment, where the trustees have no power to convert it into income and apply it as such, or **expendable endowment**, where they do have this power. (**Expendable endowment** is distinguishable from income by the absence of a positive duty on the part of the trustees to apply it for the purposes of the charity, unless and until this power to convert into income is actually exercised.) (SORP, appendix 1, para 2)

'Fixed assets for charity use'

54. All assets of material value held for use on a continuing basis in the charity's activities (SORP, para 183)

'Income'

55. All resources which become available to a charity and which the trustees are legally required to apply in furtherance of its charitable purposes within a reasonable time of receipt (the exercise of a power of accumulation is an application). **Income** includes all trading and investment income and some legacies, donations, grants, gains from disposal of fixed assets and investments, and asset revaluation gains. (SORP, appendix 1, para 13)

111

'Restricted funds'

56. Funds subject to specific trusts, which may be declared by the donor(s), or with their authority (eg in a public appeal), but still within the objects of the charity. **Restricted funds** may be restricted income funds, which are expendable at the discretion of the trustees in furtherance of some particular aspect(s) of the objects of the charity, or they may be capital funds, where the assets are required to be invested, or retained for actual use, rather than expended. (SORP, appendix 3, para 2)

57. Some trustees have power to declare specific trusts over unrestricted funds. If such a power is available and is exercised, the assets affected will form a restricted fund, and the trustees' discretion to apply the fund will be legally restricted (SORP, appendix 3, paragraph 1).

'Unrestricted funds' and 'designated' funds

58. **Unrestricted funds** are funds expendable at the discretion of the trustees in furtherance of the objects of the charity. If part of an unrestricted fund is earmarked for a particular project it may be **designated** as a separate fund, but the **designation** has an administrative purpose only, and does not legally restrict the trustees' discretion to apply the fund.

59. The following term has a statutory definition (in s96(3) of the Charities Act 1993) and is explained more fully in SORP. We give the first part of the SORP explanation:

'Permanent endowment'

60. A capital fund where there is no power to convert the capital into income is known as a **permanent endowment** fund, which must generally be held indefinitely. (SORP, appendix 3, para 7)

Chapter 8 – The statement of financial activities

8.1 Introduction

In terms of presentation, the main feature, and most controversial change introduced by the 1995 SORP was the introduction of a new statement, the Statement of Financial Activities (SOFA). This is an omnibus statement which, by including all changes to all funds, takes fund accounting to its logical conclusion. Paragraph 69 of the 1995 SORP explained the reasoning behind its introduction:

> 'A traditional income and expenditure account with the distinction between revenue and capital does not always fully explain all the charity's activities, whose primary purpose must be the provision of benefit to its beneficiaries rather than the corporate pursuit of gain for the benefit of shareholders. Furthermore, since charities often receive significant amounts of restricted income which can affect the types and level of service they provide, it is important to consider changes in the amounts of all the resources of the charity. A single accounting statement is now proposed which will analyse all capital and income resources and expenditures and contain a reconciliation of all movements in the charity's funds. Such analysis will be provided by the Statement of Financial Activities, showing total movements on all funds with supporting analyses in the notes of the movements in individual funds.'

This presentation is a logical extension of the recommendation in SORP 2 that the accounts and notes should provide information on the charity's fund structure and on the significance of each of the major fund balances.

8.2 Changes in SORP 2000

SORP 2000 retains the SOFA as the most important primary statement issued by a charity. Although the fundamental approach of the SOFA has not changed several changes have made to the detailed layout to improve understanding and address problems which arose from the application of the 1995 version of the SOFA. Therefore the format continues to require, for the current year, a columnar split between unrestricted, restricted and endowment funds with a total column, together with a total column for the previous year.

The presentation of incoming resources and resources expended has been altered to provide a more logical layout and fit in with the way in which charities handle their transactions and prepare their accounts. Incoming resources of a similar nature will be grouped together and resources expended of a similar nature will also be grouped together (paras 56-74). Categories of income and expenditure under these two headings will be consolidated on a line by line basis where there are subsidiary undertakings (instead of summarising the results of non-charitable trading activities of subsidiary undertakings on a one-line basis). This will make the accounts more transparent.

In particular:

(a) Income from non-charitable trading (described as 'incoming resources from activities for generating funds' – paras 105-108) may be combined under one heading, avoiding the necessity of splitting donated goods from bought in goods.

(b) All costs of a fundraising nature (described as 'costs of generating funds' – (paras 132-135) will be brought together and (optionally) can be deducted from total incoming resources to arrive at a sub-total 'net incoming resources available for charitable application'. This is optional because such a sub-total will not be appropriate for all charities.

(c) Investment management fees should be included under 'costs of generating funds'.

Charities with a gross income not exceeding £250,000 do not have to use the standard expenditure headings and sub-headings but can choose expenditure classifications to suit their circumstances.

8.3 The form and content of the SOFA

Paragraphs 56 to 156 set out the recommendations regarding the form and content of the SOFA. There are parallel requirements in the 2000 Regulations.

Paragraph 56 of SORP 2000 states:

'The Statement of Financial Activities is a single accounting statement with the objective of showing all incoming resources and resources expended by the charity in the year on all its funds. It is designed to show how the charity has used its resources in furtherance of its objects for the provision of benefit to its beneficiaries. It shows whether there has been a net inflow or outflow of resources, including capital gains and losses on assets, and provides a reconciliation of all movements in the charity's funds.'

The form of the SOFA is given in para 69 and reproduced below.

Description	Unrestricted funds	Restricted funds	Endowment funds	Total funds	Prior year total funds
Incoming resources analysed per para 59					
Total incoming resources	A	A	A	A	A
Resources expended analysed per para 60					
Total resources expended	B	B	B	B	B
Net incoming resources before transfers – A–B	C	C	C	C	C
Gross transfers between funds	D	D	D	D	D

The statement of financial activities

Description	Unrestricted funds	Restricted funds	Endowment funds	Total funds	Prior year total funds
Net incoming resources before revaluations and invest-ment asset disposals = C+D	E	E	E	E	E
Gains and losses on revaluations of fixed assets for the charity's own use	F	F	F	F	F
Gains and losses on revaluations and disposals of investment assets	G	G	G	G	G
Net movement in funds = E+F+G	H	H	H	H	H
Total funds brought forward	I	I	I	I	I
Total funds carried forward = H+I	J	J	J	J	J

Thus, as well as the total movements, the SOFA shows, in columnar format, for each prescribed heading, the movements in the principal types of fund (i.e., unrestricted income, restricted income and endowment). This is the minimum segregation permitted on the face of the SOFA. There is nothing to prevent a further analysis (e.g., of unrestricted funds, between general and designated funds), however, where space permits. Movements in all material underlying funds should be analysed in the notes, using the headings from, and reconciling with the figures in, the SOFA (para 49).

The SOFA should be prepared following the structure described in paras 57 to 69. However, individual charities should expand it where necessary in order to present a true and fair view and convey a proper understanding of the nature of all their activities. It is recommended that the charity's aim is to have a clear link between the incoming and outgoing resources and in particular the functional split of activities. Two examples of this are:

(a) a charity running a care home could use the sub-heading 'Residential Care Income' within para 59(ii)(a) (activities in furtherance of the charity's objects) and 'Residential Care Costs' para 60(ii)(b) (cost of activities in furtherance of the charity's objects);

(b) a charity fundraising through a shop could use the sub-heading 'shops' within para 59(ii)(b) (activities for generating funds) and para 60(i) (costs of generating funds).

Thus incoming resources and resources expended can be linked together by using similar or identical headings in different parts of the SOFA. A charity may also find it helpful to show extra columns, for instance, to highlight the financial impact of a particular activity.

Some charities may find it informative to their readers to insert an additional subtotal after para 60(i) (the cost of generating funds). Where this is done the subtotal should be called 'net incoming resources available for charitable application' and a further subtotal may be inserted for the costs in para 60(ii) (charitable expenditure).

Headings should be omitted where there is nothing to report for both the current and preceding financial years (para 73).

The 2000 Regulations require the SOFA to show the total incoming resources and their application, together with any other movements in the total resources during the financial year.

8.3.1 Examples

Example D *Aid Overseas* of CC66 contains a clear example of the layout of a SOFA for an unincoporated charity. The charity has unrestricted and restricted funds. The incoming resources are generated from a range of sources, and the analysis required by para 59 has been extended to separately report material sources of income. The analysis of expenditure, required by para 60 has also been extended to separately identify material lines of expenditure. In this example, the cost of generating funds is deducted from incoming resources to report 'net incoming resources available for charitable application'.

The charity has a subsidiary which is consolidated. SORP 2000 introduces full consolidation for the subsidiaries. Consolidation is discussed in detail in chapter **15**.

Example D   *Aid Overseas*

Consolidated Statement of Financial Activities for the year ended 30 September 2001

	Notes	Unrestricted funds £'000	Restricted funds £'000	2001 Total £'000	2000 Total £'000
Incoming resources					
Donations, legacies and similar incoming resources	2	**6,897**	3,797	**10,694**	10,991
Activities in furtherance of the charity's objects: Contracts for operational programmes	3	–	4,746	**4,746**	4,567
Activities for generating funds: Shop income	4	**8,573**	–	**8,573**	6,596
Investment income and interest	5	**190**	39	**229**	202
Total incoming resources		**15,660**	**8,582**	**24,242**	**22,356**
Less: Cost of generating funds					
Shop expenditure	4	**6,494**	–	**6,494**	6,029
Fund-raising costs	6	**1,646**	113	**1,759**	1,584
		8,140	**113**	**8,253**	**7,613**
Net incoming resources available for charitable application		**7,520**	**8,469**	**15,989**	**14,743**
Charitable expenditure					
Costs of activities in furtherance of the objects of the charity:	7				

Grants payable to partner organisations	7, 8	**1,286**	2,239	**3,525**	3,829
Operational programmes	7	**1,032**	4,578	**5,610**	5,892
Gifts in kind	7	**239**	1,092	**1,331**	1,296
Information, campaigning & education	7	**984**	9	**993**	917
Support costs	9	**1,502**	404	**1,906**	1,845
Managing and administering the charity	10	**470**	2	**472**	466
Total charitable expenditure		**5,513**	**8,324**	**13,837**	**14,245**
Total resources expended		**13,653**	**8,437**	**22,090**	**21,858**
Net incoming resources	11	**2,007**	**145**	**2,152**	**498**
Total funds brought forward		**4,006**	2,695	**6,701**	6,203
Total funds carried forward	21, 22	**6,013**	**2,840**	**8,853**	**6,701**

The statement of financial activities includes all gains and losses recognised in the year.

All incoming resources and resources expended derive from continuing activities.

Example B *Dorsetshire Drugs Advice Centre* contains a simple example of a SOFA for an incorporated charity with no subsidiaries. Reporting issues particular to an incorporated charity, such as the presentation of an income and expenditure account are discussed in chapter **16**. This charity presents a total for resources expended combining 'costs of generating funds' and 'charitable expenditure'. As in the previous example, additional analysis of the material components of expenditure has been given. The charity has unrestricted and restricted funds and a gain on revaluation of investments is reported.

Example B *Dorsetshire Drugs Advice Centre*

Statement of Financial Activities (including Income and Expenditure Account) for the year ended 31 March 2002

	Notes	Unrestricted funds £'000	Restricted funds £'000	Total funds 2002 £'000	Total funds 2001 £'000
Incoming resources					
Donations	2	–	5,000	**5,000**	6,796
Activities to further the charity's objects:					
Grants and contracts for advice and information,					

	Note				
outreach work and training project	3	95,535	150,000	**245,535**	207,304
Activities to generate funds:					
Charity shop		19,465	–	**19,465**	17,242
Investment income and interest		900	765	**1,665**	1,324
Total incoming resources		115,900	155,765	**271,665**	232,666
Resources expended					
Costs of generating funds					
Charity shop		11,773	–	**11,773**	11,225
Fund-raising and publicity		5,798	–	**5,798**	1,893
Charitable expenditure					
Advice and information		–	67,008	**67,008**	59,876
Outreach work		–	68,391	**68,391**	53,316
Training project		80,836	–	**80,836**	63,606
Management and administration		10,108	1,250	**11,358**	7,372
Total resources expended	4	108,515	136,649	**245,164**	197,288
Net incoming resources					
– Net income for the year	5	7,385	19,116	**26,501**	35,378
Gain on revaluation of investments	9	762	–	**762**	202
Net movement in funds		8,147	19,116	**27,263**	35,580
Total funds at 1 April 2001		20,249	1,316	**21,565**	(14,015)
Total funds at 31 March 2002	13	28,396	20,432	**48,828**	21,565

Movements in funds are disclosed in Note 13 to the financial statements.

(Note: *If the gross income of the entity was less than £250,000, resources expended could be analysed by natural classification (ie salaries, wages etc) rather than by activity as shown above.)*

An example of a SOFA containing unrestricted, restricted and endowment funds is presented in Example C *The Rosanna Grant Trust.* This is an unincorporated grant making charity which funds its activities from a portfolio of investments.

Example C   *The Rosanna Grant Trust*

Statement of Financial Activities for the year ended 30 September 2001

	Notes	Unrestricted funds £'000	Restricted funds £'000	Endowment Funds £'000	Total 2001 £'000	Total 2000 £'000
Incoming resources						
Investment income	2	634	103	–	**737**	680
Resources expended						
Costs of generating funds	3	14	20	90	**124**	112
Charitable expenditure:						
Grants payable	4	458	85	–	**543**	421
Support costs	5	105	5	–	**110**	81
Management and administration	6	48	3	15	**66**	63
Total resources expended		625	113	105	**843**	677
Net incoming resources/ (resources expended)		9	(10)	(105)	**(106)**	3
Other recognised gains and losses:						
Gain/(loss) on investments	10	8	12	447	**467**	(103)
Net movement in funds		17	2	342	**361**	(100)
Balance at 1 October 2000		378	5,982	20,223	**26,583**	26,683
Balance at 30 September 2001	14	395	5,984	20,565	**26,944**	26,583

8.4 Incoming resources

Paragraphs 59 and 75 to 118 of SORP 2000 set out the recommendations relating to incoming resources. The various categories of incoming resources should be analysed as appropriate to the charity and should be shown separately where material as recommended by para 59:

(a) donations, legacies and similar incoming resources (paras 87-94);
(b) incoming resources from operating activities of the charity distinguishing between (paras 101-108):
    (i) activities in furtherance of the charity's objects; and
    (ii) activities for generating funds;
(c) investment income (paras 112-113);
(d) other incoming resources (e.g., net gains on disposals of fixed assets for use by the charity) (para 118);
(e) the total by column of the above resources arising in the year.

8.4.1 Recognition of incoming resources

The 1995 SORP lacked clear guidance on the recognition of income by charities and particular problems arose with accounting for legacies and grants receivable. SORP 2000 contains a series of principles of income recognition in paras 75-82.

The value of all resources – both for income and endowment funds – accruing to the charity should be recorded in the SOFA as soon as it is prudent and practicable to do so. In all cases incoming resources should not be recognised until the conditions for receipt have been met and there is reasonable assurance of receipt. This will be dependent on the following three factors being met:

(a) entitlement – normally arises when a particular resource is receivable or the charity's right to it becomes legally enforceable;
(b) certainty – when there is reasonable certainty that the incoming resource will be received; and
(c) measurement – when the monetary value of the incoming resource can be measured with sufficient reliability.

Income therefore cannot be recognised until the trustees know that they have a right to receive some income, have a clear idea as to when that income will be received and have a reasonable understanding as to the amount that will be received.

All incoming resources should be reported gross whether raised by the charity or its agents. Netting off expenditure against income is only allowable for small fundraising events where it will not materially understate the gross incoming resources and gross resources expended for the event. However, in no case should the charity's own staff costs be netted off against the proceeds of any such events when reported in the accounts.

Some receipts can be regarded as reimbursements and can be offset against the related expenditure charged in the statement of financial activities. An example would be the receipt of an insurance payment. However, the receipt of a grant to meet resources expended already paid or accrued as a liability will not be regarded as a reimbursement and cannot be netted off against the accrued liability.

When are grants or donations to fund general or specific activities charities are normally entitled to these incoming resources when they are receivable. This is the case even if the resources are received in advance of the performance of the activity and they should not be deferred. Incoming resources may be deferred only when the donor has imposed restrictions on the expenditure of resources which amount to pre-conditions for use (e.g., the receipt in advance of a grant for expenditure in a future accounting period). However, when the conditions for receipt have been met then the charity is entitled to the incoming resources and must recognise them in the SOFA. Incoming resources cannot be deferred simply because the related expenditure has not been incurred.

Where either incoming resources are given specifically to provide a fixed asset or a fixed asset is donated (a gift in kind), the charity will normally have entitlement to the incoming resources when they are receivable. At this point, all of the incoming resources should be recognised in the SOFA and not deferred over the life of the asset. As explained in para 79 the possibility of having to repay the incoming resources does not affect their recognition in the first instance. Once acquired, the use of the asset will either be restricted or unrestricted. If its use is unrestricted the trustees should consider creating a designated fund reflecting the book value of the asset. The relevant fund will then be reduced over the useful economic life of the asset in line with its depreciation. This treatment accords with the requirements under accounting standards for the recognition of assets and liabilities and provides the most appropriate interpretation of SSAP 4 for charities.

Some incoming resources do not belong to the charity, for instance where it receives the resources in circumstances where the trustees acting as agents (and not as custodian trustees) are legally bound to pay them over to a third party and have no responsibility for their ultimate application. In these circumstances the transaction is legally a transfer of resources from the original payer (who remains the principal) to the specified third party. If the original payer retains the legal responsibility for ensuring the charitable application of the funds, the intermediary charity should not recognise the resources in the SOFA or the balance sheet (see para 248).

However, in some cases an intermediary charity may own the resources prior to transfer to the third party and its trustees will act as principal and have responsibility for their charitable application. For instance, where the trustees of the intermediary charity may have applied for the grant of the resources or are able to direct how the grant should be used by the third party or both. Other forms of funding arrangements involving intermediary charities may need their trustees to accept the legal responsibility for the transfer of the grant to the third party (and for its charitable application, where the third party is not a charity). In all of these circumstances the resources should then be included in the intermediary charity's SOFA and balance sheet (see para 249).

8.4.2 Disclosure

Where any incoming resources have been deferred the notes to the accounts should analyse the movement on the deferred account between incoming resources deferred in the current year and amounts released from previous years. Incoming resources of a similar nature can be grouped together in the notes as appropriate.

Where a charity has held resources for a third party which have not been included in the SOFA, the notes to the accounts should analyse the movement of these resources during the year relating to each party or type of party where material. Where resources have been held for related parties the required disclosure of paras 163 to 164 should be given.

Examples
The disclosure of the movement in deferred income is illustrated by Example A *Arts Theatre Trust Limited.*

Example A   *Arts Theatre Trust Limited*

14. Deferred income	Group	Charity
Balance at 1 April 2000	46	49
Amount released to incoming resources	(46)	(49)
Amount deferred in the year	55	46
Balance at 31 March 2001	**55**	**46**

Deferred income comprises admission fees received in advance and grants which the donor has specified must be used in future accounting periods.

A more complex example is given in Example F *The Higher College Charity.* In this example a school has a scheme for the payment of fees in advance.

Example F   *The Higher College Charity*

(j) **Advance fees scheme**
The school offers parents the opportunity to pay for up to seven years tuition fees in advance in accordance with a written contract. The amount received is invested and interest is accrued to contracts. This is treated as deferred income until the pupil joins the school whereupon the fees for each school term is charged against the remaining balance and taken to income. Any shortfall is treated as a deduction from school fee income and any excess accrued is treated as additional school income.

13. Advance fees scheme
Parents may enter into a contract to pay to the school up to the equivalent of seven years' tuition fees in advance. The money may be returned subject to specific conditions on the receipt of one year's notice. Assuming pupils will remain in the school, advance fees will be applied as follows:

	2001 £'000	2000 £'000
After 5 years	108	129
Within 2 to 5 years	1,316	1,291
Within 1 to 2 years	407	438
	1,831	1,858
Within 1 year	505	630
	2,336	2,488

The balance represents the accrued liability under the contracts. The movements during the year were:

	£'000	£'000
Balance at 1 September 2000		2,488
New contracts		423
Amounts accrued to contracts		165
		3,076
Amounts utilised in payment of fees:		
To the school	(646)	
To other schools	(52)	
		(698)
Capital repaid		(42)
Balance at 31 August 2001		**2,336**

8.4.3 Incoming resources subject to restrictions

The fact that an incoming resource is for a restricted purpose does not affect whether or not it is recognised in the SOFA. There is an important difference for accounting purposes between restrictions on the purposes for which a particular resource may be used and conditions which must be fulfilled prior to its receipt or use by the charity. If receipt is dependent upon preconditions which cannot be or have not been met, then the incoming resource should not be recognised in the SOFA or the balance sheet. A similar treatment should continue to be applied where the charity is unable to meet, even at a later stage, any preconditions for its use. A contingent asset may exist.

Funds received for the restricted purpose of providing fixed assets should be accounted for immediately as restricted funds. The treatment of the fixed assets provided with those funds will depend on the basis on which they are held. The terms on which the funds were received may either require the fixed asset acquired to be held in a restricted fund or the fixed assets' acquisition may discharge the restriction and the asset will be held in the unrestricted funds. There is no general rule and the treatment will depend upon the circumstance of each individual case. Where assets move from one fund to another this should be reflected as a transfer between the relevant funds.

8.5 Donations, legacies and similar incoming resources

This section of the SOFA is intended to show incoming resources of a voluntary nature usually given by the founders, patrons, supporters and the general public, government and non-statutory bodies such as businesses and charitable foundations. It will include grants which provide core funding or are of a general nature but will not include those which are specifically for the performance of a service or production of charitable goods, for instance a service agreement with a local authority. In addition it may include incoming resources from membership subscriptions, gifts in kind, intangible income and sponsorships where these are regarded as donations rather than payment for goods or services.

8.5.1 Disclosure

The material components of donations, legacies and similar incoming resources should be shown separately on the face of the SOFA or in the notes to the accounts.

8.5.2 Legacies

It is good practice to monitor a legacy from the time when notification is received to its final receipt. A charity should not, however, regard a legacy as receivable simply because it has been told about it. It should only do so when the legacy has been received or if, before receipt, it becomes reasonably certain that the legacy will be received and the value of the incoming resources can be measured with sufficient reliability.

There will normally be reasonable certainty of receipt for example, as soon as a charity receives a letter from the personal representatives of the estate advising that payment of the legacy will be made or that the property bequeathed will be transferred. It is likely that the value of the resource will also be measurable from this time. However, legacies which are not immediately payable should not be treated as receivable until the conditions associated with payment have been fulfilled (e.g., the death of a life tenant).

It is unlikely in practice that the entitlement, certainty of receipt and measurability conditions will be satisfied before the receipt of a letter from the personal representatives advising of an intended payment or transfer. The amount which is available in the estate for distribution to the beneficiaries may not have been finalised and, even if it has, there may still be outstanding matters relating to the precise division of the amount. In these circumstances entitlement may be in doubt or it may not be possible to provide a reasonable estimate of the legacy receivable, in which case it should not be included in the SOFA.

Where a charity receives a payment on account of its interest in an estate or a letter advising that such a payment will be made, the payment, or intended payment, on account should be treated as receivable.

Similarly, where a payment is received or notified as receivable (by the personal representatives) after the accounting year end, but it is clear that it had been agreed by the personal representatives prior to the year end (hence providing evidence of a condition that existed at the balance sheet date), then it should be accrued in the SOFA and the balance sheet.

8.5.3 Disclosure

Where the charity has been notified of material legacies which have not been included in the SOFA (because the conditions for recognition have not been met), this fact and an estimate, where possible, of the amounts receivable should be disclosed in the notes to the accounts.

8.5.4 Accounting examples

1. A charity with a year end of 31 December 2001 receives notification in November 2001 that it will receive payments from an estate of £20,000 in April 2002 and £25,000 in July 2002. There may be further advances but the representatives cannot determine the amount or timing. The financial statements prepared at 31 December 2001 should contain an incoming resource for this legacy of £45,000 together with a debtor of £45,000.

2. The facts are similar. The charity has long been aware that it is a potential beneficiary from the estate but details of the amounts payable to the charity are received in February 2002. The accounting, involving the recognition of the incoming resource and the debtor at 31 December 2001 will be the same, as the receipt of the payment details in February 2002 is an adjusting post balance sheet event.

8.5.5 Disclosure examples

The disclosure of legacies is illustrated by Example G *The ABC Charity*. The accounting policies explain the basis for recognising incoming resources, including legacies, and a note gives details of legacies which have not been recognised in the SOFA.

Example G   *The ABC Charity*

(d) Incoming resources

All incoming resources are included in the SOFA when the charity is legally enti-tled to the income and the amount can be quantified with reasonable accuracy. For legacies, entitlement is the earlier of the charity being notified of an impend-ing distribution or the legacy being received.

Gifts in kind donated for distribution are included at valuation and recognised as income when they are distributed to the projects. Gifts donated for resale are included as income when they are sold. Donated facilities are included at the value to the charity where this can be quantified and a third party is bearing the cost. No amounts are included in the financial statements for services donated by volunteers.

3. Legacies
The charity is the residuary beneficiary of a farm in Kent. This is occupied by a life tenant and has not been included in the financial statements. The existing unencumbered value of the farm is estimated at £400,000.

In addition, legacies with a probate value of £1,600,000 have not been included in the financial statements as no notification of impending distribution has been received.

8.6 Gifts in kind

Incoming resources in the form of gifts in kind should be included in the SOFA in the following ways:

(a) Assets given for distribution by the charity should be recognised as incoming resources for the year within 'donations, legacies and similar incoming resources' only when distributed in which case the equivalent amount should be included within charitable expenditure.
(b) Assets given for use by the charity (e.g., property for its own occu-pation) should be recognised as incoming resources when receivable. Where the donor intended the assets to be used on a continuing basis then they should be accounted for in accordance with para 80 and treated as a fixed asset for long term use by the charity.
(c) Where a gift has been made in kind but on trust for conversion into cash and subsequent application by the charity, the incoming resource should normally be recognised in the accounting period when receivable. However in certain cases this will not be practicable and the incoming resources should be included in the accounting period in which the gift is sold. The most common example is that of second-hand goods donated for resale, which, whilst regarded as a donation in legal terms, is in economic terms similar to trading and should be included within 'activities for generating funds'. In the case of second-hand goods

donated for resale, prudence dictates that no cost should be recognised until the goods, which cost nothing, are subsequently sold.

In all cases the amount at which gifts in kind are brought into account should be either a reasonable estimate of their gross value to the charity or the amount actually realised.

The principles of materiality should, of course, be applied. In many cases gifts in kind may be of negligible value and will have no material impact upon the financial statements.

8.6.1 Disclosure

The basis of any valuation should be disclosed. Where material, an adjustment should be made to the original valuation upon subsequent realisation of the gift.

Referring to (a) above, where there are undistributed assets at the year end, a general description of the items involved and an estimate of their value should be given by way of a note to the accounts provided such value is material.

In Example G *The ABC Charity* gifts in kind are immaterial but are disclosed in a note analysing the total of donations and gifts. This disclosure serves as a acknowledgement of the gift.

Example G   *The ABC Charity*

2. Donations and gifts	2001 £'000	2000 £'000
Individuals	**2,106**	1,678
Charitable foundations	**4,100**	3,500
Corporate donors	**1,100**	800
Gifts in kind	**24**	22
	7,330	6,000

Gifts in kind comprise free accommodation for the charity's Childcare team in Wimbledon kindly provided by the Packwood Foundation. A corresponding amount is included within Childcare expenditure.

8.7 Intangible income

A charity may receive assistance in the form of donated facilities, beneficial loan arrangements, donated services or services from volunteers. Such assistance is generally referred to as 'intangible income'. Common examples in practice include occupying premises rent free or with a significant discount, or the charity receiving free or heavily discounted professional services.

Such intangible incoming resources should be included in the SOFA where another party is bearing the financial cost of the resources supplied and the benefit is quantifiable and measurable. (This will not normally apply to commercial discounts except where they are clearly intended as a donation.) Where there is no financial cost borne by another party for the provision of the assistance (e.g., in the case of volunteers), the intangible income should not be included in the SOFA. The value placed on resources included in the SOFA should be the financial cost to the third party of providing them. However, where this information is not available or if the charity considers the value to be less than the costs borne by the third party, a reasonable estimate of their gross value to the charity should be given. An equivalent amount should be included as expenditure under the appropriate heading in the SOFA.

As an example a charity occupies premises rent free. The market rent is able to be determined and is estimated at £50,000 per annum. Therefore an incoming resource, together with a corresponding entry for deemed expenditure of £50,000 should be recognised in the SOFA. Recognition might not be necessary in a situation where the benefit is of nominal value. For example, where the market value of the rent is negligible because of the poor state of repair of the building or because the charity is occupying previously let space for the remainder of the period paid up by the former tenant.

The receipt of free or discounted professional services may be more difficult to account for, and more likely to be disclosed as help from volunteers. This is because the real market value of the support is difficult to determine because of its 'voluntary' nature and lack of information about charge out rates and the amount of time recorded.

Again, the principles of materiality must be remembered as often even the cost borne by the third party is not material to the charity. For example, a charity with incoming resources of £1.3m was allowed to occupy premises at a nominal rent. The market rent for the premises of £12,000 per annum is clearly immaterial.

8.7.1 Disclosure

The notes to the accounts should give an analysis of intangible incoming resources included in the SOFA distinguishing appropriately between the different major items e.g., seconded staff, loaned assets etc. Material intangible incoming resources which are not included in the SOFA (e.g., volunteers) should be commented on in the Trustees Annual Report.

Example A *Arts Theatre Trust Limited* has an accounting policy for intangible income and a note explaining why a donation in kind cannot be recognised.

Example A   *Arts Theatre Trust Limited*

Intangible income
Intangible income, which comprises donated services, is included in income at a valuation which is an estimate of the financial cost borne by the donor where such a cost is quantifiable and measurable. No income is recognised when there is no financial cost borne by a third party.

20. Related parties
The charity has a very close relationship with N Arts, which is a charity, BF Borough Council and B Town Council, all of which nominate the majority of the trustees and provide funding to enable the charity to carry out its charitable objectives. The following is a summary of transactions with those entities:

	2001 £'000	2000 £'000
Revenue funding	405	501
BF Borough Council	104	100
B Town Council	154	150
N Arts Trust	663	751

All the above funding was received under contracts with the charity to provide services, eg training in drama production, and has been included in the financial statements under the heading *Incoming Resources: from Operation of theatre and arts centre.*

The charity also received a donation in kind, from BF Borough Council, for the rent of premises, the value of which could not be quantified and therefore has not been included in these financial statements.

There are no outstanding balances with related parties at 31 March 2001 (2000–£NIL).

8.8   Incoming resources from operating activities

For the purpose of analysing incoming resources from operating activities, such activities fall into two principal categories:

(a)   activities in furtherance of the charity's objects;
(b)   activities for generating funds.

A charity should expand these broad headings appropriately to reflect the activities which it carries out. Activities may be aggregated at a suitable level with the possibility of further subdivisions being given in the notes to the accounts.

All incoming resources received for activities which are in the nature of a payment for the provision of goods or services should be combined together under the relevant activity. This will include trading income and those grants (although legally donations) which have conditions which make them similar in economic terms to trading income, such as service agreements with local authorities. However, grants which are for core funding or do not have particular service requirements or are in response to an appeal are donations and should be included in the section for 'donations, legacies and similar incoming resources'.

Activities in furtherance of the charity's objects may include:

(a) the sale of goods or services as part of the directly charitable activities of the charity (known as primary purpose trading) or the letting of non-investment property in furtherance of the objects;
(b) the sale of goods or services made or provided by the beneficiaries of the charity;
(c) incoming resources from government or public authorities where these are received in the normal course of trading under (a) or (b) e.g., fees for respite care;
(d) grants in specifically for the provision of goods and services as part of the directly charitable activities or provided by the beneficiaries;
(e) ancillary trades connected to a primary purpose in (a) and (b) where the principal aim is to provide a service to the charity's beneficiaries.

Activities for generating funds have the principal features that they are not part of the directly charitable activities but are carried out in order to generate incoming resources to support those activities. This will include fundraising events such as jumble sales, firework displays and concerts (which are legally considered to be trading activities) and those sponsorships and social lotteries which cannot be considered as pure donations.

Activities for generating funds can include selling donated goods and bought in goods, providing services to other than the charity's beneficiaries, licensing arrangements, the letting of non-investment property and many others. Whilst selling donated goods is legally considered to be the realisation of a donation in kind, in economic terms it is similar to a trading activity and should be included in this section. Therefore sales by charity shops or catalogue operations should be included in this section. Ancillary trades where the principal aim (whilst still providing a service to the beneficiaries) is to generate incoming resources to support or contribute to the other charitable activities, should also be included in this section.

It may be possible to segregate the incoming resources and resources expended for each different type of activity (this may have to be done for tax purposes) but an enterprise carrying on a mix of activities will often be viewed as a single economic unit. Charity trustees should consider the balance of the activities being undertaken to determine the most appropriate place to include the incoming resources from such enterprises but having done this the mix of incoming resources need not be segregated further. For example a shop may mainly sell donated and bought in goods, but it may also sell a small amount of goods made by its beneficiaries and incidentally provide information about the charity. It would be acceptable to class all the incoming resources from the shop as 'shop income' under 'activities for generating funds'.

8.8.1 Disclosure

An analysis of activities should be given in the notes to the accounts to supplement the analysis on the face of the SOFA. It should be sufficiently detailed so that the reader of the accounts understands the main activities carried out by the charity and the main components of the gross incoming resources receivable for each activity.

Disclosure example

A comprehensive illustration of accounting policies and supporting notes is contained in Example A *Arts Theatre Trust Limited,* a charity which generates operating resources from several sources and which has a trading subsidiary.

Example A *Arts Theatre Trust Limited*

Incoming resources

Charitable trading activities
Income from theatre admission fees is included in incoming resources in the period in which the relevant show takes place.

Commercial trading activities
Income from commercial activities is included in the period in which the group is entitled to receipt.

3. Incoming resources from operation of theatre and arts centre

	2001 £'000	2000 £'000
Admission fees	514	489
Public authority service agreements for operation of theatre	509	601
Service agreements with other charities for workshops	154	150
Other income	23	19
	1,200	1,259

4. Commercial trading operations and investment in trading subsidiary

The wholly-owned trading subsidiary, HTC Limited, which is incorporated in the United Kingdom, pays all its profits to the charity by gift aid. HTC Limited operates the bars, restaurant, coffee lounge and all commercial trading operations carried on at the Arts Theatre Trust Limited. The charity owns the entire issued share capital of 1,000 ordinary shares of £1 each. A summary of the trading results is shown below.

Summary profit and loss account

	2001 £'000	2000 £'000
Turnover	**549**	296
Cost of sales and administrative expenses	**(337)**	(280)
Interest receivable	**4**	–
Net profit	**216**	16
Amount gifted to the charity	**(216)**	(16)
Retained in the subsidiary	**–**	–
The assets and liabilities of the subsidiary were:		
Current assets	**136**	1
Creditors: amounts falling due with one year	**(135)**	–
Total net assets	**1**	1
Aggregate share capital and reserves	**1**	1

Example G *The ABC Charity* generates merchandising income through the charity and a subsidiary. A note analyses the sources and related costs.

Example G   *The ABC Charity*

4. Merchandising income and costs

	Donated goods £'000	Sale of purchased goods through ABC Enterprises Limited (see note 19)	Total 2001 £'000	Total 2002 £'000
Merchandising income	280	860	**1,140**	900
Cost of sales	–	700	**700**	620
Administrative expenses	100	70	**170**	90
Merchandising expenses	100	770	**870**	710
Surplus	180	90	**270**	190

8.9 Investment income

Incoming resources from investment assets, including dividends, interest and rents but excluding capital returns, should be included as investment income in the SOFA.

8.9.1 Disclosure

The notes to the accounts should show the gross investment income arising from each category of investment in accordance with para 238.

As a minimum this would normally include:

(a) investment properties;
(b) investments listed on a recognised stock exchange or ones valued by reference to such investments, such as unit trusts and common investment funds;
(c) investments in subsidiary or associated undertakings or in companies which are connected persons;
(d) other unlisted securities;
(e) cash and settlements pending held as part of the investment portfolio;
(f) any other investments,

together with a further analysis, for each category, of income from investment assets in and outside the UK.

FRS 16 also requires transitional relief to the disclosed.

8.9.2 Example

Example C   *The Rosanna Grant Trust* illustrates this disclosure.

(b) **Investment income**
Investment income is accounted for in the period in which the charity is entitled to receipt.

2. Investment income

	2001 £'000	2001 £'000
Dividends – UK equities	430	385
Interest – UK fixed interest securities	287	278
Interest on cash deposits	20	17
	737	680

Transitional tax relief amounting to £125,000 (2000 - £67,000) is included above.

8.10 Incoming resources from government and other public authorities

Incoming resources from the government and other public authorities arise in many and varied ways such as grants, contracts and service agreements. They include resources from the European Union and other EU bodies and incoming resources from the Community Fund (previously the National Lottery).

These resources should be treated in a similar manner to other incoming resources and included under the relevant headings of the SOFA which will normally be 'donations legacies and similar incoming resources' or 'activities in furtherance of the charity's objects'.

These resources should also be dealt with in accordance with any conditional terms which create a special trust and therefore a restricted fund, though this can be difficult to determine in practice. Sometimes the conditions may represent the authority's expectations of service provision without imposing a restriction but each case must be judged on its own merits. However, where the incoming resources are for a service (or goods) and, upon full performance of the service, any surplus funds can be retained and used for general purposes, this most likely indicates that the incoming resources and related expenditure will be unrestricted. Whereas, if upon full performance any surplus is retrievable by the authority then the resources are most likely to be restricted.

8.10.1 Disclosure

The notes to the accounts should give a description of the sources of any material incoming resources, by category. For example, this could distinguish between type of authority and resources such as fees, grants and service agreements. This is illustrated in an extract from Example D, which is given below (at **8.12**) as a comprehensive example.

8.11 Other incoming resources

Other incoming resources will include the receipt of any resources which the charity has not been able to categorise. This will be a minority of incoming resources and many charities will not need to use this category. The most common example is the gain on the disposal of a fixed asset for the charity's own use.

8.12 Comprehensive example

A comprehensive of the disclosure of varies sources of income, including donations, legacies, government and agency and grants, and gifts in kind is presented in Example D *Aid Overseas*.

Example D   *Aid Overseas*

(c) **Incoming resources**

Income is recognised in the period in which the charitable group is entitled to receipt and the amount can be measured with reasonable certainty. Income is deferred only when the charity has to fulfil conditions before becoming entitled to it or where the donor has specified that the income is to be expended in a future period.

Grants from the government and other agencies have been included as income from activities in furtherance of the charity's objects where these amount to a contract for services, but as donations where the money is given in response to an appeal or with greater freedom of use, for example government block grants.

In accordance with this policy, legacies are included when the charity is advised by the personal representative of an estate that payment will be made or property transferred and the amount involved can be quantified.'

2. Donations, legacies and similar incoming resources

	Unrestricted £'000	Restricted £'000	2001 Total £'000	2000 Total £'000
Donations				
Committed giving	4,147	–	**4,147**	4,032
Legacies	1,043	–	**1,043**	1,928
Donations, appeals and fund-raising events	1,468	854	**2,322**	1,136
	6,658	**854**	**7,512**	**8,096**
Grants from UK Government				
Department for International Development	–	**500**	**500**	**500**
Grants from other agencies				
Disaster Emergencies Committee	–	1,341	**1,341**	1,091
Other UK agencies		10	**10**	10
		1,351	**1,351**	**1,101**
Gifts in kind				
Blankets and clothing	239	–	**239**	240
Food Aid received from World Food programme	–	582	**582**	556
Food Aid received from European Union	–	510	**510**	498
	239	**1,092**	**1,331**	**1,294**
Total	**6,897**	**3,797**	**10,694**	**8,991**

137

3. Activities in furtherance of the charity's objectives

	2001 £'000	2000 £'000
Contracts for operational programmes		
UK Government – Department for		
International Development	1,415	1,296
Other UK agencies – National Lottery		
Charities' Board	25	25
European Union	1,933	1,901
United Nations agencies	269	276
Non-UK governments	1,020	991
Other international agencies	132	128
Less deferred income	(48)	(50)
	4,746	4,567

All the income arising under the above contracts is considered to be restricted to particular projects, an outline of which is given in note 7.

8.13 Resources expended

Resources expended are now to be split into two main categories being the costs of generating funds and the actual costs of charitable activities.

The required presentation, showing the relevant guidance in the SORP is as follows:

(i)   costs of generating funds (paras 132-135);
(ii) charitable expenditure showing separately:
    (a) grants payable in furtherance of the charity's objects (paras 138–146);
    (b) costs of activities in furtherance of the charity's objects (paras 147–150);
    (c) support costs for (i) and (ii) (where material) (paras 147–150); and
    (d) resources expended on managing and administering the charity (paras 151–152);
(iii) the total by column of the above resources expended in the year.

8.14 Costs of generating funds

This is a wider category than the previous 'fundraising and publicity' category. A major change is that it specifically includes investment management costs for both income generation and capital maintenance.

These are the costs which are associated with raising funds from all the possible sources of incoming resources. This will mainly be fundraising costs in attracting donations, legacies and similar incoming resources and the costs of activities for income generation. In addition it may include costs associated with raising funds for the provision of goods and services in the furtherance of the charity's objects, but it should not include any of the costs of performing or supporting those activities. For instance the costs of negotiating a contract or applying for a grant for a charitable activity could be regarded as a cost of generating funds. The costs of carrying out the activity will be costs in furtherance of the charity's objects and the costs of monitoring performance in line with the contract or grant could be support costs.

Expenditure on fundraising should be all the costs incurred in raising the fundraising proceeds shown in the accounts, including agents' costs where used. This should include publicity costs associated with fundraising or raising the profile of the charity but not those which are used in an educational manner in furtherance of the charity's objects. Such distinctions should be drawn in line with the particular nature and circumstance of each charity and its publicity material. Policies for drawing these distinctions should be disclosed.

As noted above, the costs of generating funds should also include investment management costs for both income generation and capital maintenance.

8.14.1 Disclosure

Where material, the different categories of the costs of generating funds should be shown on the face of the SOFA or in the notes to the accounts. An analysis of the major items of expenditure should be given in the notes to the accounts. This should, where possible, be linked to the incoming resource categories reflecting the funds raised. This link is illustrated above in the extract from Example G, disclosing merchandising revenue and related costs.

Example D *Aid Overseas* supports the entries on its SOFA for 'shop expenditure' and 'fundraising costs' (which make up the costs of generating funds) by two notes.

Example D   *Aid Overseas*

4. Shop income and expenditure

	Aid Overseas Trading Ltd £'000	Charitable Trading £'000	2001 Total Shop Activities £'000	2000 Total Shop Activities £'000
Turnover from donated goods	–	6,985	**6,985**	5,366
Turnover from purchased goods	1,588	–	**1,588**	1,230
Total shop income	**1,588**	**6,985**	**8,573**	**6,596**
Operating expenses	(1,012)	(4,626)	**(5,638)**	(5,187)
Management expenses	(452)	(404)	**(856)**	(842)
Shop expenditure	**(1,464)**	**(5,030)**	**(6,494)**	**(6,029)**
Net income from trading	**124**	**1,955**	**2,079**	**567**

This represents income from the sale of donated and bought-in goods through the charity's shops.

The profit of Aid Overseas Trading Limited is gifted to the charity so that there is no liability to Corporation Tax for that entity. Further details are set out in note 15 to the accounts.

6. Fund-raising costs

	Unrestricted £'000	Restricted £'000	2001 Total £'000	2000 Total £'000
Staff costs	640	100	**740**	721
Consultancy costs	501	6	**507**	427
Brochures and material	264	2	**266**	249
Office costs and other overheads	241	5	**246**	187
	1,646	**113**	**1,759**	**1,584**

8.15 Charitable expenditure

Charitable expenditure comprises all the expenditure incurred by the charity in meeting its charitable objectives as opposed to the cost of raising the funds to finance these activities and now includes management and administration costs. It should be analysed between the following sub-headings:

(a) grants payable in furtherance of the charity's objects (paras 138–146);
(b) costs of activities in furtherance of the charity's objects (paras 147–150);
(c) support costs of (a) and (b) where material (paras 147–150);
(d) costs of management and administration of the charity (paras 151–152).

Costs such as depreciation, amortisation or losses on disposal of fixed assets used wholly or mainly for charitable activities, including where the assets are written off as project expenditure, should be allocated within this section in accordance with the principles set out in para 153.

8.16 Grants payable in furtherance of the charity's objects

A grant is any payment which, in order to further its objects, a charity makes voluntarily to another institution or to an individual. A grant may or may not be repayable to the charity in certain circumstances. However, a payment which a charity must make in return for the supply of goods or services is not a grant.

SORP 2000 contains new and extended disclosures for grants made by charities and tightens up the rules for non-disclosure of grants. These principle changes are summarised as follows:

• The requirements for disclosing grants (paras 138-146) are set out more fully with the emphasis on providing the analysis and explanation necessary to understand how the grants made by a charity relate to its objects. There are different requirements for disclosure of grants to institutions and individuals.
• The rules for non-disclosure of grants (para 146) have been tightened up. Non-disclosure is regarded as exceptional and should only occur when disclosure could seriously prejudice the charity or the recipient institution. The total number, value and general purpose of non-disclosed grants should be given in the notes to the accounts and in England and Wales, prior to signing the accounts, trustees should provide the Charity Commission with full details regarding those grants which have not been disclosed and the reasons for non-disclosure. The Trustees' Annual Report should confirm that this has been done.

8.16.1 Disclosure

If grant-making is material to a charity, the charity should provide an appropriate analysis and explanation of the grants which it makes. Whether grant-making is material will to some extent depend on the size of the charity and the importance of grant-making to its overall operation. If in any accounting year a charity makes grants totalling at least 5 per cent of its total resources expended in that year the charity should regard its grant-making as material. However there may be circumstances where the value of grants to an institution in an accounting year is material compared to the total institutional grants in that year and information regarding such grants could be useful to the users of the accounts and should be disclosed.

When analysis and explanation is required, its purpose is to help the reader of the accounts understand how the grants made relate to the objects of the charity and the policy adopted by the trustees in pursuing these objects. The charity may give the analysis and explanation in the notes to the accounts, as part of the trustees' report or by means of a separate publication.

The notes to the accounts should include a reconciliation between the grant expenditure as stated in the SOFA and the details shown in the analysis and make reference to the analysis if it is in the trustees report or separate publication. When the analysis is contained in a separate publication, it should be made available to the public in the same way as the accounts. The notes to the accounts should identify the publication and state how copies of it can be obtained.

The analysis should clearly indicate whether grants are individual or institutional. An individual grant is one which is made for the direct benefit of the individual who receives it, for example to relieve financial hardship. All other grants should be regarded as institutional. For example, a grant which is made to an individual to carry out some research project should be regarded as a grant to the institution with which the individual is connected rather than as a grant to the individual.

For both individual and institutional grants, an analysis should be given which discloses the total number and the total value of the grants given for different charitable purposes. The charity should decide upon classifications which are appropriate for an understanding of its policy. For example, institutional grants may be grouped into categories covering social welfare, medical research, the performing arts, etc. Similarly, grants to individuals may be grouped in categories covering, for example, the welfare of people in financial need or help to people seeking to further their education. Some charities may decide that it is appropriate to provide further levels of analysis, for example, showing a geographical analysis of the number and value of grants made.

In addition, in the case of institutional grants the trustees should disclose details of a sufficient number of institutional grants to convey a proper understanding of the charity's grant-making activities. The number of grants which is sufficient will vary with circumstances. Where a charity has made fewer than 50 material institutional grants in a year all the grants should be disclosed. Otherwise, the disclosure should cover at least the 50 largest institutional grants or any larger number which is necessary for the proper understanding of the charity's grant-making activity. There is no requirement to disclose any grants which are below £1,000 in total.

The disclosure for institutional grants should include the name of the recipient institution and the number and total value of grants made to that institution in the accounting year. Where grants have been made to a particular institution for different charitable purposes, the number and total value of the grants made for each purpose should be disclosed. For example, a charity may have made grants to different officers of a particular university for different projects.

The analyses of grants should be clearly reconciled to the amount for grants in the SOFA. In order to demonstrate this reconciliation, it may be necessary to include in lists of grants a summary of the value and total of the institutional grants of which full details have not been disclosed, or to indicate how some grant commitments have been discounted in line with the requirements of para 125 or treated as contingent liabilities in accordance with para 124.

Exceptionally, even though the grants to a particular institution are material, it is possible that the disclosure of the details of those grants could seriously prejudice the furtherance of the purposes either of the recipient institution or of the charity itself. In these circumstances a charity may withhold details of each grant concerned but should:

(a) disclose in the notes to the accounts the total number, value and general purpose of those grants the details of which have not been disclosed;

(b) before the trustees sign the accounts, give the full details of such grants in writing to the Charity Commission (English and Welsh charities only) or other appropriate regulatory body, fully explaining the reasons why those details have not been disclosed in the accounts;

(c) state in the Trustees' Report whether or not those details have been given to the regulatory body.

It is unlikely in practice that all the material institutional grants of a charity would fall within this exception.

8.16.2 Disclosure example

A full example of the disclosures required by SORP 2000 is presented in Example C *The Rosanna Grant Trust*, a grant giving charity.

Example C   *The Rosanna Grant Trust*

(c) **Resources expended**

Grants payable are charged in the year when the offer is conveyed to the recipient except in those cases where the offer is conditional, such grants being recognised as expenditure when the conditions attaching are fulfilled. Grants offered subject to conditions which have not been met at the year end are noted as a commitment, but not accrued as expenditure.

4. Grants payable

	2001		2000	
	£'000	£'000	£'000	£'000

The amount payable in the year comprises:

Education and research
Manchester Institute of Technology
4 grants (2000–4) as follows:

	2001		2000	
to fund educational post	51		36	
genetic research	31		31	
research into awareness of symptoms of Alzheimer's in general practitioners	20		20	
the impact of Alzheimer's on family and carers	21		21	
		123		108

University of Slough
2 grants to fund educational posts

	2001		2000	
(2000–1 grant)		91		57

University of Taunton
2 grants (2000–3) as follows:

	2001		2000	
research into drug therapies	51		49	
research on nursing homes caring for patients with Alzheimer's	34		30	
compilation of registry of practitioners and hospitals specialising in Alzheimer's	–		24	
		85		103
Total Institutional grants		299		268

PhD scholarships - grants to 79 individuals

	2001		2000	
(2000 - 52 individuals)		244		153
		543		421

Reconciliation of grants payable:

	2001		2000	
Commitments at 1 October 2000		545		281
Commitments made in the year	561		431	
Grants cancelled or recovered	(18)		(10)	

Grants payable for the year	**543**	421
Grants paid during the year	**(929)**	(157)
Commitments at 30 September 2001	**159**	545
Commitments at 30 September are payable as follows:		
Within one year (note 12)	**84**	375
After more than one year (note 13)	**75**	170
	159	545

Commitments

In addition to the amounts committed and accrued noted above, the trustees have also authorised certain grants which are subject to the recipient fulfilling certain conditions. The total amount authorised but not accrued as expenditure at 30 September 2001 was £184,000 (2000: £191,000).

8.17 Costs of activities in furtherance of the charity's objects and support costs

Expenditure on activities in furtherance of the charity's objects (i.e., on the provision of services or of goods) should be appropriately analysed by the activities of the charity (functional classification) to assist the reader of the accounts in understanding how the charity spends its resources. This should mirror the operational activities in furtherance of the charity's objects in the incoming resources section but may have additional activities which do not generate incoming resources.

Where applicable, and where the amount is material, it is recommended that support costs (e.g., salaries, office, communications and other costs) identifiable as an integral part of grants payable and/or the costs of activities in furtherance of the charity's objects are shown separately in the SOFA.

'Support costs' of charitable activities comprise costs incurred directly in support of expenditure on the objects of the charity, and can therefore be considered as part of total expenditure directly relating to the objects of the charity. Such costs will include all services (either at headquarters or through a regional network) which are identifiable as wholly or mainly in support of the charity's project work or other charitable expenditure (excluding management and administration costs) if, but only if, they are an integral part of the cost of carrying out the direct charitable objectives of the charity.

Support costs may therefore be seen as a form of 'back office' cost where activities are undertaken by, say, a head office or research function to assist projects in the field. The concept of 'support costs' is difficult to apply to many charities and therefore many charities are unlikely to have material support costs.

8.17.1 Disclosure

The major items of expenditure within each type of charitable activity should be appropriately analysed in the notes to the accounts. The activities disclosed should be consistent with those disclosed for incoming resources.

An analysis of all the major items included in support costs should be given in the notes to the accounts.

A full disclosure of the cost of charitable activities and support costs is contained in Example D *Aid Overseas.*

Example D   *Aid Overseas*

(d) **Resources expended and basis of allocation of costs**

Expenditure is included when incurred.

Grants payable to partner organisations for relief and development projects are included in the SOFA when approved by the trustees and agreed with the other organisation. The value of such grants unpaid at the year end is accrued. Grants where the beneficiary has not been informed or has to meet certain conditions before the grant is released are not accrued but are noted as financial commitments.

Expenditure on operational programmes is recognised in the period in which it is incurred. A designated fund is established for expenditure which has been committed to projects, but remains unspent at the year end.

The majority of costs are directly attributable to specific activities. Certain shared costs are apportioned to activities in furtherance of the objects of the charity. Office costs and property related costs are apportioned on the proportion of floor area occupied by the activity. Staff costs and office costs are allocated in the same proportion as directly attributed staff costs.

(e) **Fund-raising costs**
These include the salaries, direct expenditure and overhead costs of the staff in offices in the UK who promote fund-raising, including events.

(f) **Support costs**
Support costs represent the cost of core field offices and the costs incurred by UK based staff, directly providing support for the international programme, including management, policy and advocacy work and supervision and technical support for emergency programmes.

(g) **Costs of managing and administering the charity**
These represent costs incurred by finance, human resources, internal audit and directorate departments, attributable to the management of the charity's assets, organisational administration and compliance with constitutional and statutory requirements.

7. Cost of activities in furtherance of the objects of the charity

	Grants Payable to Partner Organisations	Operational Programmes £'000	Gifts in Kind £'000	Information Campaigning and Education £'000	2001 Total £'000	2000 Total £'000
Health and nutrition	1,013	637	1,902	–	**2,742**	2,882
Water supply and sanitation	1,015	1,264	–	–	**2,279**	2,576
Agriculture	641	814	–	–	**1,455**	1,498
Institutional development and social organisation	556	546	–	–	**1,102**	1,076
Shelter	176	416	239	–	**831**	880
Information/ lobbying	–	–	–	520	**520**	529
Income generation/ production	–	680	–	–	**680**	702
Education and legal aid	124	322	–	202	**648**	639
Logistics support		601			**601**	576
Other	–	330	–	271	**601**	576
	3,525	**5,610**	**1,331**	**993**	**11,459**	**11,934**

Grants payable to partner organisations are considered to be part of the costs of activities in furtherance of the objects of the charity because much of the charity's development programme is carried out through grants to local organisations which support long-term, sustainable benefits for a community, which are monitored by the charity. Grants are also made to fund immediate emergency relief provision in times of crisis, catastrophe or natural disaster. Further details are given in Note 8.

The operational programme is work undertaken overseas by the charity and includes the provision of specialist services (eg to address the water and sanitation needs of refugees) and training and networking for local organisations.

The charity's information, campaigning and education programme has several key objectives. One is to contribute the experience which comes from the international programme to the curricula and methods of school teaching and youth work in the UK. Another is to inform our supporters and the wider UK public about our international experience of work with poor people. We also carry out research and analysis of the issues raised by our work, as a contribution to public debate and policy-making in the UK and the European Union, in the interests of alleviating poverty and suffering world-wide. The trustees see the programme as an important ancillary activity which furthers the charitable purposes.

Resources expended on operational programmes comprised:

	2001 £'000	2000 £'000
Staff costs	2,327	2,228
Travel and subsistence	981	993
Projects	2,302	2,671
	5,610	5,892

9. Support Costs		
Staff costs	1,167	1,124
Office costs	401	376
Communications	338	345
	1,906	1,845

8.18 Management and administration

The general principles of 'management and administration' expenditure are unchanged from the 1995 SORP. However, the expenditure is now treated as part of charitable expenditure (see **8.15** above). Expenditure on the management and administration of the charity will normally include both direct and indirect costs under this heading. Direct costs will include such items as internal and external audit, legal advice for trustees and costs associated with constitutional and statutory requirements e.g., the cost of trustee meetings and preparing statutory accounts. There should also be an apportionment of indirect costs involved in managing and administering the charity (as distinct from directly pursuing its charitable activities). This will include a proportion of management (and other staff) time and the overhead costs connected with it, e.g., office and communications costs.

8.18.1 Disclosure

There should be a clear analysis of all the main items of expenditure on management and administration in the notes to the accounts.

8.19 Allocations of costs

It is not practicable to define precisely what should be included under each expenditure heading as each charity's circumstances will be different. Furthermore, charities will often group expenditure under different headings for internal reporting purposes from those which should be disclosed in the annual accounts. In attributing costs the following principles should be applied:

(a) No part of expenditure incurred on activities falling directly within one cost category should be allocated to any other cost category.

(b) Items of expenditure which involve more than one cost category, for example the cost of running an office which houses both fundraising and charitable project support functions, should be apportioned on a reasonable, justifiable and consistent basis to the cost categories involved. For example, staff time might be allocated on a time basis, reflecting an executive role which, say, involves 40 per cent fundraising and 60 per cent charitable project work.

(c) Where costs cannot be allocated to the categories of 'costs of generating funds' and 'grants payable', 'costs of operating activities', and 'support costs' they should be included within 'management and administration'.

8.19.1 Disclosure

The basis and principles used for the allocation of all costs should be disclosed clearly in the accounting policies.

The accounting policies of Example G *The ABC Charity* illustrate the disclosure of the basis of cost allocation.

Example G *The ABC Charity*

(e) **Resources expended**

All expenditure is accounted for on an accruals basis and has been classified under headings that aggregate all costs related to the category. Where costs cannot be directly attributed to particular headings they have been allocated to activities on a basis consistent with use of the resources. Premises overheads have been allocated on a floor area basis and other overheads have been allocated on the basis of the head count.

Fund-raising costs are those incurred in seeking voluntary contributions and do not include the costs of disseminating information in support of the charitable activities. Support costs are those costs incurred directly in support of expenditure on the objects of the charity and include project management carried out at Headquarters. Management and administration costs are those incurred in connection with administration of the charity and compliance with constitutional and statutory requirements.

8.20 Transfers

All transfers, which should be shown gross, between the principal types of fund should be shown after 'net incoming resources before transfers'. Explanations supporting the transfers should be given in the notes.

Paragraph 49(d) of SORP 2000 requires that material transfers between different funds and allocations to designated funds should be separately disclosed, without netting off, and should be accompanied by an explanation of the nature of the transfers or allocations and the reasons for them.

A sub-total should then be struck for 'net incoming (or outgoing) resources for the financial year before revaluations and investment asset disposals'.

8.21 Gains and losses on revaluation and investment asset disposals

Gains and losses on revaluation of all assets and on investment asset disposals should come next (para 64). The section should record separately:

(a) gains and losses on revaluation of fixed assets for the charity's own use; and
(b) gains and losses on the revaluation and disposal of investment assets.

8.22 Gains and losses on fixed assets

Gains and losses arising on disposal, revaluation or impairment of fixed assets – whether held for the charity's own use or for investment purposes – will form part of the particular fund in which the investment or other asset concerned is or was held at the time of disposal, revaluation or impairment.

Such gains and losses should be recognised as follows:

(a) Impairment losses of assets held for the charity's own use (i.e., not investments) should be regarded as additional depreciation of the impaired asset and included appropriately in the resources expended section of the statement of financial activities.
(b) Gains on the disposal of fixed assets for the charity's own use should be included under the heading 'other incoming resources'. Losses on disposal should be treated as additional depreciation and included appropriately in the resources expended section of the SOFA.
(c) Revaluation gains or losses (which are not considered to be impairment losses) on assets held for the charity's own use should be included in the section on gains and losses on revaluations of fixed assets for the charity's own use.
(d) Any gains and losses on investment assets (including property investments) should be included under the gains and losses on the revaluation and disposal of investment assets. Realised and unrealised gains and losses may be included in a single line (but not for incorporated charities unless they prepare a separate income and expenditure account).

8.23 Net movement in funds

The net incoming resources for the financial year, together with the total of any gains or losses on revaluation of all assets and on investment asset disposals, will produce the net movement in funds for that year (para 65 of the SORP). This net movement should, then, be reconciled to the total funds, as shown in the balance sheet, as follows:

(a) net movement in funds for the year;
(b) total funds brought forward;
(c) total funds carried forward.

(Paragraph 66 of the SORP)

Chapter 9 – Balance sheet

9.1 Introduction

The balance sheet provides a snapshot of the charity's assets and liabilities at the end of its accounting year and show how the net asset position is split between the different types of funds. The balance sheet will not always include all of the assets and liabilities of a charity, nor attach an up to date valuation for all assets. Some inalienable and historic assets (see paras 208-217), or contingent liabilities (see paras 261-269) may be omitted. Where such assets and liabilities exist and are not included in the balance sheet, details must be provided in the notes to the accounts.

The objective of the balance sheet is to show the resources available to the charity and whether these are freely available or have to be used for specific purposes because of legal restrictions on their use. It may also show which of the resources the trustees have designated for specific future use. It will normally be necessary to read the reserves policy in the trustees report to gain a full understanding of the availability and planned use of the charity's funds.

SORP 2000 has had little impact upon the general presentation of the balance sheet. It has adopted the accounting treatments of the Financial Reporting Standards issued since the publication of the 1995 SORP and particular consideration must be given to the implications of FRS 15 *Tangible fixed assets* for accounting for fixed assets and FRS 12 *Provisions, contingent liabilities and contingent assests.*

9.2 Presentation

9.2.1 Structure of the balance sheet

The funds of a charity should be grouped together in the balance sheet according to their kind. It should distinguish, as a minimum, between unrestricted income funds, restricted income funds and endowments. Distinctions between permanent and expendable endowment and designated funds can also be made.

The balance sheet should show assets and liabilities under the following headings:

(i)   fixed assets, sub-divided between:
      (a) intangible assets;
      (b) tangible assets;
      (c) inalienable and historic assets;
      (d) investments.
(ii)   Current assets sub-divided between:
      (a) stocks and work-in-progress;
      (b) debtors;
      (c) investments; and
      (d) cash at bank and in hand
(sub-totals should be given for (i) and (ii) above).
(iii) Creditors: amounts falling due within one year.
(iv) Net current assets or liabilities (i.e., the amount in (ii) less the amount in (iii)).
(v)   Total assets less current liabilities (ie the amount in (i) plus (or minus) the amount in (iv)).
(vi) Creditors: amounts falling due after more than one year.
(vii) Provisions for liabilities and charges.
(viii) Net assets (i.e., the amount in (iv) less the amounts in (v) and (vi)).
(ix) The funds of the charity divided between:
      (a) unrestricted income funds;
      (b) restricted income funds; and
      (c) endowment funds.

The balance sheet can be presented in one continuous vertical format or it can be presented in columns appropriately divided between the three types of fund.

In addition, the assets and liabilities should be analysed in a way that enables the reader to gain a proper appreciation of their spread and character. For example, long-term debtors should, where the total is material, be separately stated in the balance sheet – otherwise their total amounts by category should be disclosed in the notes to the accounts.

If there are no amounts for the current and prior year then no entries need to be made on the balance sheet and the headings can be omitted.

Expenditure may be incurred in anticipation of the receipt of restricted income, possibly leading to a negative balance on a specific fund. Where such balances are material they should not simply be netted off against positive balances on the fund category in the balance sheet. This means that the balance sheet may need to separately identify positive and negative balances on restricted funds.

9.3 The principles for the inclusion of assets and liabilities in the balance sheet

9.3.1 Fixed assets

Introduction

There have been significant developments in accounting for fixed assets by the charity and charities are now subject to the same standards as commercial companies. Before the appearance of the 1995 SORP the importance of fixed assets was recognised in a paper by a group of researchers (*Charity accounting standards: Issues for charity researchers* compiled by the NCVO) which stated:

> 'We know very little about the value ... of the assets held by the charity sector, and yet the proper application of assets is probably the longest-standing area of public concern about charities ... A more accurate accounting of their true worth would paint a wholly different picture of the charitable sector, and the standards of its asset management...'.

Historically, the charity sector has accounted for expenditure on fixed assets in a variety of ways. However, the 1995 SORP recommended that, subject to the specified exceptions, all such expenditure is capitalised, the charity sector had to account for fixed assets in the same way as the commercial sector.

There are further developments in reporting in SORP 2000, mainly arising from the introduction of FRS 15 *Tangible fixed assets.* These developments particularly affect the treatment of inalienable and historic fixed assets.

Paragraph 184 of the SORP 2000 recommends that a charity's fixed assets are divided between intangible assets, tangible assets, inalienable and historic assests.

9.3.2 Intangible fixed assets

Intangible fixed assets should be included in the balance sheet in accordance with Financial Reporting Standard 10 (FRS 10) *Goodwill and Intangible Fixed Assets.*

Goodwill arising from the acquisition of another entity will tend to be rare in the charity sector, but some charities may have intangible assets representing intellectual property arising from activities subject as research and development or publishing. The costs of acquiring the intangible asset should be capitalised and amortised over an expected life which should not normally exceed 20 years.

9.3.3 Tangible fixed assets (other than investments)

Financial Reporting Standard 15 *Tangible Fixed Assets* requires that all fixed assets should be capitalised on initial acquisition and included in the balance sheet at cost or valuation. They may then be periodically revalued. Subsequent expenditure which enhances (rather than maintains) the performance of fixed assets should also be capitalised.

Within charities, tangible fixed assets (other than investments) fall into two categories, those held for charity use (including those used for the running and administration of the charity) and those classed as inalienable and historic assets. There may be some overlap in that some inalienable and historic assets may also be used in the functional activities of the charity.

General rules for the inclusion of tangible fixed assets
Tangible fixed assets should initially be included at their cost of acquisition including costs that are directly attributable to bringing the assets into working condition for their intended use.

This can include costs of interest on loans to finance the construction of such assets but only where the charity has adopted this as a policy for all tangible fixed assets and capitalisation should cease when the asset is ready for use. This applies whether assets are bought outright or through hire purchase or finance leasing.

If a fixed asset is acquired in full or in part from the proceeds of a grant it should be included at its full acquisition cost (or in the case of a joint arrangement at the gross value of the charity's share in the asset) without netting off the grant proceeds which should be shown as part of incoming resources in the SOFA.

Where functional fixed assets have been donated they should be valued at the amount of the gift included as an incoming resource in the SOFA.

Similarly where such assets are capitalised some time after being acquired, for example as a result of a change in accounting policy, they should be included at original cost or at the value at which the gift was included in the SOFA less an amount for depreciation. However, if neither of these amounts is ascertainable, a reasonable estimate of the asset's cost or current value to the charity should be used. Such a valuation will be regarded as the asset's initial carrying amount and will not be regarded as a revaluation.

Where the net book value of a fixed asset is higher than its recoverable amount, it will be impaired and should be written down to its recoverable amount.

Mixed use of fixed assets (functional and investment)

Where land and buildings are held for mixed purposes, ie partly as functional property and partly as investment, the way in which they are capitalised depends upon the primary purpose for holding the asset and the extent to which they are separable. In general the following rules should be followed:

(a) assets held primarily for charity use of which a part is leased at a commercial rent can be regarded as functional fixed assets if:
   (i) only a small part of the asset is leased; or
   (ii) the lease is for a short period of time,
(b) assets held primarily for investment purposes where a small part is used for functional purposes should be classed as investment assets; and
(c) assets which contain clearly distinguishable parts which are held for different purposes ie partly functional and partly investment and do not fall under (a) or (b) above should be split in the balance sheet between functional and investment assets.

Depreciation of tangible fixed assets (other than investments)

Most tangible fixed assets depreciate; that is they wear out, are consumed or otherwise suffer a reduction in their useful life through use, the passing of time or obsolescence. Their value is thus gradually expended over their useful economic life. This expenditure should be recognised by means of annual depreciation charged in the SOFA and shown in the balance sheet as accumulated depreciation deducted from the value of the relevant fixed assets.

Fixed assets held for use by the charity which are included in the balance sheet should be depreciated at rates appropriate to their useful economic life in each case.

Exceptions to charging depreciation may only arise if any of the following conditions apply:

(a) the asset is freehold land which is considered to have an indefinitely long useful life;
(b) the depreciation charge and accumulated depreciation are not material because:
   (i) the asset has a very long useful life; or
   (ii) the residual value (based on prices at the time of acquisition or subsequent revaluation) of the asset is not materially different from the carrying amount of the asset;

   provided the stringent conditions of paras 89-91 of FRS 15 are met and the asset is subject to an annual impairment review (except for charities under the threshold for following the FRSSE);

(c) the assets are inalienable or historic and have not been included in the balance sheet.

In general, though, the requirement to depreciate, is clear and cannot be avoided. In particular, in virtually all cases, freehold and long leasehold buildings are now subject to depreciation over the expected useful of the building.

Where a fixed asset for charity use comprises two or more major components with substantially different useful lives, each component should be accounted for as a separate asset and depreciated over its individual useful life.

The useful economic lives and residual values of fixed assets should be reviewed at the end of the accounting period and, where there is a material change, the value of the asset should be depreciated over its remaining useful life.

Disclosure
Tangible fixed assets for use by the charity should be analysed in the notes to the accounts within the following categories:

(a) freehold interest in land and buildings;
(b) leasehold and other interests in land and buildings;
(c) plant and machinery including motor vehicles;
(d) fixtures, fittings and equipment; and
(e) payments on account and assets in the course of construction.

These are broad categories and any charity may, within reason, split the headings or adopt other narrower classes that meet the definition of a class of tangible fixed assets and are appropriate to its operations.

The notes should summarise all material changes in the values of each class of functional fixed assets and reconcile the opening and closing balances. This should include, separately stated

at the beginning and end of the period:

(a) cost, valuation or revalued amount;
(b) accumulated depreciation and impairment provisions;

movements on both carrying amount and depreciation during the period:

(c) additions;
(d) disposals;

(e) revaluations;
(f) transfers;
(g) impairment losses (or reversals).

Totals should be given for all classes of assets (including a combined total) separately identifying the depreciation charged for the period.

The methods of depreciation used and useful economic lives or depreciation rates should be disclosed in the accounting policy notes.

There is often a considerable difference between the carrying value and market value of interests in land and buildings not held as investments. Where the trustees consider this to be so significant that it needs to be drawn to the attention of the users of the accounts then the difference should be included, with such precision as is practicable, in the notes to the accounts. If it is not practicable to quantify the difference a written explanation will suffice.

Inalienable and historic fixed assets

FRS 15 requires that all fixed assets should be capitalised in the balance sheet. In principle this includes fixed assets which are inalienable or historic such as ancient monuments, historic buildings or a collection of artistic or scientific works.

SORP 2000 defines an 'inalienable asset' as:

'An asset which a charity is required by law to retain indefinitely for its own use/benefit and therefore cannot dispose of without external consent, whether prohibited by its governing document, the donor's wishes or in some other way. Normally the asset will belong to the charity's "permanent endowment" where it is held on trusts which contemplate its retention and continuing use but not its disposal. However, in the case of a gift-in-kind of a "wasting asset", such as a building, a long lease or a non-durable artefact, the terms of trust may not have provided for its maintenance in perpetuity or its replacement. In that case the endowment will be expended to the extent of the aggregate amount of its depreciation or amortisation properly provided for in the annual accounts (ie based on its currently anticipated useful life).'

The SORP defines an 'historic asset' as:

'An asset of acknowledged historic, scientific (including environmental) or artistic importance, whether of former or present times, the continuing retention and use of which is in direct furtherance of the charity's objects as the primary reason for retaining it. Such assets are normally expected to be held for their lifetime and disposal should be a rare exception, while in the case of a "collection" (museums, galleries, etc) the proceeds of any individual items sold will normally be used only for their replacement in order to maintain the collection or in accordance with the terms of trust.'

Inalienable and historic assets should be included in a separate line in the balance sheet and can be further subdivided into classes appropriate to each charity e.g., churches, collections, historic houses, artefacts.

An appropriate depreciation policy should be applied in accordance with the requirements of the SORP. The very long expected life of the asset, due to its nature, value and need to be protected and preserved means that in many cases the depreciation charge will not be material and no depreciation need be applied.

In addition to assets which are legally inalienable there are some assets which can be clearly identified as historic, artistic or scientific. They are often unique and form part of the heritage of the nation, for instance ancient churches and works of art. Other assets such as war memorials or nature reserves are also preserved as part of the heritage of the nation. They can be considered as historic where they are held as the objects of the charity (rather than as a means of achieving the objects) and the charity has a policy of long term retention. Inalienable and historic assets do not normally represent a store of financial resources for the charity, and public access to them, (whether free or otherwise) is often essential to demonstrate the public benefit of holding such assets. In the case of buildings this may be achieved by using them for the charitable purposes for which they were intended.

Where an inalienable or historic asset is used for administrative or fund generating purposes, such as a visitor centre or a shop, or is held as an investment, it should not be regarded as inalienable or historic and should be capitalised within the appropriate category of fixed assets. Similarly if a decision has been made to sell an asset it should be included at its net realisable value within fixed assets or as a current asset investment.

It may be difficult or costly to attribute a cost or value to inalienable and historic assets. In such cases these assets may be excluded from the balance sheet if:

(a) reliable cost information is not available and conventional valuation approaches lack sufficient reliability; or
(b) significant costs are involved which may be onerous compared with the additional benefit derived by users of the accounts in assessing the trustees stewardship of the assets.

It may also be difficult or costly to attribute a cost or valuation to inalienable and historic fixed assets which are donated. Where assets are purchased by the charity or by another party who then shortly afterwards

159

donates the asset to the charity, the purchase price should be considered as reliable cost information and could be used as a reference point for the fair value of donations of similar assets. Where an asset is partly purchased and partly donated a reasonable estimate of the cost or value to the charity should be made.

Therefore whilst the exclusion criteria may be applied to existing inalienable and historic fixed assets held by a charity, assets acquired subsequent to the implementation of SORP 2000 should be recognised in the balance sheet.

The value of inalienable and historic assets in cultural, environmental, educational and historic terms is unlikely to be fully reflected in a financial value derived from a market mechanism or the price of such assets. It is, therefore, essential that the disclosure requirements of the SORP are met.

Charities should evaluate whether or not to attribute a cost or value to any of their inalienable and historic assets, paying particular attention to the comparison of costs against benefits of such an exercise and taking into account valuation fees, the cost of researching past records etc. In this context, examples of inalienable and historic assets for which a cost or valuation may not be attributed are:

(a) museum and gallery collections and other collections including the national archives;
(b) archaeological sites, burial mounds, ruins, monuments and statues.

For example, a charity operates nature reserves on several sites of redundant farmland. The land has been acquired from various purchases, gifts and bequests. Reliable cost or valuation may not exist for the current land holdings and it is may be difficult to determine a reliable and objective basis of valuation for the land. Therefore, it would appear appropriate to leave these assets 'off balance sheet'. However, new acquisitions are acquired for a known cost or a reliable value can be attributed to new gifts and legacies. Also, if a visitor centre were to be constructed on one of the sites, then the costs of the construction should be capitalised and depreciated.

Disclosure
Information on inalienable or historic assets (whether or not they have been capitalised) should be given in the notes to the accounts or in another publication which is referred to in the notes to the accounts and is available to the public in the same way as the accounts. This should specify why the assets are considered to be inalienable or historic and be

sufficient to enable the reader to appreciate the age and scale of these assets and what use is made of them. This can be done in aggregate for similar types of assets. These details can only be omitted if the publication of the information would prejudice the efficient working of the charity (e.g., by materially increasing the risk of theft or vandalism of the assets in question). If any inalienable and historic assets have not been capitalised or valued, a statement to this effect should be included in the notes to the accounts.

The amount spent on acquiring inalienable and historic assets during the year should be disclosed in the notes to the accounts.

The accounting policy notes should include the acquisition and disposal policy for inalienable and historic assets.

Disclosure example

The principles of SORP 2000 are illustrated in detail in Example E *The Edinburgh Educational Trust*, a charity which operates a school and day centre for disabled children. The extracts presented show the accounting policies for tangible fixed assets and the disclosure notes, including details of inalienable and historic assets.

Example E   *The Edinburgh Educational Trust*

(f)   **Tangible fixed assets**
Until 31 December 1991 neither the original cost nor improvements to freehold land and buildings were capitalised because the buildings are historic, inalienable and form part of a permanent endowment which means that these cannot be sold but must be held in perpetuity.

The original cost of the assets and improvements thereto is not available. The users of the accounts are principally the trustees, parents of children attending the school and various donors. The trustees consider the cost of carrying out a professional valuation to include these assets at a value in the accounts to be considerable compared to the limited additional benefit derived by the users of the accounts.

Since 1 January 1992, all improvements to land and buildings costing more than £1,000 are capitalised and depreciated. Other tangible fixed assets costing more than £1,500 are capitalised and depreciated over 4 years. At 31 March 2001, all such assets have been fully depreciated and eliminated from these accounts.

(g)   **Depreciation**
Depreciation is charged to write off the cost less estimated residual value of property improvements over 20 years.

9. Tangible fixed assets

	Furniture and equipment £'000	Improvements to property £'000	Total £'000
At cost			
Balance at 1 April 2000	341,206	1,591,208	1,932,414
Additions in year	–	1,401,229	1,401,229
Balance at 31 March 2001	**341,206**	**2,992,437**	**3,333,643**
Depreciation			
Balance at 1 April 2000	341,206	254,404	595,610
Charged in the year	–	149,621	149,621
Balance at 31 March 2001	**341,206**	**404,025**	**745,231**
Net book value			
At 31 March 2001	–	**2,588,412**	**2,588,412**
At 31 March 2000	–	1,336,804	1,336,804

The Trust owns the original Georgian Mansion House built in 1757 and the Victorian Hospital designed by Hippolyte Whyte and built in 1874, both of which are 'A' listed. These properties were originally gifted to the Trust to be held in perpetuity in accordance with the Trust Deed and they form part of the permanent endowment funds. The original value of the assets and the cost of improvements to them until 1991 has not been included in the balance sheet because, in the opinion of the trustees, the cost of professionally valuing these assets to include a value in the accounts outweighs the benefits to the users of the accounts. They are insured for £20,000,000 which is an estimate of their replacement cost.

9.3.4 Revaluation of tangible fixed assets (other than investments)

In accordance with FRS 15, *Tangible fixed assets* (other than investment assets) do not need to be revalued unless the charity adopts a policy of revaluation. Where such a policy is adopted, whilst it need not be applied to all fixed assets it must be applied to entire classes of fixed assets. Therefore if an individual fixed asset is revalued all other assets in that class must also be revalued. Classes of assets can be narrowly defined, within reason, according to the operations of the charity.

The initial valuation of an asset when it is donated or where it is capitalised as a result of the change in an accounting policy will not be regarded as a revaluation and hence will not require the entire class of such assets to be revalued.

Similarly where a charity is holding assets at a revalued amount at the date of commencement of this SORP this will not be regarded as a revaluation unless the trustees so choose.

Where there is a policy to revalue such fixed assets their value must be updated on a regular basis. The trustees may use any reasonable approach to valuation at least every five years subject only to obtaining advice as to the possibility of any material movements between individual valuations. Where a charity has a number of such assets it will be acceptable for valuations to be carried out on a rolling basis over a five-year period. Independent formal professional valuations are not mandatory in the case of a charity, which instead can rely on the option of a suitably qualified person who could be a trustee or employee for this purpose.

In the case of assets other than properties, such as motor vehicles, there may be an active second-hand market for the asset, or appropriate indices may exist allowing a valuation to be made with reasonable certainty by an appropriate person (but not necessarily a qualified valuer) either internal or external to the charity. Where this method of valuation is used the assets' values must be updated annually. As an alternative to market value such assets can be recorded at depreciated replacement cost.

Disclosure

Where any class of functional fixed assets of a charity has been revalued the notes to the accounts should give:

(a) the name and qualification of the valuer and whether they are a member of staff or a trustee or external to the charity;
(b) the basis or bases of valuation;
(c) where records are available, the historical cost less depreciation;
(d) date of the previous full valuation;
(e) if the value has not been updated in the reporting period, a statement by the trustees that they are not aware of any material changes since the last valuation.

9.3.5 Impairment of fixed assets for use by the charity

On rare occasions a functional fixed asset may become impaired. This occurs if its net book value (at cost or valuation) is higher than its recoverable amount. In such a case Financial Reporting Standard 11 (FRS 11) *Impairment of tangible fixed assets* would require it to be written down to its recoverable amount.

The recoverable amount is the higher of the net realisable value and the value in use. Value in use is normally the present value of the future cash flows obtainable as a result of an asset's continued use. If a fixed asset is not held for the main purpose of generating surplus cash flows either by itself or in conjunction with other assets, it is not appropriate to measure the value in use of the asset at an amount based on expected future cash flows. In such cases an alternative measure of its service potential may be more relevant, such as the intrinsic worth of the service delivery or the replacement cost of the asset. Each charity can determine its own measure of service delivery but this must be reasonable, justifiable and consistently operated.

Impairment reviews should only be carried out where this is some indication that the recoverable amount of a functional fixed asset is below its net book value. Such a review should as far as possible be carried out on individual assets or where this is not possible then certain categories of assets can be grouped.

Events or changes which may indicate an impairment are:

(a) physical deterioration, change or obsolescence of the fixed asset;
(b) social, demographic or environmental changes resulting in a reduction of beneficiaries for a charity;
(c) changes in the law, other regulations or standards which adversely affect the activities of a charity;
(d) management commitments to undertake a significant reorganisation;
(e) a major loss of key employees associated with particular activities of a charity;
(f) operating losses on activities using fixed assets primarily to generate incoming resources.

Where an impairment review is required the charity should first determine the net realisable value of the asset. If this is lower than the net book value the value in use will need to be considered. If the value in use is considered to be above the net book value the asset should be valued at the net book value. If a decision is made to sell the asset it should be valued at its expected net realisable value.

Value in use calculations should not be used to manipulate the write down of fixed assets. For instance when a new specialised asset is purchased, although it may have a low net realisable value, it is unlikely that it will suffer an impairment in service delivery within the first years after acquisition.

Where there is an impairment loss that needs to be recognised, charities should determine this in accordance with the requirements of FRS 11 (whilst being able to use alternative valuation methods for some assets). The loss should be treated as additional depreciation and included in the SOFA in accordance with para 198 of the SORP. The revised carrying amount of the asset should be depreciated over its remaining useful economic life.

Disclosure

The methods used in the impairment review to determine net realisable value and value in use should be disclosed in the notes to the accounts.

9.3.6 Investment assets

Introduction

The extent of a charity's powers of investment will be set out in its governing document. These will generally be quite wide, giving freedom to invest more or less as an individual would in a range of investments and investment products but subject to the overriding duties of trustees. However, a number of older non-incorporated charities (and a few incorporated bodies also) have historically been bound by the Trustee Investments Act 1961 – either through specific reference to this legislation or, in the absence of appropriate powers in the trust deed, by default.

The 1961 Act permitted a split of investments between two pools, the narrower range (consisting primarily of government stocks and other fixed interest securities) and the wider range (encompassing also those equities that satisfied certain conditions). The split was initially on a 50:50 basis, although this was relaxed in 1995 such that the wider range could be equal to up to three times the value of the narrower.

Because of the under-performance of gilts as opposed to equities, the terms of the Trustee Investments Act have undoubtedly been very costly for those charities subject to its restrictions. However, it had always been possible for trustees to apply to the Charity Commission for an extension of their investment powers and, in anticipation of new legislation, the Commission announced in December 1999 that it would be willing to agree to such applications more or less automatically.

The anticipated legislation came in the form of the Trustee Act 2000, which became effective from 1 February 2001 and extended to almost all charitable trusts the wide powers of investment that would be found in any modern trust deed (if trustees consider that they remain subject to restrictions that inhibit their work, the option of approaching the Charity Commission is still available). The Trustee Act 2000 does, however, impose two requirements that apply when unincorporated charities exercise any investment power:

(a) the trustees must take proper advice; and
(b) they must have regard to the 'standard investment criteria' (i.e., to the suitability of the investment proposed and to the need for diversification).

The Act also imposes a new duty of care and a requirement that, when delegating asset management functions, trustees should prepare a written policy statement to guide their appointed agent.

Although strictly applicable only to unincorporated charities, the Trustee Act 2000 contains a good deal of guidance that should be regarded as 'best practice' when it comes to dealing with investment matters.

Presentation

In effect, the SORP takes a portfolio approach to the classification of investments.

Investment assets (including investments and investment properties and cash held for investment purposes) should be classified as a separate category within fixed assets except where the intention is to realise the asset without reinvestment of the sale proceeds. In such a case, it should be reclassified as a current asset. The reason for this is that investment assets are generally held with the overall intention of retaining them long-term (i.e., as fixed assets) for the continuing benefit of the charity in the form of income and capital appreciation.

Valuation of investment assets

All investment assets should be shown in the balance sheet at market value or at the trustees' best estimate of market value as described below. Market value best represents a true and fair view of the value of these assets to the charity, given the duty of the trustees to administer the portfolio of investment assets so as to obtain the best investment performance without undue risk. Investment assets should not be depreciated. All changes in value in the year, whether or not realised, should be reported in the 'gains and losses on revaluations and disposals of investment assets' section of the SOFA.

Most freely tradable investments will have a readily available market price e.g., shares on a recognised stock exchange. For investment assets for which there is no readily identifiable market price the trustees should adopt a reasonable approach: for instance, valuing shares in unlisted companies by reference to underlying net assets or earnings or the dividend record, as appropriate. Sometimes, where there is no readily available market value for an investment asset (such as a trading subsidiary), the cost of obtaining a valuation outweighs the benefit to the users of the accounts. In such a situation the asset may be included in the accounts at cost.

For investment assets other than shares or securities, the trustees may use any reasonable approach to valuation which must be done at least every five years subject only to obtaining advice as to the possibility of any material movements between individual valuations. If there is a material movement the assets must be revalued. Where a charity has a number of such assets it will be acceptable for valuations to be carried out on a rolling basis over a five-year period.

Disclosure

Where values are determined other than by reference to readily available market prices, the notes to the accounts should disclose who has made the valuation giving their name, qualification and position (e.g., trustee, employee, external valuer) and how the valuation has been carried out.

In the rare case where the size or nature of a holding of securities is such that the market is thought by the trustees not to be capable of absorbing the sale of the shareholding without a material effect on the quoted price, the trustees should summarise the position in the notes to the accounts. If they are able to do so, the trustees should give an opinion on how much the market price should be adjusted to take this fact into consideration.

The notes to the accounts should show all changes in values of investment assets and reconcile the opening and closing book values.

The notes should also show the total value of investment assets divided between distinct types. As a minimum this would normally include:

(a) investment properties;
(b) investments listed on a recognised stock exchange or ones valued by reference to such investments, such as unit trusts and common investment funds;
(c) investments in subsidiary or associated undertakings or in companies which are connected persons;
(d) other unlisted securities;
(e) cash and settlements pending held as part of the investment portfolio;
(f) any other investments.

Items in categories (a) to (f) above should be further analysed between:

(i)   investment assets in the UK;
(ii) investment assets outside the UK.

The total value of shares or investment schemes (including unit trusts) relating to companies listed on a UK stock exchange or incorporated in the UK are treated as investment assets in the UK and no further analysis is required of whether such entities invest their funds in the UK or outside the UK.

167

Balance sheet

Further details should be given in the notes to the accounts to show how
the portfolio is structured. This should indicate direct and indirect investment in listed securities (including unit trusts), details of any material
investments (any over 5 per cent by value of the portfolio) and any material
restrictions which might apply on the realisation of any such assets.

The notes to the accounts should indicate the value of investments held in
each type of fund. This may be included in the overall analysis of assets held
in the different type of funds.

Disclosure examples
A simple example of the disclosure of investments is given in Example C
The Rosanna Grant Trust.

Example C   *The Rosanna Grant Trust*

10. Investments

	2001 £'000	2000 £'000
Market value at 1 October 2000	27,102	27,501
Acquisitions at cost	5,150	4,013
Sales proceeds from disposals	(5,720)	(4,309)
Gain/(loss) in the year	467	(103)
Market value at 30 September 2001	26,999	27,102
Investments at market value comprised:		
UK equities	18,897	18,168
UK fixed interest securities	8,102	8,934
	26,999	27,102
Historical cost as at 30 September 2001	14,303	14,121

All investments are listed UK securities.

A more complex example, including investments held in unrestricted,
restricted and endowment funds, as well as invested deferred income is presented in Example F *The Higher College Charity.*

168

Example F   *The Higher College Charity*

10. Investments Group:

Group	Unrestricted £'000	Restricted £'000	Endowment £'000	Advance fees £'000	Total £'000
Balance at					
1 September 2000	203	744	3,963	2,027	6,937
Additions	20	73	1,402	–	1,495
Disposals at book value	–	(33)	(1,605)	(41)	(1,679)
Revaluations	27	27	273	(47)	280
Balance at					
31 August 2001	**250**	**811**	**4,033**	**1,939**	**7,033**
Listed on UK Stock Exchange (Historical cost: £6,150,000)	250	711	3,783	1,939	**6,683**
Cash deposits	–	100	250	–	**350**
Charity: as above					**7,033**
Investment in Subsidiary Company (see Note 3 and below)					**7**
					7,040

The assets and liabilities of the subsidiary were:	2001 £'000	2000 £'000
Tangible fixed assets	8	12
Current assets	162	215
	170	227
Creditors: amounts falling due within one year	(155)	(215)
	15	12
Representing:		
Share capital	7	7
Profit and loss account	8	5
	15	12

Details of the subsidiary's profit and loss account are given in note 3.

9.3.7 Current assets, liabilities and long-term creditors

Current assets (other than investments, see para 232) should normally be recognised at the lower of their cost and net realisable value.

Liabilities should normally be recognised at their settlement value. In the case of provisions this will be the amount that an entity would rationally pay to settle the obligation at the balance sheet date or to transfer it to a third party at that time and may therefore involve discounting.

Disclosure
Where there are debtors or creditors which do not fit into any of the following categories the headings may be added to or adapted as appropriate to the type of debtor or creditor and nature of the charity.

Debtors should be analysed in the notes to the accounts between short term and long term (above one year) giving amounts for the following:

(a) trade debtors;
(b) amounts due from subsidiary and associated undertakings;
(c) other debtors;
(d) prepayments; and
(e) accrued income.

Where investments are held as current assets the same disclosure is required as for fixed asset investments (see **9.3.6** above).

The totals for both short-term and long-term creditors should each be separately analysed in the notes giving amounts for the following:

(a) loans and overdrafts;
(b) trade creditors;
(c) amounts due to subsidiary and associated undertakings;
(d) other creditors;
(e) accruals; and
(f) deferred income.

Where a charity is acting as an intermediary agent (as opposed to a custodian trustee) for another organisation (as described in para 81 of the SORP – see **8.4.1**) any assets held and the associated liabilities should be separately identified in the notes to the accounts but not included in the balance sheet. The notes to the accounts should provide sufficient detail so that the reader of the accounts understands the relationship and nature of the transactions between the charity, the funding organisation and the recipient of the funds.

9.3.8 Provisions for commitments

Expenditure resulting from provisions that arise due to a legal or constructive obligation (as per FRS 12) should be recognised as expenditure in the SOFA. Such provisions should be appropriately split in the balance sheet between liabilities due within one year and those falling due after one year.

The amount recognised as a liability should be the best estimate of the expenditure required to settle the present obligation at the balance sheet date or to transfer it to a third party at that time. When calculating this amount consideration should be given to:

(a) the timing of the cash flows;
(b) future events and uncertainties which may affect the amount required to settle the obligation.

Where provisions are accrued in the current financial year but are to be paid over several years then future payments may have a reduced value in today's terms (current value). Where the effect is material the outflow of resources required to settle the obligation at the balance sheet date should be discounted to their present value. The discount rate used should reflect the current assessments of the time value of money and the risks specific to the provision. The interest rate either for the cost of borrowing or investment could be an appropriate discount rate.

The best estimate of the liability should be reviewed at the balance sheet date and adjusted appropriately. If a transfer of resources is no longer needed to settle the obligation then the amount of the liability no longer representing an obligation should be deducted from the expenditure category where it was originally charged in the SOFA.

In some instances charities may receive funding for the obligations from a third party which may be regarded as reimbursements and can be netted off against the liability accrued in the statement of financial activities. But if they exist at the balance sheet date such resources must be shown as a separate asset in the balance sheet.

Some expressions of financial support are not binding upon the trustees or do not meet the definition of a constructive obligation. If they cannot be enforced and the trustees retain the option to discontinue future instalments, they should not be treated as liabilities but disclosed as an 'intention'. Where the trustees have decided to incur the expenditure out of existing unrestricted funds, they should account for such intentions by transfer to an appropriate designated fund.

Disclosure

Particulars of all material provisions for commitments accrued in the balance sheet as liabilities should be disclosed in the notes. Similarly particulars of all material commitments in respect of specific charitable projects should be disclosed if they have not been charged in the accounts.

These particulars should include the amounts involved, when the commitments are likely to be met and the movements on commitments previously reported. Particulars of all other material binding commitments should also be disclosed (e.g., operating leases).

The notes should distinguish between those commitments included on the balance sheet as liabilities and those that are intentions to spend and are not included but in both cases should detail:

(a) the reason for the commitments, giving separate disclosure for material projects;
(b) the total amount of the commitments, including amounts already charged in the accounts;
(c) the amount of commitments outstanding at the start of the year;
(d) any amounts charged in the SOFA for the year;
(e) any amounts released during the year due to a change in the value in the commitments;
(f) the amount of commitments outstanding at the end of the year and an indication as to how much is payable within one year and over one year.

Any designated funds should be separately disclosed as part of the unrestricted funds of the charity and appropriately described in the notes. The purpose of the disclosure is to identify that portion of the unrestricted funds that has been set aside to meet the commitments. Activities that are to be wholly financed from future income would not form part of such designation.

Disclosure example

Example D *Aid Overseas* includes a note which discloses commitments to pay grants which have not been accrued as well as commitments relating to leases and capital expenditure.

172

Example D *Aid Overseas*

24. Commitments

	2001 Group £'000	2000 Group £'000	2001 Charity £'000	2000 Charity £'000
At 30 September 2001, the charity had commitments as follows:				
Capital expenditure authorised but not contracted for:	**79**	**200**	**79**	**200**
Commitments in respect of grants approved for projects which have not been accrued in the financial statements but will form part of grants:				
Within one year	472	319	472	319
Between one and two years	180	165	180	165
Between two and three years	42	38	42	38
	694	**522**	**694**	**522**
Annual commitments under non-cancellable operating leases for land and buildings which expire:				
Within 1 year	185	138	137	101
In two to five years	416	281	416	281
Over five years	393	574	372	553
	994	**993**	**925**	**935**
Annual commitments under non-cancellable operating leases for motor vehicles which expire:				
Within one year	1	–	–	–
In two to five years	45	46	28	28
	46	**46**	**28**	**28**

9.3.9 Guarantees

All material guarantees given by the charity, and the conditions under which liabilities might arise as a result of such guarantees, should be disclosed in a note to the accounts.

9.3.10 Contingent assets and liabilities

A charity may have contingent assets and liabilities as defined in Financial Reporting Standard 12 (FRS 12) *Provisions, contingent liabilities and contingent assests.*

A charity should not recognise incoming or outgoing resources or gains and losses arising respectively from contingent assets or contingent liabilities in the SOFA or the balance sheet.

Contingent assets are not recognised because it could result in the recognition of incoming resources that may never be realised. However, when the realisation of the incoming resources is virtually certain, then the asset is not a contingent asset and the resource/gain arising should be included in the SOFA as an incoming resource and in the balance sheet as a debtor.

Where it becomes probable that there will be a future outflow of resources to settle an item previously regarded as a contingent liability it should cease to be contingent and should be accrued in the accounts. The amount of the liability should (except in extremely rare circumstances where no reliable estimate can be made) be capable of being estimated with reasonable accuracy at the date on which the accounts are approved.

The probability of a contingent asset or liability resulting in a future transfer of resources (to or from the charity) should be continually assessed and the recognition of the asset or liability should be reviewed as appropriate.

Disclosure
Material contingent assets and liabilities should be disclosed in the notes to the accounts unless the probability of a future transfer of resources (to or from the charity) is extremely remote – in which case no disclosure is necessary.

The accounts should disclose the nature of each contingency, the uncertainties that are expected to affect the outcome, and a prudent estimate of the financial effect where an amount has not been accrued. If such an estimate cannot be made, the accounts should explain why it is not practicable to make such an estimate.

Where there is more than one contingent asset or liability they may be sufficiently similar in nature for them to be grouped together as one class and be disclosed in a single statement.

Where a liability has been accrued but there is still a contingent liability arising from the same set of circumstances then the notes to the accounts should link the provision and the contingent liability.

9.3.11 Loan liabilities

If any specific assets (whether land or other property) of the charity are subject to a mortgage or charge given as security for a loan or other liability, a note to the accounts should disclose:

(a) particulars of the assets which are subject to the mortgage or charge;
(b) the amount of the loan or liability and its proportion to the value of the assets mortgaged or charged.

The amounts and interest and repayment terms of all inter-fund loans (summarised, if necessary) should be disclosed in the notes to the accounts. Loans made to trading subsidiaries, the security provided, the interest payable and the repayment terms should be disclosed as a separate item in the notes to the accounts.

Chapter 10 – Accounting for separate funds

10.1 Introduction

The main purpose of a charity's accounts is to give an overall view of the total resources available to a charity during the period and show how those resources have been expended, with the balance sheet showing the position at the year end.

But there are additional requirements for charities. Many receive monies which, either by the donor or by the terms of an appeal, are earmarked for special purposes. Similarly, income generated from assets held in a particular fund may be subject to donor-imposed restrictions as to its use or to the fund to which it belongs. In order to achieve these distinctions between the various funds, the accounting records need to be somewhat sophisticated, tailored to meet the circumstances so that it is known which assets and liabilities are held in which funds.

10.2 What is a 'fund'?

Paragraph 12 of Appendix 1 to SORP 2000 defines a 'fund' as:

'a pool of unexpended resources, held and maintained separately from other pools because of the circumstances in which the resources were originally received or the way in which they have subsequently been treated. At the broadest level a fund will be one of two kinds: a restricted fund or an unrestricted fund.'

10.2.1 Unrestricted funds

Unrestricted funds are expendable at the discretion of the trustees in furtherance of the charity's objects.

10.2.2 Designated funds

A designated fund is a particular form of unrestricted fund, consisting of amounts of unrestricted funds which have been allocated or designated for specific purposes by the charity itself. The use of designated funds for their designated purpose is at the discretion of the trustees. Designated funds are not to be confused with restricted funds. While the former are established as a result of a decision of the trustees, which may be later altered, or rescinded, the latter arise either from donor-imposed restrictions or by the terms of a specific appeal or the governing document in some cases. Designated funds are often employed as buffers to temper the effect on the balance sheet of, for example, future maintenance costs of buildings. Paragraph 49 to the SORP recommends that the precise purpose of such funds is given in the notes.

10.2.3 Restricted funds

Paragraph 2 of Appendix 3 to the SORP states that 'restricted funds are funds subject to specific trusts, which may be declared by the donor(s) or with their authority (e.g., in a public appeal) or created through legal process, but still within the wider objects of the charity. Restricted funds may be restricted income funds, which are expendable at the discretion of the trustees in furtherance of some particular aspect(s) of the objects of the charity. Or they may be capital (i.e., endowment) funds, where the assests are required to be invested, or retained for actual use, rather than expended'. Paragraph 1(h) of the Schedule to the 2000 Regulations requires the notes to give a description of any incoming resources which represent capital, according to whether or not that capital is permanant endowment.

If the trustees use restricted income in a way which is inconsistent with the restrictions imposed, they may be in breach of trust. Accordingly, it is essential that due care is taken to spend from a particular restricted fund only where the trusts so permit. Nonetheless, expenditure may be charged to a restricted fund which is not, at the time, in credit (or in sufficient credit), provided that there is a genuine anticipation of income which can properly be credited to that fund to meet the expenditure. In order to allow for the income not materialising, the trusts of the fund used to finance the expenditure should be sufficiently widely drawn to permit that expenditure. Expenditure charged to an unrestricted fund should not, subsequently, be recharged to a restricted fund, simply in order to increase the amount of that fund.

Where restricted income has been temporarily invested, prior to being used for a suitable charitable purpose, any income derived from the investment should be added to, and will form part of, the restricted income fund in question unless specified otherwise by the donor or the terms of the appeal. Conversely, unless a specific purpose has been declared by the donor, or the terms of the appeal, for the application of the income, in which case such income will be restricted income, that income may be applied for the general purposes of the charity.

The power may be conferred upon the trustees to convert capital funds into expendable income. Were such a power to be exercised, the relevant funds would become restricted or unrestricted income, depending on whether the trusts permit expenditure only for specific purposes or for any of the purposes of the charity.

10.2.4 Permanent endowment funds

Paragraph 3 of Appendix 3 to the SORP states that 'an endowment fund where there is no power to convert the capital into income is known as a permanent endowment fund, which must generally be held indefinitely'.

This concept of 'permanence' does not however necessarily mean that the assets held in the endowment fund cannot be exchanged (though, in some cases the trusts will require the retention of a specific asset for actual use e.g., a historic building), nor does it mean that they are incapable of depreciation or loss. What it does mean is that the permanent endowment fund cannot be used as if it were income (i.e., to make payments or grants to others), however certain payments must be made out of the endowment, such as the payment of investment management fees where these relate to investments held within the endowment. Where assets held in a permanent endowment fund are exchanged, their place in the fund must be taken by the assets received in exchange. 'Exchange' here may simply mean a change of investment, but it may also mean, for example, the application of the proceeds of sale of freehold land and buildings in the purchase or improvement of freehold property.

10.2.5 Expendable endowment funds

Appendix 3 to the SORP continues to state that 'trustees may have the power to convert endowment funds into expendable income; such funds are known as expendable endowments. (Expendable endowment is distinguishable from "income" by the absence of a positive duty on the part of the trustees to apply it for purposes of the charity, unless and until this power to convert into "income" is actually exercised.) If such a power is exercised the relevant funds become restricted or unrestricted income, depending upon whether the trusts permit expenditure for any of the purposes of the charity, or only for specific purposes'.

All incoming resources and resources expended relating to endowment funds should be included in the SOFA. Paragraph 49 of the SORP recommends that the notes disclose how the funds have arisen. As well as identifying any major individual funds, the notes should, also, analyse the funds between permanent endowment and expendable endowment.

10.3 Fund structure

Paragraph 37 of the SORP recommends that the accounts should provide information on the structure of the charity's funds so as to disclose the individual fund balances and the reasons for them. Although details of individual funds may be given in the notes, para 184 of the revised SORP recommends, that, as a minimum, the balance sheet provides a summary of the main funds, differentiating between restricted, including capital (endowment), funds and unrestricted, including designated, funds. The decision as to the most appropriate form of presentation is conferred on the trustees, who should have regard both to the complexity of the fund structure and to the need to avoid confusion between the movements on the various funds.

10.4 Reconciliation and analysis of funds

10.4.1 Reconciliation of opening and closing funds

Paragraph 48 of the revised charity SORP recommends that the SOFA should provide a reconciliation of the opening and closing balances on all of the funds of the charity. The reconciliation should be analysed between unrestricted and restricted and, in the latter case, between income and capital (i.e., endowment) funds. Further analysis of individual funds (i.e., in the case of endowment funds, between permanent endowment and expendable endowment) can be relegated to the notes. Any restricted funds in deficit should be separately disclosed and an explanation provided in the trustees' report. These analyses will show that the charity trustees have accounted for the proper administration of individual funds, in accordance with their terms.

10.4.2 Analysis of the total amount of assets and liabilities

Paragraph 49(a) of the revised SORP recommends that the assets and liabilities should be analysed between the various funds. It is important to be able to distinguish between the assets and liabilities held in the different funds in order to maintain the integrity of those funds.

10.4.3 Are the resources held in an appropriate form?

It is important to provide an indication as to whether or not sufficient resources are held in an appropriate form to enable the funds concerned to be applied in accordance with restrictions imposed. Thus, funds which are to be spent in the short-term need to be matched with assets and investments of a short-term nature. If a fund which has to be applied in the short term is represented by assets which cannot reasonably be expected to be realised in the short term, the charity may not be able to apply its funds as directed.

Paragraph 49(b) of the charity SORP recommends that the notes indicate whether or not sufficient resources are so held in an appropriate form, but not what action is being taken by the charity trustees, or what the consequences (if any) might be, if assets are not held in that form. For example, if a charity has a fund which is to be spent in the near future, it should be made clear in the notes whether or not the assets held (or expected to be received) in the fund are liquid assets.

10.4.4 Realised and unrealised elements

Realised and unrealised gains and losses, provisions for depreciation and diminutions in value on assets held in a particular fund form part of that fund. Similarly, provisions for depreciation, or for a permanent fall in value, form part of the fund in which the asset is held.

There is no recommendation to analyse the total amount of each fund between its realised and unrealised elements.

10.4.5 The nature and purpose of each fund

Paragraph 49 of the revised SORP recommends the disclosure of how each of the funds has arisen and the purpose of each fund.

Separate sets of statements may be produced for each major fund and linked to a total summary. The trustees should decide on the most suitable form of presentation, bearing in mind the complexity of the fund structure and the need to avoid confusion between the movements on the various funds.

10.5 Transfers between funds

Paragraph 49(d) of the revised SORP recommends that material transfers out of restricted funds should be shown separately from allocations to designated funds and should be accompanied by an explanation of their nature and purpose.

Paragraph 1(i) of the Schedule to the 2000 Regulations requires the notes to give an itemised analysis of any material movement between any of the restricted funds of the charity, or between a restricted and unrestricted fund, together with an explanation of the nature and purpose of each of those funds.

10.6 Overhead costs

Unless specifically forbidden by the donor or the terms of the trust a reasonable allocation of overhead expenses (e.g., management and administration, costs of generating funds) can be set against restricted funds.

10.7 Disclosures – particulars of individual funds and notes to the accounts

The notes to the accounts should provide information on the structure of the charity's funds so as to disclose the fund balances and the reasons for them differentiating between unrestricted income funds (both general and designated), restricted income funds, permanent endowment and expendable endowment as well as identifying any material individual funds among them in particular:

(a) The assets and liabilities representing each type of fund of the charity should be clearly summarised and analysed (e.g., investments, fixed assets, net current assets) between those funds.

(b) Disclosure of how each of the funds has arisen (including designated funds), the restrictions imposed and the purpose of each fund. An indication should be given as to whether or not sufficient resources are held in an appropriate form to enable each fund to be applied in accordance with any restrictions. For example, if a charity has a fund which is to be spent in the near future, it should be made clear in the notes whether or not the assets held (or expected to be received) in the fund are liquid assets.

(c) Any funds in deficit should always be separately disclosed. An explanation should be given in the Trustees' Annual Report (see para 31(f)). Designated funds should never be in deficit.

(d) Explanations should be provided for material movements in the funds. In disclosing details of movements on funds, material transfers between different funds and allocations to designated funds should be separately disclosed, without netting off, and should be accompanied by an explanation of the nature of the transfers or allocations and the reasons for them.

10.8 Disclosure examples

Example B *Dorsetshire Drugs Advice Centre* illustrates the analysis of net assets between funds.

Example B   *Dorsetshire Drugs Advice Centre*

12. Analysis of net assets between funds

	General Funds £'000	Designated Funds £'000	Restricted Funds £'000	Total Funds £'000
Tangible fixed assets	7,500	–	3,750	**11,250**
Investments	9,825	1,829	–	**11,654**
Current assets	5,170	10,000	19,138	**34,308**
Current liabilities	(5,928)	–	(2,456)	**(8,384)**
Net assets at 31 March 2002	**16,567**	**11,829**	**20,432**	**48,828**

A simple example of the disclosure of movements in funds is also given in Example B *Dorsetshire Drugs Advice Centre*. In this example, the movements on all the funds are presented in one note. As the charity has a small number of designated and restricted funds, the presentation of one note brings together the movements on all funds into one clear disclosure.

13. Movements in funds

	At 1 April 2001 £'000	Incoming Resources £'000	Outgoing Resources £'000	Transfers £'000	At 31 March 2002 £'000
Restricted funds:					
Computer equipment	–	5,000	(1,250)	–	**3,750**
Advice and information	1,316	70,000	(67,008)	–	**4,308**
Outreach	–	80,765	(68,391)	–	**12,374**
Total restricted funds	1,316	155,765	(136,649)	–	**20,432**
Unrestricted funds:					
Designated training project equipment fund	–	–	–	10,000	**10,000**
Designated revaluation fund	1,067	762	–	–	**1,829**
General funds	19,182	115,900	(108,515)	(10,000)	**16,567**
Total unrestricted funds	20,249	116,662	(108,515)	–	**28,396**
Total funds	**21,565**	**272,427**	**(245,164)**	–	**48,828**

Purposes of restricted funds

Computer equipment	The balance will fund future depreciation of computers which were originally purchased using restricted funds and which the donor specified must be retained.
Advice and information	The fund is for the advice and information activity as explained in the trustees' report.
Outreach	This is a fund for outreach work with young people who are vulnerable or falling into drug misuse. The balance arose from a delay in using grants which were given for the purpose of appointing new staff. Staff were appointed late in the year and all the fund will be utilised in forthcoming months.

Purposes of designated funds

Training project equipment	The management committee has designated funds for purchase of new equipment in the training project.
Revaluation fund	The revaluation fund is required by the Companies Act 1985 and represents the amount by which investments exceed their historical cost.

Where a charity has several designated or restricted funds, then separate notes may give more effective presentation and clearer information to the reader. Example A *Arts Theatre Trust* takes this approach. Note 16, the unrestricted funds note, contains an explanation that funds have been designated for possible repairs that may be required under a property lease. A provision for this item cannot be created because the possibility of repairs would not constitute a provision under FRS 12.

Example A   *Arts Theatre Trust*

16. Unrestricted funds of the charity

	General Fund £'000	Designated Funds £'000	Total £'000
Balance at 1 April 2000	1,263	31	1,294
Movement in funds for the year	83	–	83
Transfer of amount designated for future repairs	(136)	136	–
Balance at 31 March 2001	**1,210**	**167**	**1,377**

The trustees have designated funds for repairs which may be required under the lease for property.

17. Restricted funds

	At 1 April 2000 £'000	Incoming Resources £'000	Outgoing Resources £'000	At 31 March 2001 £'000
Piano fund	10	3	5	8
Ceramics residency	3	–	3	–
Jazz course	1	1	–	–
Clay at the park	2	–	–	2
Kennel ride	2	–	–	2
The ugly show	–	1	1	–
ATC Park capital project	–	73	73	–
	17	78	83	12

The piano fund is for the purchase of a baby grand piano, which was acquired in June 2001.

The ceramics residency fund is to support the appointment of a resident ceramist. The appointment was made at the beginning of September 2000.

The jazz course fund is specifically to underwrite the costs of the jazz weekend held in March as an attempt to bring professional and amateur musicians together.

The clay at the park fund is to publish documents and create an archive relating to the development of clay craft in the Borough.

The kennel ride fund is to assist with the charity's project with the young people of Kennel Ride.

The ugly show fund was to underwrite the costs of an exhibition from five artists held in September and October 2000 which explored notions of beauty.

The ATC Park capital project was funded by the Arts Council of England, which gave the charity a grant of £73,000. This grant was towards the cost of a further feasibility study for alterations, refurbishment and a new extension to the Theatre, which is a Grade 2, listed building. It included the appointment of consultants and the payment of professional fees.

A final example is presented from Example F *The Higher College Charity*. This example includes the disclosure of movements in endowed funds, and as with Example A breaks down the movements on each fund into separate disclosures.

Example F   *The Higher College Charity*

14. Net assets of the group's funds

The group's net assets belong to the various funds (including Advance Fees) as follows:

	Fixed assets £'000	Investments £'000	Net current assets £'000	Long-term liabilities £'000	Fund balances £'000
Endowment funds	–	4,033	–	–	4,033
Restricted funds	–	811	275	–	1,086
Unrestricted funds:					
Designated funds					
Advance fees	–	1,939	185	(1,831)	293
Tangible fixed assets fund	9,562	–	(2,000)	–	7,562
Heritage fund	–	250	2	–	252
Non-charitable trading funds	8	–	–	–	8
General Reserve	–	–	1,190	(44)	1,146
	9,570	7,033	(348)	(1,875)	14,380

Net current assets for
  Advance Fees comprised:

Cash	**397**
Advance fees due within one year	**(505)**
	(108)

14A. Endowed funds: movements in the year

	Balance at 1 September 2000 £'000	Incoming endowments £'000	Amounts expended £'000	Transfers and investment gains/(losses) £'000	Balance at 31 August 2001 £'000
Permanent endowments:					
Foundation capital	563	–	–	15	**578**
Other Special Trusts:					
Grants and allowances	1,772	8	–	66	**1,846**
Scholarships, bursaries	1,460	–	–	(17)	**1,443**
Prize and other funds	168	–	–	(2)	**166**
	3,963	**8**	**–**	**62**	**4,033**

The Foundation Capital represents the original endowment to provide free education. The income of this fund contributes to the free education of pupils whose parents live in Newshire.

The other Special Trusts consist of a number of individual trusts and prize funds set up by individual donors.

Each fund is allocated its proportion of investment income and gains and losses and bears its own expenses.

14B. Restricted funds: movements in the year

	Balance at 1 September 2000 £'000	Income £'000	Expended £'000	Transfers and investment gains/(losses) £'000	Balance at 31 August 2001 £'000
New building fund	–	320	(90)	–	**230**
Grants and allowances	157	112	(112)	(8)	**149**
Scholarships and bursaries	504	113	(86)	20	**551**
Prize and other funds	99	28	(21)	4	**110**
Foundation	44	39	(36)	(1)	**46**
	804	**612**	**(345)**	**15**	**1,086**

Included above is a transfer of £3,700 from a bursary fund to the grants and allowances fund.

14C. Unrestricted funds: movements in the year

	Balance at 1 September 2000 £'000	Income £'000	Expended £'000	Transfers and investment gains/(losses) £'000	Balance at 31 August 2001 £'000
Designated funds:					
Advance fee income	250	248	(165)	(40)	**293**
Tangible fixed assets fund	7,374	–	–	188	**7,562**
Heritage fund	219	20	–	13	**252**
General reserve	890	8,716	(8,511)	51	**1,146**
Charity	**8,733**	**8,984**	**(8,676)**	**212**	**9,253**
Non-charitable trading funds	5	1,694	(1,466)	(225)	**8**
Group	**8,738**	**10,678**	**(10,142)**	**(13)**	**9,261**

Advance fee income represents the amount set aside to cover any future short-fall on the accrued liability for advance fees.

The tangible fixed assets fund represents the net book value of tangible fixed assets less the bank facilities secured on those assets.

The Governors are setting aside, in the Heritage Fund, monies towards the costs of extensions and refurbishment of the school buildings in preparation for the school's centenary celebrations in 2006.

The general reserve fund represents those funds which are unrestricted and not designated for other purposes.

186

Chapter 11 – Cash flow statements

11.1 Introduction

Wherever prepared, para 273 of the charity SORP requires the cash flow statement to comply with FRS 1 (Revised). Paragraph 272 states that 'the object is to show the cash received and used by the charity in the accounting period'. As the cash flow statement is considered to be a 'primary statement', it should be accorded the same prominence as the SOFA and, where prepared, the summary income and expenditure account.

11.2 Exemption

Whether or not incorporated under the Companies Acts, charities are exempt from FRS 1 if they satisfy the 'small company' limits for the purposes of, *inter alia*, filing abbreviated accounts with the Registrar (para 272).

The current thresholds are shown in **14.2.1**.

11.3 Format of cash flow statements

The analysis of the cash movements should accord with the charity's operations as reported in its statement of financial activities, and be given in appropriate detail. The starting point will normally be 'net incoming/outgoing resources before revaluations and investment asset disposals'.

Paragraph 7 of FRS 1 requires the cash flow statement to list the inflows and outflows of cash for the period under the following *standard headings*:

- operating activities;
- dividends from joint ventures and associates;
- returns on investments and servicing of finance;
- taxation;
- capital expenditure and financial investment;
- acquisitions and disposals;
- equity dividends paid;
- management of liquid resources; and
- financing.

The first seven headings should be in the sequence set out above. Except in those rare circumstances where the presentation would not be a fair representation of the activities of the charity, the cash flow statement should disclose separately, where material, the individual categories of cash flows under those standard headings. In those circumstances informed judgement should be used to devise an appropriate alternative treatment. The cash flow classifications may be further divided to give a fuller description of the activities of the charity, or to provide segmental information.

Unlike the recommendations for the structure of the SOFA and reconciliation of funds, the revised SORP contains no recommendation for the cash flow statement to be presented in columnar format if the charity operates more than one fund. This creates an asymmetric presentation.

11.3.1 Operating activities

Cash flows from operating activities are, in general, the cash effects of transactions and other events relating to operating, or trading, activities. FRS 1 states that the cash flow from such activities represents the net increase, or decrease, in cash resulting from the operations shown in the income and expenditure account in arriving at operating profit.

Paragraph 7 of FRS 1 permits operating cash flows to be reported in one of two ways: either by the 'direct method' or by the 'indirect method'. The direct method reports gross operating receipts and payments, including, in the case of charities, cash receipts from fundraising, donations etc., and cash payments in respect of beneficiaries and on behalf of employees to arrive at net cash flows from operating activities. Conversely, the indirect method adjusts, in the form of a reconciliation, the operating result for, for example, depreciation, accruals and prepayments and other items which do not affect cash to arrive at the same net cash flows.

FRS 1 requires the information provided by the indirect method to be given in *all* circumstances. Where only the indirect method information is given, the FRS shows the reconciliation in a note to the cash flow statement, with the statement itself starting with 'Net cash inflow from operating activities'.

A charity may choose to add the information given by the direct method and, where the benefits to users outweigh the costs of obtaining the information, an appendix to the FRS encourages this. Most charities using the indirect method do not offer, voluntarily, the direct method information.

Where information is given in accordance with the direct method, the examples in the FRS position this on the face of the cash flow statement with the indirect method reconciliation given by way of note.

11.3.2 Returns on investments and servicing of finance

These are receipts resulting from the ownership of investments and payments to providers of finance and include interest and dividends. Also, included is the interest element of finance lease rentals and interest paid, whether or not capitalised. Excluded are those items required to be classified under other headings.

11.3.3 Capital expenditure and financial investment

The cash flows included in 'capital expenditure and financial investment' are those related to the acquisition or disposal of any fixed asset other than one required to be classified under 'acquisitions and disposals' and any current asset investment not included in liquid resources.

If no cash flows relating to financial investment fall to be included under this heading the caption may be reduced to 'capital expenditure'.

Cash inflows from 'capital expenditure and financial investment' include:

(a) receipts from sales or disposals of property, plant or equipment; and
(b) receipts from the repayment of the reporting entity's loans to other entities or sales of debt instruments of other entities other than receipts forming part of an acquisition or disposal or a movement in liquid resources, as specified respectively in paras 22–24 and 26–28 of the FRS.

Cash outflows from 'capital expenditure and financial investment' include:

(a) payments to acquire property, plant or equipment; and
(b) loans made by the reporting entity and payments to acquire debt instruments of other entities other than payments forming part of an acquisition or disposal or a movement in liquid resources, as specified respectively in paras 22–24 and 26–28 of the FRS.

FRS 1 is silent as regards the positioning of grants received for the purchase of fixed assets. While some charities classify them as investing cash flows, others classify them as part of financing.

11.3.4 Acquisitions and disposals

The cash flows included in 'acquisitions and disposals' are those related to the acquisition or disposal of any trade or business, or of an investment in an entity that is or, as a result of the transaction, becomes or ceases to be either an associate, a joint venture, or a subsidiary undertaking.

189

Cash inflows from 'acquisitions and disposals' include:

(a) receipts from sales of investments in subsidiary undertakings, showing separately any balances of cash and overdrafts transferred as part of the sale;
(b) receipts from sales of investments in associates or joint ventures; and
(c) receipts from sales of trades or businesses.

Cash outflows from 'acquisitions and disposals' include:

(a) payments to acquire investments in subsidiary undertakings, showing separately any balances of cash and overdrafts acquired;
(b) payments to acquire investments in associates and joint ventures; and
(c) payments to acquire trades or businesses.

11.3.5 Management of liquid resources

The 'management of liquid resources' section should include cash flows in respect of liquid resources.

'Liquid resources' are current asset investments held as readily disposable stores of value. A readily disposable investment is one that:

(a) is disposable by the reporting entity without curtailing or disrupting its business; and is either:
  (i) readily convertible into known amounts of cash at or close to its carrying amount, or
  (ii) traded in an active market.

Each entity should explain what it includes as liquid resources and any changes in its policy. The cash flows in this section can be shown in a single section with those under 'financing' provided that separate subtotals for each are given.

Cash inflows in management of liquid resources include:

(a) withdrawals from short-term deposits not qualifying as cash in so far as not netted under para 9(b) of FRS 1; and
(b) inflows from disposal or redemption of any other investments held as liquid resources.

Cash outflows in management of liquid resources include :

(a) payments into short-term deposits not qualifying as cash in so far as not netted under para 9(b) of FRS 1; and
(b) outflows to acquire any other investments held as liquid resources.

11.3.6 Financing

Financing cash flows comprise receipts or repayments of principal from or to external providers of finance. The cash flows in this section can be shown in a single section with those under 'management of liquid resources' provided that separate subtotals for each are given.

Financing cash inflows include:

(a) receipts from issuing shares or other equity instruments; and
(b) receipts from issuing debentures, loans, notes, and bonds and from other long-term and short-term borrowings (other than overdrafts).

Financing cash outflows include:

(a) repayments of amounts borrowed (other than overdrafts);
(b) the capital element of finance lease rental payments;
(c) payments to reacquire or redeem the entity's shares (unlikely for a charity); and
(d) payments of expenses or commissions on any issue of equity shares.

Reconciliation to net cash/debt

A note reconciling the movement of cash in the period with the movement in net cash/debt should be given either adjoining the cash flow statement or in a note. The reconciliation is not part of the cash flow statement: if adjoining the cash flow statement, it should be clearly labelled and kept separate. The changes in net cash/debt should be analysed from the opening to the closing component amounts showing separately, where material, changes resulting from:

(a) the cash flows of the entity;
(b) the acquisition or disposal of subsidiary undertakings;
(c) other non-cash changes; and
(d) the recognition of changes in market value and exchange rate movements.

Where several balance sheet amounts or parts thereof have to be combined to form the components of opening and closing net cash/debt, sufficient detail should be shown to enable the cash and other components of net cash/debt to be respectively traced back to the amounts shown under the equivalent captions in the balance sheet.

Movements in endowments

Movements in endowments should not be included in cash flows from 'operating activities' but should be treated as increases or decreases in the financing section. This is achieved as follows:

191

(a) cash donations to endowment should be treated as additions to endowment in the 'financing' section;

(b) the receipts and payments from the acquisition and disposal of investments should be shown gross in the 'capital expenditure and financial investment' section of the cash-flow statement. A single line should then be included in this section showing the net movement in cash flows attributable to endowment investments. A corresponding line should be included in the 'financing' section for the same amount. The line in the 'financing' section should reflect the cash into/(cash out of) the endowment fund whereas it will be the opposite direction in the 'capital expenditure and financial investment' section;

(c) on the rare occasion when payments are made out of permanent endowment this should be shown as a decrease in the 'financing' section;

(d) transactions which do not result in cash flows should not be reported in the cash flow statement (e.g., depreciation, revaluations, accruals,) but may need to be disclosed (see para 276).

11.4 Major non-cash transactions

Paragraphs 276(a) and 46 of the SORP and FRS 1 respectively require all material transactions not resulting in movements of cash or cash equivalents of the charity to be disclosed in the notes to the cash flow statement, if such disclosure is necessary for an understanding of the underlying transactions. This would include the inception of a finance lease. Fixed assets donated to a charity would, also, be classified as a non-cash transaction and, if material, disclosed.

11.5 Reconciliation with balance sheet figures

Paragraph 276(b) of the SORP requires the movements in cash (and any financing) movements should be reconciled to the appropriate opening and closing balance sheet amounts.

11.6 Comparatives

Paragraph 48 of the FRS requires comparatives to be provided for all items in the cash flow statement and such notes thereto as are required. This requirement should extend to the notes reconciling the balance sheet figures, i.e., the analyses of changes in cash and cash equivalents and in financing.

11.7 Disclosure examples

The cash flow statement and related notes from Example D *Aid Overseas* is presented below. The format of the statement is virtually identical to that which is used for commercial companies. In this example cash flows arising from investment income are not considered to be part of the 'operational activities' and hence have been shown within 'returns on investments and servicing of finance'.

Example D   *Aid Overseas*

Consolidated Statement of Cash Flow for the year ended 30 September 2001

	Notes	2001 £'000	2001 £'000	2000 £'000	2000 £'000
Net cash inflow from operating activities	26(a)		**1,659**		**827**
Returns on investments and servicing of finance					
Deposit interest received		221		195	
Investment income		8		7	
			229		202
Capital expenditure and financial investment					
Payments to acquire tangible fixed assets		(488)		(266)	
Receipts from sales of tangible fixed assets		46		–	
Disposal of fixed asset investments		8		–	
			(434)		**(266)**
Net cash inflow before management of liquid resources and financing			**1,454**		**763**
Management of liquid resources					
Cash added to short term deposits			(1391)		(1,170)
Increase/(decrease) in cash in the year			**63**		**(407)**
Net cash resources at 1 October 2000			1394		1801
Net cash resources at 30 September 2001	26(b)		**1,457**		**1,394**

26. Notes to consolidated cash flow statement

(a) Reconciliation of surplus of income to net cash inflow from operating activities

	2001 £'000	2000 £'000
Net movement in funds for the year	**2,152**	498
Investment income	**(229)**	(202)
Depreciation charges	**297**	291
Decrease in stocks	**185**	56
Increase in debtors	**(869)**	(21)
Increase in creditors	**569**	102
(Decrease)/increase in grants payable	**(446)**	103
Net cash inflow from operating activities	**1,659**	827

(b) Analysis of net cash resources

	2000 £'000	Cashflow £'000	2001 £'000
Cash in hand (note 18)	929	**212**	1,141
Deposits on one day notice (note 18)	567	**243**	810
Overdrafts	(102)	**(392)**	(494)
	1,394	**63**	1,457

Short term deposits on more than one days notice are considered to be liquid resources.

The format of the cash flow statement presented with Example G The ABC Charity is also 'standard'. In this case, cash flows from investment income are considered to be part of 'operational activities' as the charity considers investment activities to be an integral part of its operations.

Example G *The ABC Charity*

Consolidated Cash flow Statement for the year ended 31 March 2001

	Notes	2001 £'000	2000 £'000
Net cash inflow from operating activities	20	**2,090**	595
Capital expenditure and financial investment			
Payments to acquire tangible fixed assets		**(1,990)**	(1,000)
Proceeds from sale of tangible fixed assets		**130**	170
Purchase of investments		**(1,200)**	(865)
Proceeds from sales of investments		**2,300**	915
		(760)	(780)

194

Cash inflow/(outflow) before increase in liquid resources and financing	20	**1,330**	(185)
Financing			
Finance lease payments		**(40)**	(40)
Management of liquid resources			
Increase in short term deposits		**(400)**	(200)
Increase/(decrease) in cash in the year	20	**890**	(425)

20. Cash flow information for the group

(a) Reconciliation of changes in resources to net inflow from operating activities

	2001	2000
	£'000	£'000
Net incoming resources before revaluations	**2,155**	150
Gain on sale of tangible fixed assets	**(20)**	(30)
Depreciation	**380**	270
Decrease in stocks	**100**	450
Increase in debtors	**(765)**	(225)
Increase/(decrease) in creditors	**240**	(20)
Net cash inflow from operating activities	**2,090**	595

(b) Reconciliation of net cash flow to movement in net funds/debt

Increase/(decrease) in cash in the period	**890**	(425)
Cash outflow from decrease in lease financing	**40**	40
Cash outflow from increase in liquid resources	**400**	200
Movement in net funds and debt in the year	**1,330**	(185)
Net funds and debt at 1 April 2000	**3,020**	3,205
Net funds and debt at 31 March 2001	**4,350**	3,020

(c) Analysis of net funds/debt

	1 April 2000	Cashflow	31 March 2001
	£'000	£'000	£'000
Cash at bank and in hand	200	**890**	1,090
Liquid resources	3,000	**400**	3,400
Finance leases	(180)	**40**	(140)
	3,020	**1,330**	4,350

195

Chapter 12 – Accounting policies

12.1 Introduction

By recommending that the accounts should include an explanation of the accounting policies used to prepare them, the provisions of the charity SORP not only mirror the requirements both of the 1985 Act and of FRS 18 *Accounting policies*, but, more importantly, recognise the basic difficulty of understanding charity accounts.

12.2 FRS 18 Accounting policies

The purpose of FRS 18 is to assist in user understanding and interpretation of accounts by setting out the principles to be followed in selecting accounting policies and the disclosures needed to help users to understand the accounting policies adopted and how they have been applied.

The FRS promotes the adoption and review of accounting policies most appropriate to the particular circumstances of each entity for the purpose of giving a true and fair view and of sufficient disclosure for users to understand the policies adopted and how they have been applied. The FRS distinguishes between accounting policies which are the principles on which the accounts are prepared and estimation techniques which are the particular methods that an entity may choose to use in order to provide a monetary value for an asset, liability, gain or loss in accordance with the adopted principles in the chosen accounting policies.

The following two notions are emphasised as having a pervasive role in financial statements and hence in the selection of accounting policies:

(a) *The 'going concern' assumption*: the enterprise will continue in operational existence for the foreseeable future.
(b) *The 'accruals' concept*: the substance of transactions should be reflected in the accounts in the accounting period in which they occur rather than when any money or other form of consideration is received or paid in respect of the transactions.

The appropriateness of accounting policies and estimation techniques to each entity's particular circumstances should be judged against the objectives below balancing these against each other and against the cost of providing information with the likely benefit to the users of the accounts:

(a) *Relevance*: information is provided in a timely manner and has the ability to influence economic decisions of users of the accounts. It will have predictive or confirmatory value or both.
(b) *Reliability*: the information faithfully represents transactions being materially complete, free from bias and material error and has been prudently estimated when conditions are uncertain.
(c) *Comparability*: information can be compared from one period to another and against other entities. This can usually be achieved through a combination of consistency and disclosure. Industry practices in SORPs developed with public consultation will be particularly persuasive.
(d) *Understandability*: the information is capable of being understood by users with a reasonable knowledge of business and economic activities and accounting and a willingness to study the information with reasonable diligence.

12.3 Disclosure of accounting policies

The notes regarding the basis of preparation of the accounts should state that the accounts have been prepared in accordance with:

(a) this SORP and accounting standards or with this SORP and the FRSSE;
(b) the Charities Act or the Companies Act or other legislative requirement; and
(c) the historic cost basis of accounting except for investments (and if applicable, fixed assets) which have been included at revalued amounts.

If the accounts depart from accounting standards in any material respect, this should be stated in the accounting policies and Annual Report giving the reason and justification for the departure and the financial impact. Similarly the following details should be given for any material departure from this SORP:

(a) a brief description of how the treatment adopted departs from this SORP;
(b) the reasons why the trustees judge that the treatment adopted is more appropriate to the charity's particular circumstances; and
(c) an estimate of the financial effect on the accounts where this is needed for the accounts to give a true and fair view.

A departure is not justified simply because it gives the reader a more appealing picture of the financial position or results of the charity.

If any branches have been omitted from the accounts the reason for omission must be given although the individual branches do not need to be named. Reference should also be made to any potentially linked organisations (such as supporters associations or subsidiaries not consolidated) explaining the accounting treatment adopted.

12.3.1 Examples

Two examples are presented to illustrate how charities explain the basis of the accounting policies that they have adopted. Slight variations between the examples arise because Example A *Arts Theatre Trust Limited* is a company, whilst Example D *Aid Overseas* is unincorporated. Both charities have a subsidiary, and the note explaining the basis of group accounting also shows slight variations.

Example A *Arts Theatre Trust Limited*
Notes forming part of the financial statements for the year ended 31 March 2001

1. Accounting policies

The financial statements have been prepared under the historical cost convention and in accordance with the Statement of Recommended Practice, Accounting and Reporting by Charities (SORP 2000) issued in October 2000, applicable accounting standards and the Companies Act 1985. The principal accounting policies adopted in the preparation of the financial statements are as follows:

Group financial statements
These financial statements consolidate the results of the charity and its wholly-owned subsidiary HTC Limited on a line by line basis. A separate Statement of Financial Activities, or income and expenditure account, for the charity itself is not presented because the charity has taken advantage of the exemptions afforded by section 230 of the Companies Act 1985 and paragraph 304 of SORP 2000.

Example D *Aid Overseas*
Notes forming part of the financial statements for the year ended 30 September 2001

1. Principal accounting policies

(a) **Accounting convention**
    The financial statements are prepared under the historical cost convention as modified by the inclusion of investments at market value and in accordance with applicable accounting standards. In preparing the financial statements the charity follows best practice as set out in the Statement of Recommended Practice 'Accounting and Reporting by Charities' (SORP) issued in October 2000.

(b) **Group financial statements**

These financial statements consolidate the results of the charity and its wholly-owned trading subsidiary, Aid Overseas Trading Limited, on a line by line basis. It also includes the results of all the charity's branches, including those overseas. A separate statement of financial activities (SOFA) is not presented because the charity has taken advantage of the provisions of paragraph 304 of the SORP.

12.4 Specific policies

Trustees should explain in the notes to the accounts the accounting policies they have adopted to deal with material items. Explanations need only be brief but they must be clear, fair and accurate. Significant changes to any of the policies from the preceding year must be disclosed in detail. The following are some examples of matters on which the accounting policies should be explained where the amounts involved are material. Trustees should only include those notes which are relevant to their charity.

12.5 Incoming resources policy notes

The policy for including each type of material incoming resource should be given. This will normally be on a receivable basis but may need further details in some cases, for instance:

(a) a description of when a legacy is regarded as receivable;
(b) the basis of recognition of gifts and intangible income, specifically covering when such items are not included in the SOFA and the methods of valuation;
(c) the basis of recognition of all grants receivable, including those for fixed assets, and how the grants are split between the different types of incoming resources;
(d) whether any incoming resources are deferred and the basis for any deferrals (this will normally only apply to contractual incoming resources received or invoiced in advance);
(e) the basis for including subscriptions for life membership;
(f) whether the incoming resources from endowment funds are unrestricted or restricted;
(g) whether any incoming resources have been included in the SOFA net of expenditure and the reason for this.

12.5.1 Example

A good illustration of a policy note for incoming resources is contained in Example A *Arts Theatre Trust Limited*. The charity has several sources of income, including both charitable and commercial trading activities, and donations, grants and intangible sources of income.

Example A *Arts Theatre Trust Limited*

1. Accounting policies

Incoming resources

Charitable trading activities
Income from theatre admission fees is included in incoming resources in the period in which the relevant show takes place.

Commercial trading activities
Income from commercial activities is included in the period in which the group is entitled to receipt.

Donations and grants
Income from donations and grants, including capital grants, is included in incoming resources when these are receivable, except as follows:

- When donors specify that donations and grants given to the charity must be used in future accounting periods, the income is deferred until those periods.
- When donors impose conditions which have to be fulfilled before the charity becomes entitled to use such income, the income is deferred and not included in incoming resources until the pre-conditions for use have been met.

When donors specify that donations and grants, including capital grants, are for particular restricted purposes, which do not amount to pre-conditions regarding entitlement, this income is included in incoming resources of restricted funds when receivable.

Intangible income
Intangible income, which comprises donated services, is included in income at a valuation which is an estimate of the financial cost borne by the donor where such a cost is quantifiable and measurable. No income is recognised when there is no financial cost borne by a third party.

Interest receivable
Interest is included when receivable by the charity.

12.6 Resources expended and liabilities policy notes

Policy notes should be presented which explain how the material items of resources expended and material liabilities and provisions are treated in the financial statements.

(a) The policy for the recognition of liabilities including constructive obligations should be given. Where the liabilities are included as provisions, the point at which the provision is considered to become binding and the basis of any discount factors used in current value calculations for long term commitments should be given. This is particularly applicable to grants, the policy for which must be separately identified.

(b) The policy for including items within types of resources expended should be given. In particular the policy for including items within:

    (i)   costs of generating funds;

    (ii)   grants payable in furtherance of the charity's objects, activities in furtherance of the charity's objects and support costs;

    (iii) management and administration costs;

and in addition,

(c) The methods and principles for the allocation and apportionment of all costs between the different categories of expenditure in (b). This disclosure should include the underlying principle (i.e., whether based on staff time, staff salaries, space occupied or other). Where the costs apportioned are significant, then further clarification on the method of apportionment used is necessary, including the proportions used to undertake the calculations.

12.6.1 Example

A thorough example of an accounting policy for resources expended is presented in Example D *Aid Overseas*. The note explains the treatment of the material components of resources expended and how different costs are allocated. Separate notes are presented explaining the components of fundraising costs, support costs and management and administration costs.

Example D   *Aid Overseas*
Notes forming part of the financial statements for the year ended 30 September 2001

    (d)   **Resources expended and basis of allocation of costs**
          Expenditure is included when incurred.

          Grants payable to partner organisations for relief and development projects are included in the SOFA when approved by the trustees and agreed with the other organisation. The value of such grants unpaid at the year end is accrued. Grants where the beneficiary has not been informed or has to meet certain conditions before the grant is released are not accrued but are noted as financial commitments.

          Expenditure on operational programmes is recognised in the period in which it has incurred. A designated fund is established for expenditure which has been committed to projects, but remains unspent at the year end.

          The majority of costs are directly attributable to specific activities. Certain shared costs are apportioned to activities in furtherance of the objects of the charity. Office costs and property related costs are apportioned on the proportion of floor area occupied by the activity. Staff costs and office costs are allocated in the same proportion as directly attributed staff costs.

(e) **Fund-raising costs**

These include the salaries, direct expenditure and overhead costs of the staff in offices in the UK who promote fund-raising, including events.

(f) **Support costs**

Support costs represent the cost of core field offices and the costs incurred by UK based staff, directly providing support for the international pro-gramme, including management, policy and advocacy work and super-vision an technical support for emergency programmes.

(g) **Costs of managing and administering the charity**

These represent costs incurred by finance, human resources, internal audit and directorate departments, attributable to the management of the charity's assets, organisational administration and compliance with consti-tutional and statutory requirements.

(h) **Gifts in kind**

Blankets and clothing etc are received and given to overseas projects are included in the financial statements at market value at the time of export. Food aid from the World Food Programme, for which the charity accepts full responsibility for distribution, is included in income at its market value and as resources expended at the same value when distributed. Properties, investments, and other fixed assets donated to the charity are included as donation income at market value at the time of receipt. Items donated for resale are included in shop income when sold and no value is placed on stock at the year end.

12.7 Assets policy notes

12.7.1 Fixed assets

The policy for capitalisation of fixed assets for charity use should be stated including:

(a) whether each class of asset is included at cost, valuation or revaluation and the method of valuation where applicable;
(b) the value below which fixed assets are not capitalised;
(c) whether or not inalienable and historic assets are capitalised and if not, the reason why (e.g., lack of reliable information, cost/benefit reason etc. see para 211), specifying the acquisition and disposal policies for such assets;
(d) the rates of depreciation applying to each class of fixed asset; and
(e) the policy with respect to impairment reviews of fixed assets.

12.7.2 Example

Example F *The Higher College Charity* operates two independent schools and presents a detailed accounting policy explaining the treatment of the school

buildings and equipment. The note includes details of the most recent revaluation of the buildings and details of the charity's capitalisation policy.

Example F   *The Higher College Charity*

(h)   **School buildings and equipment**
      Capitalisation and replacement
      The college land, together with the original college buildings (which are
      all Grade 1 listed properties) was a gift to the Charity in 1903. These assets
      were professionally revalued by Inspectit & Co, Chartered Surveyors, on 31
      August 1995 at £7,500,000, with the college grounds being valued at
      £6,000,000 and the original buildings at £1,500,000. This valuation has
      been adopted as the historical cost under the transitional provisions of the
      Financial Reporting Standard 15. The Charity is responsible for keeping
      the original buildings in fit and useful condition, and these costs are
      written off as incurred.

      Building improvements and extensions subsequent to the original gift costing
      more than £5,000, together with furniture and equipment costing more than
      £1,500, are capitalised and carried in the balance sheet at historical cost.

      Depreciation
      Land is not depreciated. Depreciation of other assets is provided at rates
      calculated to write off the excess of cost over estimated residual amount
      evenly over the estimated useful economic lives of each class of asset,
      subject to annual review.

      These rates are currently as follows:

Original cost of freehold buildings	20–50 years
Buildings improvements and extensions	10–20 years
Furniture and equipment	3–10 years
Motor vehicles	4 years

      As explained in note 9, inalienable and historic assets have not been capi-
      talised or depreciated as no reliable value can be attributed.

12.7.3 Investments

The policy for including investments in the accounts should be given. This
should be at market value but may need to be modified for the valuation of:

(a) investments not listed on a recognised stock exchange;
(b) investment properties; and
(c) investments in subsidiary undertakings.

The basis of inclusion in the SOFA of unrealised and realised gains and
losses on investments should be stated.

12.7.4 Example

Normally the investments policy note is short and straightforward, as illustrated by Example C *The Rosanna Grant Trust.*

> **Example C** *The Rosanna Grant Trust*
>
> (e) **Fixed asset investments**
> Investments are included at closing mid-market value at the balance sheet date. Any gain or loss on revaluation is taken to the Statement of Financial Activities.

12.7.5 Stocks and work in progress

The basis for inclusion of material stocks and work in progress should be given.

12.8 Funds structure policy notes

A brief description should be given of the different types of fund held by the charity, including the policy for any transfers between funds and allocations to or from designated funds. Transfers may arise for example where there is a release of restricted or endowed funds to unrestricted funds or charges are made from the unrestricted to other funds.

The policy for determining each designated fund should be stated.

12.8.1 Examples

Several of the examples present an accounting policy on fund accounting which simply states

> 'The nature and purpose of each fund are explained in note X'.

Examples A and D take an approach whereby the note briefly explains the classes of funds held by the charity, before stating that more information is given in the notes.

> **Fund accounting**
>
> Funds held by the charity are either:
>
> - Unrestricted general funds – these are funds which can be used in accordance with the charitable objects at the discretion of the trustees.
> - Designated funds – these are funds set aside by the trustees out of unrestricted general funds for specific future purposes or projects.
> - Restricted funds – these are funds that can only be used for particular restricted

purposes within the objects of the charity. Restrictions arise when specified by the donor or when funds are raised for particular restricted purposes.

Further explanation of the nature and purpose of each fund is included in the notes to the financial statements.

12.9 Other policy notes

These could include policies for the recognition of the following:

(a) pension contributions;
(b) foreign exchange gains and losses;
(c) treatment of exceptional items;
(d) treatment of finance and operating leases;
(e) treatment of irrecoverable VAT.

The accounting policies in respect of these items would be determined by the SORP and accounting standards. Several of these policies are illustrated in the examples below.

12.10 Complete example

The complete statement of accounting policies for Example G *The ABC Charity* is presented below. The charity is incorporated and has a subsidiary. The charity engages in a variety of activities, and therefore this illustrative example contains a broad range of policies.

Example G   *The ABC Charity*
Notes forming part of the financial statements for the year ended 31 March 2001

1.   **Accounting policies**

(a) **Basis of preparation**
     The financial statements have been prepared under the historical cost convention, with the exception of investments which are included at market value. The financial statements have been prepared in accordance with the Statement of Recommended Practice (SORP), 'Accounting and Reporting by Charities' published in October 2000 and applicable accounting standards.

     The statement of financial activities (SOFA) and balance sheet consolidate the financial statements of the charity and its subsidiary undertaking. The results of the subsidiary are consolidated on a line by line basis.

     The charity has availed itself of Paragraph 3(3) of Schedule 4 of the Companies Act and adapted the Companies Act formats to reflect the special nature of the charity's activities. No separate SOFA has been presented for the charity alone as permitted by Section 230 of the Companies Act 1985 and paragraph 304 of the SORP.

(b) **Company status**

The charity is a company limited by guarantee. The members of the company are trustees named on page 1. In the event of the charity being wound up, the liability in respect of the guarantee is limited to £1 per member of the charity.

(c) **Fund accounting**

General funds are unrestricted funds which are available for use at the discretion of the trustees in furtherance of the general objectives of the charity and which have not been designated for other purposes.

Designated funds comprise unrestricted funds that have been set aside by the trustees for particular purposes. The aim and use of each designated fund is set out in the notes to the financial statements. Restricted funds are funds which are to be used in accordance with specific restrictions imposed by donors or which have been raised by the charity for particular purposes. The cost of raising and administering such funds are charged against the specific fund. The aim and use of each restricted fund is set out in the notes to the financial statements.

Investment income and gains are allocated to the appropriate fund.

(d) **Incoming resources**

All incoming resources are included in the SOFA when the charity is legally entitled to the income and the amount can be quantified with reasonable accuracy. For legacies, entitlement is the earlier of the charity being notified of an impending distribution or the legacy being received.

Gifts in kind donated for distribution are included at valuation and recognised as income when they are distributed to the projects. Gifts donated for resale are included as income when they are sold. Donated facilities are included at the value to the charity where this can be quantified and a third party is bearing the cost. No amounts are included in the financial statements for services donated by volunteers.

(e) **Resources expended**

All expenditure is accounted for on an accruals basis and has been classified under headings that aggregate all costs related to the category. Where costs cannot be directly attributed to particular headings they have been allocated to activities on a basis consistent with use of the resources. Premises overheads have been allocated on a floor area basis and other overheads have been allocated on the basis of the head count.

Fund-raising costs are those incurred in seeking voluntary contributions and do not include the costs of disseminating information in support of the charitable activities. Support costs are those costs incurred directly in support of expenditure on the objects of the charity and include project management carried out at Headquarters. Management and administration costs are those incurred in connection with administration of the charity and compliance with constitutional and statutory requirements.

(f) **Tangible fixed assets and depreciation**
Tangible fixed assets costing more than £1,000 are capitalised and included at cost including any incidental expenses of acquisition.

Depreciation is provided on all tangible fixed assets at rates calculated to write off the cost on a straight line basis over their expected useful economic lives as follows:

Freehold land	nil
Freehold buildings	over 50 years
Project and office equipment	over 5 years
Computer equipment	over 3 years
Motor vehicles	over 4 years
Equipment held under finance leases	over the life of the lease

(g) **Investments**
Investments are stated at market value at the balance sheet date. The SOFA includes the net gains and losses arising on revaluations and disposals throughout the year.

(h) **Stock**
Stock consists of purchased goods for resale. Stocks are valued at the lower of cost and net realisable value. Items donated for resale or distribution are not included in the financial statements until they are sold or distributed.

(i) **Pension costs**
The cost of providing pension and related benefits is charged to the SOFA over the employees' service lives on the basis of a constant percentage of earnings which is an estimate of the regular cost. Variations from regular cost, arising from periodic actuarial valuations are allocated over the expected remaining service lives of current and estimated future earnings. Any difference between the charge to the statement of financial activities and the contributions payable to the scheme is shown as an asset or a liability in the balance sheet.

(j) **Finance and operating leases**
Rentals applicable to operating leases are charged to the SOFA over the period in which the cost is incurred. Assets purchased under finance lease are capitalised as fixed assets. Obligations under such agreements are included in creditors. The difference between the capitalised cost and the total obligation under the lease represents the finance charges. Finance charges are written-off to the SOFA over the period of the lease so as to produce a constant periodic rate of charge.

(k) **Foreign currencies**
Transactions in foreign currencies are recorded at the rate ruling at the date of the transaction. Monetary assets and liabilities are retranslated at the rate

of exchange ruling at the balance sheet date. All differences are taken to the SOFA.

12.11 Small charity example

As a contrast, the accounting policies for Example B *Dorsetshire Drugs Advice Centre* are reproduced. The smaller and simpler nature of the charity's activities result in much shorter accounting policies. The basis of allocating costs in item (f) is a particular feature to note.

Example B *Dorsetshire Drugs Advice Centre*
Notes forming part of the financial statements for the year ended 31 March 2002

1. **Accounting policies**
(a) The financial statements have been prepared under the historical cost convention, as modified by the inclusion of fixed asset investments at market value, and in accordance with the Financial Reporting Standard for Smaller Entities (effective March 2000), the Companies Act 1985 and follow the recommendations in *Accounting and Reporting by Charities: Statement of Recommended Practice* issued in October 2000.
(b) Voluntary income is received by way of donations and gifts and is included in full in the Statement of Financial Activities when receivable. The value of services provided by volunteers has not been included.
(c) Grants, including grants for the purchase of fixed assets, are recognised in full in the Statement of Financial Activities in the year in which they are receivable.
(d) Incoming resources from the charity shop and from investments is included when receivable.
(e) Resources expended are recognised in the period in which they are incurred. Resources expended include attributable VAT which cannot be recovered.
(f) Resources expended are allocated to the particular activity where the cost relates directly to that activity. However, the cost of overall direction and administration on each activity, comprising the salary and overhead costs of the central function, is apportioned on the following basis which are an estimate, based on staff time, of the amount attributable to each activity:

Charity shop	0%
Fund-raising and publicity	15%
Advice and information	20%
Outreach work	20%
Training project	30%
Management and administration of the charity	15%

(g) Depreciation is provided at rates calculated to write off the cost of each asset over its expected useful life, which in all cases is estimated at 4 years. Items of equipment are capitalised where the purchase price exceed £500.

(h) Investments held as fixed assets are revalued at mid-market value at the balance sheet date and the gain or loss taken to the Statement of Financial Activities.

(i) Unrestricted funds are donations and other incoming resources receivable or generated for the objects of the charity without further specified purpose and are available as general funds.

(j) Designated funds are unrestricted funds earmarked by the management committee for particular purposes.

(k) Restricted funds are to be used for specific purposes as laid down by the donor. Expenditure which meets these criteria is charged to the fund, together with a fair allocation of management and support costs.

Chapter 13 – Other matters to be covered in the notes to the accounts

13.1 Introduction

This chapter considers the following:

- related party transactions;
- trustee remuneration;
- trustee expenses;
- indemnity insurance;
- staff costs and emoluments;
- cost of audit, independent examination or reporting accountant services and other financial services;
- ex-gratia payments; and
- note of changes in resources applied for fixed assets for charity use.

13.2 Related party transactions

This section of the SORP, primarily dealing with transactions with trustees and connected persons, has been rewritten to reflect FRS 8 *Related party disclosures* which was issued after the publication of the 1995 SORP. Although the definitions and disclosures can be complex, disclosable transactions will arise 'where the charity has a relationship with another party or parties (the related party) which might inhibit it from pursuing its own separate interests'.

Disclosure in a note to the accounts is required where the reporting charity enters iinto a related party transaction. Related parties include:

(a) a charity trustee or someone else who is related to the charity; and
(b) someone who is either connected with a charity trustee or to a person who is related to the charity.

A fuller description of related parties is given in appendix 1 to the SORP.

A charity can be a related party of another charity, for example, if one is the trustee of the other, or if one has the power to appoint or remove a significant proportion of the charity trustees of the other, or if the two charities are subject to common control (for instance a majority of trustees in common).

However, they are not necessarily related simply because a particular person happens to be a trustee of both (though if one charity subordinates its interests to the other charity in any transaction because of this relationship then the charities will be related).

Any decision by a charity to enter into a transaction ought to be influenced only by the consideration of the charity's own interests. This requirement is reinforced by legal rules which, in certain circumstances, can invalidate transactions where the charity trustees have a conflict of interest. This does not necessarily mean that all transactions with related persons are influenced by the consideration of interests other than the charity's nor that they are liable to invalidation.

However, transparency is particularly important where the relationship between the charity and the other party or parties to a transaction suggests that the transaction could possibly have been influenced by interests other than the charity's. It is possible that the reported financial position and results may have been affected by such transactions and information about these transactions is therefore necessary for the users of the charity's accounts.

Related party transactions potentially include:

(a) purchases, sales, leases and donations (including donations which are made in furtherance of the charity's objects) of goods, property, money and other assets such as intellectual property rights to or from the related party;
(b) the supply of services by the related party to the charity, and the supply of services by the charity to the related party. Supplying services includes providing the use of goods, property and other assets and finance arrangements such as making loans and giving guarantees and indemnities;
(c) any other payments and other benefits which are made to trustees under express provisions of the governing document of a charity or in fulfilment of its charitable objectives.

Only material transactions need to be disclosed in the notes to the accounts. Transactions should be disclosed whether or not they are at arms length.

The following disclosures must be given in respect of each related party transaction:

(a) the name(s) of the transacting related party or parties;
(b) a description of the relationship between the parties (including the interest of the related party or parties in the transaction);
(c) a description of the transaction;

211

(d)   the amounts involved;

(e)   outstanding balances with related parties at the balance sheet date and any provisions for doubtful debts from such persons;

(f)   any amounts written off from such balances during the accounting year; and

(g)   any other elements of the transactions which are necessary for the understanding of the financial statements.

The disclosure can be given in aggregate for similar transactions and type of related party, unless disclosure of an individual transaction or connected transactions is necessary for an understanding of the impact of the transactions on the accounts of the charity or is a legal requirement.

Some related party transactions are such that they are unlikely to influence the pursuance of the separate independent interests of the charity. These need not be disclosed unless there is evidence to the contrary. Examples are:

(a)   donations received by the reporting charity from a related party, so long as the donor has not attached conditions which would, or might, require the charity to alter materially the nature of its existing activities if it were to accept the donation (but any material grant by the reporting charity to a charity which is a related party should be disclosed);

(b)   minor or routine unremunerated services provided to a charity by people related to it;

(c)   contracts of employment between a charity and its employees (except where the employees are the charity trustees or people connected with them);

(d)   contributions by a charity to a pension fund for the benefit of employees;

(e)   the purchase from a charity by a related party of minor articles which are offered for sale to the general public on the same terms as are offered to the general public;

(f)   the provision of services to a related party (including a charity trustee or person connected with a charity trustee), where the related party receives the services as part of a wider beneficiary class of which he is a member, and on the same terms as other members of the class (for example, the use of a village hall by members of its committee of management, as inhabitants of the area of benefit); and

(g)   the payment or reimbursement of out-of-pocket expenses to a related party (including a charity trustee or person connected with a charity trustee – however, see below for disclosures of these).

13.2.1 Examples

Example A *Arts Theatre Trust Limited* contains a detailed note explaining the charity's relationship and transactions with several external organisations including local authorities and another charity.

20. Related parties

The charity has a very close relationship with N Arts, which is a charity, BF Borough Council and B Town Council, all of which nominate the majority of the trustees and provide funding to enable the charity to carry out its charitable objectives. The following is a summary of transactions with those entities:

	2001 £'000	2000 £'000
Revenue funding		
BF Borough Council	405	501
B Town Council	104	100
N Arts Trust	154	150
	663	751

All the above funding was received under contracts with the charity to provide services, eg training in drama production, and has been included in the financial statements under the heading *Incoming Resources: from Operation of theatre and arts centre.*

The charity also received a donation in kind, from BF Borough Council, for the rent of premises, the value of which could not be quantified and therefore has not been included in these financial statements.

There were no outstanding balances with related parties at 31 March 2001 (2000 – £NIL).

13.3 Trustee remuneration

Unlike in the case of the directors of commercial companies, it is not the normal practice for charity trustees, or people connected with them, to receive remuneration, or other benefits, from the charities for which they are responsible, or from institutions connected with those charities. Detailed disclosures are, therefore, required, where the related party is a charity trustee, or a person connected with a charity trustee. The following points should be borne in mind when reporting on related party transactions, where the related party is a charity trustee or a person connected with a charity:

(a) The transaction should always be regarded as material, and should, therefore, be disclosed regardless of its size, unless one of the exceptions in para 165 of the SORP applies.

(b) Each type of related party transaction must be separately disclosed. This means, for example, that particulars of remuneration paid to each charity trustee or person connected with a charity trustee, should be given individually in the notes. Where the charity has made any pension arrangements for charity trustees or persons connected with them, the amount of contributions paid and the benefits accruing must be disclosed in the notes for each related party.

(c) Where remuneration has been paid to a charity trustee or a person connected with a charity trustee, the legal authority under which the payment was made (e.g., provision in the governing document of the charity, order of the Court or Charity Commission) should also be given, as should the reason for such remuneration.

(d) Where neither the trustees nor any persons connected with them have received any such remuneration, this fact should be stated.

13.4 Trustee expenses

Where a charity has met individual expenses incurred by trustees for services provided to the charity, either by reimbursement of the trustee or by providing the trustee with an allowance or, as introduced by SORP 2000, by direct payment to a third party, the aggregate amount of those expenses should be disclosed in a note to the accounts. The note should also indicate the nature of the expenses (e.g., travel, subsistence, entertainment etc.) and the number of trustees involved.

Sometimes trustees act as agents for the charity and make purchases on its behalf and are reimbursed for this expenditure, e.g., payment for stationery or office equipment. Such expenditure is not related to the services provided by a trustee and there is no need to disclose it. Likewise there is no need to disclose routine expenditure which is attributable collectively to the services provided by the trustees, such as the hire of a room for meetings or providing reasonable refreshment at the meeting.

Where the trustees have received no such expenses, this fact should be stated.

13.5 Examples

Example G *The ABC Charity* contains a note disclosing details of expenses paid to trustees and details of transactions between the charity and trustees.

Example G *The ABC Charity*

7. Trustees' remuneration
The trustees neither received nor waived any emoluments during the year (2000: £Nil).

Out of pocket expenses were reimbursed to trustees as follows.

	2001 Number	2000 Number	2001 £'000	2000 £'000
Travel	2	3	640	530
Visit to Sudan Project	1	–	1,200	–
Other	1	1	40	65
	4	4	1,880	595

During the year payments of £2,500 were made to the Harvey Print Company for the printing of the Annual Report. Mrs W Williams, a trustee of this charity, is a director of that company. Mr H. Singh a trustee is also a trustee of the Packwood Foundation that provided free accommodation to the charity during the year valued at £24,000.

Example D *Aid Overseas* also contains a note disclosing expense payments to trustees. As there are no other transactions with trustees, the resulting note is straightforward.

Example D   *Aid Overseas*

13. Trustees' remuneration
Trustees are not remunerated. £2,142 was reimbursed for directly incurred travel expenses to 8 trustees (2000 – £1,896 to 7 trustees).

13.6 Indemnity insurance

If funds belonging to the charity have been used for the purchase of insurance:

(a) to protect the charity from loss arising from the neglect or defaults of its trustees, employees or agents; or

(b) to indemnify the trustees or other officers against the consequences of any neglect or default on their part;

these facts and the cost involved in providing such insurance should be disclosed in detail in the notes to the accounts.

Section **2.9** explains the limitations to taking out such insurance.

13.7 Staff costs and emoluments

The main changes in SORP 2000 are that the analysis of staff costs must now include costs in respect of seconded and agency staff and those employed by connected charities, and changes have been made to the disclosures relating to higher paid employees.

13.7.1 Staff costs

It is important that the accounts disclose the costs of employing staff who work for the charity whether or not the charity itself has incurred those costs. This includes seconded and agency staff and staff employed by connected or independent companies. For instance, staff working for a charity may have contracts with and be paid by a connected company. Payments may also be made to independent third parties for the provision of staff. Where such arrangements are in place and the costs involved are material (in relation to the charity's own expenditure) there should be disclosure by way of note which outlines the arrangements in place, the reasons for them and the amounts involved.

The total staff costs should be shown in the notes to the accounts giving the split between gross wages and salaries, employer's national insurance costs and pension contributions for the year. An estimate of the average number of full time equivalent employees for the year should be disclosed in the notes to the accounts providing sub-categories according to the manner in which the charity's activities are organised.

13.7.2 Higher paid staff

The notes should also show the number of employees whose emoluments for the year (including taxable benefits in kind but not employer pension contributions) fell within each band of £10,000 from £50,000 upwards. Bands in which no employee's emoluments fell should not be listed.

In addition pension details must be disclosed in total for higher paid staff as follows:

(a) contributions in the year for the provision of money purchase benefits (normally money purchase schemes); and
(b) the number of staff to whom retirement benefits are accruing under money purchase and defined benefit schemes respectively.

If there are no employees with emoluments above £50,000 this fact should be stated.

13.7.3 Examples

Example D *Aid Overseas* presents a combined employees and staff costs note which discloses details of a higher paid employee and acknowledges the support of the charity's volunteers.

216

Example D   *Aid Overseas*

12. Employees and staff costs

	2001 No	2000 No
The average number of UK contracted employees throughout the year, calculated on a full time equivalent basis, was:		
Trading operation	98	96
Market operations	47	45
Corporate functions	18	17
Programmes in the UK	38	38
Programmes overseas	11	13
	212	209
Staff based overseas on local contracts	192	194
	404	403

	2001 £'000	2000 £'000
The costs of employing those staff was:		
Salaries and wages	3,395	3,286
National insurance	325	315
Pension scheme	160	154
	3,880	3,755

In addition, a great amount of time, the value of which it is impossible to reflect in these financial statements, is donated by thousands of volunteers throughout the UK.

The emoluments of one member of staff, including benefits in kind, are within the range of £50,000 to £59,999 (2000 – one in range £60,000 to £69,999), not including retirement benefits which are accruing under a defined benefit scheme.

Example A *Arts Theatre Trust Limited* presents a combined staff costs and trustees' remuneration note. The disclosures include details of an ex-gratia payment.

Example A   *Arts Theatre Trust Limited*

7. Staff costs and trustees' remuneration

Wages and salaries	**620**	603
Social security costs	**41**	39
Pension costs	**19**	11
Ex-gratia payments	**16**	
	696	653

The ex-gratia payment was made to a former chief executive for whom no pension provision had been made. The Charity Commission approved payment on 15 December 2000.

No employee earned more than £50,000 per annum (2000 – nil).

The trustees were not paid or reimbursed for expenses during the year.

8. Staff numbers
The average number of full-time equivalent employees (including casual and part-time staff) during the year was made up as follows:

	2001	2000
	No	**No**
Arts department	**11**	11
Administration, marketing and commercial	**14**	13
Technical	**11**	10
Bars and coffee shop	**21**	17
Front of house, box office, cleaning	**20**	21
Course tutors, models	**31**	30
	108	102

13.8 Cost of audit, independent examination or reporting accountant services and other financial services

The notes to the accounts should disclose separately the amounts payable to the auditor, independent examiner or reporting accountant in respect of:

(a) the costs of their respective external scrutiny; and
(b) other financial services such as taxation advice, consultancy, financial advice and accountancy.

In addition, where a charity has incurred other non-statutory costs of external scrutiny, such as a branch audit, the total of these costs should be identified and disclosed separately.

13.9 Ex-gratia payments

The total amount or value of any:

(a) payment;
(b) non-monetary benefit;
(c) other expenditure of any kind; or
(d) waiver of rights to property to which a charity is entitled,

which is made not as an application of funds or property for charitable purposes but in fulfilment of a compelling moral obligation should be disclosed in the notes to the accounts. Where trustees require and obtain the authority of the Court, the Attorney General or the Charity Commission, the nature and date of the authority for each such payment should also be disclosed.

Payments which the trustees reasonably consider to be in the interests of the charity (more than a moral obligation) should not be treated as ex-gratia, even though there is no legal obligation to make them. For example, the trustees may think that it will motivate retained staff and hence benefit the charity if they make redundancy payments over and above the minimum legally required.

13.10 Note of changes in resources applied for fixed assets for charity use

Where resources expended during the year on the acquisition of functional fixed assets is material, this fact should be explained in a note to the accounts to help the reader understand the impact on the more liquid funds of the charity. It may be useful for this note to follow on immediately after the reconciliation of funds at the bottom of the SOFA.

The format should, where necessary, show:

(a) net movement in funds for the year (from the SOFA);
(b) resources used for net acquisitions (or obtained from net disposals) of fixed assets for charity use (i.e. the increase or decrease in the net book value of functional fixed assets);
(c) net movement in funds available for future activities (i.e., those not held in functional fixed assets).

13.10.1 Example

Example G *The ABC Charity* presents this note. For space reasons the note is not presented below the SOFA. However, a statement at the foot of the SOFA refers to where the information can be found, and the note is contained within the primary statements, because it is placed below the cash flow statement.

Example G The ABC Charity
Statement of changes in resources applied for fixed assets for charity use for the year ended 31 March 2001

	Unrestricted Funds £'000	Restricted Funds £'000	Totals 2001 £'000	Totals 2000 £'000
Net movement in funds for the year	3,065	(810)	**2,255**	400
Resources used for net acquisitions of tangible fixed assets	(1,100)	(400)	**(1,500)**	(590)
Net movement in funds available for future activities	1,965	(1,210)	**755**	(190)

Chapter 14 – Application of accounting standards

In preparing accounts which show a true and fair view charities must apply the accounting standards issued by the Accounting Standards Board and the abstracts issued by the Urgent Issues Task Force. The SORP includes most of the principles from these standards which are relevant to charities, although in respect of specific matters the original accounting standard should be consulted.

This chapter contains a commentary, which has been adapted from Appendix 2 of SORP 2000, of the accounting standards and their applicability to charities.

14.1 Statements of Standard Accounting Practice (SSAPs)

14.1.1 SSAP 4 Accounting Treatment of Government Grants

SSAP 4 deals with the accounting treatment and disclosure of government grants and other forms of government assistance, including grants, equity finance, subsidised loans and advisory assistance. It is also indicative of best practice for accounting for grants and assistance from other sources.

The SORP provides the most appropriate interpretation of SSAP 4 for charities. In particular grants for fixed assets should not be deferred though normally they will have to be accounted for in a separate fund (see paras 79 and 84).

14.1.2 SSAP 5 Accounting for Value Added Tax (VAT)

SSAP 5 follows the general principle that the treatment of VAT in the accounts should reflect an entity's role as a collector of the tax and VAT should not be included in income or in expenditure whether of a capital or revenue nature. However where the VAT is irrecoverable, it should be included in the cost of the items reported in the financial statements.

Many if not all charities will suffer irrecoverable VAT either because they are not registered or have a mixture of activities which are zero and standard rated, exempt and outside the scope of VAT. The irrecoverable tax should be included in the relevant cost headings on the face of the Statement of Financial Activities and not shown as a separate item though separate disclosure of the amount may be made in the notes to the accounts.

14.1.3 SSAP 9 Stocks and Long-term Contracts

SSAP 9 gives guidance on the values to be included in the balance sheet of stocks and long-term contracts and the criteria for recognition of income and expenditure on such items within the profit and loss account (Statement of Financial Activities for charities).

Equally applicable to charities as to other entities.

14.1.4 SSAP 13 Accounting for Research and Development

SSAP 13 provides guidance on three broad categories of activity, namely pure research, applied research and development. The standard defines these categories and specifies the accounting policies that may be followed for each.

Equally applicable to charities as to other entities.

14.1.5 SSAP 17 Accounting for Post Balance Sheet Events

SSAP 17 defines the period for post balance sheet events and describes the accounting treatment for adjusting and non-adjusting events. Adjusting events are those which provide additional evidence of conditions existing at the balance sheet date. Non-adjusting events are those which concern conditions that did not exist at the balance sheet date.

Equally applicable to charities as to other entities.

14.1.6 SSAP 19 Accounting for Investment Properties

SSAP 19 requires investment properties to be included in the balance sheet at their open market value, but without charging depreciation.

Equally applicable to charities as to other entities.

14.1.7 SSAP 20 Foreign Currency Translation

SSAP 20 generally requires, in individual financial statements, that each transaction should be translated into the entity's local currency using the exchange rate in operation at the date of the transaction. In consolidated accounts the standard allows two alternative methods of translation of a foreign entity's financial statements, depending on whether the enterprise is a separate quasi-independent entity, or a direct extension of the trade of the investing entity.

Generally applicable to charities entering directly into transactions overseas or with branches or subsidiaries overseas. Gains should be recorded as other income in the Statement of Financial Activities and losses as support costs or management and administration costs. Where the standard permits gains and losses to be taken to reserves these should be shown as a separate line in the Statement of Financial Activities after 'net incoming/outgoing resources before revaluations and investment asset disposals'.

14.1.8 SSAP 21 Accounting for Leases and Hire Purchase Contracts

SSAP 21 describes how to identify and account for finance leases, operating leases and hire purchase contracts both for the lessee and the lessor.

Equally applicable to charities as to other entities.

14.1.9 SSAP 24 Accounting for Pension Costs (being replaced by FRS 17)

SSAP 24 deals with the accounting for, and the disclosure of, pension costs and commitments in the financial statements of entities that have pension arrangements for their employees. It requires employers to recognise the expected cost of providing pensions on a systematic and rational basis over the period during which they derive benefit from the employees' services.

FRS 20 *Retirement Benefits* will replace SSAP 24. It covers pensions and other retirement benefits such as medical care. The most significant requirements are that defined benefit pension scheme assets would be measured at market value at the balance sheet date rather than at an actuarial value; scheme liabilities would be discounted at the current rate of return on a long-term AA corporate bond rate; actuarial gains and losses (variations from regular cost) would be recognised immediately in the statement of total recognised gains losses rather than spread forward in the profit and loss account, resulting in the surplus (subject to a recoverability test) or deficit in the scheme being shown on the balance sheet.

For periods ending from June 2001, the employers who provide defined benefit pension schemes must provide the disclosures require by FRS 17. The full accounting requirements apply for periods ending from June 2003.

FRS 17 does not change the accounting or disclosure requirements for defined contribution pension schemes.

Equally applicable to charities as to other entities with any references to the statement of total recognised gains and losses being the bottom part of the Statement of Financial

223

Activities for charities. However the standard does not cover the provision of voluntary retirement benefits which are provided by some charities. It may be more appropriate to use designated funds to reflect such discretionary funding arrangements.

14.1.10 SSAP 25 Segmental Reporting

SSAP 25 requires the disclosure by class of business and by geographical segment of turnover, segment result and segment net assets. The turnover disclosure is required by all companies otherwise the disclosure is mandatory only for PLCs, banking and insurance companies and those over ten times the threshold for medium sized companies.

This will only be applicable to the largest charities. The disclosure requirements in the SORP for details of activities by function meets the spirit of SSAP 25 for turnover by class of activity. The disclosure by geographical region and segment net assets would be additional.

14.2 Financial Reporting Standards (FRSs)

14.2.1 FRS 1 Cash Flow Statements (Revised 1996)

FRS 1 (Revised 1996) requires reporting entities within its scope (two of £2.8m gross turnover; £1.4m gross assets; 50 employees) to prepare a cash flow statement in the manner set out in the FRS. (Non-company charities in Scotland are bound by the limits in the Scottish Regulations 1992 being £2m gross income and £975,000 gross assets.)

Paragraphs 272 to 277 explain the applicability of FRS 1 to charities.

14.2.2 FRS 2 Accounting for Subsidiary Undertakings

FRS 2 sets out the conditions under which an entity qualifies as a parent undertaking which should prepare consolidated financial statements for its group, the parent and its subsidiaries. It also sets out the manner in which consolidated financial statements are to be prepared.

Paragraphs 299 to 319 explain consolidation and the applicability of FRS 2 to charities.

14.2.3 FRS 3 Reporting Financial Performance

FRS 3 requires a layered format for the profit and loss (income and expenditure) account split between continuing, newly acquired and discontinued operations. It has effectively outlawed extraordinary items. The standard also requires a statement of total recognised gains and losses to be shown as a primary statement. A note of historical profits, which is a memorandum item, is also required as is the disclosure of earnings per share.

The Statement of Financial Activities combines both the income and expenditure account and the statement of total recognised gains and losses and meets charity law. Exceptional items should be disclosed on a separate line within the activity to which they relate. The additional requirements for charitable companies are explained in paras 331 to 343. Earnings per share is not relevant to charities.

14.2.4 FRS 4 Capital Instruments

FRS 4 requires capital instruments to be presented in financial statements in a way that reflects the obligations of the issuer and the impact on shareholders equity.

Not generally applicable to charities following the SORP.

14.2.5 FRS 5 Reporting the Substance of Transactions

FRS 5 requires that the substance of an entity's transactions is reported in its financial statements. This requires that the commercial effect of a transaction and any resulting assets, liabilities, gains and losses are shown and that the accounts do not merely report the legal form of a transaction.

Equally applicable to charities as to other entities.

14.2.6 FRS 6 Accounting for Acquisitions and Mergers

FRS 6 sets out the circumstances in which the two methods of accounting for a business combination (acquisition accounting and merger accounting) are to be used. The FRS sets out five criteria that must be met for merger accounting to be used. If they are not met then acquisition accounting should be used.

The principles of merger accounting are applicable to charities where two or more charities merge. However where funds are merely transferred from one charity to another this may constitute a gift or in the case of a restricted fund simply the administrative transfer of the restricted fund from one set of trustees to another. Two of the five criteria apply to shareholders funds and so will not be applicable to charities. Charities cannot merge with non-charitable companies and so acquisition accounting will have to be used where such companies are acquired.

14.2.7 FRS 7 Fair Values in Acquisition Accounting

FRS 7 sets out the principles of accounting for a business combination under the acquisition method of accounting. It explains what 'identifiable assets and liabilities' means and how to determine their fair values. The difference between the sum of these fair values and the cost of acquisition is recognised as goodwill or negative goodwill.

Equally applicable to charities as to other entities where acquisition accounting is used.

14.2.8 FRS 8 Related Party Disclosures

FRS 8 determines who and what are 'related parties' and the disclosures necessary to draw attention to the possibility that the reported financial position and results may have been affected by the existence of related parties and by material transactions with them.

Paragraphs 157 to 169 explain the application of FRS 8 with respect to charities.

14.2.9 FRS 9 Associates and Joint Ventures

FRS 9 sets out the definitions and accounting treatments for associates and joint ventures, two types of interests that a reporting entity may have in other entities. The FRS also deals with joint arrangements that are not entities.

Paragraphs 320 to 330 explain the applicability of FRS 9 to charities.

14.2.10 FRS 10 Goodwill and Intangible Fixed Assets

FRS 10 requires purchased goodwill and intangible fixed assets (where marketable) to be capitalised on the balance sheet and amortised over their life, normally regarded as 20 years, subject to impairment reviews.

FRS 10 covers common occurrences of goodwill and intangible assets. Where a charity has an intangible asset which does not meet the criteria under the standard it should not be included in the primary statements but details of the asset and its financial effect must be disclosed in the notes to the accounts.

14.2.11 FRS 11 Impairment of Tangible Fixed Assets

FRS 11 sets out the principles and methodology for accounting for impairments of fixed assets and goodwill. The carrying amount of an asset is compared with its recoverable amount and, if the carrying amount is higher, the asset is written down. Recoverable amount is defined as the higher of the amount that could be obtained by selling the asset (net realisable value) and the amount that could be obtained through using the asset (value in use). Impairment tests are only required when there has been some indication that an impairment has occurred.

Paragraphs 224 to 230 explain the applicability of FRS 11 to charities.

14.2.12 FRS 12 Provisions, Contingent Liabilities and Contingent Assets

FRS 12 describes the circumstances in which a provision (a liability that is of uncertain timing or amount) may arise and how it should be measured and recognised in the financial statements. It also describes how to account for contingent assets and liabilities.

FRS 12 is generally applicable to charities. Paragraphs 119 to 130 and 250 to 269 describe some particular application points to charities.

14.2.13 FRS 13 Derivatives and Other Financial Instruments

FRS 13 specifies the disclosure for financial instruments for entities which issue such instruments (such as swaps, forwards, caps and collars, and other derivatives) by focusing on the way in which they are used by the reporting entity.

It does not specifically apply to charities, but any charities which fall within the standard should nevertheless report on their use of such instruments. Charities in England and Wales without a power to use such instruments will need to seek authorisation from the Charity Commission to do so.

14.2.14 FRS 14 Earnings Per Share

Not applicable to charities.

14.2.15 FRS 15 Tangible Fixed Assets

FRS 15 sets out the principles of accounting for tangible fixed assets, with the exception of investment properties. In principle all fixed assets must be capitalised at cost or at revalued amount. However, where an enterprise chooses to adopt a policy of revaluing some assets, all assets of the same class must be revalued and the valuations kept up to date.

The principles of FRS 15 are generally applicable to charities and are embodied in the balance sheet section of the SORP. However, there are relaxed criteria for the valuations of charity assets and certain inalienable and historic assets need not be capitalised in certain circumstances as explained in paras 208 to 217.

14.2.16 FRS 16 Current Tax

FRS 16 is generally not applicable to charities. However, the Government is paying compensation payments to charities for five years from April 1999 for the removal of ACT credits on the payment of UK dividends. These payments should be included as part of the charities investment income.

14.2.17 FRS 17 Retirement benefits

See SSAP 24 above.

14.2.18 FRS 18 Accounting policies

Applicable to charities – see chapter 12.

14.2.19 FRS 19 Deferred tax

Introduces a requirement that deferred tax timing differences should be provided for in full.

Not generally applicable to charities.

14.2.20 FRSSE Financial Reporting Standard for Smaller Entities

The FRSSE brings together the relevant accounting requirements and disclosures from the other accounting standards and UITF abstracts, simplified and modified as appropriate for smaller entities. The FRSSE is an optional standard but entities adopting it are exempt from applying all the other accounting standards and UITF abstracts. Financial reporting is continually evolving and therefore the FRSSE needs to be updated, roughly on an annual basis, to reflect new or revised accounting standards and UITF abstracts.

Paragraphs 345 to 347 explain the applicability of the FRSSE to smaller charities. Whilst it can be followed there are certain principles and notes within the SORP which apply to all charities and must be included in the financial statements.

14.3 Urgent Issues Task Force (UITF) Abstracts

14.3.1 UITF Abstract 4 Presentation of Long-term Debtors in Current Assets

Such items should be separately disclosed on the face of the balance sheet or in the notes to the accounts.

Equally applicable to charities as to other entities.

14.3.2 UITF Abstract 5 Transfers from Current Assets to Fixed Assets

Applicable in principle to charities but unlikely to arise in practice.

14.3.3 UITF Abstract 9 Accounting for Operations in Hyper-inflationary Economies

Only applicable to charities which operate in countries where such conditions exist.

14.3.4 UITF Abstract 10 Disclosure of Directors' Share Options

14.3.5 UITF Abstract 11 Capital Instruments: Issuer Call Options

Not generally applicable to charities.

14.3.6 UITF Abstract 12 Lessee Accounting for Reverse Premiums and Similar Incentives

Equally applicable to charities as to other entities.

14.3.7 UITF Abstract 13 Accounting for ESOP Trusts

Not generally applicable to charities.

14.3.8 UITF Abstract 15 Disclosure of Substantial Acquisitions

14.3.9 UITF Abstract 16 Income and Expenses Subject to Non-standard Rates of Tax

14.3.10 UITF Abstract 17 Employee Share Schemes

Not applicable to charities.

14.3.11 UITF Abstract 19 Tax on Gains and Losses on Foreign Currency Borrowings that Hedge an Investment in a Foreign Enterprise

Not generally applicable to charities.

14.3.12 UITF Abstract 21 Accounting Issues Arising from the Proposed Introduction of the Euro

Generally applicable to charities though it will have limited impact unless the UK adopts the euro.

14.3.13 UITF Abstract 22 The Acquisition of a Lloyd's Business

Not applicable to charities.

14.3.14 UITF Abstract 23 Application of the transitional rules in FRS 15

Provides transitional rules on the use of prior period adjustments where tangible fixed assets which were previously treated as a single asset are identified as having two or more major components with substantially different useful economic lives.

Equally applicable to charities as to other entities.

Chapter 15 – Consolidated accounts

15.1 Introduction

Unlike the 1985 Act, the 1993 Act and the Regulations made thereunder do not contain provisions relating to consolidation. This is a matter left entirely to the SORP; para 300 requires, subject to three exceptions (see **15.4.2** below) that consolidated accounts are prepared for a charity and the subsidiary (usually non-charitable) undertakings it controls. The purpose is to show a true and fair view of the state of affairs and activities of the charity and its subsidiary undertakings as a whole.

It is, however, the entity accounts of the accountable charity which are paramount – the consolidated accounts only supplementing those entity accounts. Apart from groups of charitable companies, where the 1985 Act determines accountability, the key to an understanding of charity control is in the definition of the entity accounts of an 'accountable' charity. A charity is accountable for any special trusts, as well as for any subsidiary charities, as determined by law. Section 97(1) of the 1993 Act defines a special trust of a charity, while s96(5) and (6) empowers the Commissioners to determine whether a charity shall be accounted for by another charity as its subsidiary.

15.2 Changes in SORP 2000

SORP 2000 requires consolidation to be performed on a line-by-line basis, bringing the SORP completely into line with FRS 2.

The SORP introduces disclosure requirements and accounting principles for associates, joint ventures and joint arrangements, which are consistent with FRS 9.

15.3 How are parent and subsidiary undertakings defined?

15.3.1 The 1985 Act and FRS 2

In summary, an undertaking is a parent undertaking to a subsidiary undertaking if:

231

(a) it holds a majority of the voting rights in the subsidiary undertaking;

(b) it is a member of the subsidiary undertaking and has the right to appoint or remove a majority of its board of directors;

(c) it has the right to exercise a dominant influence over the subsidiary undertaking by virtue of:

    (i) provisions contained in the subsidiary undertaking's Memorandum or Articles; or

    (ii) a control contract.

    (Note: It is not necessary for the parent undertaking to be a member of the subsidiary undertaking in this case);

(d) it is a member of the subsidiary undertaking and controls, alone, pursuant to an agreement with other shareholders or members, a majority of the voting rights in the undertaking; or

(e) it has a participating interest in the undertaking and:

    (i) it actually exercises a dominant influence over it; or

    (ii) it and the subsidiary undertaking are managed on a unified basis.

    (Note: A 'participating interest' is an interest held by an undertaking in the shares of another undertaking which it holds on a long-term basis for the purpose of securing a contribution to its activities by the exercise of control or influence arising from, or related to, that interest. A holding of 20 per cent or more of the shares of an undertaking is presumed to be a participating interest, although this presumption may be rebutted.)

As with the previous law, subsidiaries include sub-subsidiaries.

15.3.2 SORP 2000

'Parent undertaking' and 'subsidiary undertaking' are defined in para 22 of Appendix 1:

> 'In relation to a charity an undertaking is the parent undertaking of another undertaking, a subsidiary undertaking, where the charity or its trustees hold or control the majority of the voting rights, or have the right to appoint or remove a majority of the board of directors or trustees of the subsidiary undertaking, or have the right to exercise a dominant influence over the subsidiary undertaking. For a fuller definition, reference should be made to sections 258 and 259 Companies Act 1985.'

The SORP's definition is therefore based on that in the 1985 Act, to which reference should be made, if necessary.

Paragraphs 306 to 308 set out some guidance on applying the definition of 'subsidiary undertaking'. A non-company charity can only be regarded as a subsidiary undertaking where the parent charity can be shown to be exercising dominant influence over the subsidiary. This can arise in any of the following situations:

(a) the charity trustees and/or members and or employees of the parent charity are, or have the right to appoint or remove, a majority of the charity trustees of the subsidiary charity;

(b) the governing document of the subsidiary charity reserves to the parent charity's trustees and/or members the right to direct, or to give consent to, the exercise of significant discretions by the trustees of the subsidiary charity;

(c) the objects of the subsidiary charity are substantially or exclusively confined to the benefit of the parent charity.

The basis for treating a non-company charity as a subsidiary is that the connection between it and some other charity is such that the operating and financial policies of the former are likely to be set in accordance with the wishes of the latter. This is likely to be the case where one of the relationships described in the previous paragraph exists, but trustees may, in a particular case, be able to produce evidence to the contrary.

A further instance where the relationship is similar to that of a parent and subsidiary undertaking may arise where the parent charity transacts with another undertaking in such a way that all the risks and rewards of the transactions remain with the parent undertaking. For instance transfers of assets to another entity whilst retaining exclusive use of those assets and the costs of maintaining them. Such undertakings are regarded as quasi subsidiaries and should be accounted for in accordance with Financial Reporting Standard 5 (FRS 5).

15.4 What are the requirements governing the preparation of consolidated accounts?

15.4.1 The 1985 Act and FRS 2

Both the 1985 Act and FRS 2 (para 21) exempt a parent undertaking from preparing consolidated accounts if:

(a) the parent undertaking is a wholly-owned subsidiary undertaking and its immediate parent undertaking is established under the law of a member state of the European Union. Exemption is conditional on compliance with certain further conditions set out in s228(2);

(b) the parent undertaking is a majority-owned subsidiary and meets all the conditions for exemption as a wholly-owned subsidiary undertaking set out in s228(2) as well as the additional conditions set out in s228(1)(b);

(c) all of the parent undertaking's subsidiary undertakings are permitted or required to be excluded from consolidation by s229; or

(d) the group is small or medium-sized and is not an ineligible group, as defined in s248. A group is ineligible if any of its members is a public company, a banking institution, an insurance company, an authorised person under the Financial Services Act 1986, or a body corporate which has power under its constitution to offer its shares or debentures to the public and may lawfully exercise that power.

15.4.2 SORP 2000

Paragraphs 300 to 302 discuss whether or not consolidated accounts should be prepared. The general rule is set out in para 300. A parent charity should prepare consolidated accounts including all its subsidiary undertakings except where:

(a) the gross income of the group in the accounting period is no more than the audit threshold under the Charities Act 1993 which can be revised by Ministerial Order;
(b) the subsidiary undertaking or undertakings results are not material to the group; or
(c) the accounts have to be aggregated under charity legislation in England and Wales.

Item (a) is a change in SORP 2000, introducing exemption from consolidation for small charitable groups. The present level of gross income for audit exemption is £250,000. This applies in place of the more generous grounds for exemption on size grounds which are permitted by the 1985 Act and FRS 2.

Consolidated accounts should be prepared for the reporting charity and its charitable subsidiary undertakings whether or not the subsidiaries are also companies. However, where the subsidiary undertaking is a non-company charity it will normally be accounted for in the consolidated accounts in the same manner as a branch in accordance with paras 51 to 55 of the SORP (see chapter **17**). Similarly, charities – whether companies or not – which use non-charitable subsidiary undertakings to carry out their charitable purposes should prepare consolidated accounts for the charity and such subsidiary undertakings.

The composition of a 'charitable group' is discussed further in para 1 of Appendix 1 (which defines branches for the purposes of the SORP). This states that FRS 2 expressly disapplies its requirements where they are not consistent with a particular statutory framework. Thus, charitable bodies which are controlled by other charitable bodies will not normally be subject to the requirements of that Standard as they will be treated as 'special trusts' under the 1993 Act or will be the subject of a direction under s96(5) that they should be treated as part of the main charity for accounting purposes. That is, the main charity and the subsidiary charitable body will, in substance, be treated as one. The question of consolidation does not arise since the subsidiary charity, as a 'branch', will be included within the entity accounts of the main charity. This is one area which some charities may be able to explore further since the status of 'subsidiary charity' for accounting purposes extends also to a special trust administered 'on behalf of the main charity by a separate body of trustees, and can also be extended under s96(5) to include certain connected charities and s96(6) to charities whose only connection is that they have the same trustee body'.

15.5 Method of consolidation

SORP 2000 specifies that the 'line-by-line' method of consolidation, used in FRS 2, should be applied to the consolidation of charitable groups.

All items of incoming resources and resources expended should be shown gross after the removal of intra-group transactions. Clearly it is desirable that similar items are treated in the same way. For instance operating activities for generating funds in the charity should be combined with similar activities in the subsidiary, and charitable activities within the charity should be combined with charitable activities in the subsidiary. Similarly costs of generating funds and or administration costs in the subsidiary should be aggregated with those of the charity.

Each charity should choose appropriate line headings within the permissible format of the SOFA and suitable amalgamations of activities. The headings should be expanded and changed to reflect the underlying activities of the group. In practice it may not be possible to find exactly matching items between the subsidiary undertaking and the parent charity in which case segmental information should be provided so that the results of the parent charity and each subsidiary undertaking are transparent.

Therefore the sales of a trading subsidiary would be consolidated as an 'incoming resource from an operating activity for generating funds' whilst the cost of sales would be consolidated within 'costs of generating funds'. However, the presentation of a separate summary profit and loss account for the trading subsidiary within the notes to the financial statements would aid understanding.

15.6 What are the conditions permitting, or requiring, subsidiary undertakings to be excluded from consolidation?

15.6.1 The 1985 Act and FRS 2

Generally, all subsidiary undertakings are to be included in the consolidation. There are, however, five exceptions, four of which are permissive and one prescriptive.

A subsidiary undertaking may be excluded from consolidation where:

(a) its inclusion is not material in determining whether a true and fair view is given. However, two or more undertakings may only be excluded if they are not material, taken together;

(b) severe long-term restrictions substantially hinder the exercise of the rights of the parent over the assets or management of the undertaking;

(c) the information necessary for the preparation of consolidated accounts cannot be obtained without disproportionate expense or undue delay;

(d) the interest of the parent is held exclusively with a view to subsequent resale and the undertaking has not previously been included in the consolidated accounts prepared by the parent.

(e) The fifth exception is a requirement that a subsidiary undertaking must be excluded from consolidation where:
  - its activities are so different from those of other undertakings to be included in the consolidation that its inclusion would be incompatible with the requirement to show a true and fair view.

FRS 2 only permits subsidiaries to be excluded from consolidation on the grounds of the criteria in (b), (d) and (e), although, as the FRS does not apply to immaterial items, no special mention is required for that exclusion required by the Act. The criterion in (c) was considered by the ASB not to be an appropriate reason for excluding material subsidiaries.

Immateriality

A number of parent charities have taken the opportunity not to consolidate on the grounds of immateriality. The activities of a trading subsidiary may, for example, be immaterial when compared against the overall operations of the charity.

Different activities

The Act stresses that the requirement not to consolidate does not apply 'merely because some of the undertakings are industrial, some commercial and some provide services, or because they carry on industrial or commercial activities involving different products or provide different services'.

The same approach is taken by FRS 2. Paragraph 78(e) states (*inter alia*) that:

'The key feature of this exclusion is that it refers only to a subsidiary undertaking whose activities are so different from those of other undertakings included in the consolidation that to include that subsidiary undertaking in the consolidation would be incompatible with the obligation to give a true and fair view. Cases of this sort are so exceptional that it would be misleading to link them in general to any particular contrast of activities. For example, the contrast ... between profit and not-for-profit undertakings is not sufficient of itself to justify non-consolidation. The different activities of undertakings included in the consolidation can better be shown by presenting segmental information rather than by excluding from consolidation the subsidiary undertakings with different activities'.

Thus, exclusion from consolidation would appear to be merited only in very exceptional circumstances and consolidation will generally be required of all subsidiary undertakings. A survey of parent charity accounts reveals that subsidiary undertakings with different activities are now consolidated.

Paragraph 18A of Sch 4 to the 1985 Act and para 30 of FRS 2 require subsidiary undertakings excluded from consolidation on these grounds to be equity accounted.

15.7 Disclosures

15.7.1 All charities with subsidiary undertakings

There should be a separate comment in the Trustees' Annual Report concerning the performance of the charity's subsidiary undertakings (see chapter **6**).

The notes to the accounts should state the aggregate amount of the total investment of the charity in its subsidiary undertakings and, unless the subsidiary is not material, in relation to each one:

(a) its name;
(b) particulars of the charity's shareholding or other means of control;
(c) how its activities relate to those of the charity;
(d) the aggregate amount of its assets, liabilities and funds;
(e) a summary of its turnover and expenditure and its profit or loss for the year (or equivalent categories for charitable subsidiary undertakings).

Similar details should be provided relating to any minority interest external to the charity held in the subsidiary undertakings including any restrictions that may be placed on the groups' activities.

If a charity has a large number of subsidiary undertakings such that this disclosure would result in information of excessive length being given, the information need only be given in respect of those undertakings whose results or financial position materially affected the figures shown in the charity's annual accounts. The full disclosure must be made available (in the same way as the accounts) to any member of the public upon request.

Paragraphs 15 and 16 of Pt II of Sch 5 to the 1985 Act require the following to be disclosed for each undertaking which is a subsidiary of the parent at the end of the financial year:

(a) its name;
  (i) if it is incorporated outside Great Britain, its country of incorporation;
  (ii) if unincorporated, the address of its principal place of business;
(b) under which of the conditions the undertaking is a subsidiary; and
(c) the identity of each class of share held by the parent (and the group) and the proportion of the nominal value held.

In addition to these disclosures, para 33 of FRS 2 requires disclosure of:

(a) the proportion of voting rights held by the parent and its subsidiary undertakings; and
(b) an indication of the nature of its business.

15.7.2 Where consolidated accounts are prepared

SORP 2000 specifies that where consolidated accounts are prepared the method of consolidation should be stated in the policy notes and which subsidiaries are included and excluded from the consolidation.

Segmental information may need to be provided where the aggregation and adjustments required to consolidate financial information may obscure information about the different undertakings and the activities included in the consolidated accounts. It is important that the presentation adopted and disclosure in the notes is sufficiently detailed to distinguish the key results of the charity from those of its subsidiary undertakings. Examples of those items that should be separately disclosed include the costs of generating funds, management and administration and the costs of charitable activities.

In consolidated accounts, funds or reserves retained by subsidiary undertakings other than funds used in carrying out the charity's objects should be included under an appropriate separate fund heading in the balance sheet (e.g., 'non-charitable trading funds').

15.7.3 In the entity accounts of the parent where consolidated accounts are not (required to be) prepared

If consolidated accounts are not prepared, then the trustees should explain the reasons in a note to the charity's accounts with reference to each excluded subsidiary undertaking.

Paragraphs 1 to 4 of Pt I of Sch 5 to the 1985 Act require the following to be disclosed:

(a) the name of each subsidiary undertaking;
   (i) if it is incorporated outside Great Britain, its country of incorporation;
   (ii) if unincorporated, the address of its principal place of business;
(b) the identity of each class of share held by the parent and the proportion of the nominal value held;
(c) unless the subsidiary undertaking is included in the accounts using the equity method of accounting, the aggregate amount of its capital and reserves as at the end of its financial year and of its profit or loss for that year; and
(d) where the disclosures in (c) are provided and the subsidiary undertaking's year end is not co-terminous with that of the parent, its year end (i.e., the last before that of the parent's).

Paragraph 22 of the FRS requires a parent undertaking not preparing consolidated accounts to state that its accounts present information about it as an individual undertaking and not about its group.

15.7.4 For subsidiaries excluded from consolidation

Paragraph 15(4) of Pt II of Sch 5 to the 1985 Act and para 26 of FRS 2 require to be stated the names of subsidiary undertakings excluded from consolidation, together with the reasons for their exclusion.

Unless included in the accounts by way of the equity method of accounting, para 17(1) of Pt II of Sch 5 requires to be stated the aggregate amount of each subsidiary undertaking's share capital and reserves as at the end of its financial year and of its profit or loss for that year.

In addition, para 31 of FRS 2 requires to be disclosed:

(a) particulars of the balances between the excluded subsidiary undertakings and the rest of the group;

(b) the nature and extent of transactions of the excluded subsidiary undertakings with the rest of the group;

(c) unless the excluded subsidiary undertaking is equity accounted, any
amounts included in the consolidated accounts in respect of:
  (i) dividends received and receivable from that undertaking; and
  (ii) any write-down in the period in respect of the investment in that
  undertaking or amounts due from that undertaking;

(d) for subsidiary undertakings excluded from consolidation because of
different activities, their separate accounts. Summarised financial
information may be provided unless the excluded subsidiaries account
for more than 20 per cent of any of the group's operating profits,
turnover or net assets. The group amounts should be measured by
including all excluded subsidiary undertakings.

15.8 Approval and filing of consolidated accounts

Accounts for each member of the group, i.e. parent and subsidiary undertakings, should be prepared for approval by the respective boards of
trustees and/or directors. The consolidated group accounts should then be
prepared by the parent charity.

In para 304 the SORP contains guidance on how to meet the requirements of
the Charities Act 1993 for charities in England and Wales, which have prepared consolidated accounts, to file the individual charity's accounts with
Charity Commission. Where the group and parent charity's accounts are
included in the same set of consolidated accounts, as well as two balance sheets
there should be two SOFAs (one for the group and one for the parent).
However consolidated accounts are often filed with the Commission omitting
the SOFA for the parent charity. The Commission is prepared to accept these
accounts as long as the assets and liabilities of the charity can be distinguished
from those of its subsidiary/ies and that the turnover and results of the sub-
sidiary/ies are clearly stated. However, the Commission retains the power to
require the production and filing of any individual charity SOFA and
similarly members of the public have a legal right to request this statement.

15.9 Accounting for associates, joint ventures and joint arrangements

SORP 2000 contains extensive new guidance on the accounting for and disclosure of associates, joint ventures and joint arrangements. This guidance
applies the requirements of FRS 9 to charities.

Where associates, joint ventures and joint arrangements exist, consolidated accounts should be prepared, subject to the exemptions in para 300 of the SORP.

15.9.1 Identification

Associate

Where a charity has a long-term participating interest in another undertaking and exercises significant influence over its operating and financial policy then this is likely to be an associate undertaking. Where a charity beneficially holds 20 per cent or more of the voting rights in any undertaking, it will be presumed to have a participating interest and significant influence over its operating and financial policy, unless the contrary is shown.

Joint venture

In a joint venture situation, a separate entity is jointly controlled by two or more undertakings, all of which have a say in the operations of the joint venture, so that no one investing undertaking controls the joint venture but all together can do so. It is possible for a charity to beneficially hold 20 per cent or more of the voting rights in an undertaking but for the management arrangements to be such that control is clearly shared with the other partners and hence the undertaking is a joint venture as opposed to an associate.

Joint arrangements

Often charities also undertake joint arrangements where they may carry out activities in partnership with other bodies but without establishing a separate legal entity.

15.9.2 Methods of accounting for associates, joint ventures and joint arrangements

Associates

Associates should be included in the accounts based on the net equity method. The consolidated SOFA should show the net interest in the results for the year in the associates as a separate line after the 'net incoming/(resources expended)' line. In the balance sheet the net interest in associates should be shown as a separate line within fixed asset investments.

Where there are gains and losses on investments and unrealised gains on other fixed assets, the net share relating to associates should be shown on a separate line of the SOFA.

241

Joint ventures

Joint ventures should be accounted for on a gross equity method. This requires the reporting entity to present its share of the gross incoming resources of joint ventures on the face of the consolidated profit and loss account. However, this does not form part of the group incoming resources and must be clearly distinguished. For charities this can be achieved by including gross incoming resources from joint ventures in the SOFA on a line by line basis with an additional line showing the total share of gross incoming resources from joint ventures as a reduction in total incoming resources. In addition a line showing the net interest in the results for the year in the joint ventures as a separate line after the 'net incoming/(resources expended)' line must be included (this may be combined with that of the associates). In the balance sheet the share of the gross assets and the gross liabilities should be shown in a linked presentation within fixed assets investments.

Where there are gains and losses on investments and unrealised gains on other fixed assets, the gross share relating to joint ventures should be shown either on a separate line or combined with the appropriate lines on the statement of financial activities.

Joint arrangements

Where there is a joint arrangement the charity's gross share of the incoming resources and resources expended and the assets and liabilities should be included in the accounts in the same way as for a branch (see chapter **17**). If under the arrangement the charity is jointly and severally liable for an obligation, it should accrue the part of the obligation for which it is responsible and treat the part of the obligation which is expected to be met by the other parties as a contingent liability.

15.9.3 Disclosure

The following disclosure should be given in respect of each associate and joint venture and this will normally be compliant with FRS 9:

(a) its name;
(b) the charity's shareholding and other interests in it;
(c) the nature of the activities of the associate or joint venture;
(d) the charity's interest in the results showing separately its share in:
  (i)   gross incoming resources by type;
  (ii)   costs of generating funds;
  (iii)   expenditure on charitable activities;
  (iv)   expenditure on management and administration;
  (v)   the net results (where tax is payable the share of the results pre and post tax and the share in the tax should be shown);

(vi)   gains or losses on investments and the share in unrealised gains on other fixed assets;

(vii)   fixed assets;

(viii) current assets;

(ix)   liabilities under one year;

(x)   liabilities over one year;

(xi)   the different funds of the charity;

(xii)   contingent liabilities and other commitments;

(xiii) particulars of any qualifications contained in any audit or other statutory report on its accounts, and any note or reservation in those accounts to call attention to a matter which, apart from the note or reservation, would properly have been referred to in such a qualification.

For joint arrangements the notes to the accounts should provide appropriate details of the charity's commitments in the arrangement.

15.10 Disclosure examples

Example A *Arts Theatre Trust Limited* is a charitable company which has a trading subsidiary. The charity prepares consolidated accounts and the SOFA and balance sheets are presented below. In addition, the note explaining the activities and summarising the results of the subsidiary is also presented.

Example A   *Arts Theatre Trust Limited*
Consolidated Statement of Financial Activities (including Income and Expenditure Account) for the year ended 31 March 2001

	Notes	Unrestricted Funds £'000	Restricted Funds £'000	Total Funds 2001 £'000	Total Funds 2000 £'000
Incoming resources					
Operation of theatre and arts centre	3	1,200	–	**1,200**	1,259
Activities for generating funds:					
Commercial trading operations	4	549	–	**549**	296
Donations		12	79	**91**	79
Interest receivable		18	1	**19**	16
Total incoming resources		1,779	80	**1,859**	1,650
Less cost of generating funds:					
Commercial trading operations	4	337	2	**339**	280
Net incoming resources available for charitable application		1,442	78	**1,520**	1,370
Charitable expenditure					
Cost of operation of theatre and arts centre	5	1,209	81	**1,290**	1,230
Managing and administering the charity	6	150	2	**152**	113
Total charitable expenditure		1,359	83	**1,442**	1,343
Total resources expended		1,696	85	**1,781**	1,623
Movement in total funds for the year –					
Net income/(expenditure) for the year		83	(5)	**78**	27
Total funds brought forward		1,294	17	**1,311**	1,284
Total funds carried forward	16,17	1,377	12	**1,389**	1,311

The statement of financial activities includes all gains and losses recognised in the year.

All incoming resources and resources expended derive from continuing activities.

Consolidated and Charity Balance Sheets as at 31 March 2001

	Notes	Group 2001 £'000	Group 2000 £'000	Charity 2001 £'000	Charity 2000 £'000
Fixed assets					
Tangible assets	10	**830**	824	**830**	824
Investments	4	**–**	–	**1**	1
		830	824	**831**	825
Current assets					
Stock	11	**217**	213	**203**	212
Debtors	12	**207**	206	**272**	206
Cash at bank and in hand		**423**	319	**314**	319
		847	738	**789**	737
Creditors: amounts falling due within one year	13	**242**	195	**185**	195
Net current assets		**605**	543	**604**	542
Total assets less current liabilities		**1,435**	1,367	**1,435**	1,367
Creditors: amounts falling due after more than one year	15	**46**	56	**46**	56
		1,389	1,311	**1,389**	1,311
Unrestricted funds					
General	16	**1,210**	1,263	**1,210**	1,263
Designated	16	**167**	31	**167**	31
		1,377	1,294	**1,377**	1,294
Restricted funds	17	**12**	17	**12**	17
		1,389	1,311	**1,389**	1,311

Approved by the trustees on 16 June 2001 and signed on its behalf by
S.A. Bloggs: Chairman

Chapter 16 – Incorporated charities

16.1 Introduction

A continuing problem with charity reporting has concerned charitable companies, which are subject to the requirements of both the Companies Act 1985 and the Charities Act 1993, and which, in England and Wales, must file accounts with both Companies House and the Charity Commission. The 1995 SORP contained limited guidance on the particular problems of charitable companies. This is addressed in SORP 2000 by a separate section of guidance which addresses the main problems arising from applying the requirements of both the Companies Act 1985 and the Charities Act 1993 and the SORP.

16.2 Accounts and reports

Charitable companies must comply with the Companies Act 1985 with respect to the form and content of their accounts. This Act also stipulates the contents of the annual (directors') report. Strictly, the directors of charitable companies, in England and Wales, have to prepare both that report, and the annual (trustees) report under Pt VI of the Charities Act 1993, but the Charity Commission is prepared to accept the directors' report for filing under Pt VI if it also contains the information required under Pt VI. Charitable companies (unlike unincorporated charities) do not have an exemption to leave out the names of the directors from the annual report.

The Companies Act 1985 requires a company to prepare annual financial statements which give a true and fair view of its state of affairs at the end of the year and of its profit and loss for that year. In addition, para 3(3) of Pt 1, sA of Sch 4 to this Act requires the directors to adapt the headings and subheadings of the balance sheet and profit and loss account in any case where the special nature of the company's business requires such adaptation.

The requirement to show a true and fair view and to adapt the accounts for the special nature of charity means that there is a strong presumption that charitable companies will in all but exceptional circumstances have to comply with this SORP in order to meet the requirements of company law. Particulars of any material departures from this SORP are required to be disclosed. A departure is not justified simply because it gives the reader a more appealing picture of the financial position or results of the charity.

16.3 The statement of financial activities and the summary income and expenditure account

A long-standing confusion which arose from the 1995 SORP was whether charitable companies had to prepare both a Statement of Financial Activities and an income and expenditure account. The regulatory position is as follows:

- all charitable companies registered under the Companies Act 1985 must include an income and expenditure account in their financial statements; and
- the Statement of Financial Activities, a requirement of the SORP, is designed to include all the gains and losses of a charity which would be found in the income and expenditure account or in the statement of total recognised gains and losses as required by FRS 3.

A separate income and expenditure account is therefore not necessarily required for a charitable company. However it probably will be required where the income and expenditure account cannot be separately identified within the Statement of Financial Activities and there are items which may be open to challenge if they are included in an income and expenditure account. This might arise when there are:

(a) movements on endowment (capital) funds during the year; and
(b) unrealised gains and losses arising during the year.

Whilst unrealised gains and losses are not allowed in the income and expenditure account most of these are included in the Statement of Financial Activities below the point at which a conventional income and expenditure account would end.

In practice, considerations of materiality mean that in many cases a separate income and expenditure account will not be presented. This arises because the degree of the presentational difference between the surplus/deficit as reported in the SOFA and the net surplus/deficit as reported under the Companies Act is not deemed to be significant. Where a separate income and expenditure is not presented, a note on the face of the SOFA should disclose the amount of net income under Companies Act reporting requirements.

16.4 Presentation of the summary income and expenditure account

Where the Statement of Financial Activities of a charitable company does not include any of the items mentioned in (a) and (b) above it may not need to produce a separate summary income and expenditure account.

However the headings in the Statement of Financial Activities must be changed so that:

(a) the title clearly indicates that it includes an income and expenditure account and statement of total recognised gains and losses (if required); and

(b) there is a prominent sub total entitled 'net income/(expenditure) for the year' which replaces or is in addition to the heading of 'net incoming/(outgoing) resources for the year'.

Care must also be taken to ensure that all realised gains and losses are included in the Statement of Financial Activities in such a way that they fall within the bounds of the headings for (a) and (b) within the income and expenditure account. Particular attention may need to be given to impairment losses and reversals which, in accordance with the guidance in FRS 11 are realised in some circumstances and unrealised in others.

Where a summary income and expenditure account is required, it should be derived from and cross-referenced to the corresponding figures in the Statement of Financial Activities. It need not distinguish between unrestricted and restricted income funds but the accounting basis on which items are included must be the same as in the Statement of Financial Activities. It should show separately in respect of continuing operations, acquisitions and discontinued operations:

(a) gross income from all sources;

(b) net gains/losses from disposals of all fixed assets belonging to the charity's income funds;

(c) transfers from endowment funds of amounts previously received as capital resources and now converted into income funds for expending;

(d) total income (this will be the total of all incoming resources – other than revaluation gains – of all the income funds but not for any endowment funds);

(e) total expenditure out of the charity's income funds; and

(f) net income or expenditure for the year.

In practice, the format may need to be modified to comply with specific statutory requirements or those of the charity's own governing document.

Where consolidated accounts are prepared a summary income and expenditure account should be included for the group (when it is required).

16.5 The balance sheet format

If a columnar format is chosen then charitable companies will still have to show the funds of the charity as a single line or split between the various different types of fund in order to comply with the Companies Act requirements.

16.6 Revaluation reserve

Where fixed assets are revalued upwards a revaluation reserve will arise being the difference between the original depreciated cost or valuation of the asset and the revalued amount. Separate reporting of the reserve is not significant for charities as they do not distribute profits, but a revaluation reserve will, nevertheless, arise. This will form part of the funds in which the revalued assets are held. In certain circumstances (as described in FRSs 11 and 15) impairment losses or other downward revaluations can be offset against the revaluation reserve.

To comply with the Companies Act 1985 charitable companies must separately disclose the revaluation reserve within the funds section on the face of the balance sheet but may change the heading as appropriate. This may be best effected by use of a prominent inset.

16.7 Summary financial information

Charitable companies should follow the recommendations in paras 292 to 297 but their summary financial information must also include a statement indicating whether or not the statutory accounts for the relevant year(s) have been delivered to the Registrar of Companies.

Any summary financial information prepared by a charitable company will almost all be non-statutory (the statutory option for the publication of summary financial statements only applies to listed companies) and the auditor's report cannot be published with them without the statutory accounts to which it relates. This means in effect that companies can produce summarised accounts without the backing of an audit report.

16.8 Disclosure examples

In Example G *The ABC Charity*, which is a charitable company, technically a separate income and expenditure account is required because the 'net movement in funds' includes both realised and unrealised gains. As the difference between any surplus under Companies Acts requirements is not materially different from that presented, the difference is noted at the bottom of the SOFA.

As the SOFA incorporates an income and expenditure account, the heading of the statement refers to this fact.

Example G   *The ABC Charity*
Consolidated Statement of Financial Activities (incorporating an Income and Expenditure Account) for the year ended 31 March 2001

	Notes	Unrestricted funds £'000	Restricted funds £'000	Totals 2001 £'000	Totals 2000 £'000
Incoming resources					
Donations and gifts	2	4,130	3,200	**7,330**	6,000
Legacies	3	2,150	–	**2,150**	1,330
Building appeal	17	–	400	**400**	900
Activities in furtherance of the charity's objects:					
Government grants for residential care	17	–	700	**700**	400
Fees for residential care		1,200	–	**1,200**	1,000
Activities for generating funds:					
Merchandising income	4	1,140	–	**1,140**	900
Investment income	5	350	50	**400**	475
Net gain on disposal of fixed assets		20	–	**20**	30
Total incoming resources		8,990	4,350	**13,340**	11,035
Resources expended					
Cost of generating funds:					
Fund-raising costs		480	210	**690**	550
Building appeal costs	17	–	45	**45**	110
Merchandising costs	4	870	–	**870**	710
Investment management fees		80	10	**90**	110
		1,430	265	**1,695**	1,480
Charitable expenditure:					
Costs of activities in furtherance of the charity's objects:					
Residential care costs		1,400	1,030	**2,430**	2,545
Childcare		1,000	2,400	**3,400**	3,150
Emergency services		1,800	1,300	**3,100**	2,800
Information and Education		90	10	**100**	300
Support costs		110	80	**190**	180
Management and administration		210	60	**270**	230

		4,610	4,880	**9,490**	9,405
Total resources expended	6	6,040	5,145	**11,185**	10,885
Net incoming resources (resources expended) before transfers		2,950	(795)	**2,155**	150
Transfers between funds	17	15	(15)	–	–
Net incoming resources/ (resources expended)		2,965	(810)	**2,155**	150
Net gains on investment assets	11	100	–	**100**	250
Net movement in funds		3,065	(810)	**2,255**	400
Fund balances brought forward at 1 April	17	6,300	3,900	**10,200**	9,800
Fund balances carried forward at 31 March	17	9,365	3,090	**12,455**	10,200

All of the above results are derived from continuing activities. All gains and losses recognised in the year are included above. The surplus for the year for Companies Act purposes comprises the net incoming resources for the year plus realised gains on investments and was £2,225,000 (2000: £230,000). Page 10 gives details of changes in resources applied for fixed assets for charity use.

Example E *The Edinburgh Educational Trust* is a Scottish charity, and is required by Scottish charity accounts regulations and law to present a separate income and expenditure account. A statement of total recognised gains and losses is also presented in order to report unrealised investment gains.

Example E   *The Edinburgh Educational Trust*
Statement of Financial Activities for the year ended 31 March 2001

	Notes	Unrestricted funds £'000	Restricted funds £'000	Endowment Funds £'000	Totals 2001 £'000	Totals 2000 £'000
Incoming resources						
Donations and legacies	2	123,328	–	–	**123,328**	28,565
Millennium appeal income	2	–	1,490,367	–	**1,490,367**	372,525
Activities in furtherance of the charity's objects:						
Grants and fees for care and education of children	3	1,381,047	–	–	**1,381,047**	1,491,997
Activities for generating funds						
– rental income		11,761	–	–	**11,761**	15,576
Investment income	4	258,266	–	–	**258,266**	205,181
Total incoming resources		1,774,402	1,490,367	–	**3,264,769**	2,113,844
Cost of generating funds	5	–	(82,975)	–	**(82,975)**	(242,282)
Net incoming resources available for charitable application		1,774,402	1,407,392	–	**3,181,794**	1,871,562
Charitable expenditure						
Costs of activities in furtherance of charitable objectives:						
Teaching and care of children	6(a)	794,227	–	–	**794,227**	733,870
Running costs and maintenance of school	6(b)	793,340	–	149,621	**942,961**	706,524
Management and administration	7	69,950	14,321	–	**84,271**	62,242
Total charitable expenditure		1,657,517	14,321	149,621	**1,821,459**	1,502,636
Total resources expended		1,657,517	97,296	149,621	**1,904,434**	1,502,636
Net incoming/ (outgoing) resources before transfers		116,885	1,393,071	(149,621)	**1,360,335**	368,926
Transfers in respect of fixed assets additions	14	–	(1,401,229)	1,401,229	**–**	–
Gains on investments		–	–	209,329	**209,329**	2,550,912
Net movement in funds for the year		116,885	(8,158)	1,460,937	**1,569,664**	2,919,838
Total funds at 1 April 2000	14	194,224	(135,085)	8,185,985	**8,245,124**	5,325,286
Total funds at 31 March 2001	14	311,109	(143,243)	9,646,922	**9,814,788**	8,245,124

Income and expenditure account for the year ended 31 March 2001

	Notes	2001 £'000	2000 £'000
Income			
Donations, legacies and Millennium Appeal income	2	**1,613,695**	401,090
Grant from Scottish Executive	3	**902,978**	923,854
Local authority fees	3	**478,069**	568,143
Investment income	4	**258,266**	205,181
Rental income		**11,761**	15,576
		3,264,769	2,113,844
Charitable expenditure			
Costs of generating funds	5	**82,975**	242,282
Teaching and care of children	6	**794,227**	733,870
Running costs and maintenance of school	6	**942,961**	706,524
Management and administration expenses	7	**84,271**	62,242
		1,904,434	1,744,918
Operating surplus for the year		**1,360,335**	368,926
Realised (loss)/gain on sale of investments		**(29,843)**	109,434
Surplus for the year		**1,330,492**	478,360
Statement of Total Recognised Gains and Losses			
Surplus for the year		**1,330,492**	478,360
Unrealised gain on investment	10	**239,172**	2,441,478
Total gains and losses recognised since 31 March 2000		**1,569,664**	2,919,838

All activities relate to continuing operations.

There is no difference between the surplus on ordinary activities for the year stated above and its historical cost equivalent.

Chapter 17 – Accounting for branches

17.1 Introduction

For the first time the 1995 SORP formally required unincorporated charities to incorporate the transactions of its branches into their accounts. In many cases this meant not only a dramatic change in the format and size of the figures in charity accounts, but also formalising branch accounting procedures and, in many cases, the preparation of branch returns. SORP 2000 has similar accounting requirements but gives clearer guidelines in terms of what constitutes a branch.

Apart from a diversity of purpose, charities have a diversity of structure. Some charities have local branches which form part of the registered charity, with one charity number. If the charity is a company incorporated under the Companies Acts, s221 requires the charity to obtain returns from its branches and incorporate these in the national accounts. For such branches the charity will need to comply with s5 of the 1993 Act and state the fact that it is a registered charity on, *inter alia*, all branch notices, advertisements, cheques, invoices and receipts.

Others may have local groups, which are autonomous and, therefore, registered as main charities. They are subject to compulsory registration with the Commissioners, under s3 of the 1993 Act, if, broadly, they either use or occupy land, have permanent endowment or have gross income of more than £1,000 p.a. from any source. They will have their own accounts and their own body of trustees.

Some charities may have a mix of local branches and autonomous groups.

Who accounts for what? It is extremely important that charity trustees recognise and account for all subsidiary charitable funds, special trusts and branches it controls because the relevant income and expenditure thresholds identified in the 1993 Act relate to those of the charity as a whole, including its special trusts and controlled branches. Because many charities do not neatly fall into one category or another, this is a complex area requiring legal advice in cases of doubt. It is understood that, in any particular case, the Commissioners will provide further guidance to charity trustees on request.

17.2 What is a branch?

Before considering the accounting requirements it is essential to understand what constitutes a branch for these purposes. Branches are defined in Appendix 1 to the SORP as follows:

> 'Branches' (which may also be known as supporters' groups, friends' groups, members' groups, communities or parishes which are part of a common trust etc) are entities or administrative bodies set up, for example, to conduct a particular aspect of the business of the reporting charity, or to conduct the business of the reporting charity in a particular geographical area. They may or may not be legal entities which are separate from the reporting charity. For the purpose of this SORP a 'branch' is either:
>
> (a) simply part of the administrative machinery of the reporting charity; or
> (b) a separate legal entity which is administered by or on behalf of the reporting charity and whose funds are held for specific purposes which are within the general purposes of the reporting charity. 'Legal entity' means a trust or unincorporated association or other body formed for a charitable purpose. The words 'on behalf of' should be taken to mean that, under the constitution of the separate entity, a substantial degree of influence can be exerted by the reporting charity over the administration of its affairs; or,
> (c) in England and Wales, a separate legal entity not falling within (b) which the Charity Commission has united by a direction under section 96(5) or 96(6), Charities Act 1993 should be treated as linked to the reporting charity for accounting purposes.

This definition has been adopted to reflect the provisions of the Charities Act 1993 allocating responsibility for accounting in the case of multicellular charities.

Financial Reporting Standard 2 expressly disapplies its requirements where they are not consistent with a particular statutory accounting framework. Consequently, charitable bodies which are controlled by other charitable bodies will not normally be subject to the requirements of that standard as they will be treated as 'special trusts' under the Charities Act 1993 or will be the subject of a direction as mentioned above in sub-paragraph (c) – see the definition of 'subsidiary undertaking' below.

Some of the characteristics of a branch are:

(i) it uses the name of the reporting charity within its title;
(ii) it exclusively raises funds for the reporting charity and/or for its own local activities;
(iii) it uses the reporting charity's registration number to receive tax relief on its activities;
(iv) it is perceived by the public to be the reporting charity's local representative or its representative for a particular purpose;
(v) it receives support from the reporting charity through advice, publicity materials, etc.

If the branch exists to carry out the primary objects of the charity, typically it will receive funds from the reporting charity for its work and may be staffed by employees of the reporting charity.

If the branch is not a separate legal entity, all funds held by a branch will be the legal property of the reporting charity, whether or not the branch has a separate bank account.

Organisations which are not branches

Some charities may be known as 'branches' within a particular organisational or network structure, but if their level of administrative autonomy from the reporting charity – as determined by their constitutions – is such that legislation requires them to be treated as separate accounting entities, then they should not be regarded as 'branches' for accounting purposes but should prepare separate accounts for submission to the appropriate regulatory authority.

Other examples of organisations which are not 'branches' for the purpose of these recommendations include groups of people who occasionally gather together to raise funds for one or a number of different charities and special interest groups who are affiliated to a particular charity, but do not themselves undertake charitable activities (including fundraising for the charity).

The legal position of local branches and groups can vary. In some cases, this may create problems of an accounting nature. It may be necessary, in some circumstances, for charity trustees of the main charity to reexamine their structures so that the position is clarified.

17.3 Accounting requirements

Paragraphs 51-55 of the SORP cover the accounting requirements in respect of branches and are as follows:

Before preparing accounts, trustees must be quite clear as to the legal structure of the charity. A charity may operate through branches to raise funds and/or carry out its charitable purposes. Branches as defined in the glossary (see Appendix 1) will be accounted for as part of the whole charity. But if both reporting charity and the branches are companies, company law requires each entity to prepare its own accounts. In such a case, one annual report should normally be prepared to cover both the reporting charity and its branch(es) and consolidated accounts should be prepared in accordance with paragraph 299 to 319.

Separate legal entities which may be known as branches but do not fall within the definition of a branch in the Glossary should prepare their own Annual Report and Accounts and, if they are connected charities the relationship should be explained in the trustees report (see paragraph 31(c)).

All branch transactions should be accounted for gross in the reporting charity's own accounts excluding those transactions which net off eg branch to branch transactions of those between the branches and the head office. Similarly all assets and liabilities of the branch including, for example, funds raised but not remitted to the reporting charity at the year end should be incorporated into the reporting charity's own balance sheet. This provision need not apply where the transactions and balances of the branches in aggregate are not material to the charity's accounts.

Funds raised by a branch for the general purpose of the reporting charity will be accounted for as unrestricted funds in the accounts of the main charity. (Comment: Such funds are sometimes treated as designated funds if they are retained by the branch) Funds raised by a branch for specific purposes of the reporting charity will need to be accounted for as restricted funds in the accounts of the main charity. Funds held for the general purposes of a branch which is a separate charity should usually be accounted for as restricted funds in the accounts of the reporting charity.

Where a branch is not a separate legal entity, its accounts must form part of the accounts of the reporting charity but it may be in the interests of local supporters and beneficiaries for additional accounts to be prepared covering only the branch.

17.4 Further considerations

17.4.1 Fund accounting

In addition to the requirements of para 54 (above) there may be instances where a donor gives funds for use by, or is led to believe that funds collected will be used only for, a specific branch. In these cases the funds should normally be treated as restricted funds in the accounts of the charity (i.e., they can only be used by that specific branch).

17.4.2 Branch returns

In order to properly reflect the transactions and funds of its branches, a charity may need to consider what information it requires from the branches, either on a regular basis, or simply at the end of each financial year. Whilst this information will need to be accurate and supported by reliable records (which may be subject to audit either locally or by the auditors of the main charity), careful consideration will have to be given to the effect which any formal requirements may have on those who run the branches and who will frequently be volunteers, who do not have a detailed accounting knowledge. Trustees' responsibilities extend to branches and therefore they must satisfy themselves as to the general management and conduct of all branches, including the proper recording of transactions and details of any branch assets and liabilities at any time.

If the time taken between the year end and the preparation of the accounts is short it might be appropriate to consider branch returns being prepared to a slightly earlier date, provided the treatment is consistent each year and that there are no material transactions within the intervening period. If this policy is adopted it should be made clear in the notes to the accounts.

17.4.3 Omission of branches from accounts

Paragraph 281 of the SORP requires the reason for the omission of any branches from the accounts to be given although individual branches do not need to be named. Reference should also be made to any potentially linked organisations (such as supporters associations or subsidiaries not consolidated) explaining the accounting treatment adopted.

17.4.4 External scrutiny of branches

Trustees may need to consider either regular or periodic external scrutiny of branch accounts (alternatively they may be covered by internal audit procedures). The cost of any such scrutinies should be identified and disclosed separately in the accounts of the main charity.

17.4.5 Local branches constituted as separate autonomous bodies

Where local branches are separately registered charities and autonomous, separate accounts should be prepared and separate annual returns submitted. Whether or not this represents conclusive evidence, such branches should not be included in the accounts of the main charity, unless it seems that their public accountability might be open to question. In such a case their registration with the Commissioners should be re-examined. In determining the level of autonomy, there may be circumstances in which consideration should be given to the principles of FRS 5. Some of the questions which might be asked in the absence of the 'special trust' situation are:

- Does the main charity have legal control over the branches' constitution and administration, including the power of intervention?
- Are the branches financially dependent on the main charity, other than for grant- funding?
- Does the main charity have the right to control the use of the branches' resources for its own purposes to the detriment of the branch?
- What would happen if a branch were in financial difficulties? Would creditors have access only to the branch funds and branch trustees?
- What would happen to surplus funds if a branch were dissolved?

The litmus test of to what extent there is sufficient autonomy may be obscured in circumstances where there is a mix of independence and control. In some situations the main charity may have limited controls over the local branches, although their management and administration may, in all other respects, be independent. In others, local groups may use the national charity number for, for example, fundraising purposes, for example, but, in most other respects, may be autonomous.

17.5 Connected charities

The references to 'connected charities' in SORP 2000 are less than those in the 1995 SORP as they are now generally covered under the heading of 'related parties'. They are defined in Appendix 1 as those which have common, parallel or related objects and activities; and either:

(a) common control; or
(b) unity of administration

Within this category may be charities which come together under one umbrella organisation.

Chapter 18 – Summarised accounts

18.1 Introduction

Summarised accounts have become a regular feature of UK financial reporting. But they are not confined to companies reporting under the 1985 Act. As the Introduction to the ED of the 1995 SORP pointed out, many charities now issue such accounts for one purpose or another, in addition to their full accounts.

18.2 What are the requirements relating to summarised accounts?

There are no accounting provisions in the 1993 Act relating to the content of, or reporting on, summarised information published by unincorporated charities.

Paragraphs 25 and 292 to 297 of SORP 2000 set out the general principles for the preparation of Summary Financial Information and Statements. As the form of this information may vary, depending on the purpose for which they are prepared, the SORP acknowledges that it is impractical to provide detailed guidance on their content. Nonetheless, summary financial information should:

(a) be a fair and accurate summary of the full accounts (para 25); and
(b) contain information relating to both the SOFA and the balance sheet (para 294).

Summarised accounts should be accompanied by a statement signed on behalf of the trustees, giving the following details (para 295):

(a) that they are not the statutory accounts but a summary of information relating to both the Statement of Financial Activities and the balance sheet;
(b) whether or not the full financial statements from which the summary is derived have as yet been externally examined (whether audit, independent examination, or reporting accountants report); and
(c) where they have been externally examined whether there was an unqualified report;

(d) where the report is qualified, contains an explanatory paragraph or emphasis of matter, sufficient details should be provided in the summary financial information to enable the reader to appreciate the significance of the report;
(e) where branch accounts are produced it must be clearly stated that the summary is for the branch only and has been extracted from the full accounts of the main charity (giving its name);
(f) details of how the full annual accounts, the external examiners report (as applicable) and the trustees report can be obtained;
(g) the date on which the annual accounts were approved; and
(h) for charities registered in England and Wales, say whether or not the annual report and accounts have been submitted to the Charity Commission and, in the case of incorporated charities, to the Registrar of Companies.

If the full accounts have been externally examined (either audited, independently examined or subject to a reporting accountants report) the external examiner should attach a statement giving an opinion as to whether or not the summary financial information is consistent with the full annual accounts. This should be in accordance with the example shown in chapter **21** (at **21.12.5**) and addressed to the trustees.

Any other summary financial information in whatever form which does not include information on the Statement of Financial Activities and the balance sheet must be accompanied by a statement signed on behalf of the trustees as to:

(a) the purpose of the information;
(b) whether or not it is from the full annual accounts;
(c) whether or not these accounts have been audited, independently examined or subject to a reporting accountants report; and
(d) details of how the full annual accounts, trustees report and external examiners report (as appropriate) can be obtained.

Charitable companies are required to comply with the provisions in the 1985 Act relating to non-statutory accounts. Non-statutory accounts are any balance sheet or profit and loss account that a company publishes that relates to, or purports to deal with, any financial year, but that do not qualify as full individual accounts or full group accounts in respect of that financial year (s240(5)). For this purpose, a company publishes a balance sheet or a profit and loss account whenever it publishes, issues or circulates it (or makes it available in any other way for public inspection) with a view to its being read by the public generally or by any class of members of the public.

If a charitable company publishes non-statutory accounts, s240(3) (as amended) requires a statement to be appended, indicating:

(a) that they are not the company's statutory accounts;
(b) whether the statutory accounts have been delivered to the Registrar;
(c) whether the auditors or reporting accountant have made a report on the statutory accounts;
(d) whether the auditors' report was qualified or contained a statement under s237(2) or (3) (accounting records or returns inadequate, accounts not agreeing with records and returns or failure to obtain necessary information and explanations), or whether any report by the reporting accountant was qualified.

A charitable company must not publish either the auditors' or reporting accountant's report with the non-statutory accounts.

18.3 Example

The following example has been prepared from the full accounts of *Arts Theatre Trust Limited* (Example A in CC66), together with the relevant information statement required under SORP para 295.

Arts Theatre Trust Limited and its trading subsidiary

Summary financial information for the year ended 31 March 2001

	2001 £'000	2000 £'000
Incoming resources		
From theatre and arts centre including commercial trading operations	1,749	1,555
From other sources	110	95
	1,859	1,650
Less: Resources expended		
Operation of theatre and arts centre	1,629	1,510
Management and administration expenses	152	113
	1,781	1,623
Net income for the year	78	27
Total funds brought forward	1,311	1,284
Total funds carried forward	1,389	1,311

Being:		
Unrestricted funds	**1,377**	1,294
Restricted funds	**12**	17
	1,389	1,311
and represented by:		
Fixed assets	**830**	824
Net current assets	**605**	543
	1,435	1,367
Less: **Long term liabilities**	**46**	56
	1,389	1,311

The summary financial information above has been extracted from the full statutory accounts, which were approved on 16 June 2001 and which have been submitted to the Charity Commission and Registrar of Companies. The full statutory accounts have been audited and received an unqualified report from the auditors, CEP & Co, who have also confirmed to the Trustees that the summary financial information is consistent with the full statutory accounts.

A copy of the full statutory accounts, together with the trustees' and auditors' reports thereon, can be obtained from the registered office.

Signed on behalf of the Trustee by:

S A BLOGGS   Chairman

10 September 2001

Chapter 19 – Small charities

What is a 'small charity'?

In the context of SORP 2000 a smaller charity is one which due to its size does not have to adopt all the requirements of the SORP. However this encompasses charities of various sizes. The regulatory framework applicable to charities allows various reporting options and regulatory requirements of charities which are determined by levels of income and expenditure.

This chapter summarises the regulatory framework as it applies to smaller charities (i.e., those with a gross income not exceeding £250,000).

19.1 Introduction

The 1995 Annual Report of the Commissioners stated that, of the total number of over 180,000 registered charities, about 140,000 had an annual income of less than £10,000. Guidance for smaller charities on applying the 1995 SORP was, therefore, essential.

Many of the smaller charities are managed, and services provided, entirely by lay volunteers. More often than not, there are no professional resources, nor, if there were, would there be any, or enough, resources to pay for them. Some of those who work with these charities took the view that the proposals of the exposure draft to the 1995 SORP were onerous and likened them to the use of a sledgehammer to crack a nut. One of the major concerns was the then threshold of £25,000 for the preparation of accounts to a true and fair view standard and the burden which compliance with that would have imposed on those charities.

It is clearly important to strike a proper balance between the requirements for supervision and the need to minimise burdens. Accordingly, in August 1993, as part of the consultation process, an eighth Deregulation Task Force (additional to the seven business task forces) was established with the mission of examining the regulation of charities and voluntary organisations. (This Task Force considered a broad range of regulations and legislation, including the Charities Acts.) The Task Force published its report in July 1994. Some of the recommendations have been implemented by the Deregulation and Contracting Out Act 1994; others by statutory instrument, e.g., The Charities Act 1993 (Substitution of Sums) Order 1995 (SI 1995 No 2696).

Developments in charity reporting after the issue of the 1995 SORP continued to consider the requirements of smaller charities, and where appropriate, allow disclosure concessions.

19.2 The 1993 Act and related regulations

The current regulatory position for smaller charities is summarised in the Charity Commission publication CC61 *Charity accounts 2001: the framework.*

19.2.1 Charities whose gross income does not exceed £1,000

Charities with gross income which does not exceed £1,000 and which have neither a permanent endowment nor the use or occupation of land are not required to register. If they do register, they will be subject to the same requirements as in **19.2.2** below.

Such charities must maintain proper accounting records, can prepare their accounts on the receipts and payments basis and must make those accounts available to the public on request.

There is no statutory requirement for any form of external scrutiny, although one may be required by, for example, the governing document. There is, also, no duty to prepare a trustees' annual report or to submit the accounts to the Commissioners.

19.2.2 Charities whose gross income or total expenditure do not exceed £10,000

The 1993 Act introduced a new regulatory band – a light touch band which had not previously been in existence. It is for those charities which have neither gross income nor total expenditure which do not exceed £10,000 in a financial year.

Charity trustees must keep proper accounting records and, except in the case of a charitable company, can elect to prepare their accounts on the receipts and payments basis. As with the above band, this will allow many small charities, e.g., local lay-volunteer charities, which use treasurers who may have had little, or no, training and experience in accounting, but have diligently trained themselves in bookkeeping, to continue to act for them.

If they elect to prepare the accounts on the accruals basis, however, those accounts must be prepared in accordance with the Regulations and SORP, although these allow some concessions from disclosure. There is no requirement to:

(a) provide a statement that the accounts have been prepared in accordance with applicable accounting standards (FRSs/SSAPs or the FRSSE) and the SORP and particulars of, and reasons for, any material departure;
(b) provide particulars of the cost to the charity of providing trustees' indemnity insurance; and
(c) adhere to the standard expenditure headings in the SOFA.

There is no statutory requirement for an independent examination although, again, an examination or audit may be required by, for example, the governing document, or by the Commissioners.

The trustees must prepare an annual report, but it may be simplified. Regulation 7(4) requires the following legal and administrative details to be provided in that report:

(a) the name of the charity as it appears in the register and any other name by which it makes itself known;
(b) the charity registration number;
(c) its principal address;
(d) the names of the charity trustees, or where a charity has more than 50, the names of 50 including any charity trustee who is also an officer, e.g., chair, treasurer, of the charity and the name of any other person who has at any time during the financial year been a charity trustee.

In the case of a particular charity or class of charities, or of a particular financial year of a charity or class of charities, the regulations allow the Commissioners to dispense with the requirement(s), in (c) and/or (d) above, to give the principal address and/or name of a trustee, where they are satisfied that its/their disclosure could lead to that person, e.g., the trustee of a women's refuge, being placed in any personal danger.

The report on the activities in the annual report must specify the financial year to which the report relates (reg 7(3)) and be a brief summary of its main activities and achievements during the year in relation to its objects (reg 7(3)(a)). The annual report must be dated and signed by one, or more, of the charity trustees, each of whom must be authorised to do so (reg 7(3)(c)).

A description of the charity's trusts must be provided.

As there is no requirement for them to submit their annual report to the Commissioners, such charities do not routinely engage in the surveillance regime. If the Commissioners request the report, however, the charity trustees must submit it within the prescribed time limit. Where that request is made before the end of seven months after a financial year to which that report relates, within 10 months of the end of that financial year; in any other case, within three months of the date of the request. In either case, the Commissioners may, for any special reason, allow a longer period.

The charity trustees are required to keep, for at least six years from the end of the financial year to which a report relates, any annual report which they have not been required routinely to submit to the Commissioners.

If registered, these charities are asked – but not as statutory requirement – to provide the Commissioners with factual information to enable them to keep the public register up to date.

19.2.3 Charities whose gross income does not exceed £100,000 (but whose gross income or total expenditure exceeds £10,000)

The charity trustees must maintain proper accounting records and can (except in the case of a company) elect to prepare their accounts on the receipts and payments basis. In circumstances where the charity is trading, committed to substantial capital expenditure or has significant investment assets, previous publications such as *Charity accounts and reports: Core guide* (page 9) advised trustees to prepare their accounts on the accruals basis. Where they do so, the same concessions allowed for charities whose gross income and total expenditure do not exceed £10,000 (see **19.2.2** above) can also be taken, except as below.

To whatever standard the accounts are prepared, they must be independently examined or audited. A charity's governing document may demand a level of scrutiny higher than that required by the 1993 Act. Where an audit is required to be carried out by a registered auditor, the option to have an independent examination is removed. In certain circumstances the intention of the document may be unclear, having been constructed to comply with a then regulatory framework. In these circumstances, the trustees may seek an amendment to the document.

The accounts must be submitted to the Commissioners, together with the annual report containing the same information as required by charities in the above band, within 10 months of the end of the financial year (or such longer period as the Commissioners may allow). These charities will also have to submit an annual return.

19.2.4 Charities whose gross income exceeds £100,000 but whose gross income and total expenditure do not exceed £250,000

The accounts must be prepared on the accruals basis in accordance with the Regulations.

Provided that the financial thresholds are not exceeded for either the current or two preceding financial years, the trustees can opt for an independent examination instead of an audit (subject to the terms of the governing document – see **19.2.3** above).

The accounts must be submitted to the Commissioners, together with the annual report. As a change from the previous Regulations, the 2000 Regulations allow the report to be simplified, as outlined above.

An annual return will also need to be submitted.

19.3 The Charities Act 1993 versus the Companies Act 1985

As regards the standard to which accounts are prepared, charity trustees of all charitable companies must prepare accounts which show a true and fair view of its results for the year and its state of affairs at the year end. Accordingly, however small, they cannot take advantage of the provisions allowing the preparation of accounts on the receipts and payments basis. The 1993 Act is, however, less demanding. The charity trustees of unincorporated charities, whose gross income in a financial year does not exceed £100,000, may elect to prepare a simplified set of accounts on the receipts and payments basis. This set of accounts is not required to give a true and fair view, either of the financial activities of the year or of the state of affairs at the date of the year end. Where an unincorporated charity's gross income exceeds that figure in a financial year, a statement of accounts must be prepared to give a true and fair view and, thus complying with all applicable FRSs, SSAPs and the revised SORP.

Under the 1985 Act, a charitable company will require an audit if it does not qualify as a small company, its gross income is greater than £250,000 or if its balance sheet total is greater than £1.4m. Under the 1993 Act, an audit will be required if an unincorporated charity's gross income or total expenditure exceeds £250,000 in either a financial year or the immediately preceding two financial years.

Under the 1985 Act, a charitable small company whose gross income is greater than £90,000 but not greater than £250,000 (and where its balance sheet total is not greater than £ 1.4m) will normally require a report, an audit exemption report, to be prepared in accordance with the specified requirements. Under the 1993 Act, the charity trustees of an unincorporated charity whose gross income or total expenditure exceeds £10,000 but in neither a financial year nor the immediately preceding two financial years does not exceed £250,000, may as an alternative to audit elect to have its accounts examined by an independent examiner.

In this latter respect, the 1993 Act is more demanding. While an unincorporated charity with gross income or total expenditure greater than £10,000 but with gross income less than £90,000 will require, as a minimum, its accounts to be examined by an independent examiner, a charitable company meeting the relevant criteria is exempt from the provisions relating both to audit and to audit exemption reports. Thus, it may be possible for charity trustees to set up a charitable company, hide behind the veil of incorporation and not have the accounts subjected to any form of independent scrutiny, other than any additional monitoring which the Commissioners may choose to undertake.

The accounts of unincorporated charities with gross income and total expenditure which do not exceed £10,000 in a financial year will, like those of charitable companies satisfying the criteria, not normally be subject to any form of independent scrutiny, although the Commissioners may require an ad hoc audit.

The qualifications required of persons able to provide an audit exemption report are more demanding than those of persons able to undertake an independent examination. The Companies Act 1985 (Audit Exemption) Regulations 1994 (SI 1994 No 1935) require the audit exemption report to be prepared by a member of the ICAEW, ICAS, ICAI or ACCA who, under the rules of the body, either:

(a) holds a practising certificate and is not ineligible, on the grounds of lack of independence, for appointment as a reporting accountant; or
(b) is a registered auditor.

Conversely the 1993 Act describes, an independent examiner is one 'who is reasonably believed by the trustees to have the requisite ability and practical experience to carry out a competent examination of the accounts' (see chapter **24**). It is somewhat ironic that, while the duties placed on an independent examiner are more onerous than those of a reporting accountant, the qualifications required are less.

269

19.4 Preparing accounts on the receipts and payments basis

19.4.1 The Commissioners' guidance

There are no statutory requirements which govern the structure, presentation and content of accounts prepared on the receipts and payments basis.

SORP 2000

There are many relatively small charities with very simple structures and no control of other organisations. The vast majority of them will have cash and deposit accounts but few other assets. Apart from charitable companies (which must always prepare accruals accounts) these charities will often find that receipts and payments accounts meet both their needs and those of others who read their accounts. This form of accounts contains a summary of money received and money spent during the year and a list of assets.

Receipts and payments accounts have the following general features:

(a) The accounting statements showing what happened during the financial year summarise only cash movements (compared with resource movements in accruals accounts).
(b) A statement listing assets and liabilities is required (in place of a balance sheet required by accruals accounts).
(c) No asset valuations are required, unless an evaluation is essential to a meaningful description of the asset (they may be provided if trustees' wish).
(d) Notes to the accounts are not often necessary, although it is recommended that these are prepared where doing so would increase the user's understanding of the accounts. The regulations made under the Law Reform (Miscellaneous Provisions) (Scotland) Act 1990 require notes on certain matters to be provided where applicable. It is recommended that notes on related party transactions and trustee remuneration in accordance with para 166, should always be given, as well as information on significant non-monetary resources.
(e) They do not claim to show a true and fair view of the charity's financial activities and state of affairs. Accounting standards, which are primarily concerned with the presentation of a true and fair view, will therefore not generally apply to such accounts.
(f) The only accounting convention always applicable to receipts and payments accounts is comparability through consistency, that is they are prepared in a consistent way from year to year. Where valuations are provided the estimates should also be relevant, reliable and understandable and normally the going concern concept will also apply.

Receipts and payments accounts and statements of assets and liabilities may be organised in any way that the trustees feel appropriate. There is also flexibility in extending the titles as long as they include 'Receipts and Payments' and 'Statement of Assets and Liabilities' (Statement of Balances in Scotland). However there are some general principles that trustees should be aware of:

(a) In this context 'cash' includes near cash (bank and building society current and deposit accounts) where the amount deposited (the 'capital' sum) is not at risk and is not subject to withdrawal term conditions.

(b) Bank balances must be reconciled for unpaid cheques and deposits before the receipts and payments accounts are drawn up. Cheques paid out but not cleared through the bank must not be counted as creditors. Cash received but not yet banked is still cash in the hands of the charity and must be accounted for.

(c) Trust law requires that trustees should be able to account separately for each trust fund they manage. It will therefore be important for trustees to account separately for cash belonging to unrestricted funds, restricted funds and endowment funds. This may be achieved by using a columnar receipts and payments account (similar to the Statement of Financial Activities) or by having three (or more) separate accounts. As with accruals accounts it is acceptable to add together all restricted funds in one statement and all endowment funds in another, though the book-keeping records must enable accounts to be drawn up for each separate trust fund.

(d) Receipts and payments accounts will normally summarise the cash movements in that all payments for similar purposes (e.g., wages) and receipts for similar purposes (e.g., donations) should be grouped together and not shown separately. Two forms of grouping of expenditure are normally used: by nature (wages, rent, electricity, etc.) or by function (charitable expenditure, fund raising costs, etc).

(e) When summarising, any form of grouping of receipts and payments is acceptable.

(f) The statement of assets and liabilities should be adequate to show the readers of the accounts what assets are controlled by the trustees. There is no need to list all individual assets but the list should be comprehensive in covering all classes of asset held by the charity trustees. No valuation of assets held is required, unless an evaluation is essential to a meaningful description of the asset, for example in the case of cash and other monetary assets, the cash value would be given. Trustees may add values if they wish and the valuation rules given earlier in relation to accruals accounts should be followed in this case.

Where receipts and payments accounts are subjected to external examination this will normally be done by an independent examiner. However the

271

Charities Auditing Practice Note 11 does allow for the audit of receipts and payments accounts by a registered auditor (though a 'true and fair' opinion cannot be given) and so an audit provision does not demand the production of accruals accounts. Occasionally, there is a requirement (e.g., by the governing document or by a donor) for both an audit by a registered auditor and for accruals accounts to be prepared.

The recommendations given by the SORP are minimum ones and charities should feel free to include more information if they think this will help readers understand the accounts.

Accounting for the smaller charity
The Commissioners have prepared a guide, *Accounting for the smaller charity* ('the Guide'), for those charities preparing their accounts on the receipts and payments basis. Although the Guide predates SORP 2000 its recommendations remain useful and are discussed below.

The Guide comprises three parts: an introduction; guidance on the preparation of the receipts and payments account and statement of assets and liabilities; and guidance on the content of the trustees' annual report. There are various appendices, including examples of small charity accounts.

19.4.2 General principles
The only accounting policy which applies to accounts prepared on the receipts and payments basis is that of consistency.

The principle of materiality applies. Trustees should regard an item as material unless they 'can justify its omission ... on the grounds that it is too trivial to influence the reader. In cases of doubt, the item should be regarded as material and should be included in the accounts or report'.

A note to the accounts should state that they have been prepared under the receipts and payments basis. That note should also state that the accounts comply with the appropriate legal requirements, i.e., that the gross recorded income from all sources did not exceed £100,000 and the charity is not a company incorporated under the Companies Acts.

Where a charity has branches, or local groups, which raise funds in the charity's name, funds raised, and any expended, and any assets and liabilities should be included in the charity's receipts and payments account and statement of assets and liabilities. This will mean obtaining accounting returns from branches, or groups, to add to the figures for head office. To avoid double-counting, intra-charity transactions should be eliminated.

Where both restricted and unrestricted funds are held, the receipts and payments account should distinguish cash received and paid between the funds. This can be done in several ways; for example, by preparing separate receipts and payments accounts for each fund or by preparing one receipts and payments account which is appropriately sectionalised.

Comparatives should be provided for all headings.

19.4.3 Classification of receipts and payments

The Guide lists headings under which receipts and payments may be classified. Given that all charities are different, these headings are not obligatory and trustees are free to use headings which are more appropriate to their charity.

19.4.4 The receipts and payments account

All cash receipts, including receipts in respect of grants, should be included in the receipts and payments account when the cash is actually received. Non-monetary benefits can present accounting problems. Donations in the form of assets should be included only when the assets are sold. If the assets have not been sold at the year end, and are still in the trustees' possession, they should be included in the statement of assets and liabilities with a note of the fund of which they form part. Donations for onward distribution, e.g., clothing, are not cash and should not appear in the receipts and payments account but described in the annual report. Other benefits received, e.g., in the form of intangible income, should be described in the annual report in a way which properly illustrates their value and importance to the charity.

Legacies which the charity has been informed of but not received at the year end should be included in the statement of assets and liabilities only if the trustees have a legally enforceable right to receive them. They should be described, not as the assets themselves, but as the right to the assets. The description should also explain the circumstances under which the rights have arisen.

All trading receipts, whether or not directly connected with the charity's purposes, should be shown gross, as should proceeds from fundraising events. Profits covenanted by non-charitable companies carrying out activities which the charity may not should be shown separately from other receipts.

Tax recovered on interest or other income received should be shown separately from the income to which it relates. Refunds claimed but not received at the year end should be included in the statement of assets and liabilities with a suitable explanation.

19.4.5 The statement of assets and liabilities

Cash and bank deposits should be shown as the first heading. (Note: Deposits held for fixed periods should be classified as investments, as the trustees do not have immediate access to the funds.)

Debts and other monies owed, e.g., loans, tax refund claims, to the charity should be classified as other monetary assets.

Assets or property held by the charity for investment purposes should be classified as investment assets. This will include stocks and shares, cash deposits held for a fixed term, interests in land and shares in a charity's own non-charitable trading company. Their value to the charity should be given in the notes. If an asset is difficult or expensive to value, the note should include the estimated market, or insured, value at the year end. In the case of land (with or without buildings), the note should provide the address and a brief description of the property. The Guide believes it will be helpful to disclose the original cost to the charity of the land and briefly to describe the age and condition of any buildings. Where the charity is subject to the Trustee Investments Act 1961, a note should analyse investments between each of the ranges.

Assets held by the charity for its own use should be separately categorised. This will include land and buildings, motor vehicles, office and any specialised equipment and shares in a charity's non-charitable company providing charitable services. All assets should be included, including those being purchased under a hire purchase agreement or finance lease and those which cannot be sold because the governing document prohibits disposal. A note should provide information to allow a user to gain a clear picture of their value to the charity. The age, condition and estimated market (or insured) value of each major asset should be given. If an asset has no market value either because the law or the governing document prohibits its sale, or because the asset is not saleable (e.g., a statue or monument), this fact should be disclosed.

Liabilities should be analysed between current and non-current liabilities. For 'major' liabilities, the actual date on which the liability falls due should be given, if known.

Where a liability, e.g., a hire purchase liability, relates directly to an asset, the relationship should be explained. The number and frequency of instalments, together with the amount of each instalment should be provided.

If a charity has undertaken to make a charitable payment on some future date, it should be shown as a liability only if the charity is legally bound to make the payment, or the payment is unavoidable in the interests of the charity. A commitment is not to be treated as a liability if it only becomes legally binding if, and only if, a condition is fulfilled in the future. Conditional charitable liabilities should be described separately from current and non-current liabilities.

Guarantees given by the charity should be disclosed, as should their nature and likely expiry date.

Any other liability which the trustees think likely to become payable at some future time should also be disclosed, together with an explanation of how and why it arises.

It should be stated to which fund each asset and liability relates.

19.4.6 Trustees' annual report

For charities preparing their accounts on the receipts and payments basis, the trustees' annual report is likely to be their main publicity document. To be effective, every effort should be made to get the best use from the report by conveying useful information in a clear and convincing manner.

The Guide recommends that the report should 'identify the charity, how it is constituted, its aims and officers, and provide a brief but comprehensive review of the year's activities and achievements, including the main features of the accounts'.

Legal and administrative details
The following details should be provided:

(a) the charity's full name;
(b) the charity's registered number;
(c) its principal address.
   (Note: The Guide states that, if the charity does not have use of its own office, this will be the address of the person acting as the charity's correspondent);
(d) the nature of its governing document;
(e) the names of the charity trustees which should include officeholders, e.g., chair, treasurer, together with the persons who can appoint trustees.
   (Notes: 1 If there are more than 50 charity trustees, the Guide and the Regulations allows only 50 to be given;

2 The Guide recommends disclosure of the following: if the charity trustees are incorporated, a statement to that effect; the names of its directors [or other persons managing it] of any corporate trustee acting as a sole trustee; the names of any custodian trustees; and, the principal officers or employees of the charity);

(f) the names and addresses of the charity's main advisers;

(g) a note of any restrictions, which limit the charity's activities, imposed by the governing document;

(h) a brief summary of any specific investment powers in the governing document.

The disclosures recommended in (d), (f), (g) and (h) are revised SORP recommendations only.

The Guide states that the Commissioners may dispense with the recommendation to disclose the principal address of the charity trustees where they are satisfied that its disclosure could lead to that person being placed in any personal danger. The Guide is unclear, however, whether the names of the trustees need not be disclosed in similar circumstances.

Narrative information

The Guide states that the following information 'should enable the reader to gain a proper understanding of the financial information given in the accounts'.

(A) Aims and organisation

In order to explain what the charity is trying to achieve and how it is going about it, the Guide recommends that the following are provided:

(a) a brief summary of the charity's trusts;

(b) an explanation of how the charity is organised;

(c) details of, and reasons for, any major changes in aims or organisation since the last report.

(B) Review of progress and achievements

A brief summary of the charity's main achievements during the year in relation to its objects should be provided. This should show how the charity's work has developed towards fulfilling its aims, what progress has been made on any special projects and how the charity has responded to any important events of the year.

(C) Review of financial activities and affairs

As regards the review of the financial activities and affairs, the Guide recommends that the following information is disclosed insofar as it is applicable:

(a) a review of any major cash or non-cash transactions, showing how the charity's activities have been financed;

(b) any important events which have occurred since the year end;

(c) where available, figures demonstrating the impact the charity is making. (Note: The Guide suggests numbers of beneficiaries helped, calls on the charity's services etc., compared with the estimated number of those in need and the charity's existing capacity to help);

(d) in order to pursue its work, the extent of the charity's reliance on the future continuance of any substantial voluntary help, gifts-in-kind, unquantifiable free facilities or services received by the charity during the year;

(e) a review of the trading performance of any subsidiary company;

(f) if the charity has any substantial liabilities, obligations or commitments, a review of the adequacy and availability of its cash and non-cash resources to meet them;

(g) a list of any assets mortgaged as security for a loan or other liability. The amount of the loan outstanding at the year end should also be given and compared with the current value of the assets mortgaged;

(h) brief particulars, with names of recipients, of any grants of cash or other assets to the value of £1,000 or more made in the year to institutions (including other charities);

(i) if there have been any transactions with connected persons, an explanation of the nature of the relationships and a description of the transactions;

(j) any payments (including repayments of expenses) made to the trustees out of the charity's funds or by connected persons;

(k) any trustee indemnity insurance premiums paid from the charity's funds;

(l) the total of any *ex gratia* payments made by the charity, i.e., where the trustees believe that they are under a moral obligation but cannot justify the payment as being within the charity's objects. The trustees should confirm that any necessary authority, e.g., an Order of the Commissioners, has been received and provide the date on which it was given;

(m) where the charity acts as custodian trustee:
  - details of any assets for which it is responsible;
  - the name and aims of the charity concerned;
  - particulars of any special arrangements made for segregation and safe custody of the assets; and
  - how this activity furthers its own objects.

Other than (m), these disclosures are additional to those required by statute and allow a reader to understand better the charity's work.

The Guide states that disclosures in (g), (h), (j), (k) and (l) are only to be provided in the annual report 'if not disclosed in the accounts or explanatory notes'.

Change in accounting basis

For each year in which the charity changes from accruals accounts to receipts and payments accounting or vice versa, the corresponding amounts for the previous financial year should be restated on the basis of the new accounting policy.

19.5 Accruals accounting for the smaller charity

The Commissioners also published a further publication *Accruals accounting for the smaller charity*, for those unincorporated charities which:

(a) have gross income of not more than £100,000 for a financial year;
(b) do not have branches or investment assets.

This publication lifts those parts from the 1995 SORP which are likely to be of relevance to these charities when they choose to prepare their accounts on the accruals rather than the receipts and payments basis. Again, this publication continues to be of relevance to the smaller charity which wishes to prepare accruals accounts.

19.6 The application of the Financial Reporting Standard for Smaller Entities (FRSSE)

Any charity (whether or not it is a company) which is under the thresholds for small companies as described in the Companies Acts can follow the Financial Reporting Standard for Smaller Entities (FRSSE) in preparing its financial accounts except where it conflicts with this SORP in which case this SORP should be followed. Where consolidated accounts or receipts and payments accounts are produced smaller entities cannot follow the FRSSE in preparation of their accounts.

In following the FRSSE the accounts will meet most of the requirements of the SORP for such entities. They will, however, have to include a Statement of Financial Activities in place of a profit and loss account and statement of total recognised gains and losses, and adopt the principles of fund accounting throughout the accounts. This will include appropriate descriptions of the funds and notes showing the composition of the funds and the differentiation of funds on the balance sheet. Charities which follow another SORP or have to prepare additional accounts in a format required by other bodies, such as HM Treasury, may find that they cannot follow the FRSSE for these purposes.

In addition the following specific points must be followed:

(a) all investments including investment properties must be shown at market value;

(b) those foreign exchange gains and losses which may be allowed to be taken to reserves (as prescribed in the FRSSE) must be shown in the bottom of the Statement of Financial Activities; and

(c) those exceptional items which are required to be shown after operating profit must be shown in an appropriate place on the Statement of Financial Activities.

19.7 Charities with gross income not exceeding £250,000 (England and Wales)

Charities with gross income not exceeding £250,000 preparing accounts on the accruals basis do not have to use the expenditure headings and subheadings set out in para 60 of the SORP. They may choose expenditure classifications to suit their circumstances (e.g., salaries and wages, office costs, repairs and maintenance, etc).

Chapter 20 – Risk management

20.1 Introduction

The requirement for charities to confirm in the trustees' report that they have identified the major risks to which the charity is exposed, and that systems are in place to mitigate them was introduced in chapters **5** and **6**. This disclosure requirement is possibly the most significant change in SORP 2000 and this chapter explains further the issues that trustees' should consider when managing risk. The chapter also explains why risk management is an important issue for charities.

20.2 Why risk management?

Responding to risk is something that all organisations, including charities and other non-profit organisations, are doing on a daily basis, at one level or another. But how do organisations know that these responses, whether through individual or collective efforts, are complete, appropriate and effective?

Dictionary definitions describe risk as 'a chance or possibility of danger, loss, injury or other adverse consequences'. Being 'at risk' means being exposed to danger or loss. These definitions reinforce the widely held perception that risk has primarily negative connotations.

Risk is being used increasingly in the context of the business environment to refer to real and potential events which reduce the likelihood of an organisation achieving its business objectives. Business objectives can be threatened through opportunities not being spotted or gains not being maximised, as well as things going wrong. This introduces an important upside to risk as it includes the potential for reward, opportunities and change.

Risk management is about containing/minimising the downside and exploiting the upside/opportunities. It is about taking risks knowingly rather than by mistake and without due care.

The 'wheel' diagram, below, suggests some of the factors which interlink to form a credible starting point for effective risk management. Fundamental to the process is the development of a critical risk register based around the charity's key objectives.

280

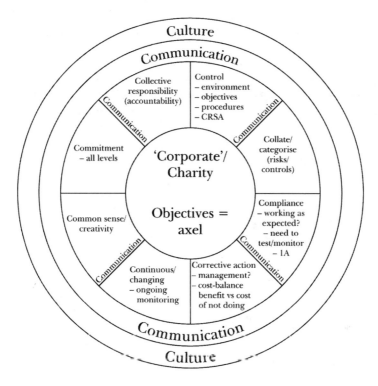

20.3 Charity objectives

Central to the risk management process, and the 'hub' of the wheel, are the charity's objectives. In order to identify the risks the charity faces there is a prerequisite to understand what it is trying to achieve. Connecting the management of the charity and the achievement of its objectives to the management of the risks threatening these objectives is necessary to ensure that the process is relevant, effective and sustainable.

20.4 Critical risk register

Once the charity's objectives have been made explicit, the process of identifying the threats to their achievement, or 'risks', can begin. The board of trustees should be able to formally identify the significant risks faced by the charity, or at least review and endorse the process by which they have been identified. The trustees should also be able to show that they are aware of such risks and that they have thought about how they may evolve.

One way to do this is to develop a 'Critical Risk Register'. The precise format the Register takes will depend on the needs and nature of the organisation

281

concerned. It is more likely to be used on an ongoing basis if it is con-structed as a user friendly, practical and straightforward document.

It is important that at this level the risks are not defined too narrowly. A thought-provoking, if not uncomfortable, starting point might be to think about what sort of events keep the trustees 'awake at night', or what sort of headlines would be a disaster for the charity if reported in the press. It may also be helpful to think about the near misses (or actual misses) of the past – either in relation to the charity or to others in a similar position. Think about the actual or potential losses made (not necessarily just financial), as well as instances when opportunities were spotted and taken.

A key risk for a children's charity, for example, might be the infiltration of a paedophile in terms of the actual danger posed to children and the damage to the charity's reputation. Similarly, the risk of sensitive infor-mation about vulnerable service users and potential or actual offenders getting into the wrong hands would also pose a significant concern. A risk to a health trust may be the employment of a bogus surgeon. In these examples, the financial risks are not paramount although there would clearly be financial implications.

20.5 Collate, prioritise and categorise

The ability to prioritise and focus on the important and the likely risks is key to critical risk management. For each risk identified, there should be a balanced assessment of the probability of its occurrence and its impact on the charity should it materialise. Categorising the risks into 'high', 'medium' or 'low' may be enough as long as there is a clear, shared under-standing by the Board on what is and is not acceptable.

It is important to remain focused on the significant risks and not to get dis-tracted, therefore the charity should only be concerned at this stage with those risks which threaten the achievement of the high-level objectives identified in the first stage of the exercise.

There are various ways of classifying risks – for example, by function within the charity ('Fundraising', 'Personnel' etc) or by category (strategic, oper-ational, regulatory, financial). The categories the charity chooses must be relevant and clearly defined – classifying by function may be the easiest way initially but it is important to ensure that cross-functional risks are not missed. The charity may decide that the classification is not as important as being able to show how the rules relate to the charity's objectives.

At this stage, it should be assumed that there are no or only very weak con-trols in place – effectively the charity may want to prioritise the 'gross risk'.

20.6 Controls

Having identified and prioritised the 'gross' risk, it is important to review the control processes the charity has in place which prevent the risks occurring in the first place, and those which mitigate the impact of the risks should they occur. At this level, it is important to identify the strength of the overall control environment, before diving into the lower level detail of the individual controls and processes themselves.

Assessing the strength of the perceived controls on a high, medium and low basis should be a good starting point, again as long as these terms are defined and clearly understood. Once the key elements of the internal control system have been identified and evaluated, it is then possible to arrive at a 'net' or 'residual' risk position.

At this point, the charity should have the basis of an effective critical risk register, which identifies the main threats (risks) to the achievement of the charity's objectives and links these to the main control processes which are already in place. But this is only the starting point.

20.7 Continuity and change

The trustees will need to know that the risks are being managed on an ongoing basis and that the controls identified continue to operate effectively and as expected.

The environment in which the charity is operating is changing, so are the risks it faces. For example, how will the charity ensure that risks previously categorised as non-critical ones remain that way, and that no new ones have emerged? The type and level of risk the trustees are prepared to accept may change over time depending on external factors as well as the charity's 'appetite' for risk. The nature or effectiveness of the controls may also change as staff move on or processes become more streamlined or technological.

The review process needs to be clearly defined in terms of, for example, the scope and frequency of reviews, who should perform them, the nature of reporting and the actions which will be taken to address the findings.

The trustees may find that they need an independent function such as internal audit to assist in these reviews. The need for this, whether in-house or outsourced, should be periodically reviewed.

The use of Control Risk Self Assessment (CRSA) techniques which involve staff at all levels in identifying and managing risk in their own areas may also be considered as a way of helping to ensure that the risk management process is effective at an operational level.

20.8 Commitment and responsibility

Effective risk management relies on the commitment of the trustees, management and staff at all levels. Trustees should expect to set the scene and demonstrate commitment to drive the risk management process. The key is to get people involved. Different contributions can be valuable in ensuring that there is awareness of issues facing others as well as of the cumulative effect. This is one of the benefits of introducing a CRSA process.

An effective ongoing risk management process also depends on the clear allocation of responsibilities and accountability – of the board, management, other employees, and internal audit (if relevant). The key is to ensure that the respective roles and responsibilities are properly aligned and are agreed and understood.

20.9 Communication

Communication throughout the risk management process is paramount. For example, some of the key matters which may need to be actively defined communicated and discussed are:

- Agreement of the charity's objectives.
- Is there adequate information being communicated about the objectives and the risks?
- Is it timely, relevant and reliable communication? Does it look at the future and not just review the past?
- What about communication should things go wrong?
- Authority, roles and responsibility and accountability to ensure that people understand what is expected of them. Clearly define these so they are not misinterpreted.
- The Board should make it clear what its risk management expectations are – of itself, of management and other staff and internal audit – in relation to identifying, evaluating, monitoring and reporting of risk

The charity may also want to communicate with its stakeholders and users – whether in the initial stages of risk identification or later into the process when the charity wants to highlight the positive steps that it is taking in relation to risk management. It is important, however, not to get distracted by specific requests and issues and to keep a balanced perspective.

20.10 Creativity

An example of a risk register page has deliberately not been presented in this chapter as the key to its success is for each charity to find something which works for them. Factors have been highlighted which are instrumental in making the process work, without being precise about the output itself. It is up to each organisation concerned to adapt these, be creative and come up with something relevant and appropriate for its own circumstances – something which works and which captures the essence of the organisation – its passion, its objectives and its work.

There will be elements of judgement, disagreements, perception – this is all part of the art of risk management. It is important to capture the spirit of risk management and make it more than merely another set of procedures.

20.11 Costs

There will be a cost to this process, particularly in terms of people's time. However, this needs to be weighed up against the cost of not doing anything – and also the fact that additional opportunities and rewards may not otherwise be identified. The charity may also find that, when identifying the controls relevant to the critical risks, it uncovers processes occurring which are unnecessary. Savings may be made in resources or staff time.

20.12 Culture

Whatever the precise way that is employed to manage risk, it needs to fit with the culture of the organisation, and also to become part of that culture. If the process does not take account of this then the risk management process will not go anywhere. The better the process is aligned to the culture of the organisation, the less bumpy the ride will be.

Ultimately then this means that the risk management activities should be incorporated into the charity's normal management and governance processes and not be seen as exercises divorced from what the charity is trying to achieve. Do not underestimate the cultural change which may be required, or the 'people issues'.

20.13 Common sense

One of the factors to successful risk management is to keep the process simple and straightforward. For example, use existing systems where possible and formalise processes which may already be occurring. Harness existing knowledge, expertise and information. Charities do not necessarily have to start with a blank sheet of paper – they must assess where they are now. At least initially, they should concentrate on the significant risks, keep the register relevant to the activities of the charity and keep it up to date. It should be more than a box-ticking exercise but it is important that initiative is not stifled.

20.14 Conclusion

The ideas presented in this chapter should provide a challenging and practical starting point for any organisation to embark on effective risk management.

It is important that there is a response to risk – just because a charity may not want to actively identify the key risks facing the organisation does not mean that they are not there. The process is called risk management, not risk elimination – it will not necessarily make the risks go away but, performed properly, the exercise should enable a more informed response to them. Risk identification and management should be viewed positively and real benefits sought, such as the identification and maximisation of opportunities. The process should assist the achievement of the charity's objectives – more efficiently or quickly – and not be a hindrance.

Unfortunately, it will not stop poor human judgement, human error, deliberate circumvention of procedures, management override and unforeseen circumstances, but it should help the charity to anticipate these, detect them quickly and at least mitigate the effects.

The Charity Commission have issued further detailed guidance on risk replacement.

Annex – 'Charities' case study – risk assessment review

Charities, by their very nature, often operate in inherently 'risky' areas. They are the organisations which tend to deal in the areas which private and commercial sectors shy away from – for example, working with the minorities, the homeless, the abused, or those in care and rehabilitation. Charities often represent the under-privileged or those people, or animals, which need someone to lobby on their behalf. Or charities may be pursuing areas of medical research where the prospect of monetary return or profit is remote.

Our charity client approached the Risk Management Team at Chantrey Vellacott DFK to request assistance in identifying and assessing the critical risks it faced. The charity was proactive in realising that it operated in a risky environment – it wanted to understand and manage these risks knowingly, rather than be taken by surprise. The charity was also encouraged by a desire to follow perceived 'best practice' in the commercial sector. This need was underlined by the requirement in the revised Statement of Recommended Practice (SORP) 'Accounting and Reporting by Charities' for the Trustees to state that they have identified all major risks facing the charity, and that systems are in place to mitigate them. Our client also felt that it wanted independent confirmation that what it was doing to mitigate risks was sufficient, and that resources were being used effectively.

We worked with the charity to ensure that we fully understood its objectives and operations. We immersed ourselves on-site reading the charity's key documentation which gave us a valuable insight into its constitution, procedures, policies (or lack of), financial performance, future plans and strategy, threats and opportunities.

We knew that the risk review had to be more than a 'box-ticking' exercise – we had to demonstrate that it added value to the work of the charity, and was not yet another diversion of management time and resources. In order to achieve this, we linked the exercise closely into the charity's business plan. By identifying the key business objectives first, we were then able to highlight the key factors which could prevent the charity from achieving these objectives, that is, the risks. And it wasn't always negative events which we came across – there were also examples of areas which weren't being fully exploited – of opportunities, for example in areas of fundraising and e-Commerce, which were being overlooked.

The most valuable source of information for the risk review came from the people who worked in the charity – after all, they are the people who have the expert knowledge of the charity's operations on a day-to-day level. Our role was to extract and capture this information in one place through facilitating discussion groups and asking lots of questions. There were many benefits to this approach – for example, it brought staff together in the charity who did not usually liaise with each other, therefore encouraging the sharing of ideas, it helped mutual understanding of their roles and responsibilities, and it helped to identify risks which, although small in each individual functional area, were quite significant on a cumulative charity-wide scale.

Our team also shared its experience of similar organisations and highlighted a few areas which had not, until then, been considered, for example, certain regulatory risks. We analysed all the risks in terms of likelihood of occurrence, and the impact on the charity's operations. This then enabled us to identify the 'serious' areas, so that the charity could focus resources accordingly.

As well as identifying the main risks, we also identified the key systems and controls that the charity had in place to mitigate these risks. This came as a relief to some extent, after the previous, rather daunting focus on the risks. Sometimes these factors prevented the risk occurring in the first place; in some cases, controls were in place to mitigate the risk and in other instances the impact of the risk was transferred, for example, through the purchase of insurance. An added bonus was that we were also able to identify areas where there was too much control compared to the nature of the risk – areas where resource could be more effectively targeted to other areas of the business. Often we found that adequate systems were in place to mitigate the risks – the issue was, however, that management and the Trustees had often not connected the two, nor did they have sufficient processes in place to monitor that all was operating as they expected on an ongoing basis.

The main outcome of the exercise was a comprehensive risk register, structured around the key business objectives. It aligned the main systems and controls which were in place to mitigate or prevent the risks identified. We also highlighted areas for further thought, as well as suggesting improvements in overall monitoring and governance. We were keen to encourage the charity to maintain the momentum of the exercise – our documents were passed to the charity on disk for internal updating. We advised management and the Trustees on practical ways of monitoring the risks and controls, for example, through a Control Risk Self Assessment (CRSA) process, and through a form of internal audit function. We were also able to work with the participants to identify key 'risk indicators' – events, statistics or other information which could indicate when things were not quite right. After all, risks are always evolving and it is important that the assessment is kept up to date and that any new risks are captured and addressed on a timely basis.

Feedback we received praised the hands-on and user-friendly approach we took, and specifically commented on the effort we made to understand the charity's operations and tailor the outcome of the review to the charity's circumstances. Perhaps the most encouraging comment, however, was that the Trustees now feel confident that they understand the risks facing the charity and, whilst it is not possible or desirable to eliminate them completely, they are also confident that they are focusing the charity's resources effectively to address them.

Chapter 21 – Audit of charities

21.1 Introduction

The regulatory framework governing the audit of charities is more fully discussed in chapter **3**.

Audits of charities may only be carried out by registered auditors or other persons authorised by statute or to whom the Charity Commission may grant dispensation. When conducting audits, registered auditors are required to comply with Statements of Auditing Standards (SASs).

In conducting an audit of a charity, including that of an unincorporated charity whose gross income does not exceed £100,000 and where the accounts may be prepared on the receipts and payments basis, auditors should have regard both to the SASs, in general, and to Practice Note No 11 *The audit of charities* ('the Practice Note'), issued by the APB in October 1996, in particular. At the time of writing an Exposure Draft to revise the Practice Note was under discussion, and where appropriate, this chapter reflects changes proposed by the Exposure Draft.

As with all Practice Notes issued by the APB, their purpose is to assist auditors in applying Auditing Standards of general application to particular circumstances and industries. While the Practice Notes are persuasive, rather than prescriptive, they are indicative of good practice, even though they may have been developed without due process.

The Practice Note compares audit and independent examination. The detailed guidance on independent examination published by the Commissioners is discussed in chapter **22**.

21.2 The special audit features of charities

In planning and performing the audit of a charity, auditors should have regard to the special features of charities. These features have an impact upon the assessment of risk, upon the consideration of compliance with laws and regulations and the detailed collection of audit evidence, as well as the reporting of the results of the audit.

21.2.1 Trustees' responsibilities

Overall responsibility for the preparation and presentation of the trustees' report and the annual financial statements of an individual charity rests with the trustees. Trustees have responsibility for losses which the charity may incur from mismanagement of its funds, which can include supporting charitable projects which are outside the objects detailed in the charity's constitution or investing funds in investments not permitted by the constitution. The Charity Commission may take action against individual trustees, which can include disqualification from acting as trustee of any charity. Auditors must ensure that trustees of their charity clients fully understand their duties and responsibilities. Many trustees have traditionally seen their appointment as a mark of their support for the charity and therefore do not appreciate the full magnitude of their responsibilities. An effective audit service must include, where necessary, a process of trustee education to ensure that responsible controls and leadership is given.

21.2.2 Understanding the charity

Each charity is different and the forms of constitution can very widely through the sector. Understanding the client is therefore vital and a full permanent file is essential. SAS 210 *Knowledge of the business* refers to the importance of proper understanding of the activities, organisation and constitution of individual clients. In respect of charities, auditors should be particularly aware of:

- the constitution – which will come in many forms depending upon the original origins of the charity and charity's structure;
- the constitutionally defined objectives and investment powers;
- the accounting system and controls established by the charity;
- the operational structure of the charity and the nature of its relationship with branches, affiliated groups and other supporters; and
- the principal sources of income of the charity which may include fundraising activities which can be difficult to audit for completeness and trading activities which can give rise to threats to the taxation status of the charity.

21.2.3 Operating structures and branches

Where a charity undertakes activities through branches or other affiliated groups, rather than through a central structure, the accounting treatment is determined by the legal relationship between the various entities. If the branches come under the control of the trustees of the main charity, the SORP requires the branches to be accounted for in the financial statements of the main charity. Many charities have excluded branches from their accounts in the past, and therefore, they are now including them in the full financial statements for the first time.

The inclusion of branches in the financial statements gives rise to a series of audit problems. The aggregation may prove to be complex, including many small entities whose local treasurers may be difficult to contact and slow to complete and return the 'consolidation packs'. In total these branches may be material, and a process of review by rotation may be needed. This may impact upon the assessment of audit risk, and because of the implications for the level of audit work, upon the fee quotation.

If the charity has subsidiaries, then they must be consolidated. Similar considerations to the audit of branches apply. Charitable companies are not permitted to take advantage of the statutory exemption from preparing group accounts which apply to small and medium-sized companies. If the subsidiary undertakes trading or fund-raising activities, then difficulties in auditing the completeness of its income may impact upon the audit opinion given for the 'group' as a whole.

21.2.4 Sources of income

Many charities derive a significant proportion of their income from voluntary sources such as donations in the form of cash, cheques or kind. There is unlikely to be any supporting documentation to these sources of income and the pattern of income may be difficult to predict with any degree of accuracy.

Audit procedures which can be applied to test income for completeness and accuracy include placing reliance upon the control procedures implemented by the charity. Relevant controls may include post opening procedures to ensure that all cheques received are recorded or the strict controls that should be operated when a charity conducts a public collection. Some analytical procedures may be appropriate such as reviewing actual collections against expectations, budgets and prior years. If a charity tends to expend the funds it raises and historically maintains a low level of reserves, then matching expenditure to income may be an appropriate audit test.

Income generated by branches and other supporting groups may also be difficult to test for completeness and accuracy because of the lack of control of the main charity over the supporting group and variations in the fund-raising activities of individual groups. In this case, it is particularly important to review the charity's procedures for ensuring that funds are remitted by its supporters and that the charity's income recognition policy has been complied with.

21.2.5 Restricted funds

Charities may not use restricted funds for general purposes, and must separately disclose their funds in the financial statements. Misuse of restricted funds constitutes a breach of duty by the trustees. As a result auditors must give close attention to the presentation of restricted funds and the reporting of movements in these funds. Therefore, the normal principals of materiality do not apply when reviewing and testing restricted funds.

21.2.6 Trading activities

The existence of trading activities needs to be taken into account when planning the audit and the implications of any breaches in the taxation status of the charity must be considered. Charities may engage in primary purpose trading or trade for the purposes of raising funds. If, however, the charity is deemed to be trading for profit or engages in any trade which is contrary to charity law, or its constitutional objects, then its exemption from taxation may be questioned.

21.2.7 Whistleblowing

Auditors have a duty to report to the Charity Commission on any matters which they believe are of 'material significance' to the Commission. Usually, a matter is 'materially significant' if the actions of the trustees have put the funds of the charity at risk or are likely to put the funds at risk. Such matters would include, for example, the discovery of expenditure not in accordance with the trust deed, material weaknesses in the trustees' control over the charity's affairs or where insufficient explanations or records were available to enable the audit or examination to be completed satisfactorily. This arrangement is similar to those for other regulated bodies such as pension schemes and registered financial services entities.

No additional audit procedures need to be performed to seek to identify such matters. However, all staff involved in the audit need to be aware of this reporting responsibility, and the firm of auditors needs to have in place procedures for reporting and assessing matters which gave rise to concern and a possible need to 'whistleblow'.

21.2.8 Public interest

As a final consideration, the charity sector has a high public profile and an individual charity will typically receive greater public interest in its activities than would a similar sized trading activity. Charities handle large sums of monies given by the general public and receive generous taxation exemptions. Charities often receive grants and other allowances and must be seen to properly account for these. The auditors may receive unwelcome attention as a result of deficiencies which are identified in the accounts of a charity client, or because of general comments or concerns which arise regarding the activities of the charity. The audit of a charity has high risks attached to it in terms of public exposure and the importance of its proper conduct must be communicated to all members of the engagement team. Equally, of course, the importance of the auditors' duty of confidentiality, and the confidential nature of the procedures for 'whistleblowing' to the Charity Commissioners must also be emphasised.

21.3 Reporting requirements

The audit opinion of an unincorporated charity must explicitly state whether the accounts:

(a) are properly prepared in accordance with the requirements of the Charities Act 1993;
(b) give a true and fair view of the state of affairs at the year end and the incoming resources and application of the resources in the year.

If the charity is incorporated under the Companies Act 1985, the audit opinion must explicitly state whether the accounts:

(i) are properly prepared in accordance with the Companies Act 1985; and
(ii) give a true and fair view of the state of affairs at the year end and the incoming resources and application of the resources, including its income and expenditure, in the year.

The auditors of a charity, whether incorporated or unincorporated, must also report by exception if:

- proper accounting records have not been kept;
- accounts do not agree to the accounting records; or
- they have not received all the information or explanations that they require.

The reporting requirement is modified for an unincorporated charity which prepares receipts and payments accounts. In this case the auditor must explicitly report that:

- the receipts and payments account and the statement of assets and liabilities are properly prepared in accordance with the Charities Act 1993;
- the account and the statement adequately distinguish any material special trust or other restricted fund of the charity.

21.4 Terms of engagement

SAS 140 *Engagement Letters* states that the auditors and the client should agree on the terms of engagement, which should be recorded in writing. Therefore, written terms of engagement should be in existence for all charity audit clients, regardless of the charity's legal form.

The engagement letter should clearly summarise the responsibilities of the trustees and of the auditors, the scope of the engagement and the form of the reports to be given.

The particular characteristics of charities give rise to several considerations when setting out the terms of engagement.

Addressee

The engagement letter should be addressed to the authority within the charity who had the responsibility to appoint the auditor. Usually, for an unincorporated charity, this will be the trustees, although the auditors should review the constitution of the charity to confirm the appointing authority. The trustees should be asked to return to the auditors a signed copy of the letter which acknowledges their confirmation of the terms of engagement. If the trustees are not involved in the day-to-day management of the charity a copy of the letter should be sent to the persons who have this responsibility.

Scope of the audit

The engagement letter should state the legislation or regulations which govern the requirement for the charity to have an audit and should state which subsidiary or branches and funds of the charity fall within the scope of the audit.

Form of reports

An outline of the form of report to be given should be specified in the letter, together with the details of any other special report which the auditors are required to give. Such a report might arise when the charity is in receipt of special income such as government or local authority grants.

21.4.1 Example engagement letter for an unincorporated charity audit in England & Wales

(Accruals basis for accounts preparation is used)

This letter has been reproduced from Appendix 4 of Practice Note 11.

The Trustees

Charity

Dear Sirs

1 The purpose of this letter is to set out the basis on which we [are to] act as auditors of the charity and the respective areas of responsibility of the Trustees and of ourselves.

Audit

2 As trustees of the (above charity) you are responsible for ensuring that the charity maintains appropriate accounting records and for preparing financial statements which give a true and fair view and have been prepared in accordance with the Charities Act 1993 and regulations thereunder. You are also responsible for making available to us, as and when required, all of the charity's accounting records and all other relevant records and related information, including minutes of trustees' and meetings and of all appropriate management meetings.

3 As trustees of a charity, you are under a duty to prepare an annual report for each financial year complying in its form and content with regulations made under the Charities Act 1993. You are also required to have regard to the Statement of Recommended Practice 'Accounting by Charities', issued in October 2000 by the Charity Commissioners for England & Wales.

4 We have a statutory responsibility to report to you as trustees whether in our opinion the financial statements comply with the requirements of regulations made under the Charities Act 1993 and give a true and fair view of the state of affairs of the charity at the end of the financial year and of the incoming resources and application of the resources of the charity in that year. In arriving at our opinion, we are required to consider the following matters, and report on any in respect of which we are not satisfied:

4.1 whether accounting records have been kept by the [charity] in accordance with Section 41 of the Charities Act 1993;

4.2 whether the financial statements are in agreement with the accounting records;

4.3 whether we have obtained all the information and explanations to which we are entitled for the purpose of our audit;

4.4 whether the information in the trustees' statutory annual report is consistent with that in the financial statements.

5 In addition, there are certain other matters which, according to the circumstances, may need to be dealt with in our report. For example, non-compliance with a requirement of Regulations to be made under the Charities Act 1993.

Duty to report to Charity Commissioners

6 Under the Charities (Accounts and Reports) Regulations 2000 you are required to report as to whether you have given consideration to the major risks to which the charity is exposed, and to the systems designed to mitigate those risks. Compliance with the Charities SORP requires you to confirm that those risks have been reviewed and that systems have been established to mitigate those risks. We are not required to audit this statement, or to form an opinion on the effectiveness of the risk management and control procedures.

7 We have a statutory duty to report to the Charity Commissioners such matters (concerning the activities or affairs of the charity or any connected institution or body corporate) of which we become aware during the course of our audit which are (or are likely to be) of material significance to the Commissioners in the exercise of their powers of inquiry into, or acting for the protection of, charities (Regulation 6(5) The Charities (Accounts and Reports) Regulations 1995).

8 We have a professional responsibility to report if the financial statements do not comply in any material respect with applicable accounting standards, unless in our opinion the non-compliance is justified in the circumstances. In determining whether or not the departure is justified we consider:

8.1 whether the departure is required in order for the financial statements to give a true and fair view; and

8.2 whether adequate disclosure has been made concerning the departure.

9 Our professional responsibilities also include:

9.1 including in our report a description of the trustees' responsibilities for the financial statements where the financial statements or accompanying information do not include such a description; and

9.2 considering whether other information in documents containing audited financial statements is consistent with those financial statements.

Scope of audit

10 Our audit will be conducted in accordance with the Auditing Standards issued by the Auditing Practices Board, and will include such tests of transactions and of the existence, ownership and valuation of assets and liabilities as we consider necessary. We shall obtain an understanding of the accounting systems and internal controls in order to assess their adequacy as a basis for the preparation of the financial statements, and to establish whether appropriate accounting records have been maintained by the charity. We shall expect to obtain such relevant and reliable evidence as we consider sufficient to enable us to draw reasonable conclusions therefrom.

296

Reporting to the Council and Management

11 The nature and extent of our procedures will vary according to our assessment of the charity's accounting system and, where we wish to place reliance on it, the internal control system, and may cover any aspect of the charity's operations that we consider appropriate. Our audit is not designed to identify all significant weaknesses in the charity's systems but, if such weaknesses come to our notice during the course of our audit which we think should be brought to your attention, we shall report them to you. Any such report may not be provided to third parties without our prior written consent. Such consent will be granted only on the basis that such reports are not prepared with the interests of anyone other than the charity in mind and that we accept no duty or responsibility to any other party as concerns the reports.

Representations by management/trustees

12 As part of our normal audit procedures, we may request written confirmation of oral representations which we have received during the course of the audit on matters having a material effect on the financial statements.

Documents issued with the financial statements

13 In order to assist us with the examination of your financial statements, we shall request sight of all documents or statements, including the trustees' report, which are due to be issued with the financial statements. If it is proposed that any documents or statement which refer to our name, other than the audited financial statements, are to be circulated to third parties, please consult us before they are issued.

Irregularities, including fraud

14 The responsibility for the prevention and detection of fraud, error and non-compliance with law or regulations rests with yourselves. However, we shall endeavour to plan our audit so that we have a reasonable expectation of detecting material misstatements in the financial statements or accounting records (including those resulting from fraud, error or non-compliance with law or regulations), but our examination should not be relied upon to disclose all such material misstatements or frauds, errors or instances of non-compliance as may exist.

Other matters

15 (Where appropriate) We shall not be treated as having notice, for the purposes of our audit responsibilities, of information provided to members of our firm other than those engaged on the audit (for example, information provided in connection with accounting, taxation and other services).

16 Once we have issued our report we have no further direct responsibility in relation to the financial statements for that financial year. However, we expect that you will inform us of any material event occurring between the date of our report and that of the Annual General Meeting which may affect the financial statements.

Other services

17 You have requested that we provide other services in respect of .... The terms under which we provide these other services are dealt with in a separate letter. We will also agree in a separate letter of engagement the provision of any services relating to investment business advice as defined by the Financial Services Act 1986 (to be replaced by the Financial Services and Markets Act 2000).

Fees

18 Our fees are computed on the basis of the time spent on your affairs by the partners and our staff, and on the levels of skill and responsibility involved. Unless otherwise agreed, our fees will be billed at appropriate intervals during the course of the year and will be due on presentation.

Applicable law

19 This engagement letter shall be governed by, and construed in accordance with, [English] law. The Courts of [England] shall have exclusive jurisdiction in relation to any claim, dispute or difference concerning the engagement letter and any matter arising from it. Each party irrevocably waives any right it may have to object to an action being brought in those Courts, to claim that the action has been brought in an inconvenient forum, or to claim that those Courts do not have jurisdiction.

Agreement of terms

20 Once it has been agreed, this letter will remain effective from one audit appointment to another until it is replaced. We should be grateful if you would confirm in writing your agreement to these terms, [either by acknowledging it or] by signing and returning the enclosed copy of this letter, or let us know if they are not in accordance with your understanding of our terms of engagement.

Yours faithfully

....

Auditors

We agree to the terms of this letter.

....

Signed, for and on behalf of Charity   Date

....

Position

Alternative paragraphs where the charity is based in England & Wales, is unincorporated and prepares accounts on a receipts and payments basis

1 Para 3: In accordance with the Charities Act 1993 Section 42(3), where the charity's gross income in any financial year does not exceed £100,000, the charity's trustees may elect to prepare a receipts and payments account and a statement of assets and liabilities [as its annual statement of accounts]. [You have elected to prepare such an account and statement.]

2 References in paragraphs 4, 9, 10 and 12 of the letter will be to the 'account and statement' rather than to 'statement of account/financial statement'.

3 The reference in paragraph 4 to the consistency of the trustees' annual report to the financial statements will be dropped.

4 The statutory requirement for the auditor to report if the financial statements do not comply with applicable accounting standards does not apply, so paragraph 7 is dropped.

Alternative paragraphs where the charity is incorporated under the Companies Act 1985

1 Para 1: The first paragraph can refer to 'charitable company' rather than 'charity', and the first reference to 'Trustees' is followed in brackets by the words 'being company directors'.

The numbered paragraphs are changed as follows:

2 Para 2: As directors of the above charitable company, you are responsible for ensuring that the company maintains proper accounting records and for preparing financial statements which give a true and fair view and have been prepared in accordance with the Companies Act 1985 [in the case of charities incorporated under other legislation, the reference will be to the applicable legislation]. You are responsible for making available to us, as and when required, all the company's accounting records and all other relevant records and related information, including minutes of meetings of members, trustees and management.

3 Para 3: The reference in paragraph 3 is to 'charitable company' rather than charity, but the obligations to prepare an annual report complying in the form and content with the Charities 1995 Regulations are the same. The accounts of all charitable companies and audit report which are annexed to the annual report are prepared in accordance with the Companies Act 1985.

4 Para 4: We have a statutory responsibility to report to the members whether in our opinion the financial statements give a true and fair view and whether they have been properly prepared in accordance with the Companies Act 1985. In arriving at our opinion, we are required to consider the following matters, and to report on any in respect of which we are not satisfied:

4.1 whether proper accounting records have been kept by the company and proper returns adequate for our audit have been received from branches not visited by us;

4.2 whether the company's balance sheet and income and expenditure account are in agreement with the accounting records and returns;

4.3 whether we have obtained all the information and explanations which we consider necessary for the purposes of our audit; and

4.4 whether the information given in the trustees' annual report (directors' report) is consistent with the financial statements.

5 Para 5: In addition, there are certain other matters which, according to the circumstances, may need to be dealt with in our report. For example, where the financial statements do not give details of directors' remuneration or other their transactions with the company, the Companies Act 1985 requires us to disclose such matters in our report.

There is no statutory duty for auditors of charitable companies to report to the Charity Commissioners. However, auditors may wish to refer to the possibility that circumstances may arise that will cause them to report to an appropriate authority in the public interest.

6 Paras 10 to 16: These paragraphs on the scope of the audit are replaced by the wording in paragraphs 2.1 to 2.7 from the example engagement letter in the appendix to SAS 140.

21.5 Audit planning

21.5.1 Features of charity audits

When planning the audit of a charity, auditors should consider the following special features of their client and how these features may affect their audit approach:

(a) existence of special regulations governing the conduct of charities;

(b) sources of income which may include grants from public authorities or funds held on trust. Breaches of the conditions relating to the use of such income can have serious implications for the charity;

(c) tax relief dependent upon the charity complying with the governing document submitted to the Inland Revenue;

(d) activities of the charity which bring it within the scope of other regulations as well as those relating to charities;

(e) the level of involvement in the administration of the charity which can be expected of (typically unpaid) trustees; and

(f) the way in which the charity is managed on a day to day basis (for example, systems within the organisation for controlling income, expenditure and staff resources).

21.5.2 The regulatory framework

At the planning stage of the audit, the auditors must ascertain and understand the law and regulations under which the client operates, and be aware of any changes in these since the last audit. The form of law and regulations under which the charity operates will influence both the charity's reporting responsibilities and the duties of the auditor.

21.5.3 The operations of the charity

The auditors must then undertake and review the details of the charity's activities and organisation, as this is essential for assessing the risk of misstatement arising from potential fraud, error or non-compliance with the relevant law and regulations. Information can be built up from sources within the charity such as minutes, budgets and plans, and procedures manuals, and from external sources such as specialist publications and information providers.

21.5.4 The structures of the charity

The reporting structures of the charity and the resulting audit approach will be determined by the legal form that the charity has adopted for its operations. The main structures which could be adopted are:

(a) groups, in which activities are conducted by separate legal entities which are controlled by the charity;

(b) associated undertakings, where the charity has a participating interest in the other undertaking and exercises a significant degree of influence over its operations;

(c) operations conducted by a separate administrative entity such as a sub-committee of the charity which does not have a separate legal identity from the charity itself;

(d) 'sub-contracting' by the charity of its activities to non-controlled organisations; and

(e) branches.

21.5.5 Groups

When planning the audit of a charity which has a group structure, the auditors must ascertain if audits of the members of the charity's group are to be performed and whether they or another firm has been engaged to perform the audits which are required. If the results or financial position of the other members of the group are material in relation to the principal charity, the auditors must determine the level of evidence which they require to support their opinion on the group accounts from the auditors of the members of the group, and issue written instructions to those auditors setting out the information and reports which are required.

21.5.6 Branches

A branch of a charity may or may not be a separate legal entity. It may be either a part, either geographical or functional, of the overall operation of the charity or it may be a separate legal entity which for accounting purposes requires to be grouped with the main charity. The SORP requires the main charity to prepare accounts which aggregate (i.e.,consolidate) its results, assets and liabilities with those of its branches. The auditors must plan their procedures to ensure that they are able to conclude that proper returns have been received from the branches which they have not visited. Usually, the auditors will visit, by rotation, a number of the branches of the charity to review branch transactions and procedures.

If the branch is a separate legal entity, then although aggregation is required, it must also prepare separate accounts and receive an audit or independent examination if its income or expenditure falls within the relevant qualification bands.

21.5.7 Overseas operations

If the charity has overseas operations, the auditors must, as part of their planning, ensure that they have a clear understanding of the relationship between the overseas operation and the main charity. If the overseas operation constitutes a separate legal entity which is controlled by the main charity, consolidated accounts should be prepared which incorporate the charity and its overseas operation. If the overseas operation constitutes a branch, its results and financial position should be aggregated together with those of the main charity. If grants or donations are paid to a local entity, then it is unlikely that a branch or subsidiary relationship arises.

21.6 Materiality

SAS 220 makes a distinction between the auditors'consideration of materiality in planning the audit, and that at the time of evaluating the results of audit procedures. The assessment of materiality at the planning stage determines the nature, timing and extent of audit tests. The materiality of matters found in the course of audit work is considered both in relation to their possible impact on the financial statements, and in relation to applicable regulations and other factors governing the conduct of individual charities. If the auditor is engaged to make additional reports, for example in respect of restricted grants, it will be appropriate for the auditors to make a separate assessment of materiality specifically for the purposes of such additional engagements.

Where a charity operates through branches or subsidiaries, their contribution to the result and financial position of the charity may not be known at the time of planning the audit. In this case, the auditors consider how to decide the likely results of branches or subsidiaries by reference to procedures such as:

- discussion with management;
- consideration of problems or particular issues encountered in previous years to see whether there is an identifiable pattern suggestive of weak management or fraud, for example;
- consideration of prior year figures; and
- any budgeted or preliminary results;

and incorporate the resulting best estimate into the materiality calculation for the audit as a whole.

Often, a split materiality figure is appropriate for the audit of a charity because of the different magnitude of current income and expenditure reported in the SOFA and fixed assets and investments presented on the balance sheet.

Restricted funds

Many charities may receive funds which are subject to specific trusts, which must be accounted for separately (unless grouped together if, individually, they are comparatively small) in accordance with the Charities SORP. It is not necessary in every case to set a different monetary materiality level for such funds: however, SAS 220 indicates that materiality may be influenced by considerations such as legal and regulatory requirements, which may result in different materiality consideration being applied to particular aspects of the financial statements. Auditors therefore consider whether this is appropriate when planning the nature and extent of their work in relation to restricted funds. Any breaches of the terms of trusts relating to restricted funds which come to the auditors' attention in the course of their work, regardless of materiality to the financial statements as a whole, need to be considered in terms of their significance to the auditors' report on the financial statements and brought to the attention of trustees, as a failure on their part to comply with the terms of trusts may place them in breach of their responsibilities.

21.7 Consideration of laws and regulations

SAS 120 requires auditors to be alert for instances of possible or actual non-compliance with law or regulations. In the case of charities, relevant laws and regulations include trust law, and hence specific requirements as to the use of restricted funds and preservation of any permanent endowments (capital funds).

The regulatory framework relevant to the operations of a charity can be divided into the following categories:

1. those relating directly to the preparation of the charity's financial statements, or the inclusion or disclosure of specific items in the financial statements;
2. those which relate to the independent audit or review of the charity's financial statements;
3. those which provide a legal framework within which the charity conducts its activities and which are central to the charity's ability to conduct its activities.

Auditors need to be aware of the regulatory framework applicable to each charity that they act for. Details of the framework should be recorded on the permanent file and the implications of regulatory changes must be considered. The auditors must consider the implications of any regulatory breach that they become aware of upon the financial statements, the audit opinion and whether a whistleblowing duty arises.

The regulatory structure of a charity is determined by its own constitution and by conditions imposed upon it by statute, regulators, the courts and other third parties.

21.7.1 Charity governing documents

In addition to the external regulations which govern the activities of a charity, the charity's own governing documents will define the objects of the charity and the powers and responsibilities of its trustees. The documents may contain special provisions as to the disclosure of information in the financial statements or extend the reporting requirements of the auditors.

The charity's governing documents are extended by any subsequent will, trust or other instruction, which imposes a restriction upon any present or future funds of the charity.

21.7.2 Laws relating directly to the preparation of the financial statements

As part of their audit, auditors must ensure that the charity is presenting its financial statements in accordance with the reporting regulations and the SORP, as well as any special reporting requirements imposed by the charity's own governing documents. Normally this is evidenced by the use of a disclosure checklist together with a file note explaining how compliance with any special requirements has been checked.

Auditors should also check whether charities' governing documents contain any special provisions as to the disclosure of information in the financial statements or reporting requirements for the auditors. Users of the financial statements of a charity reasonably expect that the transactions recorded within them are authorised by the governing document of the charity and in furtherance of the charity's objects. In order to give a true and fair view, due regard needs to be given to disclosure of any non-compliance with the governing document.

Auditors therefore familiarise themselves with charities' governing documents and in planning and conducting their audit:

- ensure that their audit procedures cover compliance with the governing document;
- consider any changes in the charity's activities proposed by the trustees to ensure that these comply with the governing document; and
- are alert to new or unusual transactions which may not be in accordance with the governing document.

21.7.3 Laws and regulations central to the charity's conduct of its business

SAS 120.3 requires auditors to carry out specified steps to help identify possible or actual instances of non-compliance with those laws and regulations which fall into the category of those central to the entity's ability to conduct its business.

Laws and regulations which are central to the charity's ability to conduct its activities are those where:

(a) compliance is a prerequisite of obtaining a licence to operate; or
(b) non compliance may reasonably be expected to result in the charity ceasing operation, or call into question its status as a going concern.

If these laws and regulations are breached, the following consequences may arise:

(i) appointment by the Charity Commission of a receiver and manager (due to primary breaches of laws and regulations applying to charities generally);
(ii) loss of necessary licences to continue a major element of the charity's work;
(iii) financial effects resulting in liabilities which are likely to exceed the available resources of the charity.

Examples of laws which apply to the activities of charities include:

- laws on raising funds through lotteries, including betting, gambling, lotteries and amusements legislation;
- laws relating to the generation of income by commercial and professional fundraisers;
- laws relating to the generation of income through house-to-house or street collections;
- The Trustees Investment Act 1961 (to be replaced by the Trustee Act 2000).

Specific regulations which apply to the operations of individual charities would include:

- Children Act requirements in respect of day care or respite care;
- Registered Homes Act requirements in respect of nursing homes;
- clinical waste requirements under the Environmental Protection Act and its implications for hospitals and hospices;
- food safety and hygiene regulations and their implications for residential care homes, village halls and community buildings.

Breaches of laws and regulations which apply to a particular type of activity may also result in fines, the financial consequences of which may, in particular instances, be significant. Severe financial consequences may also arise from failure to comply with grant conditions or taxation law.

Compliance with grant conditions
Charities receiving grants of public funds (including lottery funds) are normally required to meet certain specific conditions. Expenditure outside grant conditions can lead to disallowance and repayment. Such conditions might include for example, the requirement to produce audited accounts regardless of the size of the charity.

Compliance with taxation law
Charities are exempt from tax on most (but not all) types of income and on capital gains, provided the income and capital gains are applicable, and are applied to, qualifying charitable purposes. There is, however, no general exemption from VAT for charities.

21.8 Accounting systems

The auditors are required by SAS 300 *Accounting and internal control systems and audit risk assessments* to obtain an understanding of the accounting and internal control systems sufficient to enable them to plan the audit and develop an effective audit approach.

The trustees of a charity must then determine the extent of the internal control systems which are appropriate for the charity. However an effective control system is important because the trustees have a duty to protect the property of the charity and to secure its application in accordance with the objects of the charity. If the trustees fail to protect the charity's property, they may be personally liable for any loss which the charity suffers.

21.8.1 Reports on the internal controls

Certain charities (for example, those which are also registered friendly societies), are subject to specific reporting requirements in respect of internal controls. In such cases, the auditors should plan their audit to enable them to give an opinion that there is a satisfactory system of control over transactions.

21.8.2 The control environment

Although the nature of the control environment will vary between charities depending upon their size, and the nature of their operations, the features detailed below are likely to exist in an effective control environment of any charity.

21.8.3 The smaller charity

Smaller charities are unlikely to have a formal system of internal control and their internal procedures are likely to lack features such as segregation of duties and may be performed by staff who lack training or relevant qualifications. Volunteers may be involved with the control system of the charity and may resent the imposition of formal procedures or direction by the trustees. In such an environment, the auditors may be unable to place formal reliance on the control system and may also identify a risk that they will not be able to obtain adequate assurance as to the completeness of the transactions of the charity. This risk may be addressed by placing reliance on the close involvement of the trustees in reviewing or supervising the activities of the charity.

21.8.4 Examples of control

The examples given below illustrate the types of internal control that should be expected to be present in most charities, although the practical application would, of course, vary depending upon the size, structure, and special characteristics of the individual charity.

The examples are indicative of steps that can be taken by trustees rather than providing a comprehensive list of controls: the basic measures will be adapted and extended as necessary by trustees to fit the circumstances of different charities.

(a) Donations – collecting boxes and tins.
   - Numerical control over collecting boxes and tins.
   - Satisfactory sealing of boxes and tins so that any opening prior to recording is apparent.
   - Regular collection and recording of proceeds from collecting boxes.
   - Dual control over counting and recording of proceeds.

(b) Donations – postal and cash.
   - Dual control over the opening of mail.
   - Immediate recording of donations on the opening of mail or receipt of cash.

(c) Donations in kind.
   - All types of activity: immediate recording of donated assets.

(d) Deed of covenant.
   - Regular checks and follow-up procedures to ensure due amounts are received.
   - Regular checks to ensure all tax repayments have been obtained.

(e) Legacies.
   - Comprehensive correspondence files maintained in respect of each legacy, numerically controlled.
   - Search agency reports of legacies receivable.
   - Regular reports and follow-up procedures undertaken in respect of outstanding legacies.

(f) Fundraising activities.
   - Records maintained for each fundraising event.
   - Comparable controls maintained over receipts as for normal donations.
   - Comparable controls maintained over expenses as for administrative expenses.

(g) Central and local government grants and loans.
   - Regular checks that all sources of income or funds are fully exploited and appropriate claims made.
   - Ensuring income or funds are correctly applied in accordance with the terms of the grant or loan.
   - Comprehensive records of applications made and follow-up procedures for those not discharged.

(h) Branches.
   - Any branch, office or individual representative of the charity should make regular reports or returns to the charity, and checks should be made to ensure that all these are received.
   - Any report of the misuse of the charity's name should be promptly investigated.
   - Wherever the trustees of the charity have direct control over the branches, internal controls should be of equivalent standard to those of the main charity.
   - Consideration of an accounts manual and the standardisation of procedures at all branches.

- Proper acknowledgements of remittances to and from abroad.
- Clarity of instructions and guidelines as to receipt and transfer of income to identify the point at which it belongs to the main charity.

(i) Fixed assets (including investments).
- A register of fixed assets, including donated assets.
- Donated assets recorded at approximate market value, where appropriate.
- Depreciation calculated and recorded as for commercial enterprises.
- Authority for purchase of investments and safe custody of documents of title.

(j) Specific funds – records maintained of the following.
- Separate revenue and assets.
- Terms controlling application of fund moneys.
- Application of fund moneys.

(k) Grants to beneficiaries.
- Records maintained of all requests for material grants received and their treatment.
- Checks made of the *bona fides* of applicants for substantial grants, and that amounts paid are *intra vires*.
- Minutes maintained of all Grants Committee Meetings with records of decisions made including the recording of conflicts of interest.
- Adequate documentation given to the committee for them to base their decision on the accurate facts.

(l) Bank records (in small charities the following controls will have particular significance).
- Prompt banking of receipts.
- Independent agreement of banking records to receipts records.
- Regular bank reconciliations.
- Adequate arrangements for bank signatories.
- Controls operated by banks/building societies over the opening of new accounts.

(m) Overseas operations. The responsibilities of charity trustees to maintain appropriate controls apply equally to all the operations of the charity, wherever they are carried out. However, trustees will need to adapt internal controls to the circumstances of specific overseas operations. Appropriate internal controls for overseas operations include the following.
- Controls over recruitment and appointment of staff to run overseas operations.
- Defined authorisation limits and responsibilities for local staff in ordering and paying for goods and services.
- Periodic, summary returns to the charity's head office and a mechanism for monitoring branch activities, for example by comparison of expenditure to budget.

Where the charity makes grants for charitable purposes (for example to other charities or to individuals) in accordance with its objects, the auditors must consider what controls are operated by the charity to ensure that the money is properly spent for the specified purpose. The charity may attach conditions to the grant, such as a requirement for the recipient to make a return, with supporting documentation or auditors' report, of expenditure. The need for the trustees or professional management of the charity to make and enforce such conditions depends on the materiality of the grants made. Where a charity's activities include the making of a number of grants which are immaterial individually, but amount to a material sum in aggregate, controls instituted by it could be expected to include a set format for applications, including proof of need. Charities should also have in place systems for monitoring grants to other bodies including, where appropriate, visits to such bodies on a rotating basis. This will enable trustees to discharge their duty to ensure that grants are used for the purposes intended.

Where the system of controls appears to be weak or where breaches of internal rules or procedures have occurred and have not been corrected, the auditors should consider the implications. The auditors may need to report these matters to the trustees, the management, or relevant external authorities.

21.9 Audit risk

When developing their audit approach auditors are required to assess the risk of misstatement of material account balances and classes of transactions, whether arising from the characteristics of the charity as a whole or the characteristics of the individual balances or class of transactions.

Certain features of charities may increase the risk of fraud or error. These include:

- the complexity and extent of regulation;
- the significance of donations and cash receipts;
- the extent of donations over the internet or by credit card;
- difficulties of the charity in establishing ownership and timing of voluntary income where funds are raised by non-controlled bodies;
- lack of predictable income or precisely identifiable relationship between expenditure and income which makes it difficult for the charity to ensure that income to which it is entitled is actually received;
- uncertainty of future income which can make consideration of future operations and viability of the charity difficult;
- the objects and powers given by charities' governing documents are often narrower than in the equivalent documents for commercial entities. Failure to act in accordance with those objects and powers is more likely to have consequences for the financial statements, and therefore the

auditors' report, than a transaction by a commercial company which is not permitted by its Memorandum or Articles of Association;

- restricted funds held by many charities which require special considerations as to use and accounting;
- the extent and nature of trading activities must be compatible with the entity's charitable status;
- the complexity of tax rules (whether income, capital, value added or local rates) relating to charities;
- the sensitivity of certain key statistics, such as the proportion of resources used in administration and fundraising; and
- the need to maintain adequate resources for future expenditure while avoiding the build up of reserves which could appear excessive to potential donors or be incompatible with the entity's charitable status.

When planning the audit of a charity the following specific features should be considered when assessing audit risks.

21.9.1 Understatement or incompleteness of income

It may be difficult to ensure the completeness and accuracy of the recording of income from donations and fundraising activities. The charity may not be able to control collections by unpaid volunteers, and it may not be possible to form an opinion on the completeness of postal receipts or legacies, and there may be no formal policy for the recognition of donations in kind.

21.9.2 Central and local government grants and loans

The terms under which the grant or loan is given to the charity may be complicated and subject to specific conditions. The auditors must also seek to understand how the loan or grant should be treated in the financial statements.

21.9.3 Branches

This arises over the relationship between the charity and its associated entities, and whether the relationship is such that the entity is a branch which should be included within the main charity's financial statements. Branches which require inclusion in the financial statements may be managed by volunteers and there may be few controls over the completeness and accuracy of transactions at branch level.

21.9.4 Overseas activities

As with branches, the auditors must identify the overseas activities of the charity and assess its relationship with them. If the overseas charities meet the SORP's definition of a 'branch' they must be included within the charity's accounts and the auditors must obtain sufficient and relevant audit evidence as to the results and state of affairs of the branches. If the charity makes payments to overseas affiliates which are not branches, then risk arises as to the control and use of the funds remitted.

21.9.5 Specific funds

All funds under the control of the trustees must be included in the financial statements of the charity. These funds must be identified and information must be obtained that they have been correctly accounted for and applied. The trustees may be unwilling to acknowledge they have full control over all specific funds.

21.9.6 Grants to beneficiaries

Risk arises as to the charity's procedures for giving grants, establishing the bona fides of beneficiaries and monitoring that funds have been correctly applied for the purpose for which they are allocated.

21.9.7 Trustees and volunteers

The trustees may be volunteers who delegate the day-to-day management of the charity to full-time executive officers. The trustees might not be willing to accept their statutory duties and responsibilities, and may not impose effective control and stewarding over the executive officers. In a charity where all the activities are undertaken by volunteers, the resistance to control may be extended.

21.10 Audit evidence

Auditors must collect sufficient appropriate audit evidence to enable them to form conclusions on which to draw their audit opinion. In this section, emphasis is placed upon the forms of audit evidence which should be collected in order to address the risk characteristics and planning considerations which have been considered earlier.

21.10.1 Sources and completeness of income

The income of charities depends upon a number of different sources, ranging from grants from government departments to occasional cash donations by members of the public in response to street collections. Whilst it is the trustees' responsibility to safeguard the assets and income of the charity, the voluntary nature of some elements of its income raises considerations concerning the methods available to the trustees for the purposes of ensuring that all income to which the charity is entitled is correctly accounted for. These considerations differ from those in commercial concerns: the amount of voluntary donations cannot be determined in advance, nor can a charity be regarded as necessarily entitled to funds, even when the amounts can be predicted, before they are donated to it. Trustees of a charity cannot be held responsible for the security of money or other assets which are intended for its use until that money or assets are within the control of the charity.

The most effective source of audit evidence as to the completeness of income is from the operation of the charity's system of internal control. The auditors should document the income recording systems, identify the controls within the system, and perform tests on these controls to ascertain if the controls are effective. Controls which the auditors could seek to place reliance upon would include:

(a) controls over postal receipts such as:
    (i) unopened mail to be kept securely,
    (ii) incoming post to be opened in the presence of at least two people,
    (iii) maintenance of a post log,
    (iv) recording of cheques and cash received,
    (v) checking to agree paying-in slips to the record of receipts,
    (vi) regular bank reconciliations to ensure that recorded receipts are in fact paid into the bank account;
(b) controls over street and similar cash collections such as:
    (i) collecting boxes to be individually numbered, sealed and controlled,
    (ii) collections to be counted in the presence of the collector and receipted;
(c) controls over fundraising events such as:
    (i) separate records to be kept for each event,
    (ii) procedures for controlling cash and cheque receipts similar to those for cash collections,
    (iii) use of pre-numbered tickets for events when tickets are sold, and reconciliation of those to recorded income.

Audit evidence for the completeness of income may also be drawn from using internal historical data as a guide to the level of income that may be expected from the charity's various fundraising activities. Assurance may also be drawn from assessing and placing reliance upon the budgeting and internal management reporting procedures of the charity.

Receipts from legacies
The auditors must ensure that the charity's accounting policy has been consistently applied. Usually, legacies are recognised on a receipts basis, which is a departure from the strict principles of accruals accounting. However, such an approach can be justified on the grounds of both uncertainty as to the timing and amount of the receipt and prudence.

Evidence as to the completeness of legacies can be obtained from review of minutes and from placing reliance on the charity's controls over cash receipts.

Receipts from fundraisers
If the charity makes use of external fundraisers the auditors should check the fundraising agreement which is required by the Charities Act 1992, and any other relevant documentation, to ascertain the basis on which the receipts due to the charity are to be computed and when these funds were transferred to the charity.

Receipts from branches, associates and supporters' associations
The auditors should ascertain the nature of the relationship between the charity and its branches and other associated organisations to determine the basis on which funds are raised for the charity and how the funds are to be remitted.

If control over fundraising events is imposed by the main charity, the auditors should identify the relevant controls and seek to place reliance upon them. If funds are raised by an associated body which is not controlled by the main charity, the same control conditions apply as for other donations. Audit reliance can be obtained from the past history of volume and timing of receipts from associated bodies. The auditors may also seek to request associate bodies to confirm directly to them details of the amounts remitted.

Income from grants
In the case of grant funded charities, an examination of the grant applications and correspondence is a useful way of verifying completeness of income. It may also be possible to obtain direct confirmation of the amounts receivable from the grant provider

Non-cash donations
Satisfactory operation of internal controls may enable the auditors to obtain sufficient appropriate audit evidence as to the recognition and measurement of donations made by way of goods, other assets or services. The trustees of a charity should develop procedures for recording donations in kind and ensure that the policy for valuing the assets or services received is consistent with the Charities SORP. The basis of any valuation of non-cash donations should be clearly stated in the notes to the financial statements and consistently applied. The auditors consider whether the policy is reasonable in the circumstances and has been properly applied.

Loss of income through fraud
Auditors consider the possibility that the charity's records of income to which it is legally entitled may be incomplete as a result of fraud. A common

type of fraud against charities is the diversion of donations to bank or building society accounts which they do not control. Sources of audit evidence as to whether income from appeals and other 'non-routine' sources has been fully recorded can involve the assessment and testing of the sort of internal controls described in the section on SAS 300, and comparison of donations actually received by the charity to past results for similar appeals and statistics for response rates for charities in general.

21.10.2 Expenditure

Verification of the accuracy and validity of the charity's expenditure should include consideration that the charity's expenditure is properly applied in accordance with the terms of the governing document. If funds are expended on non-charitable activities tax reliefs may be forfeited and actions may be brought against the trustees.

If the charity has made donations of goods, services or other funds, the auditors must obtain evidence that these were for charitable purposes which fall within the charity's objectives. Audit evidence can be obtained from the assessment of the charity's controls for making and awarding donations, and for monitoring the use of the donation by the recipients.

In some cases, expenditure may be difficult to test. For example, the charity may operate in a war or disaster zone or it may undertake a significant amount of cash expenditure and hold few supporting records for this expenditure.

21.10.3 Branches, subsidiaries and overseas operations

If the charity does not fully control a branch or an associated operation, the auditors must consider the nature of the controls which have been instituted to ensure that the assets and income arising from these operations are recognised and safeguarded, and that the information received is reliable. Returns made by the branch to the charity should be reviewed by the auditors to ensure that all returns have been received and reviewed by the charity, and any matters arising have been addressed.

Where a branch, subsidiary or associated operation which is to be included in the main accounts of the charity is audited or examined by another auditor/examiner the principal auditor should seek to obtain sufficient appropriate audit evidence by:

(a) issuing instructions to the secondary auditors/examiners detailing the scope of the work to be performed and the form of the report to be issued;
(b) issuing a standard questionnaire for completion by the secondary auditors/examiners;

(c) requesting a report of the principal matters arising and conclusions direct from the secondary auditors/examiners.

If the reports from the other auditor/examiner indicate potential problems and in particular qualified opinions, which in aggregate could cover a substantial part of the charity's transactions, the principal auditors should assess whether it is possible for additional audit procedures to be performed, in order to obtain further evidence so that an unqualified opinion can be given.

21.10.4 Fixed assets (including investments)

Evidence must be obtained that the fixed assets of the charity exist and that none are omitted from the financial statements. In particular, auditors must ensure that all donated fixed assets have been recognised in the financial statements both as an asset and as income, and that the value given to the asset is appropriate. Evidence needs to be obtained that the charity has title to its fixed assets, by inspection of deeds, invoices or from review of the terms under which gifts were received. If an asset has not been capitalised because it is deemed to be inalienable or historic or because neither a cost nor a market value can be attached to it, the auditors should assess whether the treatment is appropriate and whether the disclosures regarding the treatment in the financial statements are sufficient.

Audit evidence as regards investments will include ensuring that the trustees have title to all investments, that all investment transactions are properly authorised, that the charity is complying with any constitutional restrictions that it may have on its investment powers, that investment income is complete, and that all investments, gains or losses (realised and unrealised), and income are allocated to the correct fund.

21.10.5 Charitable loans

If the charity has made loans of a charitable nature, then doubt may arise as to their recoverability. In particular, provision would be expected if the loan is unsecured, has 'soft' terms or there are doubts as to the whereabouts of the recipient.

21.10.6 Application of funds

Evidence must be obtained that the charity has properly accounted for its individual funds in accordance with the terms of its constitution and the terms of trust for the individual funds. The auditors should ensure that all funds are correctly classified and should ensure that they have a correct record of the terms of each fund. Checks should be performed to ensure that the movements on each fund are authorised and properly recorded. If a fund has ceased during the year, evidence must be obtained that any remaining balances have been properly expended or transferred. Auditors should ensure that all income and expenditure, and assets and liabilities have been correctly allocated between relevant funds.

21.10.7 Analytical review

Analytical procedures may prove to be an efficient and effective source of audit evidence because certain of the transactions of a charity, and particularly many of a charity's sources of income, lack detailed documentary support. There may also be a high degree of predictability regarding the income and expenditure of a charity with both the major income raising programmes and expenditure projects placed well in advance. The administrative expenditure of the charity may be relatively fixed and therefore straightforward to predict.

Analytical procedures which could be used to generate relevant audit evidence could include:

- comparison of actual income and expenditure to prior years' figures and trends;
- comparison of actual to budgeted results;
- comparison of actual expenditure to the auditors' own estimate of expenditure that would be reasonable for the particular transaction under review;
- comparison of results between branches;
- checking the sales revenue of shops and trading activities to an estimated sales value of stocks sold;
- comparison of actual cash donations received as a result of fundraising activities to the amount which could have been expected on the basis of available charity statistics;
- appropriate ratios.

21.11 Audit completion

21.11.1 Representation letters

As with any audit, the auditors should obtain a representation letter, in the case of a charity the usual source being the trustees. In many charities executive management is separate from the trustees – in these situations the letter of representation must still be received from the trustees as they have the responsibility for preparing and presenting the financial statements. The example letter, given below, is appended to the Practice Note.

To:

[Auditors]

Dear Sirs

We confirm to the best of our knowledge and belief, and having made appropriate enquiries of other trustees/directors and officials of the charity, the following representations given to you in connection with your audit of the charity's financial statements for the year ended ... .

General

1 We acknowledge as directors our responsibility under the Companies Act 1985 [Charities Act 1993 (unincorporated charity)] for the financial statements which give a true and fair view and for making accurate representations to you. All the accounting records have been made available to you for the purpose of your audit and all the transactions undertaken by the charity have been properly reflected and recorded in the accounting records. All other records and related information, including minutes of [shareholders], trustees, members and management meetings, have been made available to you.

Going concern

2 We believe that the charity's financial statements should be prepared on a going concern basis on the grounds that current and future sources of funding or support will be more than adequate for the charity's needs. We believe that no further disclosures relating to the charity's ability to continue as a going concern need to be made in the financial statements.

Law and regulations

3 We are not aware of any irregularities, including fraud, involving management or employees of the charity; nor are we aware of any breaches or possible breaches of statute, regulations, contracts, [or] agreements [or the company's Memorandum and Articles of Association (charitable company)] [which might prejudice the charity's going concern status or that might result in the charity suffering significant penalties or other loss]. No allegations of such irregularities, including fraud, or such breaches have come to our notice.

Loans and arrangements

4 The charity has not had nor entered into at any time during the year, any arrangement, transaction or agreement to provide credit facilities (including loans, quasi-loans or credit facilities) for directors nor to guarantee or provide security for such matters [charitable company].

Transactions with related parties
5 We are not aware of any transactions with related parties requiring disclosure in the financial statements. Or: All transactions with related parties have been disclosed in the financial statements. We have made available to you all relevant information concerning such transactions and are not aware of any other matters which require disclosure in order to comply with the requirements or the Charities Act 1993 or accounting standards.

Post-balance sheet events
6 There have been no events since the balance sheet date which necessitate revision of the figures included in the financial statements or inclusion of a note thereto. Should further material events occur, which may necessitate revision of the figures included in the financial statements or inclusion of a note thereto, we will advise you accordingly.

Grants and donations
7 All grants, donations and other income, the receipt of which is subject to specific terms or conditions, have been notified to you. There have been no breaches of terms or conditions during the period in the application of such income

Restricted grants and donations are as follows/listed overleaf:

Yours faithfully

....

Signed on behalf of the board of directors/trustees   Date

Examples of other matters where confirmation of representations may be necessary

- Material accounting estimates – confirming basis of estimation
- Lack of evidence – material representations where no other evidence available
- Trustees/directors opinions – confirmations of opinions concerning (e.g.)
- Provisions for doubtful debts
- Contentious legal matters
- Accounting policies – confirming appropriately adopted and disclosed
- Bank or loan facilities – confirming no breaches of covenant or terms.

21.11.2 Review of financial statements

The objective of the review of the financial statements is to consider the overall view presented, together with the conclusions formed on the audit evidence collected, to ensure that there is a reasonable basis for the audit opinion.

The view conveyed by the financial statements should be consistent with and reflect the operations of the charity during the year and the auditor's knowledge of the charity. There should be consistency between the financial statements and non-financial information issued by the charity and with the impression of the charity's activities conveyed by internal documents such as the minutes of meetings of its trustees and committees.

Other points which should be considered when reviewing the financial statements include:

- disclosure of income from fundraising activities;
- the capitalising of expenditure on fixed assets;
- apportionment of administrative expenses;
- recognition of income from donations and legacies;
- treatment of exceptional items;
- presentation of special or irregular income or expenditure.

21.11.3 Going concern

Auditors need to give consideration as to the going concern of the charity that they are reporting upon and consider the appropriateness of any disclosures which the trustees have given with regard to going concern. As with any entity, the auditors may need to refer to these disclosures in their report or qualify their opinion.

Basis for preparation of financial statements

In considering factors relating to a charity' status as a going concern, it is necessary to take account of the particular circumstances of that charity which may affect its ability to continue its activities. Auditors consider the availability of future funding and whether uncertainties exist which require disclosure in the financial statements. The charity's purpose may also require consideration: some charitable activities are focused on a specific purpose, and once this is achieved, the charity may cease to operate.

Circumstances where a charity may cease to be a going concern

The following list gives examples of conditions that can give grounds for concern that a charity may not be a going concern:

- inability to finance its operations from its own resources;
- decision by the trustees to curtail or cease activities;
- transfer to, or take-over by, another entity of the charity's activities;
- loss of essential resources or key staff;

- existence of tax liabilities which cannot be met from existing resources;
- loss of clients, for example where a public authority ends a practice or contract to refer (and pay for) clients to the charity;
- loss of operating licence (for example, for a residential care home);
- significant changes in strategy of major funders; and
- significant decline in donations by the public.

There are many indicators of potential going concern problems. The examples of indicators contained in para 31 of SAS 130 apply as much to charities as to commercial entities and include pointers such as an excess of liabilities over assets. Although the most significant factor ensuring the future viability of many charities is public goodwill, it is difficult, if not impossible, to value and cannot be included in the balance sheet, nor can auditors rely solely on the existence of goodwill as evidence to support the going concern assumption.

The operations of charities
The timing of cash flows may present special considerations in the audit of charities. This is particularly true of charities receiving grants of money from central government, as moneys are only voted on an annual basis even though there may be a working presumption that funding will continue for future years. Some charities may be unable to finance long-term commitments other than through short-term fundraising. There may be difficulty or delays in converting current assets into cash, for example, where a grant is obtained for reimbursement of expenses already incurred but is not paid for a number of months.

It may also be difficult for charities to cut back on a project or grant funding in the event of a liquidity problem, because it may not have the discretion to do so under the terms of its own funding. It is possible for a charity to have an apparently large bank balance, but to be unable to meet general liabilities as they fall due because the balance in question belongs to one or more restricted funds.

It is particularly important to consider whether the balance sheet of the charity includes **restricted funds or similiar assets** which **cannot be applied to meet the general liabilities** of the charity. Auditors also check whether short-term liabilities are matched by short-term, unrestricted assets, and whether any commitments for future expenditure are reasonable.

Assessment of a charity's financial strength or weakness is complicated by the uncertainty of future income to which most charities are subject. Regular or predictable income, from sources such as deeds of covenant, endowments and investments, forms a comparatively small part of most charities' revenues and it would be impossible to obtain confirmation of future giving from donors. Charities generally see themselves as competing for scarce resources, and the impact of competition, such as another charity operating in the same sector or area, can be profound. Other factors outside the control of charities are constraints on spending by members of the public, either through loss of personal income, or through a change in spending patterns.

Obtaining evidence

The trustees' report may contain an indication of future expected income based on past donations or patterns of giving. In addition to this information, the auditors consider the level of skills available to the charity in its trustees and staff, and their track record and commitment. Under SAS 130 the auditors' opinion on the financial statements is only qualified if they consider that the scope of their work is limited due to inadequate or inappropriate consideration of going concern by the trustees, or that there is insufficient disclosure of relevant circumstances to enable the financial statements to give a true and fair view, or that the basis used in the preparation of the financial statements was inappropriate. Where there is fundamental uncertainty about the future viability of the charity, but the auditors consider that both the measures taken by the trustees in relation to assessment of going concern and disclosure of any matters needed for a proper understanding of the circumstances were adequate, their opinion would not be qualified in respect of going concern. In these circumstances, the auditors include an explanatory paragraph in the basis of opinion section of their report.

In considering going concern, it may be helpful for the auditors to include the following points in discussions with trustees:

- the nature of management information systems covering future income and expenditure;
- the level of forecast future expenditure, divided between that which is committed and that which is discretionary;
- the level of 'known' future income (deriving from sources such as endowments, investments, and deeds of covenant – assessment of the latter making allowances for deeds terminated due to unforeseen circumstances);
- where the charity relies for a significant part of its funding on one or more major institutional donors or granting authorities such as local authorities, whether it would be practical to obtain a degree of comfort from such funders as to their future support for the charity;
- shortfall of identifiable future income on forecast expenditure needing to be made up by voluntary donations of cash or other resources;
- past patterns of income and expenditure;
- lists of projects supported or awards made in the year and planned for the following year;

- the level of uncommitted reserves remaining available to the charity;
- comparison of previous budgets to actual performance;
- the reasonableness of the assumptions underlying the current budgets;
- any reliance on support by the charity's bankers, major donors, or public authorities;
- concentration on provision of services to a particular category of beneficiaries or objects for which future funding or demand may be limited; and
- any special operating licences or similar conditions.

21.11.4 Related parties

The principles of FRS8 apply to charities together with a series of disclosures given in the SORP in respect of transactions with trustees and connected persons. The auditors consider the steps taken by the trustees to identify and record related party transactions and remain alert, in carrying out their audit, for evidence of such transactions which are not included in the information provided by the trustees.

It is a fundamental principle of trust law that a trustee should not benefit directly or indirectly from his or her trust. This means that neither charity trustees nor persons connected with them should transact business with the charity (or with any company owned by the charity), except where the transaction, and any benefit (including remuneration) derived from it, is either expressly permitted by the charity's governing document, or permission has been obtained from an appropriate authority (for example, the Charity Commission for charities based in England and Wales).

21.11.5 Other information presented with the financial statements

Other information may be issued by the charity in a combined publication with the audited financial statements. Auditors check such information to ensure that there are no inconsistencies which could either confuse readers of the accounts, or cast doubt on the reliability of the audited information. Examples include:

- statements by the patron, president, chairman of the trustees and/or chief executive of the charity;
- an operating and financial review;
- a statement concerning arrangements for corporate governance, based on the Combined Code of Best Practice for listed companies;
- a treasurer's report;
- financial summaries; and
- projections of future expenditure based on planned activity.

Additional care will be needed where, for example, the annual report and the financial statements are prepared at the same time but by different personnel, so that their content is largely independent.

The Charities SORP requires charity trustees to state in their report that the major identified risks to which the charity is exposed have been reviewed and that systems have been established to mitigate such risks. SAS160.1 requires auditors who become aware of any apparent misstatements or inconsistencies in other information published together with the audited financial statements to seek to resolve them. Whilst auditors are not expected to verify any risk management statement made by trustees they are likely to become aware of the steps taken by the trustees to identify and mitigate identified financial risks through their work in assessing audit risk under SAS 300. They may also become aware of non-financial risks during the course of their audit. If, after discussion with the trustees, any significant misstatement or apparent inconsistency identified by auditors in relation to a corporate governance or risk management statement remains in a Trustees' Report, the auditors consider reporting this in the opinion section of their report. It should be noted that, as this does not give rise to a qualified audit opinion on the financial statements, the auditors' comments may be included under the heading 'other matter' as illustrated in the APB Bulletin 1999/5.

Where trustees include information concerning corporate governance in a charity's annual report, they may request the auditors to review and report on that information. In such cases, auditors refer to the guidance set out in the APB's prouncements on this subject.

21.12 Audit reports

The form and content of the auditors' report on the financial statements of a charity should follow the general principles of SAS 600 'Auditors' reports on financial statements', whether the charity is incorporated or not. A review of the detailed requirements of the reports is given below followed by examples of unqualified reports in respect of:

(a) incorporated charities;
(b) unincorporated charities;
(c) receipts and payment accounts.

These reports have been taken from the exposure draft for the revised Practice Note 11. The report formats are consistent with the changes in the style of company audit reports which the APB introduced in 2001 in *Audit Bulletin 2001/2.*

21.12.1 Review of contents of audit reports

Addressee

The audit report of a charity which is a company should be addressed to the members, as this is a requirement of the Companies Act 1985. In respect of unincorporated charities, the Regulations specify that the report should be addressed to the trustees, unless the auditors have been appointed by the Charity Commission in which case the report should be addressed to the Commission.

Statement of trustees' responsibilities

Although the general duties of charity trustees are identical regardless of the constitution, the specific responsibilities will vary according to the constitution and legal status of the charity.

In respect of charitable companies, the duties of the trustees are specified in the Companies Act 1985, and the form of responsibility statement recommended in SAS 600 should normally be used.

Where a charity is not subject to regulation, apart from that applicable to charities, the form of words set out below should either be included in the text of the auditors' report or the report should contain a reference to the page in the package of report and accounts where it is situated.

The statement of trustees' responsibilities for an unincorporated charity could take the following form.

> Law applicable to charities in England and Wales requires the trustees to prepare financial statements for each financial year which give a true and fair view of the charity's financial activities during the year and of its financial position at the end of the year (unless the charity is entitled to prepare accounts on the alternative receipts and payments basis). In preparing financial statements giving a true and fair view, the trustees are required to:
>
> * select suitable accounting policies and then apply them consistently;
> * make judgements and estimates that are reasonable and prudent;
> * state whether applicable Accounting Standards and Statements of Recommended Practice have been followed, subject to any departures disclosed and explained in the financial statements (note that this is only required for unincorporated charities producing financial statements on an accruals basis);
> * prepare the financial statements on the going concern basis unless it is inappropriate to presume that the charity will continue in operation.
>
> The trustees are responsible for keeping proper accounting records which disclose with reasonable accuracy the financial position of the charity and which enable them to ensure that the financial statements comply with the Charities Act 1993. They are also responsible for safeguarding the assets of the charity and

hence for taking reasonable steps for the prevention and detection of fraud and other irregularities.

Responsibilities of the auditors

The responsibilities of the auditors will be defined by the reporting regime to which the charity is subject and the form of opinion that the auditors are required to give. In respect of a charitable company, the auditors are reporting under the Companies Act 1985 to the members and the responsibility statement set out in SAS 600 should be given. If the charity is unincorporated the responsibility statement should state what the auditor is required to report upon, and specify that the auditors have been appointed under and are reporting in accordance with the requirements of the Charities Act 1993.

Basis of opinion

Whether the auditors have been appointed under and are reporting in accordance with the Companies Act 1985 or the Charities Act 1993, the basis of forming the opinion is essentially the same. The auditors are required to apply Auditing Standards to form the opinion and have similar rights under both Acts to receive all required information and explanations.

Opinion

The wording of the opinion paragraph must reflect the regulations to which the charity is subject.

Charitable companies

The auditors must give an opinion on the truth and fairness of the view given of the state of affairs (balance sheet) of the charity at the reporting date and of its incoming resources and application of resources (statement of financial activities) for the period to that date. An opinion must also be given on the truth and fairness of the view given by the income and expenditure account for the period to the reporting date. The financial statements must be properly prepared in accordance with the primary legislation, the Companies Act 1985.

Unincorporated charities

The auditors' opinion differs from that for a charitable company because the Regulations specify that an opinion is required on the truth and fairness of the view given by the balance sheet and the statement of financial activities. No mention of income and expenditure is required. The financial statements must be properly prepared in accordance with the primary legislation, the Charities Act 1993.

Signature and date

The normal requirements regarding the signature and the date of the auditors' report apply to charities. Whether the charity is constituted as a company or is unincorporated, the designation 'Registered Auditors' must be used.

21.12.2 Example audit reports

Unqualified opinion: charity incorporated under the Companies Act in the United Kingdom

Independent Auditors' Report to the members of XYZ Charity Ltd.

We have audited the financial statements of (name of charity) for the year ended … which comprise (state primary financial statements such as the Statement of Financial Activities, the Balance Sheet, the Cash Flow Statement) and related notes. These Financial Statements have been prepared under the historical cost convention [as modified by the revaluation of certain fixed assets] and the accounting policies set out therein.

Respective responsibilities of trustees and auditors

The trustees' (who are also the directors of XYZ Charity Ltd for the purposes of company law] responsibilities for preparing the Trustees' Report and the financial statements in accordance with applicable law and United Kingdom Accounting Standards are set out in the Statement of Trustees' Responsibilities. Our responsibility is to audit the financial statements in accordance with relevant legal and regulatory requirements and United Kingdom Auditing Standards.

We report to you our opinion as to whether the financial statements give a true and fair view and are properly prepared in accordance with the (Companies Act 1985) (Companies (Northern Ireland) Order 1986). We also report to you if, in our opinion, the Trustees' Report is not consistent with the financial statements, if the charity has not kept proper accounting records, if we have not received all the information and explanations we require for our audit, or if information specified by law regarding trustees' remuneration and transactions with the charitable company is not disclosed.

We are not required to consider whether the statement in the Trustees' Report concerning the major risks to which the charity is exposed covers all existing risks and controls, or to form an opinion on the effectiveness of the charity's risk management and control procedures.

We read other information contained in the Trustees' Report (or, where appropriate, the Annual Report), and consider whether it is consistent with the audited financial statements. We consider the implications for our report if we become aware of any apparent misstatements or material inconsistencies with the financial statements. Our responsibilities do not extend to any other information.

Basis of opinion

We conducted our audit in accordance with United Kingdom Auditing Standards issued by the Auditing Practices Board. An audit includes examination, on a test basis, of evidence relevant to the amounts and disclosures in the financial statements. It also includes an assessment of the significant estimates and judgments made by the trustees in the preparation of the financial statements, and of whether the accounting policies are appropriate to the charitable company's circumstances, consistently applied and adequately disclosed.

We planned and performed our audit so as to obtain all information and explanations which we considered necessary in order to provide us with sufficient evidence to give reasonable assurance as to whether the financial statements are free from material misstatement, whether caused by fraud or other irregularity or error. In forming our opinion we also evaluated the overall adequacy of the presentation of information in the financial statements.

Opinion

In our opinion the financial statements give a true and fair view of the state of the charitable company's affairs as at 31 December 20.. and of its incoming resources and application of resources, including its income and expenditure, for the year then ended and have been properly prepared in accordance with the (Companies Act 1985) (Companies (Northern Ireland) Order 1986.

Registered auditors　　　　　　　　　　*Address*
Date

Unqualified opinion for an unincorporated charity in England and Wales preparing financial statements under the Charities Act 1993 s.42(1)

Independent Auditors' Report to the trustees of XYZ charity

We have audited the financial statements of (name of charity) for the year ended … which comprise (state primary financial statements such as the Statement of Financial Activities, the Balance Sheet, the Cash Flow Statement) and the related notes. These financial statements have been prepared under the historical cost convention [as modified by the revaluation of certain fixed assets] and the accounting policies set out therein.

Respective responsibilities of trustees and auditors

The trustees' responsibilities for preparing the Trustees' Report and the financial statements in accordance with applicable law and United Kingdom Accounting Standards are set out in the Statement of Trustees' Responsibilities.

We have been appointed as auditors under section 43 of the Charities Act 1993 and report in accordance with regulations made under section 44 of that Act[1]. Our responsibility is to audit the financial statements in accordance with relevant legal and regulatory requirements and United Kingdom Auditing Standards.

We report to you our opinion as to whether the financial statements give a true and fair view and are properly prepared in accordance with the Charities Act 1993. We also report to you if, in our opinion, the trustees' report is not consistent with the financial statements, if the charity has not kept proper accounting records, or if we have not received all the information and explanations we require for our audit.

We are not required to consider whether the statement in the Trustees' Report concerning the major risks to which the charity is exposed covers all existing risks and controls, or to form an opinion on the effectiveness of the charity's risk management and control procedures.

We read other information contained in the Trustees' Report (or, where appropriate, the Annual Report), and consider whether it is consistent with the audited financial statements. We consider the implications for our report if we become aware of any apparent misstatements or material inconsistencies with the financial statements. Our responsibilities do not extend to any other information.

Basis of opinion

We conducted our audit in accordance with United Kingdom Auditing Standards issued by the Auditing Practices Board. An audit includes examination, on a test basis, of evidence relevant to the amounts and disclosures in the financial statements. It also includes an assessment of the significant estimates and judgments made by the trustees in the preparation of the financial statements, and of whether the accounting policies are appropriate to the charity's circumstances, consistently applied and adequately disclosed.

We planned and performed our audit so as to obtain all the information and explanations which we considered necessary in order to provide us with sufficient evidence to give reasonable assurance that the financial statements are free from material misstatement, whether caused by fraud or other irregularity or error. In forming an opinion we also evaluated the overall adequacy of the presentation of information in the financial statements.

Opinion

In our opinion the financial statements give a true and fair view of the state of the charity's (and its subsidiaries')affairs as at 31 December 20.. and of its (their) incoming resources and application of resources in the year then ended and have been properly prepared in accordance with the Charities Act 1993.

Registered auditors   *Address*
Date

21.12.3 Receipts and payments accounts

An unincorporated charity whose gross income is not more than £100,000 per annum may prepare receipts and payments accounts rather than full accruals accounts. If such a charity elects to receive an audit of its accounts the audit report reflects, with the statement of trustees' responsibilities, that the accounts have been prepared in accordance with the Charity Commission's guidance for smaller charities. The auditors are required, in this situation, to report on the presentation of the assets and liabilities, at the reporting date, and the receipts and payments for the period to that date, as well as on the proper preparation of the accounts. There is no requirement to report on the accounts in terms of their truth and fairness.

Unqualified opinion for an unincorporated charity in England and Wales preparing a receipts and payments account and statement of assets under the Charities Act 1993 s 42(3)

Independent Auditors' Report to the trustees of XYZ charity

We have audited the receipts and payments account and statement of assets and liabilities of (name of charity) for the year ended.... , and the related notes.

Respective responsibilities of trustees and auditors

The trustees' responsibilities for preparing the account and statement in accordance with applicable law and United Kingdom Accounting Standards are set out in the Statement of Trustees' Responsibilities. The account and statement have been prepared under section 42(3) of the Charities Act 1993 following the guidance for accounting for smaller charities issued by the Charity Commission.

We have been appointed as auditors under section 43 of the Charities Act 1993 and report in accordance with regulations made under section 44 of that Act Our responsibility is to audit the account and statement in accordance with relevant legal and regulatory requirements and United Kingdom Auditing Standards.

We report to you our opinion as to whether the account and statement are properly presented and prepared in accordance with the Charities Act 1993. We also report to you if, in our opinion, the Trustees' Report is not consistent with the account and statement, if the charity has not kept proper accounting records, or if we have not received all the information and explanations we require for our audit.

We read the Trustees' Report and consider the implications for our report if we become aware of any apparent misstatements within it. We are not required to consider whether the statement in the Trustees' Report concerning the major risks to which the charity is exposed covers all existing risks and controls, or to form an opinion on the effectiveness of the charity's risk management and control procedures.

Basis of opinion

We conducted our audit in accordance with United Kingdom Auditing Standards issued by the Auditing Practices Board. An audit includes examination, on a test basis, of evidence relevant to the amounts and disclosures in the account and statement. It also includes an assessment of the significant estimates and judgments made by the trustees in the preparation of the account and statement and of whether the accounting policies are appropriate, in the context of the applicable accounting requirements, to the charity's circumstances, consistently applied and adequately disclosed.

We planned and performed our audit so as to obtain all the information and explanations which we considered necessary in order to provide us with sufficient evidence to give reasonable assurance that the statements are free from material misstatement, whether caused by fraud or other irregularity or error. In forming our opinion we also evaluated the overall adequacy of the presentation of information in the account and statement, including whether any material special trust or other restricted fund is adequately distinguished.

Opinion
In our opinion the account and statement properly present the receipts and payments of the charity for the year ended 31 December 20.. together with its statement of assets and liabilities as at that date and have been properly prepared in accordance with the provisions of the Charities Act 1993 applicable to smaller charities.

Registered auditors   *Address*
Date

21.12.4 Fundamental uncertainties and qualified opinions

The reporting of a matter arising from the audit of a charity which gives rise to a fundamental uncertainty or of circumstances which require the auditors to present a qualified opinion should follow the principles of SAS 600.

21.12.5 Reports on summarised accounts

Where a charity prepares summarised accounts, the SORP requires that there should be a statement from the auditor/independent examiner stating whether or not the summarised accounts are consistent with the full accounts. Practice Note 11 recommends that the report is made to the trustees in the following form:

Independent Auditors' statement to the Trustees of XYZ charity
We have examined the summarised financial statements of (name of charity).

Respective responsibilities of trustees and auditors
The trustees are responsible for preparing the (summarised annual report) in accordance with applicable law.

Our responsibility is to report to you our opinion on the consistency of the summarised financial statements within the (summarised annual report) with the full financial statements and Trustees' Report. We also read the other information contained in the (summarised annual report) and consider the implications for our report if we become aware of any apparent misstatements or material inconsistencies with the summarised financial statements.

Basis of opinion
We conducted our work in accordance with Bulletin 1999/6 'The auditors' statement on the summary financial statement' issued by the Auditing Practices Board for use in the United Kingdom.

Opinion

In our opinion the summarised financial statements are consistent [are not consistent] with the full financial statements and trustees' report of XYZ charity for the year ended 31 December 20xx (in the following respects....)

Registered auditors   *Address*
Date

21.13 Reporting to the charity commissioners

The Regulations require the auditors of unincorporated charities to communicate to the Charity Commissioners certain matters of which they become aware in their capacity as auditors of the charity. This provision does not apply to the auditors of charitable companies.

The Regulations specify that auditors are required to communicate matters which are of 'material significance' in the context of the Commissioners' powers to institute enquiries or act for the protection of charities.

- Matters which are of 'material significance' will primarily arise from the identification of a significant loss or misapplication of a charity's property or funds, or from the identification of a significant risk to the charity's property or funds resulting from maladministration or misuse of assets.

The Commissioners do not expect to receive reports on minor matters, which have been resolved and where the charity has suffered no loss.

Listed below are examples of matters that are likely to be of 'material significance' to these regulatory functions. The first category provides examples of matters that will always give rise to a duty to report, matters arising within the second category will give rise to a strong presumption of reportability and the third category may be reportable in certain circumstances.

21.13.1 Matters always giving rise to a duty to report

(a) Matters suggesting dishonesty or misuse of charitable funds. Indicative examples include:
   - evidence of false accounting, theft or misappropriation of assets by any charity trustee or senior employee;
   - evidence of a material application of charitable funds for a non-charitable purpose;
   - evidence that gives reasonable cause to doubt the honesty or integrity of a charity trustee or the trustee body;
   - evidence that any charity trustee is a person disqualified from acting as a charity trustee under s72 of the 1993 Act and not having obtained a waiver from disqualification (disqualification may arise

from a conviction involving dishonesty or deception, undischarged bankruptcy, sequestration, a composition or arrangement with creditors, a disqualification or removal order);

- evidence of a charity trustee, employee or agent knowingly or recklessly providing the Charity Commission with information which is false or misleading in a material respect. (Section 11 of the 1993 Act).

(b) A serious breach of a legislative requirement or of the charity's trusts. Indicative examples include:

- a significant breach of the law relating to fund raising undertaken by professional fund raisers or commercial participators. In particular a failure to make the required statement as to the method of remuneration, the failure to pay all cash and cheques so raised to the charity gross, and a failure to enter into a proper agreement with the charity (Pt II of the Charities Act 1992 (ss58 to 64 as amended) and the Charitable Institutions (Fund-Raising) Regulations 1994);
- a material inaccuracy in the completion of an annual return made under s48 of the 1993 Act which is not immediately corrected on identification;
- receipt by any charity trustee (or person connected with a trustee) of remuneration or other benefits from the assets of the charity without proper powers or consents;
- a charity entering into a significant transaction with a charity trustee (or person connected with a charity trustee) without proper authority which give rise to a conflict of interest or may be to the benefit of the trustee or connected person;
- a significant *ex-gratia* payment or waiver of entitlement given to any person connected with the charity without proper authority under s27 of the 1993 Act;
- a significant breach of law or regulation, not specific to a charity, that could prevent the charity from undertaking a significant part of its activities e.g., loss of registration in a residential care charity;
- a reckless investment made contrary to the proper advice and investment criteria requirements of the Trustee Act 2000.

21.13.2 Matters that are likely to be reportable

Where the auditors identify a matter within this category, there is a strong presumption that such a matter will be of material significance to the Charity Commission's regulatory function. The auditors would be expected to be able to document and justify the basis of any decision not to report a matter falling within this category.

All such matters which are judged by the auditor not to be a matter of material significance are nevertheless likely to be matters that need to be drawn to the attention of charity trustees by a report under SAS 610.

Where a matter, which was judged not to be reportable, arises again in the subsequent accounting period then a reoccurrence of the matter will require particular consideration by the auditors. A matter falling within this category and identified in a report to the trustees and management under SAS 610 in the previous period that has not been addressed and remedied or reoccurs in the subsequent accounting period should be regarded as reportable.

(a) Serious deficiencies in the arrangements made by the charity trustees in relation to the management and control of charitable funds. Indicative examples include:
   - evidence that the trustee body as a whole have failed to exercise proper control over the administration and management of the charity's affairs and activities, having due regard to the nature of its trusts and activities;
   - evidence of recklessness on the part of the trustee body as a whole giving rise to a significant risk of a material loss or misapplication of charitable funds;
   - adequate arrangements have not been made by the charity trustees to monitor functions delegated to third parties;
   - uncertainty exists as to who are the charity trustees;
   - a lack of adequate security or control over the assets of the charity;
   - the auditors have been prevented from continuing with or completing the audit as a result of insufficient records being available or insufficient explanations being given in answer to questions raised.

(b) A significant breach of a legislative requirement or of the charity's trusts. Indicative examples include:
   - a significant *ex-gratia* payment or waiver of entitlement given to any third party unconnected with the charity without proper authority under s27 of the 1993 Act;
   - a significant breach of an order made under the 1993 Act prohibiting a particular transaction or granting consent on particular terms;
   - evidence of a material application of funds for purposes, whilst charitable, that are outside the charity's objectives or contrary to any special trust;
   - the auditors being obstructed by the action or inaction of any charity trustee from obtaining all information or explanations necessary for the purposes of the statutory audit (Reg 8 of the Regulations (E&W);
   - failure by the charity trustees to register with the Commission a registerable charity as required by s3 of the 1993 Act.

(c) Matters suggesting dishonesty (that does not involve senior management) or misapplication of the charity's funds. Indicative examples include:
   - evidence existing of any significant theft or misappropriation by any charity employee (other than a senior employee which should be

treated as reportable), volunteer, agent or third party and this matter has not been reported to the Police Authorities or the Commission;

- knowingly making significantly inaccurate or misleading claims in relation to the charity or its activities in its publicity or fundraising material.

21.13.3 Matters that may give rise to a duty to report

In considering a matter arising identified as falling within this category, the auditors will also consider whether the matter arising is an isolated incident or of a recurring nature or pattern. Where the matter reoccurs or several separate matters arise within this category then a duty to report is more likely to exist due to the pervasive nature of such instances. The auditors will also need to consider the cumulative impact of such matters.

Matters falling within this category are often capable of remedy with the co-operation of the trustee body. Where such issues have been identified and remedied by the Trustees and the auditors are satisfied that there is no ongoing risk to the proper application of charitable funds then a duty to report is unlikely to arise.

Where a matter is identified which is judged not to be a matter of material significance the auditors are likely to address such matters in reports to trustees and management under SAS 610.

Where a matter, which is judged in itself not to be reportable, arises again in the subsequent accounting period then the recurring nature of the event will require particular consideration. A matter identified in a report to the trustees and management under SAS 610 in the previous period has not been addressed and remedied or it reoccurs then there will be a strong presumption that such matters are likely to be reportable.

(a) Other breaches of a legislative requirement or of the charity's trusts. Indicative examples include:
  - evidence existing of a failure to account for any material liability to any direct or indirect tax;
  - a failure to obtain Inland Revenue agreement for any non- qualifying loan or investment;
  - a failure, without first obtaining official consent, to obtain and consider proper advice prior to the mortgaging of charity land as required by s38 of the 1993 Act;
  - a breach of the duty to keep accounting records, as required by s41 of the 1993 Act, which is so material or pervasive that the auditors are unable to express an opinion on the financial statements;

- a charity undertaking a significant non-charitable trade falling outside current taxation exemptions or extra-statutory concessions available to charities.

21.13.4 Ceasing to hold office

In addition to the duty to report matters of material significance, reg 6(6) of the 1995 Regulations (E&W) provides that where an auditor appointed by charity trustee ceases for any reason to hold office he shall send to the charity trustees a statement of any circumstances connected with his ceasing to hold office which he considers should be brought to their attention or, if he considers that there are no such circumstances, a statement that there are none; and the auditor shall send a copy of any statement sent to the charity trustees under this paragraph (except a statement that there are no such circumstances) to the Commission.

Matters that may require consideration in relation to this duty include:

- disagreement over opinions expressed or to be expressed in an auditors' report;
- disagreement over any disclosure made or to be made to the Commission in respect of a matter of material significance;
- disagreement over any accounting policy, assumption, financial judgement or disclosure made in the accounts or in the preparation of the accounts;
- concerns over any matter which is believed to give rise to a material risk of a loss of charitable funds; and
- lack of co-operation or obstruction in the context of an audit.

21.13.5 Discussing matters of material significance with trustees

The trustees are the persons principally responsible for the management of the charity. Auditors will therefore normally bring a matter of 'material significance' to the attention of the trustees and seek agreement on the facts and circumstances. However, SAS 620.5 stresses that where the auditors conclude that a duty to report arises they should bring the matter to the attention of the regulator without undue delay. The trustees may wish to report the matters identified to the Charity Commission themselves and detail the actions taken or to be taken. Whilst such a report from the trustees may provide valuable information, it does not relieve the auditors of the statutory duty to report directly to the Charity Commission.

The Charity Commission has indicated that where a matter that is potentially of material significance is identified by the auditors, but has already been rectified by the trustees, then a reporting duty will not arise unless there has been significant pecuniary loss to the charity or the matter casts doubt on the honesty and integrity of the trustees. If the auditors are uncertain as to whether a matter has been rectified it would be advisable to report to the Charity Commission.

21.13.6 Auditors' right to report to the Charity Commission

In the case of unincorporated charities in England and Wales, the circumstances giving rise to a duty to report are equivalent to those applicable to regulated entities in the financial sector. In the financial sector a separate statutory right (as opposed to a duty) to report to the appropriate regulator also exists and may be used by auditors. Similarly auditors may become aware of circumstances which in their opinion do not give rise to a duty to report to the Charity Commission but which should be brought to the attention of the Charity Commission. Such matters should be considered in conjunction with SAS 120 *Consideration of law and regulations*, and where any report is made auditors rely on the protection afforded by general law.

21.13.7 Contents of a report to the Charity Commission

The Charity Commission has indicated that a report concerning a matter of material significance should be sent to the 'reporting officer' at the relevant office of the Charity Commission. SAS 620.8 provides details of the information that should be included in report to a regulator. The Charity Commission has indicated that a report should follow the format provided by the standard, that is to:

(a) state the name of the charity and its registration number;
(b) state that the report is made under reg 6(5) or (6) of the 1995 Regulations (E&W);
   - state that the report is prepared in accordance with SAS 620;
   - describe the context in which the report is given;
   - describe the matter giving rise to the report;
   - request that the Charity Commission confirms that the report has been received; and
   - state the name of the auditors, the date of the report, the date of any verbal report made to the Charity Commission and the name of the officer to whom the report was made.

The report is required to be in writing (the Charity Commission has indicated that reports sent by e-mail are not, however, acceptable at present). Auditors are not relieved of their duty to make a written report where an oral report has been previously made to the Charity Commission or by any informal discussions of the issue with Charity Commission staff. Similarly, auditors are not relieved of their duty to report on the basis that any other party has provided relevant information, whether written or oral, to the Charity Commission.

The report sets out such information as is relevant to a proper under-standing of the matter reported. It explains how the matter was identified, and the extent to which it has been investigated and discussed with the charity's trustees. The report also describes any steps taken by the trustees to rectify the reportable matter.

Where trustees wish to make a submission to the Charity Commission as to the circumstances and steps being taken to address a reportable matter, the auditors may attach such a memorandum or report prepared by the trustees to their report. Where such additional information is provided auditors refer to the additional information in their report, and indicate whether or not they have undertaken additional procedures to determine whether any remedial actions described have been taken.

Chapter 22 – Independent examination

22.1 Introduction

Current charity law now embodies the concept that, for most charities, some form of independent external scrutiny of accounts is required.

The trustees of unincorporated charities whose gross income and total expenditure is less than £250,000 in the current year and in both the preceding two years, may elect to have an independent examination subject to any other formal regulatory or constitutional requirement. This requirement applies to financial years commencing on or after 1 March 1996. (Note: As regards the threshold for previous financial years, this requirement applies only to previous financial years which commence on or after that date.) For charities whose gross income and total expenditure are each less than £10,000 in a particular year, there is no statutory requirement for any form of independent scrutiny. Trustees may, of course, seek the assurance of an examination where they consider it appropriate. Incorporated charities cannot have an independent examination.

22.2 What is an 'independent examination'?

Independent examination is a new term introduced by the 1993 Act and inserts a new layer into the scrutiny process. Independent examination provides a higher level of assurance than an audit exemption report, but is a less onerous form of scrutiny than an audit. As there is a fine dividing line between a full audit and no meaningful scrutiny, the aim of an independent examination is to find some middle ground. The more onerous requirements imposed on the independent examiner are a recognition of greater public expectation, as regards the level of assurance provided of the proper administration of the charity and its funds by the charity trustees.

The examiner is not required to form an opinion as to whether the accounts show a true and fair view. Rather, the objective of the examination is to enable the examiner to state whether, on the basis of procedures carried out, anything has come to his attention that causes him to believe that the account and statement (or, statement of accounts) is not prepared, in all material respects, in accordance with the financial reporting framework. In other words, it is a form of negative assurance. For the purposes of expressing negative assurance, the examiner should be able to obtain sufficient appropriate evidence primarily through enquiries and analytical procedures to be able to draw conclusions.

Other matters which may cause concern are reported on an exception basis, if they arise during the course of the examination.

Section 43(7)(b) of the 1993 Act enables the Commissioners to give directions, as they consider appropriate, with respect to the carrying out of such an examination and these are given in their booklet *Independent Examination of Charity Accounts 2001* (CC63) which updates their original publication. (The carrying out of an independent examination: *Directions and guidance notes* (CC56), issued in March 1996). There are 12 specific directions which the examiner must address, eight of which apply to all accounts and a further four (7, 8, 9 and 10) which apply only when a statement of accounts is prepared on the accruals basis. Each direction, which must be followed, is accompanied by explanatory guidance. The Commissioners stress that, as with any guidance, the procedures suggested and examples given cannot meet all circumstances that may arise in the course of examination and judgement will need to be exercised by examiners in the context of their work. The directions and guidance in CC63 are reproduced below (see **22.8**), together with a commentary thereon.

22.3 Who is an independent examiner?

An independent examiner is defined in s43(3)(a) as 'an independent person who is reasonably believed by the trustees to have the requisite ability and practical experience to carry out a competent examination of the accounts'.

It seems somewhat ironic that, while the level of assurance provided by an independent examination is higher than that provided by an audit exemption report, the qualifications required of an independent examiner are less demanding.

In accordance with s43(7)(a), the Commissioners have given guidance to charity trustees in connection with the selection of an independent examiner. For ease of reference, that guidance is given as Annex 1 to this chapter. Charity trustees should take all necessary steps to satisfy themselves that the examiner is independent, has the requisite ability and practical experience to discharge the responsibilities. If charity trustees follow this guidance, the guidance states that they can be satisfied that they will have taken all reasonable steps to obtain a competent independent examination of their accounts.

22.4 Who is an 'independent person'?

For an examiner to be independent, the guidance states that the individual should have no connection with the charity's trustees which might inhibit the impartial conduct of the examination. Whether or not such a connection exists will depend on the particular circumstances, but the guidance lists those persons who, as a minimum, would normally be considered to have such a connection.

Examiners should have regard to appropriate ethical considerations: these include integrity, objectivity, independence, professional competence and due care and confidentiality.

22.5 Which persons would have the 'requisite ability'?

During the debates in the House of Lords on the Charities Bill, the persons, other than accountants, who were thought to have the requisite ability included bank and building society managers and local authority treasurers. At that stage, however, the upper limit for independent examination was intended as £100,000, not £250,000.

The suitability of an independent examiner and the quality both of the examiner's credentials and of their evidence will depend on the particular circumstances and the size and nature of the charity's transactions. As regards the quality of evidence of credentials, trustees should consider obtaining references.

The Commissioners strongly recommend that where a charity's:

(a) gross assets exceed £1 million;
(b) gross income exceeds £100,000 (but is below £250,000) that a qualified accountant (or an individual with similar qualifications in charity finance at an appropriate level) should carry out the examination.

In any event if the accounts are prepared on the accruals basis a greater understanding of accounting principles and accounting standards would be required.

The standard of scrutiny which an examiner can be expected to exercise is likely to vary depending on his qualifications and experience and this should be reflected in the trustees' decision on the appointment of a suitable person. A higher standard of care would be required of a qualified accountant.

For charities seeking an independent examiner, who is not necessarily a qualified accountant, the Association of Charity Independent Examiners can provide assistance and names of suitably qualified examiners, who act within a code of ethics.

CC63 refers to this Association who can be contacted at:

36 Acomb Wood Drive
York
YO24 2XN
(Telephone: 01904 788885)

22.6 What is 'practical experience'?

Prospective independent examiners should have practical experience which is relevant to the charity. This could be achieved by:

(a) having had an involvement in the financial administration of a charity of a similar nature;
(b) having acted successfully as an independent examiner on previous occasions for such charities; or
(c) relevant practical experience in accountancy or commerce.

22.7 Selection procedures

Charity trustees should:

(a) discuss fully with the prospective examiner the work of the charity and their expectations;
(b) ensure that the prospective examiner is familiar with:
  (i) the Commissioners' directions to independent examiners and the nature of the report required;
  (ii) where a statement of accounts is prepared in accordance with s42(1), the form and content of the Regulations, the methods and principles with which that statement must be prepared and the SORP; and
(c) ensure that the letter of engagement recognises and does not limit the examiner's statutory duties.

22.8 The Commissioners' Directions

The Directions (which must be followed) are reproduced in bold print.

22.8.1 Examination and accounting thresholds

Direction

1 **Carry out such specific procedures as are considered necessary to provide a reasonable basis on which to conclude that an examination**

is required under section 43(3) and that section 43(2) (audit) does not apply to the charity, and where accounts are prepared under section 42(3), that the charity trustees may properly elect to prepare accounts under this sub-section.

Guidance

1.1 Trustees may elect for independent examination (under section 43(3) or for the preparation of receipts and payments accounts (under section 42(3)). For either election to be valid, the charity must be within the relevant income and/or expenditure bands specified by legislation. The examiner should therefore ascertain:

- the charity's gross income and total expenditure for the financial year concerned, as well as the two previous years;
- whether the charity's governing document stipulates any form of professional audit; and
- whether any grant condition demands an audit.

1.2 Carrying out these procedures at an early stage should prevent the work of the examiner being duplicated by professional audit which would add to the expense for the charity.

1.3 In cases where the charity's gross recorded income or total expenditure for the year of the accounts, or either of the two years preceding, exceeds the threshold level of £250,000 (below which an independent examination can be carried out), the accounts should be referred back to the charity trustees for an auditor to be appointed under section 43(2).

1.4 Examiners should also familiarise themselves with the various other threshold bands and their effect on the accounting procedures for charities:

- Where the charity's gross recorded income and total expenditure is £10,000 or less, there is no statutory requirement for an independent examination. In such cases the examiner should refer the accounts back to the charity trustees for confirmation as to whether the examination should proceed.
- Where the accounts comprise a receipts and payments account and statement of assets and liabilities, prepared under section 42(3), the examiner should begin by ascertaining that the gross income of the charity does not exceed the £100,000 threshold for that year. If it appears that the threshold has been exceeded, the accounts should be referred back to the charity trustees for preparation on the accruals accounting basis under section 42(1).

1.5 The examiner should consider at an early stage of the examination the levels of income and expenditure disclosed by the accounting records and by the trial balance. The examiner does, however, need to remain alert to any additional information which may come to attention during the course of the examination which indicates that an income or expenditure threshold has been crossed.

1.6 The level of income or expenditure should be calculated in accordance with the methods set out in Appendix 3. If accounts are prepared on the accruals basis then the level of income or expenditure should be considered on the accruals basis. Where accounts are prepared on the receipts and payments basis then the level of income or expenditure should be considered on the basis of money actually received and expended.

Comment

The examiner must always maintain an awareness that an audit may be a requirement:

(a) of the charity's governing document; or
(b) under another parallel statutory regime; or
(c) placed on the charity by a donor as a condition of accepting a grant, or other finance.

Many charities have related charitable funds or branches with varying degrees of independence and differing constitutions. Given that the relevant income and expenditure thresholds identified by the 1993 Act relate to those of the charity as a whole, including its special trusts and controlled branches, the examiner needs to ensure that these entities are properly constituted and accounted for.

The examiner should be aware that, under s96(5) of the 1993 Act, the Commissioners are able to direct that, for all or any of the purposes of that Act, an institution established for any special purposes of, or in connection with a charity, shall be treated as forming part of the charity, or as forming a distinct charity Further, the Charities (Amendment) Act 1995 has inserted subsection 95(6) into the 1993 Act, enabling the Commissioners to direct that, for all or any purposes of the Act, two or more charities having the same charity trustees shall be treated as a single charity.

The specific procedures appear more demanding than those in respect of an audit exemption report, where the reporting accountant is required to perform such procedures as are necessary to provide a reasonable basis on which to form an opinion on whether, having regard only to, and on the basis of, the information in the accounting records, the company is entitled to exemption from audit. The reporting accountant will accept the information contained in those records and will not attempt to verify further, or substantiate, the basis on which entitlement to the exemption is claimed by the directors. Conversely, in order to verify the level to which the accounts should be prepared and subject to scrutiny, the examiner must remain alert to any information which comes to light indicating that income or expenditure may have been unrecorded and that, consequently, a threshold has been exceeded. For example, income may have been deferred to a future financial year to circumvent the preparation of a statement of accounts or an audit being carried out.

Where it becomes apparent that the gross income or total expenditure has exceeded the limits above which an audit is required, the examiner will need to notify the trustees. Provided that he is a registered auditor, a fresh engagement can be agreed with the charity.

CC63 contains a flowchart regarding the eligibility requirements for independent examination and this is reproduced as Annex 4 to this chapter.

CC63 also contains information on how to calculate gross income and total expenditure, summarised in chapter **3** (**3.4.2**).

22.8.2 Understanding the charity

Direction

2　**Obtain an understanding of the charity's constitution, organisation, accounting systems, activities and nature of its assets, liabilities, incoming resources and application of resources in order to plan the specific examination procedures appropriate to the circumstances of the charity.**

Guidance

2.1　For a proper examination to be carried out it is important for the examiner to have an understanding of the operations, structure and objectives of the charity. This understanding will help the examiner to plan appropriate examination procedures. The steps taken by an examiner would normally include:

- consideration of the governing document of the charity, paying particular attention to the charity's objects, powers and obligations;
- discussions with trustees and, where appropriate, the charity's staff to ascertain the structure, methods and means by which the charity seeks to achieve its objects;
- discussions with the trustees and, where appropriate, the charity's staff about the affairs and activities of the charity in order to gain an insight into any special circumstances and problems affecting the charity;
- reviewing the minutes of trustees' meetings to ascertain details of major events, plans, decisions and changes to the trustee body; and
- obtaining details of accounting records maintained and methods of recording financial transactions.

Comment

The examiner should properly plan his work. His knowledge of the charity, its constitution, organisation, activities and accounting systems and the nature of its assets, liabilities, incoming resources and their application is necessary so that he can design appropriate procedures and make relevant enquiries of the charity trustees.

Although the independent examiner is required to make a positive statement in his report if there has been any material expenditure or action which does not appear to be in accordance with the charity's trusts, a separate direction is not provided. Nonetheless, while the examiner is not required to carry out specific procedures to identify such breaches, he needs to have an understanding of the objectives and activities of the charity to be able to identify such breaches when carrying out the work he is required to do.

The examiner should use the same materiality as would be applied were an audit carried out. This is because the judgement as to what is, or is not, material is made by reference to the information on which he is reporting and the needs of those relying on that information, and not on the level of assurance provided.

Many charities publish summarised accounts in addition to the full accounts required by law. In planning the examination of the full accounts, the examiner should ascertain whether summarised accounts are to be prepared.

It will usually be more efficient for the examiner to carry out his work on the summarised accounts at the same time as carrying out the examination of the full accounts. In the past, some charities have published their annual reviews, containing summarised accounts, after publication of the full accounts. The examiner should encourage the trustees to take this into account when they are planning the timetable for the preparation of the full accounts.

22.8.3 Documentation

Direction

3   **Record the examination procedures carried out and any matters which are important to support conclusions reached or statement provided in the examiner's report.**

Guidance

3.1   The working papers should provide details of the work undertaken and support any conclusions reached, and record any judgemental matters (see 8.1) which may arise. Working papers should normally be retained by the examiner for six years from the end of the financial year to which they relate, and would normally include:

- a letter of engagement from the independent examiner to the trustees, together with evidence that this has been accepted by the trustees (for example a return copy of the letter signed by a representative of the trustees);
- relevant information extracted or obtained from the governing document, trustees' meeting minutes and a record of discussions with the charity trustees and the charity's staff;
- details of procedures carried out during the examination, with conclusions reached and any areas of concern identified;
- notes as to how any areas of concern have been resolved together with details of any verification procedures used;
- schedules showing the breakdown of accounting items that have been aggregated for accounts disclosure purposes;
- copies of any trial balance, accounts and trustees' annual report; and
- copies of any written assurances obtained from the trustees confirming amounts included within the accounts.

Comment

The examiner should document all matters which are important in providing the evidence to support his report.

In addition to the above, the documentation should include:

(a) a description of the accounting records and systems and a conclusion as to whether proper accounting records have been maintained;
(b) evidence of the planning process;
(c) any disclosure checklist which has been used;
(d) a letter of representation.

A separately documented work programme is not considered to be necessary, provided that the work planned and performed and the conclusions reached are fully recorded.

22.8.4 Comparison with accounting records

Direction

4 **Compare the accounts of the charity with the charity's accounting records in sufficient detail to provide a reasonable basis on which to decide whether the accounts are in accordance with such accounting records.**

Guidance

4.1 It is necessary to compare the accounts with the underlying accounting records. Where prepared on the accruals basis, all balances in the accounts will need to be compared with the trial balance or any nominal ledger maintained. Where accounts are prepared on the receipts and payments basis a direct comparison with the cash records of the charity should be carried out if no nominal ledger is kept.

4.2 Test checks will also be necessary of the posting of entries from books of prime entry (e.g., petty cash book, any sales or purchase ledgers or day books) to any nominal ledger and/or to the trial balance itself. Similar checks are also necessary even where accounting records are maintained by using computer accounting packages.

4.3 A review of bank reconciliations, payroll summaries and control accounts prepared will provide a useful check as to the completeness of posting from books of prime entry.

4.4 There is no requirement for accounting entries to be checked against source documents (e.g., invoices, supplier statements, purchase orders etc.) unless concerns arise during the course of the examination which cannot be resolved by seeking explanations.

4.5 Whilst the charity trustees are responsible for the preparation of accounts, on occasions the examiner may also prepare accounts on behalf of the trustees. The preparation of accounts will not generally impinge on independence (see Appendix 1) provided the examiner ensures that the requirements of the Directions are met and avoids involvement in the management or administration of the charity. Where reliance is placed on work undertaken in the course of preparation of the accounts (e.g., posting of accounting entries) the examiner should consider whether separate procedures as set out above are also necessary to ensure this Direction has been met.

Comment

Postings from the books of prime entry to the general ledger should be test-checked in each direction. There is no initial requirement for accounting entries to be checked against source documents (e.g., invoices). Unlike an audit exemption report, however, source documents may need to be checked if concerns arising during the course of the examination cannot be resolved by explanation.

22.8.5 Accounting records

Direction

5 **Review the accounting records maintained in accordance with section 41 in order to provide a reasonable basis for the identification of any material failure to maintain such records.**

Guidance

5.1 The charity trustees are responsible for maintaining the accounting records.

5.2 The examiner is required to review the accounting records with a view to identifying any material failure to maintain such records in accordance with section 41(1).

5.3 The review procedures are not aimed at identifying the occasional omission or insignificant error, but at any gross failure to maintain records in a manner consistent with statutory requirements.

5.4 Accounting records should be well organised and capable of ready retrieval and analysis. The records may take a number of forms, for example book form, loose-leaf binder or computer records.

5.5 The accounting records should:
  • be up to date;
  • be readily available; and
  • provide the basic information from which the financial position can be ascertained, not only at the year end, but also on any selected date.

5.6 The accounting records should contain:
  • details of all money received and expended, the date, and the nature of the receipt or expenditure; and
  • details of assets and liabilities.

5.7 Smaller charities may not maintain formal ledgers to record assets and liabilities, and in such instances the requirements can generally be met by maintaining files for unpaid invoices and amounts receivable. A record of fixed assets is generally necessary to meet the accounting requirements.

Comment

The reporting accountant is required to carry out procedures as are necessary to provide reasonable assurance on which to express an opinion on whether the accounts are in agreement with the accounting records, but not as to whether proper accounting records have been kept. Conversely, the examiner is required to state whether any matter has come to his attention, in connection with his examination, which gives him reasonable cause to believe either that the accounts are not in agreement with the accounting records or that proper accounting records have not been kept. The requirement to keep and maintain proper accounting records is fundamental to the administration, protection and use of funds for the purposes for which they have been given. An audit exemption report would provide no assurance about that requirement.

It is worth noting that the Commissioners expect that a record of fixed assets is generally necessary to meet the accounting requirements. Thus, for those charities which have not yet done so, a fixed asset register will need to be compiled.

22.8.6 Analytical procedures

Direction

6   Carry out analytical procedures to identify unusual items or disclosures in the accounts. Where concerns arise from these procedures, the

examiner must seek explanations from the charity trustees. If, after following such procedures, the examiner has reason to believe that in any respect the accounts may be materially misstated then additional procedures, including verification of the asset, liability, incoming resource or application, must be carried out.

Guidance

6.1 It is important that the examiner looks carefully at the final accounts to see if they reveal any unusual items, unexpected fluctuations, or inconsistencies with other financial information. This procedure is called analytical review. Steps taken would normally include:
- comparing the accounts with those for comparable prior periods;
- comparing the accounts with any budgets or forecasts that have been produced;
- considering whether incoming resources and the application of resources are consistent with known fundraising sources, payroll details, activities, and the objectives of the charity. It is important to have obtained a proper understanding of the nature of the charity's activities and affairs for this aspect of the review to be successful;
- considering whether the liabilities and current assets disclosed are consistent with the scale and type of activities undertaken;
- considering whether fixed assets investments are producing income consistent with the nature of assets held; and
- considering whether the tangible fixed assets are consistent with the scale and type of activities undertaken by the charity.

6.2 Where analytical review procedures identify any unusual items, unexpected fluctuation or inconsistency then explanations should be sought from the charity trustees or, where appropriate, the charity's staff.

6.3 If the explanations provided by the charity trustees or, where appropriate, the charity's staff do not satisfy the examiner, then additional procedures will be necessary. Such procedures may include:
- physical inspection of a tangible fixed asset;
- verification of title to an asset;
- inspection of third party documentary evidence (e.g. invoice, contract or agreement) to verify an expense or liability or to confirm an amount of income received or receivable;
- third party certification of a bank balance, or other asset held including the custody of investment certificates; and
- checking of a post year end receipt or payment to confirm recoverability of a debt or the amount of a liability.

6.4 A comprehensive list of analytical procedures, and of additional procedures where concerns arise is beyond the scope of this publication, and will to an extent be an area in which the examiner will need to exercise judgement and to draw on experience.

Comment

The examiner is required to carry out analysis and review procedures of the accounts to identify any unusual items, disclosures or omissions.

Where concerns arise, the examiner must seek and obtain satisfactory information and explanations from the charity trustees. If, after making these enquiries, the examiner still has reason to believe that the accounts may be materially misstated, he must carry out additional procedures as are necessary to give that negative assurance. These additional procedures take the form of audit procedures and include the verification of an asset or liability, or the vouching of an incoming resource or application of that resource.

Analytical procedures may include:

(a) comparing the accounts with those of previous periods and, if available, with budgets and forecasts;

(b) obtaining explanations from the trustees for any unusual fluctuations or inconsistencies;

(c) considering the effect of any unadjusted errors – individually and in aggregate, bringing those to the attention of the trustees and determining how they will influence the report on the examination;

(d) reading the accounts to consider, on the basis of the information which has come to the examiner's attention, whether the accounts appear to conform with the basis of accounting indicated;

(e) considering the adequacy of the disclosures and their suitability as to classification and presentation;

(f) enquiring of the trustees concerning, for example: whether all transactions have been recorded;
   • whether the accounting policies comply with applicable accounting standards and SORPs, whether they have been applied appropriately and consistently and, if not, that the disclosures have been made of any changes;
   • changes in the charity's activities and accounting principles and practices;

(g) reading the minutes of trustees' and any executive committees) meetings in order to identify matters which could be important to the examination;

(h) enquiring about the existence of transactions with related parties, how such transactions have been accounted for and whether related parties have been properly disclosed;

(i) enquiring about commitments and contingencies;

(j) obtaining a letter of representation.

A full understanding of the objectives and activities of the charity will be necessary in order for the analytical review work to be properly performed.

22.8.7 Form and content of accounts

Direction

7   Carry out such detailed procedures as the examiner considers neces-
     sary to provide a reasonable basis on which to decide whether or not
     the accounts prepared under section 42(1) comply with the require-
     ments of the Regulations as to the form and content of charity
     accounts.

Guidance

7.1 Where accounts are prepared under section 42(1) (the accruals basis),
     the 1995 and 2000 Regulations lay down the requirements as to the
     form and content of such accounts. Which set of Regulations apply
     depends on the commencement date of the financial year in question,
     and, in some cases, on the choice of the charity trustees.

7.2 For any period which commenced on or after 1 January 2001, the 2000
     Regulations apply. In some cases, charity trustees may decide to
     prepare accounts in accordance with the 2000 Regulations for periods
     which commenced before this date. Note, however, that trustees
     should use one framework or the other – a mixture of the two is not
     acceptable.

7.3 The 1995 Regulations draw heavily on the recommendations of the
     Statement of Recommended Practice – Accounting by Charities (the
     Charities SORP, published in October 1995). Similarly, the 2000 Regu-
     lations draw heavily on the recommendations of the Statement of Rec-
     ommended Practice – Accounting and Reporting by Charities (SORP
     2000, published in October 2000). In either case, the examiner will
     require access to the relevant SORP and an understanding of its
     general principles to ensure compliance with the Regulations. In par-
     ticular the 2000 Regulations require the accounts and certain notes to
     the accounts to be prepared in accordance with the methods and prin-
     ciples set out in SORP 2000.

7.4 The examiner should be conversant with the relevant Regulations as
     to the form and content of charity accounts prepared on the accruals
     basis and should examine the accounts in sufficient detail to ensure
     compliance with these Regulations. Further detail is also available in
     our Accruals Accounts Pack 2001 (CC65).

7.5 The 1995 and 2000 Regulations do not specify the form and content
     of accounts prepared on a receipts and payments basis. Guidelines on
     the form and content of such accounts can be found in notes included
     in our Receipts and Payments Accounts Pack 2001 (CC64).

Comment

This procedure differs from that in respect of an audit exemption report. An
independent examiner is required to state whether or not any matter

has come to his attention which causes him to believe that the statement of accounts does not comply with any of the requirements (except the requirement to show a true and fair view) of the Regulations which prescribe the form and content of the statement of accounts. A reporting accountant is, however, only required to state whether the accounts have been drawn up in a manner consistent with the specified accounting requirements. The use of the words 'comply with' implies that the focus is on whether the statement of accounts complies with the substance of the legal requirements and not merely on whether it is in the required legal form.

For the majority of charities, a disclosure checklist should be completed.

As regards fixed assets, for example, detailed procedures may include the following:

(a) obtaining, or preparing, a lead schedule;

(b) considering whether fixed assets are included in the balance sheet under the appropriate caption in the format prescribed by the Regulations and recommended by the SORP;

(c) considering whether they are included on a basis permitted by the SORP;

(d) discussing with the trustees the capitalisation policy, additions to, and disposals from, fixed assets and enquiring whether all movements and profits and losses have been properly accounted for;

(e)* if necessary, vouching additions and disposals to supporting documentation;

(f)* if necessary, verifying fixed assets by establishing title or physical verification;

(g) discussing with the trustees the policy for depreciation and whether it is consistent with previous years. Considering whether fixed assets are being written off systematically over their useful economic lives. Comparing depreciation rates with prior periods. Considering whether fixed assets have suffered a permanent diminution in value;

(h) enquiring of the trustees that all information, e.g., regarding fixed assets not capitalised, is disclosed in the accounts;

(i) enquiring of the trustees whether any of the fixed assets are subject to any form of security and, if so, that the details are fully disclosed in the statement of accounts;

(j) discussing with the trustees whether all lease agreements are properly reflected in the statement of accounts;

(k) enquiring of the trustees whether all capital commitments are identified and properly disclosed.

*Only if the explanations received are not satisfactory

22.8.8 Accounting policies, estimates and judgements

Direction

8   When accounts are prepared under section 42(1), review the account-
     ing policies adopted and consider their conformity with fundamental
     accounting concepts, consistency of application and their appropri-
     ateness to the activities of the charity. The examiner must also con-
     sider and review any significant estimate or judgement that has been
     made in preparing the accounts.

Guidance

8.1 Where accounts are prepared under section 42(1) (the accruals
     basis), the accounting policies adopted, and also any estimates or
     judgements made in preparing the accounts, may have a material
     effect on both the financial activities and state of affairs disclosed by
     the accounts. Such matters therefore require careful consideration by
     the examiner.

8.2 The examiner should be satisfied that accounts are prepared on a basis
     consistent with the going concern assumption and accruals concept,
     and that the accounting policies adopted and applied are appropriate
     to the activities of the charity and to ensure a relevant, reliable, com-
     parable and understandable accounts presentation.

8.3 Where accounts are produced under the 1995 Regulations the exam-
     iner will consider whether the values at which assets and liabilities are
     recorded in the accounts are determined by the methods and prin-
     ciples set out in SORP 1995.

8.4 Where accounts are produced under the 2000 Regulations the exam-
     iner should consider whether the accounting policies adopted are con-
     sistent with the methods and principles set out in SORP 2000.

8.5. The examiner must consider the reasonableness of any estimates or
     judgements where they are material to the accounts. Matters that may
     require consideration include:
     • transfers to or from designated fund accounts;
     • valuation of gifts in kind;
     • valuation of fixed asset investments where no market prices exist;
     • estimates resulting from transactions not being fully recorded in the
       accounting records; and
     • where applicable, the allocation of costs between the various expen-
       diture categories of the Statement of Financial Activities.

8.6 If accounts are prepared on the receipts and payments basis under
     section 42(3), the only fundamental accounting concept which applies
     is that of consistency. Accounting policies and judgemental issues have
     less relevance since the receipts and payments account is simply a
     factual record of money actually received and expended. The state-
     ment of assets and liabilities is a straightforward schedule of infor-

mation. This direction therefore does not apply to such accounts, unless other examination procedures have given rise to concerns that need to be addressed in this way.

8.7 Further guidance as to the form and content of receipts and payments accounts can be found in notes included in our Receipts and Payments Accounts Pack 2001 (CC64).

Comment

The policies adopted by the charity trustees should comply with the fundamental accounting concepts and be appropriate to the activities of the charity. Unlike a reporting accountant, the examiner would need to consider, for example, the going concern concept.

Unlike a reporting accountant, the examiner must consider the reasonableness of any estimates or judgements which are material to the statement of accounts and whether that statement complies with applicable accounting standards and SORPs.

Paragraphs 279 and 280 of SORP 2000, which apply to all charities, are as follows:

'279. **AA** The notes regarding the basis of preparation of the accounts should state that the accounts have been prepared in accordance with:

(a) this SORP and accounting standards or with this SORP and the FRSSE (see paragraphs 345–347);

(b) the Charities Act or the Companies Act or other legislative requirements; and

(c) the historic cost basis of accounting except for investments (and if applicable, fixed assets) which have been included at revalued amounts.

280. **AA** If the accounts depart from accounting standards in any material respect, this should be stated in the accounting policies and Annual Report giving the reason and justification for the departure and the financial impact. Similarly the following details should be given for any material departure from this SORP:

(a) a brief description of how the treatment adopted departs from this SORP;

(b) the reasons why the trustees judge that the treatment adopted is more appropriate to the charity's particular circumstances; and

(c) an estimate of the financial effect on the accounts where this is needed for the accounts to give a true and fair view.'

A departure is not justified simply because it gives the reader a more appealing picture of the financial position or results of the charity.

22.8.9 Events subsequent to the year end

Direction

9   When accounts are prepared under section 42(1), enquire of the charity
     trustees as to material events subsequent to the year end of the accounts
     examined which may require adjustment or disclosure in the accounts.

Guidance

9.1   Where accounts are prepared under section 42(1) (the accruals basis)
      an event occurring after the balance sheet date may have a material
      effect on both the financial activities and state of affairs disclosed by
      the accounts.

9.2   The events that have occurred subsequent to the year end should
      therefore be discussed with the charity trustees and, where appropri-
      ate, with the charity's staff. Any effects on the accounts under review
      should be considered. The matters that should be discussed include:
      • whether any income anticipated and accrued into the accounts at
        the year end has proved irrecoverable;
      • discovery of an error or fraud;
      • crystallisation of a taxation liability;
      • repayment of a grant or donation received;
      • a valuation of a property indicating a permanent diminution in
        value.

9.3   Where an event occurring subsequent to the year end affects the
      amount or disclosure of an item in the accounts this should be
      brought to the attention of the charity trustees with a view to the
      accounts being amended.

9.4   If accounts are prepared on a receipts and payments basis under section
      42(3) of the 1993 Act, then there is no requirement to consider events
      subsequent to the year end, unless other examination procedures have
      given rise to concerns which need to be addressed in this way.

Comment

The examiner's responsibility is limited to making enquiries of the trustees
as to whether there are any events subsequent to the date of the statement
of accounts. He is not required to take the more active approach, i.e., to
obtain sufficient appropriate evidence, required by SAS 150 Subsequent
events. The examiner may however, ask for confirmation of this matter in
a letter of representation.

22.8.10 Trustees' annual report

Direction

10   When accounts are prepared under section 42(1), compare the
     accounts to any financial references in the charity trustees' annual
     report (if any); identifying any major inconsistencies and consider the

significance such matters will have on a proper and accurate under-standing of the charity's accounts.

Guidance

10.1 The trustees' annual report provides a report of the charity's activities during the financial year. The 1995 Regulations or, as the case may be, the 2000 Regulations specify the information that is to be con-tained in such reports.

10.2 Procedures should be directed at identifying inconsistencies with the accounts which are misleading or which contradict the financial infor-mation contained in the accounts.

10.3 Where inconsistencies are identified which may have a significant effect on the proper understanding of the accounts, this should be drawn to the attention of the charity trustees. If no appropriate amendment is made to the annual report then details of the matter should be provided in the examiner's report.

10.4 If accounts are prepared on a receipts and payments basis under section 42(3) there is no requirement placed on the examiner to con-sider the trustees' annual report. The examiner may, nevertheless, find the annual report a useful guide to the activities of the charity.

Comment

Any material inconsistency between the report and the accounts is expressed with reference to the accounts, as this relates to the relevant power in the 1993 Act. Conversely, the equivalent provision in the 1985 Act is with reference to the directors' report.

22.8.11 Examiner's report

Direction

11 **Review and assess all conclusions drawn from the evidence obtained from the examination and consider the implications on the report to be made under Regulation 7 of the 1995 Regulations. If the examiner has cause to make a positive statement on any matter arising from the provisions of Regulation 7(e) or 7(f), or to make a statement on any matter arising from the provisions of Regulation 7(g), then the exam-iner must ensure so far as practicable that the report so made gives a clear explanation of the matter and of its financial effects on the accounts presented.**

Guidance

11.1 The requirements as to the form and content of the examiner's report are set out in the 1995 Regulations. These are produced in Appendix 2, together with illustrative examples of such reports. The examiner needs to consider carefully the conclusions drawn from the procedures undertaken in accordance with the Commissioners' directions, and the impact of these conclusions on the examiner's report.

11.2 In providing the examination report the examiner must state whether or not any matter has come to attention, in connection with the examination, which gives reasonable cause to believe that in any material respect:

- accounting records have not been kept in accordance with section 41;
- the accounts do not accord with the accounting records; or
- whether accounts which are prepared on the accruals basis fail to comply with regulations in respect of their form and content.

11.3 Where any of the above concerns have been identified there should be a clear explanation of the nature of the failure and of its financial effects on the accounts. If the financial effect cannot be ascertained due to uncertainty, the nature of the uncertainty should be explained. If the concern relates to non-compliance with the relevant Regulations as to the form and content of accounts, this should be raised with the charity trustees to seek the necessary amendment to the accounts.

11.4 The examiner is also required to state whether or not any matter has come to attention in connection with the examination to which, in the examiner's opinion, attention should be drawn in the report to enable a proper understanding of the accounts to be reached.

11.5 Where such matters have come to attention, then they should be brought to the attention of the charity trustees with a view to seeking an amendment or adjustment to the accounts. If concerns remain the matter should be addressed in the examiner's report. The matter concerned should be fully explained together with the financial effects on the accounts.

11.6 There is also a requirement to provide a statement if the following matters have become apparent to the examiner during the course of the examination:

- any material expenditure or action which appears not to be in accordance with the trusts of the charity;
- any failure to be provided with information and explanation by any past or present trustee, officer or employee that is considered necessary for the examination; and
- in the case of accruals accounts any material inconsistency between the accounts and the trustees' annual report.

11.7 In order to identify any material expenditure or activities undertaken outside the objects of the charity an understanding of the stated objects of the charity, as set out in its governing document, is necessary. The guidance provided under Direction 2 (Understanding the charity) will be of particular relevance in obtaining a background understanding of the charity's objectives and activities. Small or immaterial levels of expenditure on purposes outside of the objects of the charity will not generally be included in the examiner's report unless they are of a recurrent nature. Material expenditure or significant actions contrary to the trustees of the charity would be a major concern and details should be included on the examiner's report. The examiner need not carry out specific checks or procedures to identify such breaches, but such matters when identified must be included in the examiner's report.

11.8 Any failure to be provided with information and explanations may seriously hamper an examination. If information and explanations requested are not provided this matter must be included in the examiner's report.

11.9 In the case of accounts prepared on an accruals basis any major inconsistency between the accounts and the trustees' annual report may give rise to misunderstanding. This should be brought to the attention of the charity trustees with a view to the amendment of the discrepancy. Where concerns still exist this must be stated in the examiner's report.

Comment

The report should contain a clear expression of negative assurance. The examiner should review and assess all conclusions drawn from the evidence obtained as the basis for that expression.

Matters may come to the examiner's attention which cause him to express a qualification, in the relevant parts of his report, of the negative assurance provided. For example, the Regulations require the examiner to state whether, during his examination, a matter has come to his attention which causes him to believe that the statement of accounts does not comply with the requirements of the Regulations. This might be the case where a current asset is stated at cost, rather than at its net realisable value, in which case an 'except for' report may be appropriate. Alternatively, there may be circumstances, for example the non-consolidation of a subsidiary, where the matter is so material to the statement of accounts that an 'adverse' statement should be given.

Paragraph 7(f) of the 1995 Regulations requires the examiner to state whether or not any matter has come to his attention, in connection with the examination, to which, in his opinion, attention should be drawn in the report to enable a proper understanding of the accounts to be reached. Example 3 in Appendix 2 to the Commissioners' booklet gives an example of a qualification in these circumstances and is reproduced as part of Annex 2 to this chapter.

There may have been a limitation on the scope of the examiner's procedures. For example, a limitation of scope may be imposed by circumstances (e.g., where parts of the accounting records have been lost or destroyed). Alternatively, a limitation of scope may have been imposed by the directors (e.g., where they refuse to provide information or explanations requested by the examiner). In this latter circumstance, paragraph 7(g)(ii) of the 1995 Regulations requires the examiner to make a positive statement to that effect.

Verification of the completeness of voluntary donations can often be a problem for the auditors of charities. Given the scope of the examination, however, that problem should not arise for the examiner. The procedures he will need to adopt will be restricted to:

(a) comparing the results with previous years and those expected for the current year and discussing significant variations with the trustees:

(b) discussing with the trustees whether the recognition of income has taken place in the correct accounting period; and

(c) ensuring that, where accruals accounts are prepared, the accounting policy is clearly stated and that the accounting records have been maintained in accordance with that policy.

Examples of examiners' reports are provided in Appendix 2 to the booklet and, for ease of reference, are reproduced as Annex 2 to this chapter.

22.8.12 Reports to the Charity Commissioners

Direction

12 **Inform the Charity Commissioners in writing if, whilst acting in the capacity of the examiner of a charity, information or evidence is obtained which gives the examiner reasonable cause to believe that any one or more of the charity trustees has been responsible for deliberate or reckless misconduct in the administration of the charity.**

Guidance

12.1 If the examiner believes that one or more of the charity trustees have been responsible for deliberate or reckless misconduct in the administration of a charity then a separate written report of the matter must be forwarded to the Charity Commission. A reporting requirement would not arise through mere inadvertence or error of judgement on the part of a trustee whilst endeavouring honestly to carry out trustee duties. It is also unlikely that a reporting duty will arise unless a material loss or misapplication of funds has resulted or could result.

12.2 The duty to report relates to information or evidence obtained from the examiner's work undertaken in fulfilling the Commissioners' Directions or whilst acting in the capacity of the examiner of a charity. It is not intended that the examiner should report on small or insignificant matters, particularly where such matters have been satisfactorily resolved internally.

12.3 The reporting duty relates primarily to the actions of the charity trustees. However, in considering individual actions, the examiner must take into account the trustees' overall responsibilities of management and control.

12.4 Where a reporting duty arises the examiner should report the matter in writing to the 'Reporting Officer' at the office of the Charity Commission that normally deals with the charity. The examiner should state:

- the charity's name and registration number;
- state that the report is made in accordance with 'Direction 12' provided in this guidance;
- describe this matter giving rise to concern and, where possible, provide an estimate of the financial implications; and
- where the trustees are attempting to redress the situation a brief description of any steps being taken.

12.5 Examples of the types of matters that will give rise to a reporting duty are set out in Appendix 4.

Comment

Examples of the types of matter that may give rise to a reporting duty are reproduced as Annex 3 to this chapter.

In order to avoid deluging the Commissioners, matters which do not lead to a material loss or misapplication of funds, and which belong to a report to the trustees, should not be reported.

22.9 Reporting on summarised accounts

There is no statutory requirement for an independent examiner of an unincorporated charity to report on summarised accounts. The terms of engagement may, however, include the provision of a separate report to enable the trustees to follow the SORP's principles. Paragraph 296 of the SORP 2000 recommends that, where the full accounts have been examined, there should be a statement by the examiner giving his opinion as to whether or not the summarised accounts are consistent with the full accounts.

Where summarised accounts are issued, the procedures which the independent examiner will adopt should be similar to those which auditors will adopt. These are discussed in chapter **18**.

Annex 1 – Guidance on the selection of an examiner
Charity Commission guidance under section 43(7)(a) of the Charities Act 1993

Guidance from the Charity Commissioners to charity trustees on the selection of a person for appointment as an independent examiner. References to sections are references to the 1993 Act.

1   The requirement for an independent examination

1.1   The following criteria determine eligibility for independent examination:

(a) **Charitable companies are not eligible for independent examination; they must follow the provisions of the Companies Act and Regulations made under it.**

(b) Unincorporated charities with a gross income or total expenditure in the current year exceeding £10,000 must have their accounts independently examined, or may choose to have the accounts audited.

(c) All charities whose gross income or total expenditure is more than £250,000 in the current year or either of the two preceding years must have a professional audit. Trustees cannot opt for an independent examination if this threshold is exceeded.

(d) All charities whose governing document requires them to have an audit must do so (although if this means a higher level of scrutiny is necessary than otherwise required by the 1993 Act we are prepared to consider an amendment to the governing document to accord with the 1993 Act provisions).

1.2   The charity trustees should take steps to ensure that a competent examination takes place and they will therefore wish to consider most carefully the suitability of a prospective independent examiner.

1.3   Charity trustees are entitled to pay reasonable remuneration to an independent examiner for services rendered and if they are unable to obtain the services of a competent examiner on a voluntary basis, should be prepared to pay such remuneration and regard it as a proper charge on the assets of the charity.

2.   The independent examiner

2.1   An independent examiner as described in section 43(3)(a) is 'an **independent person** who is reasonably believed by the charity trustees to have the **requisite ability** and **practical experience** to carry out a **competent examination** of the accounts' (our emphasis).

3.   An independent person

3.1 For an examiner to be **independent** that individual should have no connection with the charity trustees which might inhibit the impartial conduct of the examination.

3.2 Whether this connection exists will depend upon the circumstances of a particular charity but the following persons at least will normally be considered to have such a connection.

(a) the charity trustees or anyone else who is closely involved in the administration of the charity;

(b) a major donor to or major beneficiary of the charity; or

(c) a close relative, spouse, partner, business partner or employee of any person who falls within sub-paragraph (a) or (b) above.

4. Requisite ability

4.1 In the House of Lords' debate on the Charities Bill, it was stated that 'an independent examiner must obviously be competent for the task that he is to do and he must be familiar with accounting methods, but he need not be a practising accountant. We have in mind ... people such as bank or building society managers, local authority treasurers or retired accountants. They would all be suitable as independent examiners'.

4.2 The quality of evidence of ability which is required will depend upon the size and nature of the charity's transactions. Charity trustees should consider taking independent references on the capability of the prospective independent examiner to carry out this function.

4.3 It is strongly recommended that the trustees of charities with gross assets in excess of £1,000,000 or gross income of more than £100,000 but below the compulsory audit threshold, should select a qualified accountant (or an individual with similar qualifications in charity finance at an appropriate level) to carry out the independent examination. In other cases where accounts are prepared on the accruals basis in accordance with regulations, a commensurate understanding of accountancy principles and accounting standards will still be needed.

5. Practical experience

5.1 Charity trustees should satisfy themselves that prospective examiners have **practical experience** relevant to the charity in question which might be by virtue of that person having:

• had an involvement in the financial administration of a charity of a similar nature; or

• acted successfully as an independent examiner on previous occasions for such charities; or

• relevant practical experience in accountancy or commerce.

6. Selection procedures

6.1 Charity trustees should discuss fully with the prospective examiner the work of the charity and their expectations. They should ensure that the prospective independent examiner is conversant with the Charity Commission Directions to independent examiners and the nature of the independent examiners' report prescribed by relevant Regulations made under section 44(1)(c). Where the accounts are prepared under section 42(1), the examiner should also be conversant with the Regulations made under section 42(1) as to the form and content of those accounts and the relevant SORP.

6.2 Charity trustees should take all necessary steps to satisfy themselves as to the matters referred to in paragraphs 3 to 5 above.

6.3 Charity trustees should ensure that any written terms of engagement recognise and do not limit the examiner's statutory duties.

6.4 Charity trustees who follow these guidelines and gain suitable assurances from prospective examiners and from any references can be satisfied that they have taken all reasonable steps to obtain a competent independent examination of their accounts for the period in question.

Annex 2 – Examples of examiner's reports

Example 1: Examiner's unqualified report

Independent Examiner's Report to the Trustees of 'ABC' Trust

I report on the accounts of the Trust for the year ended 30 April 2002, which are set out on pages 00 to 00.

Respective responsibilities of trustees and examiner

The charity's trustees are responsible for the preparation of the accounts. The charity's trustees consider that an audit is not required for this year (under section 43(2) of the Charities Act 1993 (the 1993 Act)) and that an independent examination is needed.

It is my responsibility to:

- examine the accounts (under section 43(3)(a) of the 1993 Act);
- to follow the procedures laid down in the General Directions given by the Charity Commissioners (under section 43(7)(b) of the 1993 Act); and
- to state whether particular matters have come to my attention.

Basis of independent examiner's report

My examination was carried out in accordance with the General Directions given by the Charity Commissioners. An examination includes a review of the accounting records kept by the charity and a comparison of the accounts presented with those records. It also includes consideration of any unusual items or disclosures in the accounts, and seeking explanations from you as trustees concerning any such matters. The procedures undertaken do not provide all the evidence that would be required in an audit, and consequently I do not express an audit opinion on the view given by the accounts.

Independent examiner's statement

In connection with my examination, no matter has come to my attention:

(1) which gives me reasonable cause to believe that in any material respect the requirements:
  - to keep accounting records in accordance with section 41 of the 1993 Act; and
  - to prepare accounts which accord with the accounting records and comply with the accounting requirements of the 1993 Act.

have not been met; or

(2)   to which, in my opinion, attention should be drawn in order to enable a proper understanding of the accounts to be reached.

Name:
Relevant professional qualification or body:
Address:
Date:

Example 2: Examiner's qualified report – failure to disclose investments at market value

Independent examiner's report to the trustees of 'ABC' Trust
I report on the accounts of the Trust for the year ended 30 April 2002, which are set out on pages 00 to 00.

Respective responsibilities of trustees and examiner
The charity's trustees are responsible for the preparation of the accounts. The charity's trustees consider that an audit is not required for this year (under section 43(2) of the Charities Act 1993 (the 1993 Act)) and that an independent examination is needed.

It is my responsibility to:

- examine the accounts (under section 43(3)(a) of the 1993 Act);
- to follow the procedures laid down in the General Directions given by the Charity Commissioners (under section 43(7)(b) of the 1993 Act); and
- to state whether particular matters have come to my attention.

Basis of examiner's statement
My examination was carried out in accordance with the General Directions given by the Charity Commissioners. An examination includes a review of the accounting records kept by the charity and a comparison of the accounts presented with those records. It also includes consideration of any unusual items or disclosures in the accounts, and seeking explanations form you as trustees concerning any such matters. The procedures undertaken do not provide all the evidence that would be required in an audit, and consequently I do not express an audit opinion on the view given by the accounts.

Independent examiner's qualified statement
The Trust held shares listed on a recognised stock exchange as a fixed asset investment with a market value at the balance sheet date of £x. These assets have been included in the accounts at their cost of £y, resulting in their value being understated by £z in the balance sheet. This matter gives me reasonable cause to believe that in this respect the accounts do not comply with the accounting requirements of the 1993 Act.

In connection with my examination, no other matter except that referred to in the above paragraph has come to my attention:

(1)   which gives me reasonable cause to believe that in any material respect the requirements:

- to keep accounting records in accordance with section 41 of the 1993 Act; and
- to prepare accounts which accord with the accounting records and comply with the accounting requirements of the 1993 Act.

have not been met; or

(2)   to which, in my opinion, attention should be drawn in order to enable a proper understanding of the accounts to be reached.

Name:
Relevant professional qualification or body:
Address:
Date:

Example 3: Examiner's qualified report – a matter to be brought to attention in the report

Independent examiner's report to the trustees of 'ABC' Trust

I report on the accounts of the Trust for the year ended 30 April 2002, which are set out on pages 00 to 00.

Respective responsibilities of trustees and examiner

The charity's trustees are responsible for the preparation of the accounts. The charity's trustees consider that an audit is not required for this year (under section 43(2) of the Charities Act 1993 (the 1993 Act)) and that an independent examination is needed.

It is my responsibility to:

- examine the accounts (under section 43(3)(a) of the 1993 Act);
- to follow the procedures laid down in the General Directions given by the Charity Commissioners (under section 43(7)(b) of the 1993 Act); and
- to state whether particular matters have come to my attention.

Basis of examiner's statement

My examination was carried out in accordance with the General Directions given by the Charity Commissioners. An examination includes a review of the accounting records kept by the charity and a comparison of the accounts presented with those records. It also includes consideration of any unusual items or disclosures in the accounts, and seeking explanations from you as trustees concerning any such matters. The procedures undertaken do not provide all the evidence that would be required in an audit, and consequently I do not express an audit opinion on the view given by the accounts.

Independent examiner's qualified statement

In connection with my examination, no matter has come to my attention which gives me reasonable cause to believe that, in any material respect, the requirements:

- to keep accounting records in accordance with section 41 of the 1993 Act; and
- to prepare accounts which accord with the accounting records and to comply with the accounting requirements of the 1993 Act

have not been met.

The accounts disclose the receipt of a restricted grant of £x, of which £y was expended in the year. A concern exists that the unexpected balance of £z, which has been carried forward as a fund balance, may need to be repaid to the donor.

No other matter has come to my attention in connection with my examination to which, in my opinion, attention should be drawn in order to enable a proper understanding of the accounts to be reached.

Name:
Relevant professional qualification or body:
Address:
Date:

Annex 3 – Examples of deliberate or reckless misconduct

Reports to the Commissioners

Deliberate or reckless misconduct in the administration of a charity

Matters which give rise to a reporting duty primarily concern the improper use of charity assets which has resulted, or could result from the deliberate or reckless misconduct of one or more of the charity trustees in the administration of the charity. The following are examples of such misconduct.

1 Where a deliberate abuse of charity assets by one or more of the charity trustees has come to the examiner's attention, a reporting duty will arise. Matters that require consideration will include:
   • evidence of false accounting by any charity trustee;
   • evidence of theft or misappropriation by any charity trustee; and
   • evidence giving rise to doubts as to the honesty or integrity of any charity trustee.
2 A breach of legislative requirement or an action contrary to the trusts of the charity may also need to be reported. However a reporting duty will only arise if information or evidence exists which indicates that such an action was taken or sanctioned deliberately or recklessly by a charity trustee. Moreover, a reporting duty would only arise if, as a result of such action, the charity suffered or was likely to suffer a material loss or misapplication of its assets. Matters that may require consideration include:
   • a material application of funds clearly outside the objects of the charity;
   • a breach of law or regulation that could jeopardise future activities or result in a material pecuniary loss (e.g. an attempt to evoke any direct or indirect tax properly payable); and
   • an attempt by any charity trustee to obtain an improper pecuniary benefit for himself or another and/or to the detriment of the charity.
3 The charity trustees are responsible for the control and management of a charity's affairs. Where there has been a gross neglect of these duties which has resulted or could result in a material loss of charity assets, consideration will need to be given as to whether this has arisen from deliberate or reckless misconduct by the charity trustees in the administration of the charity. Factors that will require consideration include:
   • a failure of the trustee body to meet or consider issues affecting the charity;
   • a gross failure on the part of the trustee body to keep accounting records;
   • evidence of indifference or recklessness on the part of a charity trustee or the trustee body – e.g. evidence that professional advice has been disregarded without due consideration or a failure to take action in the case of fraud within or affecting the charity.

Annex 4 – Flowchart indicating eligibility requirements for independent examination

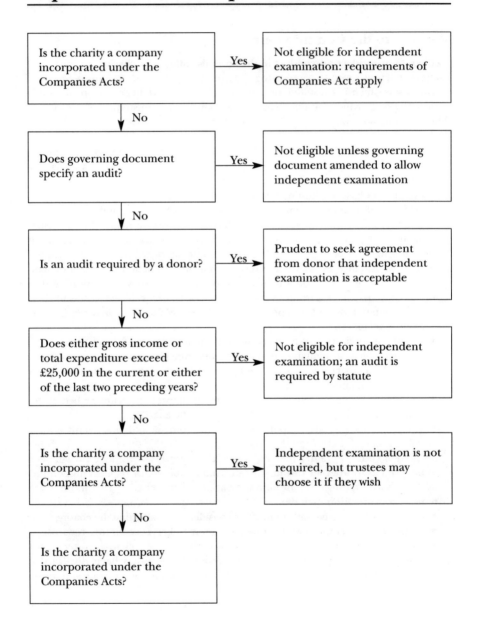

Is the charity a company incorporated under the Companies Acts?

Yes → Not eligible for independent examination: requirements of Companies Act apply

No ↓

Does governing document specify an audit?

Yes → Not eligible unless governing document amended to allow independent examination

No ↓

Is an audit required by a donor?

Yes → Prudent to seek agreement from donor that independent examination is acceptable

No ↓

Does either gross income or total expenditure exceed £25,000 in the current or either of the last two preceding years?

Yes → Not eligible for independent examination; an audit is required by statute

No ↓

Is the charity a company incorporated under the Companies Acts?

Yes → Independent examination is not required, but trustees may choose it if they wish

No ↓

Is the charity a company incorporated under the Companies Acts?

Chapter 23 – Business/trading income

23.1 Main statutory exemption

The main statutory exemptions from tax for the income of a charity are contained in s505 Income and Corporation Taxes Act 1988 (ICTA 1988). These exemptions relate to

(a) income from land;
(b) income assessable under Case III of Sch D, such as bank interest, gift-aid payments, and annual payments;
(c) trading income.

In this chapter the various trading income exemptions are considered.

The restrictions which apply to trading income received by charities are more restrictive than for all other types of income except that received under Sch D Case VI. A charity is exempt from tax on the profits of any trade carried on in the UK or elsewhere which is either:

(a) exercised in the course of the actual carrying out of a primary purpose of the charity;
(b) is mainly carried out by beneficiaries of the charity; or
(c) the turnover of a non-primary purpose trade falls below certain limits

provided it is applied solely for charitable purposes.

In light of the above the aim of this chapter is to explain how the Inland Revenue treats trading profits of charities for tax purposes. It will also look at the exemptions from tax available for trading profits under statute, mentioned above, and by concession. It will then look at some common trading activities and also give some guidance on calculating the amount of the profits of a trade carried on by a charity. Towards the end of the chapter there is a section describing ways in which non-exempt trading profits can be passed to a charity in such a way that no tax will be payable. Finally the factors to take into account when a charity invests in a trading company are examined.

23.2 What is a trade?

Many charities often fail to take account of the possibility of trading because they are of the opinion that 'we are not trading because we are not a commercial body'. However what matters from a tax point of view is not the type of body you are but what activity you are carrying on. The key question to consider is therefore 'does the activity we, the charity, amount to the carrying on of a trade for income tax purposes?'. The definition of a trade is considerably wide. Section 832 ICTA 1988, states that 'trade includes, every trade, manufacture, venture or concern in the nature of trade'. This is a very wide definition and over the years the courts have established a number of so-called 'badges of trade'. These are:

- profit-seeking motives;
- existing trade connections;
- repetition;
- method of finance;
- interval between purchase and sale;
- selling organisation;
- inheritance or donation – method of acquisition;
- operations pending sale; and
- nature of asset.

This is not the place to review all the decided cases on trading but normally a trade involves the sale of goods or services to customers as part of a commercial enterprise. A one-off or occasional venture may be treated as a trade for tax purposes if it involves the sale of goods or the provision of services for profit.

In most cases it will be clear whether an activity is, or is not, a trade. However, sometimes it will not be easy to decide whether there is a trade, for example when a one-off transaction has taken place. Professional advice should therefore be sought in such circumstances and there will be a need to look at all of the circumstances surrounding the activity.

At this stage when deciding whether an activity amounts to a trade it is irrelevant that the profits are intended to be used for charitable purposes.

'The profit cannot be taxable because we are using it for a charity' is a very popular misunderstanding which can be very expensive. A clear distinction must be drawn between the earning of income and the paying away of that income. It is necessary to distinguish clearly between expenditure which is incurred in the earning of the income, and expenditure which effectively amounts to the paying away of the profits. The former will be an allowable expense in calculating the profit (or loss) from the venture whilst the latter has no immediate bearing on the tax position at all.

Trading by charities can take a number of different forms. But in general such trades which are carried on by charities fall into one of two broad categories:

(a) trades which are exercised in the course of the actual carrying out of a primary purpose of a charity (a religious charity selling Bibles, for example) or the trade is carried on mainly by its beneficiaries (the manufacture and sale of poppies by ex-servicemen); or

(b) trades which are not themselves part of the primary purpose of the charity but which are designed to raise funds to be applied for charitable purposes (sales of promotional items, for example).

23.3 Statutory exemption from tax

The Taxes Act provides very limited exemption from tax for the profits of a trade carried on by charities. To qualify for exemption the profits must be used solely for the purposes of the charity. In addition the trade must satisfy one of the three following conditions:

(a) the trade must be exercised in the course of the actual carrying out of the primary purpose of the charity (a 'primary purpose trade') or is ancillary to this primary purpose trade, or

(b) the work in connection with the trade must be mainly carried out by beneficiaries of the charity, or

(c) the turnover of a non-primary purpose trade falls below certain limits.

If a trade does not satisfy one of the above conditions, the profits of the trade will not be exempt from tax regardless of whether or not they are used for the purposes of the charity. However some fundraising events may qualify for a concessionary relief under an extra statutory concession which will be described in more detail below.

23.4 Trading activities of charities

It will be helpful before we look at the above exemptions to look at some of the various types of activities of charities which could be regarded as trading.

(a) Sponsorship

Sponsorship is often an important source of funds for many charities. If it is no more than a straight donation, with nothing required in return, then there will be no question of trading. It should however be borne in mind that the sponsor could not expect to get any tax relief against profits for their payment. For this reason sponsors usually look for some tangible return for their generosity, i.e., a prominent display of their name, the opportunity to advertise in the event programme or perhaps complementary tickets to a function. Once this happens the charity moves into a much greyer area where trading becomes a possibility.

The activity will move into a trade where a charity incorporates large and prominent displays of the sponsor's logo or corporate colours or mentions specific products or services in publicity for events. Where the charity in return for sponsorship allows the sponsor access to its membership mailing list once again we will have a trading situation. Similarly where a charity takes steps to actively endorse a product of the sponsor that too will be regarded as trading.

Once it has been determined that sponsorship payments are trading income in the charity's hands the next step is to consider whether the sponsorship arrangement is a trade in its own right or part of income of a wider trade.

Where the sponsorship is intended to fund an activity of the charity which is in itself a trade, the payment will be regarded as part of the income of that trade so that the tax treatment will follow the tax treatment of the profits of that trade. For example where a business sponsor sponsors a stage production of a theatre the sponsorship payments will be regarded as part of the income of a trade of putting on the stage production. Whether or not the sponsorship income in such a case would be exempt from tax would depend on whether the trade was exercised in the course of the actual carrying out of a primary purpose of the charity or not.

(b) Lotteries

Charities may run lotteries in order to raise funds for their charitable purposes as defined in ss3 and 5 of the Lotteries and Amusements Act 1976. Lotteries are undertaken on a clear profit motive.

The profits of such lotteries, that are promoted by charities or by subsidiary companies on their behalf, are exempt from tax provided the lottery is conducted within the requirements of this Act and the lottery profits are applied solely to the purpose of the charity.

Where a subsidiary company, rather than the charity, is registered as the society under s5 of the Lotteries and Amusements Act 1976 the lottery profits will belong to the company and not to the charity for tax purposes. The exemption will not apply and the company will need to pass the profits to the charity under gift aid (see below) to obtain relief from tax.

(c) Charity shops
Charity shops are a common feature of many high streets.

To the extent that the shops sell only donated goods, such as clothes or bric-a-brac, there will be no problem because the Inland Revenue accept that the charity is merely turning donations in kind into cash donations. This is so even where the donated goods are sorted, cleaned and given minor repairs. If however the goods are subjected to significant refurbishment or to any process which brings them into a different condition for sale purpose other than that in which they were donated, the sale proceeds may be regarded as trading income.

Many charity shops also buy in a variety of goods in which case the sale proceeds of those goods will be seen as a trading activity. Where a charity shop sells both donated goods and bought-in stock then the trading activities will need to be separately identified from the non-trading activities.

(d) Christmas cards
Christmas cards are a common means of fundraising. The activity is clearly a commercial one and is in competition with commercial card manufacturers and is therefore seen as a trading activity.

(e) Affinity card schemes
Affinity card schemes are an ever-increasing way in which charities raise money. They operate in a way under which the charity allows their name to be used by credit card companies who produce specifically designed cards. The key advantage for the credit card company is access to the membership of the charity who will be encouraged to use the card because the charity will benefit both from the original take-up of the card and from the usage of it. In such cases there are usually two transactions involved – the license of the charity name and logo which will not be regarded as a trading activity (see below) and the sale by the charity of its mailing list of members. That is a commercial asset and its exploitation, as mentioned above, will be regarded as a trading activity.

(f) Payments for use of a charity's logo
Where a charity allows its logo to be used, in return for payment, by a business as an endorsement for one or more of the business' products or services, and the charity likewise promotes the endorsement in its own literature, the payments are likely to be trading income of the charity.

Payments **solely** for the use of a charity's logo may be annual payments rather than trading income. Whether payments for use of the logo are considered to be annual payments will depend on the precise terms of the agreement for the use of the logo. The payment must be made under a legal obligation, recur each year and be a pure donation in the hands of the charity. The charity can reclaim the tax that the payer deducts when making annual payments, provided the income is applied solely for charitable purposes.

23.5 Primary purpose trades

As mentioned above, trading activities that are exercised in the course of the actual carrying out of a primary purpose of the charity are exempt from tax. A 'primary purpose trade' is one that is exercised in the course of the actual carrying out of the primary purposes or charitable objects of the charity. These will be identified from the charity's trust deed, constitution or other governing document.

Some typical examples of primary purpose trading would include:

(a) a school charging fees will be fulfilling the primary object of advancement of education;
(b) the holding of an exhibition by an art gallery or museum in return for admission fees;
(c) the sale of tickets for a theatrical production staged by a theatre which has charitable status;
(d) provision of health care services by hospitals in return for payment;
(e) the provision of residential accommodation by a residential care charity in return for payment; and
(f) the sale of certain educational goods by an art gallery or museum.

In each of the above examples it is assumed that the organisation carrying on the activity is a charity and that it is part of the organisation's charitable objects to undertake the activity described.

The exemption from tax also extends to other trades which are not primary purpose activities in themselves but which are ancillary to the carrying out of a primary purpose so that they can still be said to be exercised in the course of the actual carrying out of a primary purpose. Examples would be:

(a) the sale of relevant books for the benefit of students by a school or college;
(b) the provision of a crèche for the children of students by a school or college in return for payment;
(c) the sale of food and drink in a cafeteria to visitors to exhibits by an art gallery;

(d) the sale of food and drink in a restaurant or bar to members of an audience by a theatre; and

(e) the sale of confectionery, toiletries and flowers to patients and their visitors by a hospital or by a league of friends.

Finally in this section, looking at primary purpose trades, there are situations where trades are not wholly primary purpose trades. In such cases a trade might amount in part to a primary purpose trade but may not be wholly a primary purpose trade. For instance the letting of accommodation for students in term time, and for tourists outside of term time by a school or college. Similarly the sale of food and drink in a theatre restaurant both to members of the audience and to the general pubic. In such circumstances the trade might not qualify as a primary purpose trade because part of the trade is not related to a primary purpose. In practice the Inland Revenue will accept that all of the profits of the trade will be within the exemption of tax if:

(a) the part of the trade which is not within the primary purpose is not large in absolute terms; and

(b) the turnover of that part of the trade is less than 10 per cent of the turnover of the whole trade.

The turnover for the part of the trade which is not primary purpose of £50,000 or less would be considered as 'not large' for the purposes of the first part of the test. So, a mixed trade with non-primary purpose turnover of less than £50,000 and representing less than 10 per cent of the total trade turnover would satisfy this test.

Where the profits of the trade cannot be exempted because part of the trade is not related to a primary purpose and it represents 10 per cent or more of the whole trade, the whole of the profits may be liable to tax, including that part of them which is related to a primary purpose.

23.5.1 Trades where the work is carried out by the beneficiaries of the charity

If the trade does not fall within the definition of primary purpose trades, the profits may be exempt because the trade is mainly carried out by the beneficiaries of the charity. This exemption was introduced originally to provide exemption for the sale of works provided by disabled people and its introduction in 1921, just three years after the end of the Great War, reinforces that. That type of activity would clearly still be relevant today as would the sale of goods produced in Third World countries and sold through aid shops or through mail order.

Where work carried out by beneficiaries has a therapeutic, remedial or educational value the profits from the trade will often also qualify for exemption from tax as a primary purpose trade. But the exemption of tax is not restricted to such trades. It covers all trades where the work is mainly carried out by beneficiaries. Examples include:

(a) a farm operated by students of an agricultural college;
(b) a restaurant operated by students as part of a catering course which is part of a further education college;
(c) the sale of goods manufactured by disabled people who are beneficiaries of a disability charity.

Often, as is the case in the above examples, part of the work of the trade may be carried out by employees, contractors or volunteer workers who will not rank as beneficiaries of the charity. In these circumstances exemption will still be available provided it can be shown that the greater part of the work in connection with the trade is carried out by beneficiaries of the charity.

Also a charity may wish to pay salaries to beneficiaries who work in a trade carried out by the charity. This will mean that the beneficiaries will become employees of the charity. Provided that they can still properly be regarded as beneficiaries of the charity, the exemption of the trading profits will not be affected. PAYE and NIC must operate on the earnings of beneficiaries who are employed by a charity in the same way as for other employees.

23.5.2 Exemption for small trading

In addition to the above exemptions, from April 2000 there is a statutory exemption for profits of small trading carried on by charities that would not otherwise be already exempt.

Before a charity considers whether this particular statutory exemption applies it should first consider whether the statutory concession for fundraising activities is of relevance (see below).

The new exemption applies to the profits of all trading activities that are not already exempt from tax provided:

• the total turnover from all of the activities does not exceed the annual turnover limit; or
• if the total turnover exceeds the annual turnover limit the charity had a reasonable expectation that it would not do so; and
• the profits are used solely for the purposes of the charity.

The annual turnover limit is:

- £5,000, or
- if the turnover is greater than £5,000, 25 per cent of the charity's gross income, subject to an overall limit of £50,000

These limits are reduced proportionally if the chargeable period is less than a year.

The following table represents the application of these rules.

Total gross income of the charity	Maximum permitted sales turnover
Under £20,000	£5,000
£20,000–£200,000	25% of charity's total gross income
Over £200,000	£50,000

The definition of sales turnover is income which would be taxable under Schedule D Case 1 as a trade, or under Case VI, and which is not exempt under any other section. Gross income means the total receipt of the charity for the year from all sources (grants, donations, investment income, trading receipts, etc).

Example 1
A charity sells Christmas cards to raise funds to enable it to carry out its objects. Such a trade is not primary purpose nor does it fall to be considered under the Extra Statutory Concession because it does not form part of the income from a fundraising event.

The sales turnover from the Christmas cards is £3,000 in the year. Assuming that this is the only taxable trading activity, any profits will be exempt from tax because the turnover does not exceed £5,000.

Example 2
A charity has sales turnover amounting to £8,000 for the year. Its gross income is £100,000 (including the £8,000 sales turnover). Profits will be exempt from tax because the sales turnover from non-exempt trades does not exceed either:

- 25 per cent of the gross income (i.e. £25,000), or
- the overall limit of £50,000.

Example 3
The facts are the same as in the previous example except that trading turnover is £30,000. The £30,000 sales turnover exceeds the annual turnover limit of £25,000.

However, the profits on sales will still be exempt from tax for this year if the charity had a reasonable expectation at the start of the year that the sales turnover would not exceed the limit.

This could happen either because the turnover was underestimated or the gross income of the charity was overestimated. It will be necessary in such cases to convince the Inland Revenue that the 'reasonable expectation' existed. The Inland Revenue will consider any evidence the charity may have to satisfy the reasonable expectation test.

The Inland Revenue has indicated that the type of evidence needed to demonstrate the levels of turnover and income which were expected might include minutes of meetings at which that matter was discussed, copies of cashflow forecasts, business plan and the previous year's accounts.

It may be the case that the charity has carried on the trading activity for a number of years and might be able to show that the turnover increased unexpectedly compared with early years. Alternatively the charity might have started carrying out the trading activity in the year in question and might be able to show that the turnover was higher than it forecasted when it decided to start the activity. Similarly the charity's gross income might be lower than if forecast, for example because the charity did not receive a grant for which it had budgeted or it was received in a subsequent accounting period.

23.6 Concessional relief for fundraising activities

As indicated above before a charity considers whether an exemption for small trading applies it should first determine whether the Extra Statutory Concession for fundraising activities is of relevance.

This extra statutory concession applies specifically to fundraising events. If an event falls within the concession the Inland Revenue will not seek to tax the profits arising from it. The full text of the concession is set out below and you will see that it mirrors the VAT exemption for similar activities.

23.6.1 The concession

Certain events arranged by voluntary organisations or charities for the purpose of raising funds for charity may fall within the definition of 'trade' in s832 ICTA 1988, with the result that any profits will be liable to income tax or corporation tax. Tax will not be charged on such profits provided:

(a) the event is of a kind which falls within the exemption of VAT under Group 12 of Sch 9 of the VAT Act 1984; and
(b) the profits are transferred to charities or otherwise applied for charitable purposes.

As this is primarily a VAT exemption, HM Customs and Excise will decide whether the extra statutory concession applies in individual cases. The charity does not have to deal separately with the Inland Revenue and HM Customs and Excise to determine whether fundraising events qualify for exemptions. If the events meet the criteria for VAT exemption, then they will automatically qualify for the purposes of exemption from income tax and corporation tax.

HM Customs and Excise regard the following as events which may be held for fundraising purposes:

- balls, dinner-dance, disco or barn dance;
- performance; such as concert, stage production, and any other event which has a paying audience;
- film showing;
- fete, fair or festival;
- horticultural show;
- exhibition – such as art, history or science;
- bazaar, jumble sale, car boot sale, good-as-new sale;
- sporting participation (including spectators), such as sponsored walk, or swim;
- sporting performance;
- game of skill, contest, quiz;
- endurance participation;
- fireworks display;
- dinner, lunch, barbecue; and
- auction of bought in goods (auction of donated goods is zero rated).

Although the above list is quite extensive, there are other factors such as frequency and turnover which are considered by Customs and Excise.

Eligible events are restricted to 15 events of the same kind in any one location by a charity (including its trading subsidiary) or qualifying body in the charity's financial year. The restriction prevents distortion of competition with other suppliers of similar events which do not benefit from tax exemption. If the charity holds 16 or more events of the same kind at the same location during their financial year none of the events would qualify for exemption.

Location means held in the same place. Similar kinds of events held in different locations would qualify for exemption provided all other conditions were met. For example 20 balls held by a national charity each in different towns in the same financial year would all qualify for relief.

All fundraising events where the gross takings are no more than £1,000 per week, such as coffee mornings, are VAT exempt and are excluded from the 15-event limit.

The £1,000 limit relates to the income of the event prior to any costs being deducted.

To ensure that commercial businesses are not put at a disadvantage if a commercial organisation alleges disadvantage Customs and Excise would look carefully into the matter and any subsequent action would depend upon the particular circumstances. A charity would have the right to appeal against the decision.

If an event falls outside the terms of the concession, and is not covered by the statutory exemptions, the profits may be taxable.

If the charity believes that a particular event or series of events will not fall within the concession, it may be possible to organise the events so as to mini- mise the amount of tax payable. For instance, the charity might set a basic minimum charge (which will be taxable) and invite those attending the event to supplement this with a voluntary donation. The additional contri- bution will not be taxable if all of the following conditions are met:

(a) it is clearly stated on all publicity material, including tickets, that anybody paying only the minimum charge will be admitted without further payment;

(b) the additional payment does not give you any particular benefit (for example, admission to a better seat in an auditorium), the extent of further contributions is ultimately left for the ticket holder to decide (even if the organiser indicates a desired level of donation). These further contributions may be made under the Gift Aid scheme, subject to them meeting the requirements of the scheme;

(c) for film, or theatre performances, concerts, sporting fixtures and similar events the minimum charge is not less than the usual price for the particular seat of a normal commercial event of the same type; and

(d) for dances, dinners and similar functions, the sum of the basic minimum charge is not less than the total cost incurred in arranging the event.

23.7 Calculating the profits of the trade

The profits of trades carried on by charities which fall outside the statutory and concessional exemptions described will be taxable. The whole of the profits will be taxable despite the possibility that part of the activities of a trade might be said to fall within one of the exemptions. The profits includ- ing capital allowances, if applicable, should be calculated in the same way as for any other trader. However, there are some factors that may be par- ticularly relevant when calculating the profits of a trade carried on by a charity.

As well as deducting direct expenditure of the trade when calculating the profits, the charity should deduct indirect expenditure which it has incurred and which is attributable to the trade. For example it would be right and proper to allocate to the trade part of the cost of premises, employee costs and other related expenditure.

The proper basis of apportionment of indirect costs will depend on the facts.

It should be noted that where a charity receives goods or services in their trade at no cost or at less than their full market value the Inland Revenue will only charge those profits calculated on a commercial basis. Thus, where a charity has received goods or services free, or at less than their full market price, the charity may deduct a notional market price when computing the profits of the trade.

23.8 Using a trading company

Charities carrying a trade outside the statutory and concessional exemptions usually arrange for the trade to be carried on by a wholly owned trading company. Using this approach it is possible for the trading profits to be applied for charitable purposes tax free. This is done by donating all the trading company's profits to the charity by way of either a profit-shedding deed of covenant or by Gift Aid.

Prior to 1 April 2000, trading companies invariably used profit-shedding deeds of covenant to pass all or part of their profits to the charity. There is nothing to prevent a trading company continuing to base the amount of profits to be transferred on a legally binding agreement such as deed of covenant. However, from 1 April 2000, all charitable payments made by a company to a charity will attract tax relief under the Gift Aid scheme (see chapter **26**).

23.9 Financing the trading company

This is an important area particularly when the trading company is about to start and considerable funds are required. One way is shares but it must be remembered that the greater the shareholding by the charity the greater is the risk to the funds of the charity. There are two other options; loans from the charity and outside funding.

The Charity Commission do not like to see large amounts of unsecured funding and/or lending by a charity to its trading subsidiary. They regard such an arrangement as putting the assets of the charity at too great a risk.

The preferred option of the Charity Commission is for there to be some outside funding of the trading company. This would come from a financial institution such as a bank. Any such borrowing would involve a commercial rate of interest, which would usually increase with the level of risk that the bank manager perceives to be involved.

Whilst it is important to get the initial funding of a company right, the problems often come after trading has begun and can often arise directly as a result of the tax planning which has triggered the creation of the company. The basic arrangement of a profit-shedding deed of covenant is that all taxable profits are transferred back to the charity. The result is that the company will never be in a position to build up reserves of profits to fund its own development and the charity will be continually required to keep putting in funds.

In reality the same money could go round in a circular route of company profit > payment to charity > loan from charity to company. Unless some money actually comes to rest in the charity the whole venture would be somewhat pointless. The potentially circular system is one that concerns both the Charity Commission and the Inland Revenue.

Chapter 24 – Charities and employment taxes

There is a popular, but erroneous belief, that because charities are exempt from tax on their own income they are also outside the scope of other requirements of the Taxes Acts. Unfortunately this approach seems to colour the view that many charities take toward their responsibilities as employers but this is extremely dangerous. It is perhaps not surprising that in light of the above far too many charities appear before employment tribunals.

Notwithstanding the fact that the taxation of employees is a complex area and is fraught with many difficulties it is an area where charities, as like other employers, need to have a sound understanding of both statute law and case law.

24.1 Casual, temporary and volunteer workers

A recent Employment Protection case, *Carmichael and another v National Power plc* (House of Lords) upheld that individuals engaged on a casual 'as required basis' are not employees. This ruling will be of significance to the many charities that use casual, temporary and/or volunteer workers. In such cases there is usually a need to avoid an employment relationship because of the fact that employees qualify for an increased amount of statutory rights including minimum notice periods, redundancy payments, maternity pay and the right not to be unfairly dismissed.

In the case in question the individuals had agreed to work for National Power plc. as guides showing visitors around as and when work arose. While they did not have to accept work neither did the company guarantee to provide it. Since National Power was not obliged to offer work and the worker was not obliged to accept work when requested there was no employment relationship. There was no 'mutuality of obligation' which is an essential feature of any contract of employment.

Many charities often enter into similar relationships with workers. The essence of the relationship being that work will be irregular and that the individual is only paid for work that he or she does and that the charity has no obligation to provide work. The relationship must not include the understanding that the worker is obliged to accept the work offered despite the fact that it might be irregular.

The more difficult area to monitor is to ensure that the pattern of work has not led to an expectation on the part of the worker that he or she will be offered work when he or she is available and in preference to others. If this were the case it could be argued that the worker has become a part-time employee. Unfair dismissal in such cases could result in an award of up to £50,000.

The benefits of the *Carmichael* case that provided clarification of employment law as it currently stands could however be short lived. There are indications that the Government is about to abandon the concept of an 'employee' status and replace it with a definition of 'worker' in extending statutory employment protection. This term is already used in various pieces of employment legislation. Where used, a 'worker' is defined as including any individual who contracts to do or perform any work or services personally, but excludes those in business on their own account. Casual and temporary charity workers would appear to come within that broader definition.

The Government has also stated that it is committed to examining what it considers to be the abuse of 'zero hour' contracts. By including the term 'worker' as opposed to 'employee' in more recent employment legislation this would tackle many of these perceived abuses. One would hope that there would still be a place for casual arrangements that are based on the genuine wishes of both parties without giving rise to statutory rights.

We are in the process where both the status of casual, temporary and volunteer workers and also the rights to which they are entitled are likely to change. It is therefore important that all charities that use such workers become clear of the changes as soon as they are implemented and how they will affect the working relationship with what is often an invaluable part of their total workforce.

24.2 Employed or self-employed?

The above question in identifying whether an individual is an employee or self-employed is one which affects both income tax and National Insurance. A person who is self-employed cannot be in receipt of income assessable under Schedule E and so the PAYE regulations cannot be applied.

The problem with whether or not a charity worker is an employee is often a hard one to resolve. The very nature of charity work, which often implies a strong sense of vocation, is an additional complicating factor. It is therefore important to look at all the circumstances surrounding the relationship between the two parties and to come to some conclusion about the nature of that relationship.

The Inland Revenue have explained what constitutes an employment in their view in booklets IR56 'Employed or Self-Employed? A guide for Tax and National Insurance' and also IR175 'Applying Services through a Limited Company or Partnership'. The trouble with these booklets is that they are biased towards the Inland Revenue's interpretation of significant amounts of case law. Much of this case law relates to employment law rather than tax law.

The first fact to note in looking at any employment or self-employment position is that there is no statutory definition of 'employment', rather it is a term that has evolved, and continues to evolve, over many years in the courts. Certain key factors need to be considered and it is these that help detail whether or not a particular contract is one of employment.

Relevant factors are:

Control
A worker will not be an employee unless there is a right to exercise 'control' over the worker. The right of control is important and not the actual control. Where 'the charity' has the right to determine 'how' the work is done this is a strong pointer towards employment. But it is not an essential feature. Equally a right to determine 'what' work is carried out is also a strong pointer toward employment. A working relationship, which involves no control, is unlikely to be one of employment.

Control would include being told what work is to be carried out at any particular time by a team leader. It would also include the right to say 'how the work should be carried out' even if in practice such control is not normally necessary. If however the contractor has a free hand over how his or her work is carried out and when, even though there may be an overall deadline for completion, control will be limited. This would be the case even if the worker is required to keep the charity fully informed about progress and the charity has the right to require the worker to modify proposals if any of them seem unsatisfactory.

The right to get a substitute or helper to do the job
Personal service is an essential element of a contract for employment. If a worker has the freedom to choose whether to do the job himself or hire somebody else to do it for him or her they are probably self-employed. Similarly if they can hire someone else to provide substantial help they are also probably self-employed.

A right of substitution must relate to the key components of the contract and not just some ancillary part of the contract.

It will probably not be sufficient to merely include a right of substitution in a contract. Rather there will be a need for the worker to be able to satisfy the Inland Revenue that either substitution actually took place or there was a real possibility that substitution could have taken place. In other words the charity was in reality willing to accept a suitably qualified substitute.

Provision of equipment

A self-employed worker generally provides whatever equipment is needed to do the job. The provision of significant equipment that is fundamental to the engagement is of particular importance. For example if an IT consultant is engaged to undertake a specific piece of work and works exclusively at home, using his own computer equipment, this will be a strong pointer toward self-employment. If on the other hand the consultant is provided with office space and computer equipment this would point toward employment.

Financial risk

Financial risk, supports a case for self-employment, and this can take many forms. For example quoting a fixed price for a job with the consequent risk of bearing the additional cost if the job overruns or having to correct any bad workmanship in one's own time. This could apply where there is a ceiling on the number of days or hours that the charity is willing to pay for in relation to a specific project unless unforeseen difficulties arise. Financial risk would also occur where the worker purchases materials and assets needed for the task in hand.

Basis of payment

Employment usually results in a fixed wage or salary paid weekly or monthly and may include payments of overtime and/or a bonus scheme. Self-employment tends to result in a fixed sum for a particular job. Where a worker gets paid an hourly rate this would point toward employment. The basis of the payment is closely linked to whether or not there is an opportunity to profit from sound management. People who are paid by the job will often be in this position.

Rights of employment

Employees are often entitled to sick pay, holiday pay, pensions, those on expenses etc. However not all employees receive such entitlements, i.e., short-term engagements. Self-employed individuals working for a charity would not expect to receive such entitlements. Similarly a right to terminate an engagement by giving notice of a specified length is a common feature of employment. It is less common in a self-employment situation where termination normally ends on the completion of the task or if the terms of the contract are breached.

Length of engagement

Long periods working for one charity may be typical of employment but are not conclusive. It is still necessary to consider all the terms and conditions of each contract.

The above are some of the factors that would influence a decision on whether or not there is an employment situation. The final decision is not however taken by merely adding up the number of factors pointing toward employment and comparing that result for the numbers pointing toward self-employment. The correct approach is to stand back and look at the picture as a whole to see if the overall effect is that of a person in business in his own account or of a person working as an employee in somebody else's business. Mummery J made this point in *Hall v Lorimer* (1994) when he remarked

> 'It is a matter of evaluation of the overall effect of the detail, which is not necessarily the same as the sum total of the individual details. Not all details are of equal weight or importance in any given situation. The details may also vary in importance from one situation to another'.

It follows from this that there are no hard and fast rules which can be applied. In general terms each case must be considered on its own facts, with key factors isolated. For this reason if a charity is in doubt as to whether or not a particular worker is an employee or not they should seek appropriate professional advice.

The problem with just accepting the Inland Revenue booklet is that they give a rather simplistic view of the question of determining employment vs. self-employment. As explained above there is no statutory definition of these terms. Rather our understanding of what constitutes employment or self-employment has come from many court cases. The problem is that case law sometimes gives a somewhat mixed message.

This can be seen by considering two recent cases on the issue of 'substitution'. It is considered that much of the argument in future with the Inland Revenue will revolve around the 'substitution' clause when determining the question of employment vs. self-employment.

In the case of *Express and Echo Publications v Tanton* (Mr Tanton, a delivery driver employed by Express and Echo) there were many factors in this case that pointed toward Mr Tanton being under a contract of employment. However included within the contact was a clause as follows;

> 'In the event that the contractor is unable or unwilling to perform the services personally he shall arrange at his own expense entirely another suitable person to perform the services'.

In addition the contract stated:

> 'In the event that the contractor provides a relief driver, the contractor must satisfy the company that such a relief driver is trained and is suitable to undertake the services'.

Gibson L J held:

> '… that, where a person who works for another was not required to perform his services personally, as a matter of law the relationship was not one of employee or employer; and accordingly, Clause 3.3 of the contract (not to perform any services personally) was a provision wholly inconsistent with the contract being one of service'.

The case should be compared with the more recent case of *MacFarlane and Skivington v Glasgow CC* heard by the employment appeal tribunal. The appeal raised the issue of whether the two appellants, qualified gymnastic instructors, were employees of the City Council or self-employed. The appellants lodged a claim for unfair dismissal and constructive dismissal (i.e., on the basis that they were employees). The council required them to sign a new contract but the appellants contended that the new contract would effectively make them self-employed. The Council contended they had been self-employed all along.

The tribunal went through the facts of the situation and noted the following provision in their contract:

> 'If for any reason one of the applicants was unable to take a class she would contact a replacement from the register of coaches maintained by the respondent, and arrange for her class to be covered by a member of the register'.

It was the applicant who was enabled to select the replacement coach rather than the Council, but the substitute had to come from the Council's list. The arrangement for the replacement was to be made by the applicant not the Council. A provision for substitution would only be available when an applicant was 'unable' to take a class although the inability could be for any reason.

The tribunal was of the opinion that the applicants were employees except for one fact that a substitute could be provided. This was in light of the *Tanton* case.

The employment tribunal found the following differences between the two cases:

• The appellants in this case could not simply choose not to attend or not to work in person. Only if the appellant was unable to attend could she arrange for another to take her class.

- The appellants could not provide just anyone who was suitable as a replacement for her but only someone from the Council's own registers. To that extent the Council could veto a replacement and also could ensure that such persons that were named on the register were persons in whom the Council could have trust and confidence.
- The Council itself sometimes organised the replacement.
- The Council would not pay the appellant for the time served by the substitute but instead paid the substitute direct. There is no finding as to what the substitutes were paid nor that they were paid the same as the appellants nor that the appellants had any say in what the substitutes were paid.

The Employment Appeal Tribunal allowed the appeal.

What we can learn from these two cases is that the more restricted the limitations are on acceptance of substitution the less likely it is that substitution will support an argument for self-employment.

Despite the above difficulties in deciding whether or not somebody is employed or self-employed the question of status is one which the charity employer should not duck. It is vital for any situations where categorisation could be an issue that this should be highlighted at an early stage and a decision taken with professional help. Whilst there is a strong incentive for a charity to argue that workers are self-employed as a way to avoid the need to pay the cost of secondary (employer's) NIC, such an incentive needs to be tempered by reality.

It is often argued that a statement by a worker that he is self-employed because he is able to provide a letter from his accountant is sufficient evidence. This is not the case as it is possible that the circumstances of the engagement with the charity may be very different from his normal activities.

As explained above if a charity is in any doubt they should seek professional advice. Failure to deal with the matter properly could mean that the charity is required to meet not only the tax which should have been deducted from payments, but also the associated employee and employers NIC. This could of course happen after the employee has left the employ of the charity with little chance of obtaining any recompense from the employee in question.

Chapter 25 – Charities/VAT

25.1 Introduction

Unlike their treatment under the direct tax system there is no universal VAT relief for charities. A charity is generally treated like any other person or business within the VAT system.

There are, however, some reliefs in the VAT system especially for charities. Some of these will apply to all charities regardless of whether they are VAT registered. Others are designed to relieve VAT registered charities of VAT in certain circumstances.

Before looking at the special reliefs, which are available to all charities, first we must consider how the normal rules of the VAT system will apply to charities generally. In particular, there is the crucial question of what is meant by the term 'business'.

25.2 VAT and how it works

VAT is designed to be a tax on consumption. It works by VAT registered persons charging VAT to their customers, and recovering VAT that their suppliers have charged to them. A VAT registered person can only recover VAT which is a cost of their business. VAT relating to non-business activity is non-recoverable.

The concept of 'business' is therefore a fundamental one. It governs both someone's obligation to charge output VAT and also their ability to recover input VAT. It is important to note, that 'business' for VAT purposes has a different meaning from 'trading' as used by the Charity Commission and/or the Inland Revenue.

An entity is generally seen as being in 'business' in VAT terms if it does something for consideration i.e., in money or payment in kind. This something could be providing goods or services. It does not matter why the entity undertakes the activity (e.g., it can be inspired by altruism), whether it can ever be a profitable activity, or indeed who pays for the goods and services provided. What matters, is that the entity make a compulsory charge to someone for providing something to them in return.

This fairly wide meaning to the term 'business' means that charities that have separate trading companies may still find that the charity itself still undertakes business activities for VAT purposes. If the value of the business supplies exceed the annual registration threshold (currently £54,000 per year) then the charity may potentially be automatically registerable for VAT if it is not already so registered.

25.3 Business and grant funded activities

When someone provides a grant, the VAT system does not generally recognise that the grantor is buying goods or services. This is because in most cases, they are not themselves consuming what they pay for. The reason for them making the payment is to enable the grant recipient to undertake its activities. It is not paid so that the grantor will receive a particular service or goods itself! The VAT system therefore generally treats grants, as being outside the scope of VAT, and so VAT is not chargeable on them. An activity which is entirely funded by grants, will automatically be 'non-business' for VAT purposes.

In practice, there is often a grey area between what is a grant and what is a genuine payment for a good/service, which falls within the VAT system. Increasingly, grant making organisations are setting stricter criteria on how their money is spent and whom it is spent on. Consequently, in many cases, it is now possible to make the argument that grants are in fact payments for a supply to the grant provider.

In some cases, treating the payment as taxable may be beneficial. If the person providing the grant is able to recover any VAT charged to them, then treating the payments as being within the VAT system will be beneficial for the charity. This is because the charity will be able to recover any VAT that they incur when undertaking the activity. It must be pointed out that this is a very technical and contentious area of the tax and one where it usually pays to take professional advice.

25.4 Donations

Donations are treated as outside the scope of VAT, when the person paying the money has no right to receive anything in return other than a token e.g., a flag/sticker.

If for example, a charity gives a major donor free/discounted attendance at dinners or pre-determined publicity events, then their payment will be within the VAT system and taxable.

25.5 Examples of business and non-business activities

Paid admissions	Business
Free admissions	Non-business
Advertising	Business
Affinity/promotion cards	Business (may also have non-business donational elements if organised correctly)
Catering	Business
Export of goods	Business
Free services	Non-business
Organising leagues	Non-business
Sponsorship	Business/non-business depending on what is produced
Subscriptions	Business

25.6 Business membership/supporters subscriptions

If someone has to pay a fee in order to receive a particular benefit be that benefit admission, publications or even the right to vote then this is a business activity. Organisations which provide benefits (be it publications, admissions or facilities) may well find that registering for VAT means that they are able to obtain ongoing refunds of VAT on their associated costs (see section on membership subscriptions).

25.7 VAT reliefs that apply to all charities

Some VAT reliefs apply to all charities regardless of whether they are VAT registered.

25.7.1 Advertising

No VAT should be charged to charities on advertising that they purchase.

Since 1 April 2000 this relief has been widened to all charity advertisements purchased for whatever purpose. Therefore, it includes advertisements for recruitment as well as fundraising and making known a charity's objects. Prior to 1 April 2000 only advertisements designed to communicate a charity's objects were relieved.

The relief applies to all forms of advertising media that the charity may purchase. It therefore includes:

- badges;
- balloons;
- banners;
- carrier bags;
- cinema;
- flags;
- Internet;
- posters;
- radio;
- television;
- Teletext; and
- skywriting by light aircraft.

To obtain the relief, the charity may need to demonstrate to their supplier that they qualify.

The relief applies to purchases of space/time in advertising media that is owned and controlled by third parties. It is not designed to allow charities to buy VAT-free goods. Therefore although the owner of a light aircraft will be able to zero rate any supply of any sky writing he might undertake for a charity, he could not sell the actual plane at a zero rate if the charity wanted to buy it. A different concession (covered later) allows charities to obtain some fundraising goods VAT free.

It is also important to note that the relief only applies to advertisements provided *to* the charity. It does not apply to advertisements provided *by* the charity. If the charity gets advertising income through its website or magazine this is not zero-rated.

Exceptions
It should be noted that there are some important exceptions.

The relief applies only to charities and not to their associated trading companies or other people.

It excludes selective adverts
Zero rating does not apply to selective advertising such as direct mail, e-mail or telesales.

In practice this exclusion can be problematic. If a charity obtains direct advertising through a supplier who produces and prints general leaflets to a selected audience then in theory, there are two liabilities. The production of the written material would normally be zero-rated. However the supply of the mailing service, e.g., the data processing, labelling etc., will be standard rated.

As Customs' policy is now to see single supplies as much as possible the old option of apportioning is not always available – although some suppliers will still apply this policy and even have permission to do so. If there is a single supply and the direct mail element is the most prominent (and in practice direct mail lists are often the largest expense) then it will be a single standard rated supply.

If charities do obtain direct marketing services involving printed matter, then it may pay to take advice as planning here can obtain sizeable savings.

In-house costs
Supplies of goods or services that are purchased by charities to enable them to produce or design their own advertisements are excluded from the relief.

25.8 Donated goods

The donation of goods to a charity which will be sold, let or exported is zero rated.

This relief means that donors who supply equipment to charities do not have to account for output VAT. This is a useful relief for charity shops.

The relief applies to charities and also persons (organisations and private individuals) who have agreed in writing to donate any profits from the sale or leasing of the goods to the charity. Therefore, private individuals or companies can obtain zero rating on goods provided to them which they are bound to use to raise money (through sale or lease).

25.8.1 Sales of donated goods by charities

The sale or letting (hire) of donated goods by a charity is zero rated. This relief also applies to persons who have agreed in writing to donate any profits they make from the sale to a charity.

This means not only sales of these goods by charities are zero rated but also sales by their trading subsidiaries and indeed any other person/organisation that agrees to raise money on their behalf.

For the zero rating to apply the sale or letting must be to the general public rather than a selected few. The exception to this is goods which charities sell specifically to people who are handicapped or on forms of State Benefit. This rule means that, for example, a corporate donor cannot buy a new mainframe computer and donate it to a charity on the understanding that it will then be leased back to them VAT free.

25.9 Goods used by charities to collect donations

A charity may obtain certain goods VAT free which it intends to use for collecting donations.

This relief applies to the following:

(a) lapel stickers, ribbons or attachments which are intended to be given away in return for an anticipated donation of £1 or less;
(b) collecting receptacles designed specifically for collecting donated money such as moulded plastic collecting boxes, or other receptacles which bear the name of the charity. The relief does not cover receptacles which incorporate an element of amusement e.g., 'helter skelter' boxes.
(c) bucket lids designed to provide a secure seal for collecting money;
(d) pre printed letters appealing solely for money for the charity;
(e) envelopes which are overprinted with an appeal request; and
(f) pre-printed collecting envelopes used for door-to-door collection.

It should be noted that these reliefs are provided by Extra Statutory Concession rather than legislation. Unfortunately this means that they are effectively in Customs' gift and able to be interpreted as strictly or loosely as a Customs officer may decide.

25.10 Reliefs for medical goods

The legislation provides for a number of quite complex reliefs for charities who buy goods to provide care, carry out medical or surgical treatment for human beings or animals or are engaged in medical research. As they are quite specialised they are outside the scope of this chapter.

Charities engage in this type of work should take advice either from professional advisors or Customs as to whether they will apply.

25.11 Charity buildings

25.11.1 New buildings

Normally, anyone purchasing construction services will be charged VAT by the builder, architect etc. For normal businesses that are VAT registered and able to recover any VAT charged to them this is not a problem. Unfortunately for charities that are likely to engage in a sizeable amount of non-business activity it is. In order to assist charities the legislation allows them to obtain zero-rated construction services providing certain conditions are met.

The principle condition is that the charity may obtain zero rated construction of a building which it intends to use for a non-business purpose. (For guidance on what is a non-business purpose see **25.5** above.)

Customs are prepared to accept that a building can be treated as being used for a non-business activity if:

(a) the building is used solely for non-business activity for 90 per cent or more of the time it is available for use;

(b) 90 per cent or more of the floor space of the building is used for non-business activity; or

(c) 90 per cent or more of the people using the building are engaged solely on non-business activity.

It should be noted that methods (a) and (b) can only be applied to the whole of a building and permission must be obtained from Customs.

In practice many charities will be in a position where the relief will not apply because charities will often have commercial or trading activities meaning the building will be used for business activities for more than 10 per cent of the time. This is an area where it is possible to obtain VAT savings by careful planning and on which it pays to take professional advice.

If a charity constructs a building for non-business use and subsequently the use of the building changes, there are provisions within the legislation which require the charity to pay back the VAT it has saved.

25.11.2 Listed buildings

One of the most peculiar features of the VAT system is the way that it treats listed buildings. Normal repairs to such buildings will always attract VAT. However alterations which require listed building approval can in certain circumstances be zero rated.

If a charity owns a listed building and makes alterations to it and it intends to use that building for a non-business charitable purpose or residential purposes (for example, as a dormitory) (see above) then it can obtain the work zero rated.

25.12 VAT reliefs that apply to VAT registered charities only

25.12 1 Fundraising

Fundraising events can be treated as VAT exempt.

The VAT legislation incorporates an exemption for fundraising events held by charities. An exempt supply is one where although no VAT needs to be accounted for sales, no VAT is recoverable on expenses. It follows that although, in theory, exemption applies to all charities, in practice it will only be of benefit to charities which would otherwise need to account for VAT i.e., VAT registered ones.

Legislation allows a charity to exempt its supply of goods or services in connection with an event whose primary purpose is the raising of money and which is promoted as such e.g., it is advertised as a fundraiser.

The exemption will apply to all income raised as part of an event unless it is an aspect of it which would otherwise be zero rated. Thus it would apply to admission charges and the sale of advertising but need not apply to the separate sale of programmes or auctioned goods.

Fundraising events include:

- dinners, balls or discos;
- concerts or stage performances;
- films;
- fairs or fetes;
- garden shows;
- exhibitions;
- car boot sales or jumble sales;
- sponsored walks;
- sports events;
- games of skill such as quizzes;
- endurance events;
- firework displays; and
- auctions of goods which have been purchased.

The relief is only designed to apply to fundraising events rather than to a charity's normal trading activities. In order to make this distinction, the legislation incorporates rules which state that if more than 16 similar events are held in the same place within the year then the exemption cannot apply. In practice this means that nearly all fundraising events can be covered by the exemption. The exemption will not apply if the event includes the provision of accommodation.

The downside of a VAT exemption as opposed to zero rating is that VAT on associated purchases cannot be recovered. This means that in some cases treating an event as exempt may not be a sensible option. If for example, the people attending the event would be able to recover any VAT charged to them on admission then there is no point in treating the event as exempt. If however, the attendees are members of the public and the charity suffers little VAT when putting on the event, then the exemption is a benefit. Fortunately, because of the way the legislation is designed, it is normally possible for a charity to change what would otherwise have been an exempt event into a taxable one if it will benefit by doing so.

Chapter 26 – Giving to charities

There are currently five ways in which an individual can give to charity in a tax-efficient manner; Gift Aid; deeds of covenant, give-as-you-earn schemes; legacies and gifting shares and securities.

The first two are most widely used and are more efficient from a charity's point of view than a give-as-you-earn scheme, principally because a give-as-you-earn scheme mainly benefits the donor and not the charity. However the last method of giving to charity by gifting shares and securities is relatively new and as will be seen is a particularly tax-effective way of giving.

This section deals with the characters of each together with some associated pitfalls.

26.1 Gift Aid

26.1.1 Gift Aid pre-April 2000

The original Gift Aid Scheme was introduced in 1990. It enabled United Kingdom resident individuals and companies to give single gifts of money to charity tax-efficiently but it required a minimum amount to be given. Non-close companies could give any amount.

The individual or company made a donation net of basic rate tax and gave the charity a certificate. The individual must have had at least as much income chargeable at the basic rate as the amount of the gross donation. Companies were required to deduct basic rate tax from a donation and pay it over to the Inland Revenue. If an individual paid tax at a higher rate he or she could get relief on the difference between the basic and higher rate on the grossed up amount. A company could deduct the grossed up amount of the donation as a charge in its corporation tax computations.

Charities receiving Gift Aid donations could reclaim basic rate tax on the donations provided they were in receipt of a valid certificate from the donor and could demonstrate a clear audit trail linking the donation to the donor.

If the donor received benefits from the charity worth more than 2.5 per cent of the net gift, the gift would not qualify for gift aid. The maximum total benefits received by the donor from any one charity in a tax year could not be worth more than £250.

26.1.2 Gift Aid for individuals from 6 April 2000

The Gift Aid scheme was simplified for donations made by individuals on or after 6 April 2000, the aim being to encourage charitable giving within the United Kingdom.

The main changes were to:

- abolish the £250 minimum limit for Gift Aid donations so that the scheme now applies to any donations whether large or small, regular or one-off;
- replace the requirement for donors to give a Gift Aid certificate with each Gift Aid donation to a particular charity with a new simpler and more flexible Gift Aid declaration;
- allow donors to give a written Gift Aid declaration by post, by fax or by internet or an oral declaration over the phone or face-to-face;
- extend the class of individuals that can use the new Gift Aid scheme;
- apply the new Gift Aid measures to covenanted payments falling due on or after 6 April 2000 and all other donations made on or after that date.

As explained above from 6 April 2000 the £250 minimum limit for Gift Aid donations was abolished. From that date charities have been able to reclaim tax on any donation made by individuals, whether large or small, regular or one-off – provided the other conditions which are shown below for the tax relief are satisfied.

From an administrative point of view each charity will need to decide, from its own circumstances, whether it wishes to reclaim tax on small Gift Aid donations. For some charities it may not be cost effective to claim on donations below a certain threshold. For other charities it may be cost-effective to claim on all Gift Aid donations.

Whether or not the charity decides to make a claim on a Gift Aid donation it will still be possible for a donor to claim higher rate tax relief on the gross amount of the donation provided he or she has completed a Gift Aid declaration and has met the other conditions of the scheme.

From 6 April 2000 the following individuals have been able to make valid Gift Aid payments:

- donations by individuals who are resident in the UK;
- donations by individuals who are Crown Servants or members of the UK Armed Forces serving overseas;

- donations by other non-resident individuals, provided they have income or capital gains charged to UK tax at least equal to the gross amount of the donation.

Donations must be a payment of a sum of money and cannot be made in kind.

From 6 April 2000 the donors have to pay an amount of income tax and/or capital gains tax whether at the basic rate or some other rate equal to the tax deducted from the donations. Prior to that date they needed to have paid income tax at the basic rate equal to the tax reclaimed by the charity on their donations.

The change means that donors who previously may have paid tax at a marginal rate between the lower and basic rate of tax (and therefore had not paid enough tax at the basic rate to cover the tax reclaimed by the charity) will no longer have additional tax to pay.

Prior to 6 April 2000 donors could only claim higher rate tax relief on donations against income tax they paid. From 6 April 2000 donors have been able to claim higher rate tax relief for their donations against both income tax and/or capital gains tax.

It should be noted that the position of taxpayers making Gift Aid donations can change from one tax year to the next. Charities are therefore recommended to remind donors on a regular basis of the need for them to have paid sufficient income and/or capital gains tax on their donations. This could be done for example by way of a newsletter and does not have to be a separate letter to each donor.

26.1.3 Gift Aid declarations

As mentioned above Gift Aid certificates for each donation to a charity have been replaced by a new simpler and more flexible Gift Aid declaration.

Before a charity can reclaim tax on a donation by an individual it must have received a Gift Aid declaration from the donor containing certain information and confirming that the donation is to be treated as a Gift Aid donation. Without this declaration, a donation from an individual will not qualify under the Gift Aid scheme.

Donors will be able to give the charity a declaration:

- in advance of their donation, at the time of their donation, or at any time after their donation (subject to the normal time limit within which tax can be reclaimed – normally within six years);

- to cover a single donation or any number of donations (i.e., all donations to a particular charity since 6 April 2000);
- in writing (e.g., by post, by fax or electronically through the internet) or orally e.g., over the phone or face-to-face.

Oral declarations must be confirmed by written notification from the charity showing the information set out below plus a note explaining that the oral declaration can be cancelled retrospectively within 30 days. The notification should also include the date on which the donor gave the charity the declaration and the date on which the charity sent the written record to the donor.

The amount of information required by law on a Gift Aid declaration has been kept to the minimum and all Gift Aid declarations must contain:

- the donors name;
- the donors address;
- the charity's name;
- a description of the donation to which the declaration relates;
- a declaration that the donations are to be treated as Gift Aid donations; and
- a note explaining the requirement that the donor must pay an amount of income tax and/or capital gains tax equal to the tax deducted from his or her donations.

There is not statutory requirement for a declaration to be signed and dated. However a date is needed on the declaration where it serves to identify that a particular donation or donations are to come within the scheme.

For example if the declaration states that 'all donations I make from today are to be Gift Aid donations', clearly a date would be required. A date would not be required, however, where the declaration stated, for example, 'all donations I make to the charity from 6 April 2000'.

Other than the information required by law charities may well wish to add further information and notes of their own on their declaration forms. It may also be necessary to add further information to satisfy other legal requirements. For example if:

- the charity plans to use the information provided by the donor for any use other than reclaiming tax, the Data Protection Act 1998 requires you to explain this;
- a charity registered in England and Wales incorporates a Gift Aid declaration in appeals literature, the Charities Act 1993 requires a charity to

include a statement that it is a registered charity. Under Scottish law, Scottish charities are required to include a statement that they are recognised charities.

Gift Aid declarations can be incorporated into other documents, such as standing order mandates for deeds of covenant.

The Inland Revenue do not produce an official Gift Aid declaration and charities are required to design their own Gift Aid declarations. The Inland Revenue do however provide in their Guidance Notes to Charities an Inland Revenue model declaration form which charities can use or adapt if they wish.

It should be noted that donors are entitled to cancel the declarations at any time. They may do so by notifying the charity in any form of communication. The charity should keep a record of the cancellation of a declaration, including the date of the donors' notification.

Subject to oral declarations, the cancellation of a declaration only has effect in relation to donations received by the charity on or after the date on which the donor notifies the charity of the cancellation, or such later date as the donor may specify in the cancellation.

As regards oral declarations as mentioned above these can be cancelled within the period of 30 days after being sent their written record. The cancellation will have retrospective effect so that it will be as if the declaration had never been made.

26.1.4 Declarations linked to sponsored events

The person being sponsored (participant) may ask the sponsors to make a separate declaration to the charity for which he or she is raising the money. This is likely to be a one-off donation type of declaration supplied to the participant by the charity.

Since the money raised by a sponsored event does not belong to the individual who has been sponsored and is not his or hers they cannot give the sum to the charity as a Gift Aid payment.

Rather than one-off donation types of declaration it is possible for charities to design a sponsorship form that can also be used as a joint declaration form. The Inland Revenue suggests that the declaration is placed at the head of each sheet with each sponsor being able to opt to have his or her sponsorship money paid to the charity as a Gift Aid donation by, for example, ticking a box. The recommended method is to have the following boxes below the declaration for each sponsor to complete:

- sponsors full name;
- address (including post code);
- amount pledged;
- amount collected;
- date collected ;
- tick box to have amount treated as a Gift Aid donation;

The details outlined in the first three bullet points above will be collected from the sponsors by the participant prior to the event with the other details being entered on the form when the money is collected.

26.1.5 Gift Aid for companies from 1 April 2000

From 1 April 2000 Gift Aid donations made by companies to charities must be paid without deduction of income tax. Since no income tax is deducted no declarations are required. Charities cannot therefore reclaim tax on donations it receives from a company on or after 1 April 2000.

If a company incorrectly deducts tax from its donation the company should be told about the new rules and asked to pay to the charity the sum it has incorrectly deducted.

Charities often set up 100 per cent wholly owned subsidiaries to carry out trading activities that fall outside the tax exemptions offered to charities. Such companies often enter into a profit shedding deed of covenant with the parent charity, or Gift Aid arrangements, under which they pay to the charity a sum equivalent to the profits assessable to corporation tax.

Unlike other types of companies, charity-owned companies have nine months from the end of the accounting period in which to determine the amount they wish to give or are obliged to pay to the charity under a profit-shedding deed or Gift Aid payment. They are then able to claim the deduction against the corporation tax profits of the accounting period to which the payment relates.

26.2 Deeds of covenant

Deeds of covenant have been a popular form of giving to charity for some time. In many cases they still remain popular despite the relaxation of the various Gift Aid regulations. To satisfy the requirements of the Inland Revenue there are a number of criteria which must be fulfilled. The way in which the covenant is worded is of paramount importance.

(a) A covenant form must state that it is a deed.
(b) It must be signed and delivered by the covenantor in the presence of a witness.

(c) A covenant must provide for annual payments to made year by year and must cover a minimum period which must be capable of lasting more than three years and in practice covenants are usually drawn up for a four-year period.

(d) A covenant cannot be back-dated.

As for Gift Aid, regular payments made by individuals and companies pre-April 2000 to a charity under a deed of covenant were paid after the deduction of basic rate tax. The charity could claim back from the Inland Revenue the basic rate tax deducted from the payment.

The individual must have paid at least as much income tax at the basic rate as the amount of tax reclaimed by the charity on the payment. If the amount reclaimed by the charity exceeded the amount paid by the covenantor, the Inland Revenue might require the individual to pay the tax difference. Companies were required to deduct basic rate tax from the covenanted payment and pay it over separately to the Inland Revenue.

If the individual paid tax at the higher rate, he or she could get relief on the payment on the difference between the basic and higher rate on the grossed up amount. A company deducted the gross amounts of the payments they charge in its corporation tax computation.

From 6 April 2000 there is no longer a separate tax relief for payments made by an individual (or a company) under a deed of covenant – in future all tax relief for such payments is under the Gift Aid scheme. As a transitional measure charities do not have to get a Gift Aid declaration in respect of payments under a deed of covenant that were already in existence before 6 April 2000. The deed of covenant will stand in place of the Gift Aid declaration. However, any donation made outside the terms of the deed, or after expiry of the deed must be covered by a separate Gift Aid declaration.

Payments made under a deed of covenant executed on or after 6 April 2000 must be covered by a Gift Aid declaration. Where a charity wishes to continue with the use of deeds of covenant for donors, these can also be used as declarations provided all the information required in the declaration is given in the deed.

The abolition of a separate tax relief for payments made under a deed of covenant to a charity does not mean, of course, that such deeds will cease to exist. It does mean that they are no longer required.

Some charities have decided to maintain deeds of covenant from their supporters in order to secure a regular flow of income. If they do so, they will need to make sure they also obtain a Gift Aid declaration from the donor, or ensure the deed contains the necessary elements required in such a declaration.

26.3 Benefits received by donors

Charities may wish to give a token of appreciation by way of a thank you to donors for their donations. Modest benefits received in consequence of making a donation will not stop the donation from qualifying as a Gift Aid donation, provided their value does not exceed certain limits.

The donor benefit rules contains two limits for the value of the benefit that a donor, or a person connected with the donor, may receive in consequence of making a donation. If the value of the benefits received exceeds either of these limits, the donation will not qualify as a Gift Aid donation. A donation will not qualify if:

- the value of the benefits exceed the limits in the table set out below

The limits for the relevant value tests are:

Amount of donation	Value of benefits
£100	25% of the donation
£101–£1000	£25
£1,001 +	2.5% of the donation

These limits apply separately to each donation. Nor will a donation apply if:

- the value of the benefit plus the value of any benefits received in consequence of any Gift Aid donation made by the same donor to the same charity earlier in the same tax year exceeds £250.

In addition to satisfying the relevant value test the value of the benefits received in consequence of donation must also satisfy the aggregate value test if the donation is to qualify as a Gift Aid donation. In other words

- the value of the benefits received in consequence of making the donation
- plus the value of any benefits received in consequences of any gift aid donations by any donor to the same charity earlier in the same tax year

must not exceed £250.

The valuation of donors' benefits can be difficult. The starting point should be to look at the value of the benefits made available. Where the item or service, or a comparable item or service, is sold to the public (whether by the charity or someone else) on arms-length terms (for example a ticket to attend a sporting event), the value of the benefit will generally be the sale price to the public. Where the value of the benefit is less immediately obvious, the charity will need to determine how much someone dealing with it at arms length would be prepared to pay for the benefit. Evidence might be obtained from similar transactions in the commercial sector.

The value to be arrived at is the value to the recipient. Consideration in the form of third-party discount could cost the charity nothing to provide but will still be of value to the recipient.

Where a charity sends literature to its donors, the Inland Revenue will accept that the value is nil provided the material is produced for the purpose of describing the work of the charity. The material must be relevant to and distributing furtherance of the objects of the charity. The fact that the literature has a cover price and is also on sale to members of the public is not relevant.

26.4 Payroll giving (give-as-you-earn)

Payroll giving provides tax relief at source for individuals who give to charity by direct deduction from their pay. Once an employee has signed up to the scheme the employer simply deducts the relevant amounts from the employee's pay before deducting tax under PAYE and sending the payment to the agency/charity.

From 6 April 2000 a number of improvements were made to payroll giving and these include the following:

- there are now no limits on the amount that can be given (in the past the limit was £1,200 per annum); and
- all gifts made between 6 April 2000 and 5 April 2003 attract a 10 per cent supplement from the Government payable to the charity.

Other than the transitional 10 per cent supplement, payroll giving benefits the donor rather than the charity so will not be discussed in any detail.

As explained above the mechanism of the scheme is that the employer deducts amounts specified by the employee from gross pay and this amount is not taxable on the employee. In most cases the employee will receive a book of vouchers, similar to a chequebook, from the Charities Aid Foundation (CAF) or other such agencies which he or she can then use to make gifts to charities of his or her choice. The charity is not entitled to reclaim any further tax on these payments.

The agency acts as a type of clearing house and pays funds into the charity concerned at the request of the employee. It performs a similar service for individuals who can set up an account for using covenanted donations. The donor issues instructions to the agency to pay amounts to specified charities from the account.

26.5 Legacies

Transfers to charities are exempt from inheritance tax and thus reduce the tax burden on an estate. There are a number of ways in which wills can be drafted to maximise the effect of this relief, particularly where the estate is substantial and the testator wishes to split the disposition between a charity or charities and individuals. A certain amount of planning can ensure that even a small pecuniary legacy to a charity can be structured so as to take advantage of maximum tax reliefs available.

26.6 Gifting shares and securities

Since 6 April 2000, individuals can get income tax relief on gifts of certain shares, securities and other investments to charities. This is in addition to the existing capital gains tax relief on gifts of assets to charities.

Since 1 April 2000 companies can get corporation tax relief on gifts to charities for the same type of investments. Companies can get this relief in addition to relief from corporation tax on capital gains on gifts to charities of shares, securities and other assets.

As far as the charity is concerned this investment can be sold immediately, or later, and the proceeds used for charitable purposes or they can be retained by the charity as an investment.

The type of investment that qualifies for the new tax relief is as follows:

- shares and securities listed or dealt in on the UK Stock Exchange, including the Alternative Investment Market;
- shares and securities listed or dealt in on any overseas recognised stock exchange;
- shares in a UK-authorised unit trust;
- shares in a UK open-ended investment company; and
- holdings in certain foreign collective investment schemes (broadly, these are schemes established outside the UK that are equivalent to unit trust and open-ended investment companies).

Individuals normally claim their relief in their self-assessment tax returns. Companies should claim the relief in their corporation tax self-assessment returns.

The amount of relief that can be claimed is the market value of the investment on the day that it is given to the charity. The date on which the gift is made is the day on which the whole of the beneficial ownership of the investments is transferred to the charity. This is usually the date on which the donor signs the stock transfer form. There might be additional costs of making the gift; for example a brokers fees can also be claimed. Any amount of consideration or the value of any benefits received by the donor, or persons connected with them, in connection with the gift must be deducted from the amount of the relief.

The following examples illustrate how the amount of relief is calculated.

Example 1
Charles owns 5,000 shares in ABC Ltd, a company quoted on the London Stock Exchange. The shares are given to a charity when they are worth £5 each. A broker's fee of £50 is charged for handling the transaction. As a token of gratitude the charity gives the donor tickets to an event worth £250.

The deduction that the donor can make is

	£
The value of the shares	25,000
Plus the brokers fees	50
	25,050
Less the value of the benefit received	250
	£24,800

Charities are able to ask donors to sell shares on their behalf. In such instances the donor can still obtain these tax reliefs. The donor will however require evidence from the charity, such as an exchange of letters, showing that they have made the gift of the investment to the charity and that the charity asked them to dispose of the investments on their behalf. Otherwise the donor will be treated as having made a disposal on his own account and the cash gift to the charity may be treated as a Gift Aid donation. No capital gains tax relief (as detailed below) would however be available in that case.

In addition to income tax and corporation tax relief there is existing relief on capital gains tax or corporation tax on chargeable gains for gifts of assets to charities. Conversely, a donor cannot take advantage of a loss for CGT purposes. This relief relates to all chargeable assets gifted to charities and not just assets that qualify for the income tax and corporation tax relief.

411

Where assets are given to a charity, or sold to a charity for no more than their cost, the donor is treated as having disposed of them for such an amount as gives rise to neither a gain nor a loss.

On any subsequent disposal by a charity the calculation of any gain is based on the date and cost of the donors original acquisition.

It is often asked whether it is more advantageous to sell the investment and give the proceeds to the charity using Gift Aid?

For companies, it will usually be better to give the shares to the charity. If no chargeable gain will arise on the sale then there is no difference between the two methods. For an individual, it depends on their circumstances and whether they wish the charity or themselves to gain the greater benefit from the tax relief. The following example demonstrates the difference.

Example 2

Claudette is a higher rate taxpayer, her shares are worth £100,000. If she sells them, she makes a net gain of £25,000 after all reliefs and allowances, and be liable to capital gains tax. The first option is for Claudette to sell the shares and give the proceeds to the charity under Gift Aid.

	£
Gross proceeds of sale of shares	100,000
Less capital gains charged	
(£25,000 @ 40%)	10,000
Net proceeds after tax	£90,000

Under Gift Aid, the charity can recover from the Inland Revenue the amount of basic rate tax.

	£
£90,000 x 22/78 which equals	£25,834
When this is added to the gift the charity receives in total £90,000, plus £25,384	£115,384
Claudette claims tax relief at the difference between the basic rate (22%) and higher rate (40%) on £115,384 (18% x £115,384) =	20,769
So the gift has cost her £100,000 – £20,769	£79,231

The second option is for Claudette to gift her shares to the charity.

	£
The charity receives shares to sell or retain as investments	100,000
Claudette gets tax relief on £100,000 at higher rate of tax (40%)	40,000
So the gift has cost Claudette £100,000 – £40,000 =	£60,000

In the above you can see under the first option the charity has received £115,384 as opposed to £100,000 under the second option. The gift has however cost Claudette £79,231 under the first option yet only £60,000 under the second option.

Appendix 1 – The Charities (Accounts and Reports) Regulations 2000 (SI 2000 No 2868)

Made	*19th October 2000*
Laid before Parliament	*25th October 2000*
Coming into force	*15th November 2000*

The Secretary of State, in exercise of the powers conferred upon him by sections 42, 44, 45 and 86(3) of the Charities Act 1993[1] and after such consultation as is mentioned in section 86(4) of that Act, hereby makes the following Regulations:

Citation and commencement

1. These Regulations may be cited as the Charities (Accounts and Reports) Regulations 2000 and shall come into force on 15th November 2000.

Interpretation

2. In these Regulations –

'director' includes any person occupying the position of a director, by whatever name called, and in relation to a body corporate whose affairs are managed by its members means a member of the body corporate;

'ex gratia payment' means any such application of the property of a charity, or any such waiver by a charity of any entitlement to receive any property, as may be authorised under section 27(1) of the 1993 Act;

'the 1993 Act' means the Charities Act 1993;

'the 1995 Regulations' means the Charities (Accounts and Reports) Regulations 1995;

'financial year' shall be construed in accordance with regulation 5 of the 1995 Regulations[2];

'fixed assets' means the assets of a charity which are intended or use or investment on a continuing basis;

'fund' means particular assets of a charity held on trusts which, as respects the purposes for which those assets are held, or as respects the powers of the charity trustees to use or apply those assets, are not identical with those on which other assets of the charity are held;

'income reserves' means those assets in the unrestricted fund of a charity which the charity trustees have, or can make, available to apply for all or any of its purposes, once they have provided for the commitments of the charity and its other planned expenditure;

'institution or body corporate connected with the charity' has the same meaning as in the 1995 Regulations;

'the SORP' means the Statement of Recommended Practice for Accounting and Reporting by Charities, issued by the Charity Commissioners on 17th October 2000;

'special case charity' means a charity which is either –

(a) a registered social landlord within the meaning of the Housing Act 1996[3] and whose registration has been recorded under section 3(3) of that Act; or

(b) has during the financial year in question –
   (i) conducted an institution in relation to which a designation made, or having effect as if made, under section 129 of the Education Reform Act 1988[4] or section 28 of the Further and Higher Education Act 1992[5] has effect;
   (ii) received financial support from funds administered by a higher education funding council or further education funding council within the meaning of the said Act of 1992 in respect of expenditure incurred or to be incurred by the charity in connection with that institution; and
   (iii) incurred no expenditure for charitable purposes other than the purposes of that institution or any other such institution;

'trustee for a charity' includes a custodian trustee and a nominee;

'unrestricted fund' means a fund which is to be used or applied in any way determined by the charity trustees for the furtherance of the objects of a charity, and 'restricted fund' means any other fund of a charity.

Form and content of statements of accounts

3. – (1) This regulation applies to a statement of accounts prepared by the charity trustees of a charity (other than a charity specified or referred to in regulation 4 of the 1995 Regulations) in accordance with section 42(1) of the 1993 Act in respect of a financial year –

(a) which begins on or after 1st January 2001; or
(b) which begins before that date if –
   (i)   the charity trustees determine that this regulation, rather than regulation 3 of the 1995 Regulations, shall apply to the statement of accounts; and
   (ii) the charity trustees have not, before the date when these regulations come into force, either approved the accounts of the charity in respect of that financial year, or authorised the signature of an annual report in respect of that financial year in accordance with regulation 10(1)(c) of the 1995 Regulations.

(2) If the charity trustees make a determination under sub-paragraph (b) above, they shall also make a determination under regulation 7(1)(b) below, if they are required to prepare an annual report in respect of the financial year in question.

(3) The requirements as to form and content of a statement of accounts to which this regulation applies are those set out in the following provisions of this regulation.

(4) The statement shall consist of –
   (a) a statement of financial activities which shall show the total incoming resources and application of the resources, together with any other movements in the total resources, of the charity during the financial year in respect of which the statement is prepared; and
   (b) a balance sheet which shall show the state of affairs of the charity as at the end of the financial year in respect of which the statement is prepared.

(5) The statement shall be prepared in accordance with the following principles, namely that –
   (a) the statement of financial activities shall give a true and fair view of the incoming resources and application of the resources of the charity in the financial year in respect of which the statement is prepared;
   (b) the balance sheet shall give a true and fair view of the state of affairs of the charity at the end of that year;
   (c) where compliance with the following requirements of this regulation would not be sufficient to give a true and fair view, the necessary additional information shall be given in the statement of accounts or in notes to the accounts;

(d) if in special circumstances compliance with any of those requirements would be inconsistent with giving a true and fair view, the
charity trustees shall depart from the requirement to the extent
necessary to give a true and fair view.

(6) The statement –
   (a) shall be prepared in accordance with the methods and principles
   set out in the SORP; and
   (b) subject to the following three paragraphs of this regulation, shall,
   with respect to any amount required to be shown in the statement
   of financial activities or in the balance sheet, also show the corresponding amount for the financial year immediately preceding
   that to which the statement or balance sheet relates.

(7) Where that corresponding amount is not comparable with the
amount to be shown for the item in question in respect of the financial year to which the statement of financial activities or balance sheet
relates, the former amount shall be adjusted.

(8) Where in the financial year to which the statement of accounts relates
the effect of paragraph (5) and paragraph (6)(a) above is that there
is nothing required to be shown in respect of a particular item, but an
amount was required to be shown in respect of that item in the statement of accounts for the immediately preceding financial year, those
provisions shall have effect as if such an amount were required to be
shown in the statement of accounts in the financial year to which the
statement relates, and that amount were nil.

(9) Where a charity has more than one fund, only amounts corresponding to the entries in the statement of financial activities relating to
the totals of both or all of the funds of the charity need be shown.

(10) There shall be provided by way of notes to the accounts the information specified in the Schedule to these Regulations, and proviso (ii)
to regulation 5(4) of the 1995 Regulations shall have effect as if for
the reference to regulation 3(4) of those Regulations there were substituted a reference to this paragraph of this regulation.

(11) The balance sheet shall be signed by one or more of the charity trustees
of the charity, each of whom has been authorised to do so, and shall
specify the date on which the statement of accounts of which the
balance sheet forms part was approved by the charity trustees.

Audit and independent examination

4. In relation to a statement of accounts to which regulation 3 applies –
   (a) regulation 6(2)(e) of the 1995 Regulations shall have effect as if,
   for the reference to regulation 3 of those Regulations, there were
   substituted a reference to regulation 3 above; and
   (b) regulation 7(e)(iii) of the 1995 Regulations shall have effect as if,
   for the reference to regulation 3 of those Regulations, there were

substituted a reference to regulation 3 above, and as if, for the reference to paragraph 1 of Part III of Schedule 1 to the 1995 Regulations, there were substituted a reference to sub-paragraphs (a) and (b) of paragraph (5) of regulation 3 above.

Form and content: special cases

5. – (1) This regulation applies to a statement of accounts prepared by the charity trustees of a special case charity in accordance with section 42(1) of the 1993 Act in respect of a financial year which begins on or after 1st January 2001.

(2) The requirements as to form and content of a statement of accounts to which this regulation applies are those set out in the following provisions of this regulation.

(3) The statement shall consist of an income and expenditure account and a balance sheet as at the end of the financial year in respect of which the statement of accounts is prepared.

(4) The statement shall be prepared in accordance with the following principles, namely that –

    (a) the income and expenditure account shall give a true and fair view of the income and expenditure of the charity for the financial year in respect of which the statement of accounts is prepared; and

    (b) the balance sheet shall give a true and fair view of the state of affairs of the charity at the end of that year.

Audit and independent examination

6. In relation to a statement of accounts to which regulation 5 applies –

    (a) regulation 6(2)(e) of the 1995 Regulations shall have effect as if, for the reference to regulation 4 of those Regulations, there were substituted a reference to regulation 5 above and as if for the words 'incoming resources and application of the resources' there were substituted the words 'income and expenditure'; and

    (b) regulation 7(e)(iii) of the 1995 Regulations shall have effect as if, for the reference to regulation 4 of those Regulations, there were substituted a reference to regulation 5 above, and as if for the reference to paragraph 1 of Part III of Schedule 1 to those Regulations, there were substituted a reference to regulation 5(4) above.

Annual reports

7. – (1) This regulation applies to an annual report prepared by the charity trustees of a charity (other than a charity specified in regulation 10(4) of the 1995 Regulations) in accordance with section 45(1) of the 1993 Act in respect of a financial year –

(a) which begins on or after 1st January 2001; or

(b) which begins before that date if –

    (i) the charity trustees determine that this regulation, rather than regulation 10 of the 1995 Regulations, shall apply to the annual report; and

    (ii) the charity trustees have not, before the date when these Regulations come into force, either authorised the signature of an annual report in respect of that financial year in accordance with regulation 10(1)(c) of the 1995 Regulations or approved a statement of accounts which has been prepared for the charity in respect of that financial year under regulation 3 of those Regulations.

(2) If the charity trustees make a determination under sub-paragraph (b) above, they shall also make a determination under regulation 3(1)(b) above, if they prepare a statement of accounts under section 42(1) of the 1993 Act in respect of the financial year in question and the charity is one to which regulation 3 above may apply.

(3) The report on the activities of a charity during the year which is required to be contained in the annual report in respect of each financial year of the charity prepared under section 45 of the 1993 Act shall specify the financial year to which it relates and shall –

    (a) in the case of any financial year of a charity in which its gross income does not exceed £250,000, be a brief summary of the main activities and achievements of the charity during the year in relation to its objects;

    (b) in the case of any financial year of a charity in which its gross income exceeds £250,000 –

        (i) be a review of all activities, including –

            (aa) material transactions, significant developments and achievements of the charity during the year in relation to its objects;

            (bb) any significant changes in those activities during the year;

            (cc) any important events affecting those activities which have occurred since the end of the year and any likely future developments in those activities; and

            (dd) where any fund of the charity was in deficit at the beginning of the financial year, the steps taken by the charity trustees to eliminate that deficit; and

        (ii) contain a statement as to whether the charity trustees have given consideration to –

            (aa) the major risks to which the charity is exposed; and

            (bb) systems designed to mitigate those risks; and

    (c) in either case, be dated and be signed by one or more of the charity trustees, each of whom has been authorised to do so.

(4) Subject to paragraphs (5) to (8) below, the information relating to a charity and to its trustees and officers which is required to be contained in that annual report shall be –

(a) the name of the charity as it appears in the register of charities and any other name by which it makes itself known;

(b) the number assigned to it in the register and, in the case of a charitable company, the number with which it is registered as a company;

(c) the principal address of the charity and, in the case of a charitable company, the address of its registered office;

(d) particulars, including the date if known, of any deed or other document containing provisions which regulate the purposes and administration of the charity;

(e) a description of the objects of the charity;

(f) the name of any person or body of persons entitled by the trusts of the charity to appoint one or more new charity trustees, and a description of the method provided by those trusts for such appointment;

(g) the name of any person who is a charity trustee of the charity on the date when the authority referred to in paragraph (3)(c) above is given, and, where any charity trustee on that date is a body corporate, the name of any person who is a director of the body corporate on that date;

(h) the name of any other person who has, at any time during the financial year in question, been a charity trustee of the charity;

(i) the name of any person who is a trustee for the charity on the date referred to in sub-paragraph (g) above;

(j) the name of any other person who has, at any time during the financial year in question, been a trustee for the charity;

(k) a description of the policies (if any) which have been adopted by the charity trustees –

(i) for the purpose of determining the level of income reserves which it is appropriate for the charity to maintain in order to meet effectively the needs designated by its trusts;

(ii) for the selection of investments for the charity; and

(iii) for the selection of individuals and institutions who are to receive grants out of the assets of the charity;

(l) a statement regarding the performance during the financial year of the investments belonging to the charity (if any);

(m) a description of the organisational structure of the charity; and

(n) a description of any assets held by the charity or by any charity trustee of, or trustee for, the charity, on behalf of another charity, and particulars of any special arrangements made with respect to the safe custody of such assets and their segregation from assets of the charity not so held and a description of the objects of the charity on whose behalf the assets are held.

(5) The Commissioners may, where they are satisfied that, in the case of a particular charity or class of charities, or in the case of a particular financial year of a charity or class of charities –

    (a) the disclosure of the name of any person whose name is required by any of sub-paragraphs (f) to (j) of paragraph (4) above to be contained in the annual report of a charity could lead to that person being placed in any personal danger; or

    (b) the disclosure of the principal address of the charity in accordance with paragraph (4)(c) above could lead to any such person being placed in any personal danger, dispense with the requirement –

        (i) in any of sub-paragraphs (f) to (j) of that paragraph, so far as it applies to the name of any such person; or

        (ii) in sub-paragraph (c) of that paragraph, so far as it applies to the principal address of the charity,

as the case may require.

(6) In the case of a charity having more than 50 charity trustees on the date referred to in paragraph (4)(g) above –

    (a) that sub-paragraph shall have effect as if for the words 'name of any person who is a charity trustee of the charity' there were substituted the words 'names of not less than 50 of the charity trustees of the charity, including any charity trustee who is also an officer of the charity'; and

    (b) paragraph (4)(h) shall have effect as if, at the end of the sub-paragraph, there were inserted the words 'other than the name of any charity trustee whose name has been excluded from the report in pursuance of sub-paragraph (g) above'.

(7) In the case of a report prepared under section 46(5) of the 1993 Act (excepted charities which are not registered), paragraph (4) above shall have effect as if –

    (a) in sub-paragraph (a) the words from 'as it appears in the register of charities' to the end, and

    (b) in sub-paragraph (b) the words 'the number assigned to it in the register and,',

were omitted.

(8) In the case of a report in respect of a financial year of a charity in which its gross income does not exceed £250,000, paragraph (4) above shall have effect as if sub-paragraphs (l) to (n) were omitted.

Minor amendments to the 1995 Regulations

8. – (1) In regulation 2(1) –
   (a) after the words 'deposit fund established by a scheme' there shall be inserted the words 'under section 22A of the Charities Act 1960[6] or'; and
   (b) after the words 'investment fund established by a scheme' there shall be inserted the words 'under section 22 of the Charities Act 1960 or'.

(2) For regulation 4(7)(a) there shall be substituted the following –
   '(a) is a registered social landlord within the meaning of the Housing Act 1996 and whose registration has been recorded under section 3(3) of that Act; or'.

(3) In regulation 9(2) –
   (a) in sub-paragraph (b), after the words 'Comptroller and Auditor General' there shall be inserted the words 'or by the Auditor General for Wales'; and
   (b) in sub-paragraph (c), after the words 'have been' there shall be inserted the words 'or will be'.

Paul Boateng
Minister of State

Home Office
19th October 2000

SCHEDULE – Regulation 3(10)

NOTES TO THE ACCOUNTS

1. Subject to paragraph 2 below, the information to be provided by way of notes to the accounts shall, insofar as not provided in the statement of financial activities or in the balance sheet, be as follows:
   (a) particulars of any material adjustment made pursuant to regulation 3(7) above;
   (b) a description of the accounting policies of, and assumptions made for the purposes of preparing the statement of accounts by, the charity trustees, including any material change in these, the reason for such change and its effect (if material) on the accounts, in accordance with the methods and principles set out in the SORP;
   (c) a description of the nature and purpose of all material funds of the charity in accordance with the methods and principles set out in the SORP;
   (d) such particulars of the related party transactions of the charity, or of any institution or body corporate connected with the charity, as may be required by the SORP to be disclosed;

(e) such particulars of the cost to the charity of employing staff as may be required by the SORP to be disclosed;

(f) such particulars of the emoluments of staff employed by the charity as may be required by the SORP to be disclosed;

(g) particulars of the cost to the charity of –

   (i) any policies of insurance against loss arising from the neglect or default of any of the charity trustees or trustees for the charity; or

   (ii) indemnifying the charity trustees, or trustees for the charity, or any of them, in respect of the consequences of any such loss;

(h) a description of any incoming resources which represent capital, according to whether or not that capital is permanent endowment;

(i) an itemised analysis of any material movement between any of the restricted funds of the charity, or between a restricted and an unrestricted fund of the charity, together with an explanation of the nature and purpose of each of those funds;

(j) the name of any institution or body corporate connected with the charity, together with a description of the nature of the charity's relationship with that institution or body corporate and of its activities, including, where material, its turnover and net profit or loss for the corresponding financial year of the institution or body corporate and any qualification expressed in an auditor's report on its accounts;

(k) particulars of any guarantee given by the charity, where any potential liability under the guarantee is outstanding at the date of the balance sheet;

(l) particulars of any loan outstanding at the date of the balance sheet –

   (i) which was made to the charity, and which is secured by an express charge on any of the assets of the charity; or

   (ii) which was made by the charity to any institution or body corporate connected with the charity;

(m) particulars of any fund of the charity which is in deficit at the date of the balance sheet;

(n) particulars of any remuneration paid to an auditor or independent examiner in respect of auditing or examining the accounts of the charity and particulars of any remuneration paid to him in respect of any other services rendered to the charity;

(o) such particulars of any grant made by the charity as may be required by the SORP to be disclosed;

(p) particulars of any ex gratia payment made by the charity;

(q) an analysis of any entry in the balance sheet relating to fixed assets, debtors and creditors, according to the categories set out in the SORP;

(r) an analysis of all material changes during the financial year in question in the values of fixed assets, in accordance with the methods and principles set out in the SORP;

(s) the following particulars of any contingent liability existing at the date of the balance sheet, that is to say, its amount or estimated amount, its legal nature and whether any valuable security has been provided by the charity in connection with that liability and, if so, what;

(t) particulars of any other financial commitments which are outstanding at the date of the balance sheet, and which have not been provided for and are relevant to assessment of the state of affairs of the charity;

(u) if the market value (as at the date of the balance sheet) of any land forming part of the property of the charity differs substantially from the amount at which that land is included in the balance sheet, and the difference is, in the opinion of the charity trustees, of such significance as to require that attention be drawn to it, particulars of that difference;

(v) in the case of any amount required by any of the preceding sub-paragraphs (other than sub-paragraph (i), (o) or (r) to be disclosed), the corresponding amount for the financial year immediately preceding that to which the accounts relate;

(w) a statement as to whether or not the accounts have been prepared in accordance with any applicable accounting standards and statements of recommended practice and particulars of any material departure from those standards and statements of practice and the reasons for such departure;

(x) where the charity trustees have exercised their powers under sub-paragraph (a) or (c) of regulation 5(4) of the 1995 Regulations so as to determine an accounting reference date earlier or later than 12 months from the beginning of the financial year, a statement of their reasons for doing so;

(y) if, in accordance with regulation 3(5)(d) above, the charity trustees have departed from any requirement of that regulation, particulars of any such departure, the reasons for it, and its effect; and

(z) any additional information –
   (i) which is required to ensure that the statement of accounts complies with the requirements of regulation 3 above; or
   (ii) which may reasonably assist the user to understand the statement of accounts.

2. Sub-paragraphs (g) and (w) of paragraph 1 above shall not apply in the case of any financial year of a charity in which the gross income of the charity does not exceed £250,000.

EXPLANATORY NOTE

(This note is not part of the Regulations)

These Regulations, which extend only to England and Wales, make new provision with respect to the form and content of the accounts of Charities and the annual reports of charity trustees for financial years which begin on or after 1 January 2001. They replace provision made by the Charities (Accounts and Reports) Regulations 1995 (S.I. 1995/2724) ('the 1995 Regulations'). There is an option for trustees to prepare accounts and reports in accordance with the new provision, rather than the 1995 Regulations, for earlier financial years.

The requirements relating to the audit or examination of charity accounts continue to be set out in the 1995 Regulations, subject to the minor modifications made by regulations 4, 6 and 8.

Regulation 3 prescribes the form and content of statements of accounts prepared by charity trustees under section 42(1) of the Charities Act 1993, and the methods and principles applicable. Regulation 3 and the Schedule prescribe the information to be provided by way of notes to the accounts.

Regulation 5 prescribes the form and content of statements of accounts of registered social landlords and charities conducting higher and further education institutions.

Regulation 7 deals with the annual reports which charity trustees are required to make to the Charity Commissioners.

The Statement of Recommended Practice for Accounting and Reporting by Charities, which is referred to in Regulation 2, may be obtained from the Charity Commission, Harmsworth House, 13-15 Bouverie Street, London EC4Y 8DP, and from its website www.charity-commission.gov.uk

Notes:

[1]   1993 c. 10; section 42 was amended by the Charities Act 1993 (Substitution of Sums) Order 1995 (S.I. 1995/2696) and section 45 was amended by section 29 of the Deregulation and Contracting Out Act 1994 (c. 40) and by Part II of Schedule 1 to the Companies Act 1985 (Audit Exemption) Regulations 1994 (S.I. 1994/1935).

[2]   S.I. 1995/2724.

[3]   1996 c. 52.

[4]   1988 c. 1. Section 129 was amended by section 72(1) of the Further and Higher Education Act 1992.

[5]   1992 c. 13. Section 28 was amended by paragraph 109 of schedule 37 to the Education Act 1996 (c. 56) and by paragraphs 33 and 38 of schedule 30 to the School Standards and Framework Act 1998(c. 31).

[6]   1960 c. 58: section 22A was inserted by the Charities Act 1992 (c. 41).back

Appendix 2 – The Charities (Accounts and Reports) Regulations 1995 (SI 1995 No 2724)*

Made	*17th October 1995*
Laid before Parliament	*20th October 1995*
Coming into force	*1st March 1996*

The Secretary of State, in exercise of the powers conferred upon him by sections 42, 44, 45 and 86(3) of the Charities Act 1993[1], and after such consultation as is mentioned in section 86(4) of that Act, hereby makes the following Regulations:

Citation and commencement

1. These Regulations may be cited as the Charities (Accounts and Reports) Regulations 1995 and shall come into force on 1st March 1996.

Interpretation

2.– (1) In these Regulations, the expression –

'common deposit fund' means a common deposit fund established by a scheme under section 25 of the 1993 Act;

'common investment fund' means a common investment fund established by a scheme under section 24 of the 1993 Act, other than a fund the trusts of which provide for property to be transferred to the fund only by or on behalf of a participating charity of which the charity trustees are the trustees appointed to manage the fund;

'financial year' shall be construed in accordance with regulation 5 below;

'institution or body corporate connected with the charity', in relation to a charity, means an institution or body corporate which –

---

* As modified to eliminate legislation superseded by SI 2000 No 2868 (see App. 1).

(a) in the case of an institution, is controlled by,

(b) in the case of a body corporate, in which a substantial interest is held by, the charity or any one or more of the charity trustees acting in his or their capacity as such;

'recognised stock exchange' has the meaning assigned to it by section 841 of the Income and Corporation Taxes Act 1988(b); and

'the 1993 Act' means the Charities Act 1993.

(2) For the purposes of these Regulations, a person is connected with a charity trustee if –

(a) he is the child, parent, grandchild, grandparent, brother or sister of the charity trustee;

(b) he is the spouse of the charity trustee or of any person connected with him by virtue of sub-paragraph (a) above;

(c) he is a trustee of any trust, not being a charity, the beneficiaries or potential beneficiaries of which include the charity trustee or any person connected with him by virtue of sub-paragraph (a) or (b) above and is acting in his capacity as such;

(d) he is a partner of the charity trustee or of any person connected with him by virtue of sub-paragraph (a), (b) or (c) above and is acting in his capacity as such; or

(e) the person is a body corporate, not being a company which is connected with a charitable institution within the meaning of section 58(5) of the Charities Act 1992(a), in which the charity trustee has, or the charity trustee and any other charity trustee or trustees or person or persons connected with him by virtue of sub-paragraph (a), (b), (c) or (d) above, taken together, have, a substantial interest.

(3) Any expression in this regulation which also appears in Schedule 5 to the 1993 Act shall be construed in accordance with paragraphs 2 to 4 of that Schedule.

Financial year

5.–(1) The financial year of a charity shall, for the purposes of the 1993 Act and regulations made thereunder, be determined in accordance with the following provisions of this regulation.

(2) The first financial year of a charity shall be –

(a) in the case of a charity which is established before the date on which these Regulations come into force, the period beginning with the day immediately following the end of the period in respect of which a statement of accounts was required to be prepared under any statutory provision contained in or having effect under an Act of Parliament applicable to that charity before the coming into force of section 42 of the 1993 Act and ending with the accounting reference date of the charity or such other date, not more than seven days before or after the accounting reference date, as the charity trustees may determine;

(b) in the case of a charity which is established on or after the date on which these Regulations come into force, the period beginning with the day on which the charity is established and ending with the accounting reference date of the charity or such other date, not more than seven days before or after the accounting reference date, as the charity trustees may determine.

(3) Subsequent financial years of a charity begin with the day immediately following the end of the charity's previous financial year and end with its accounting reference date or such other date, not more than seven days before or after the accounting reference date, as the charity trustees may determine.

(4) The accounting reference date of a charity shall, for the purposes of this regulation, be –

(a) in the first financial year of a charity which is established before the date on which these Regulations come into force, such date, not less than 6 months nor more than 18 months after the date on which that financial year began, as the charity trustees may determine;

(b) in the first financial year of a charity which is established on or after the date on which these Regulations come into force, such date, not less than 6 months nor more than 18 months after the date on which the charity was established, as the charity trustees may determine;

(c) in any subsequent financial year of a charity, the date 12 months after the previous accounting reference date of the charity or such other date, not less than 6 months nor more than 18 months after the previous accounting reference date of the charity as the trustees may determine:

Provided that –

(i) the charity trustees shall not exercise their powers under sub-paragraph (c) of this paragraph so as to determine an accounting reference date in respect of any financial year which is consecutive, or follows immediately after a financial year which is consecutive, to a previous financial year in respect of which that power was exercised; and

(ii) the charity trustees shall exercise their powers under sub-paragraph (a) or (c) of this paragraph so as to determine a date earlier or later than 12 months from the beginning of the financial year only where satisfied that there are exceptional reasons to do so (which reasons shall, in the case of a charity subject to the requirements of regulation 3(4) or 4(4) above, be disclosed in a note to the accounts).

Annual audit of charity accounts

6. (1) The duties of an auditor carrying out an audit of the accounts of a charity under section 43 of the 1993 Act(a) shall be those specified in the following provisions of this regulation.

(2) Where a statement of accounts has been prepared under section 42(1) of the 1993 Act for the financial year in question the auditor shall make a report on that statement to the charity trustees which –

(a) states the name and address of the auditor and the name of the charity concerned;

(b) is signed by him or, where the office of auditor is held by a body corporate or partnership, in its name by a person authorised to sign on its behalf and states that the auditor is a person falling within paragraph (a) or, as the case may be, (b) of section 43(2) of the 1993 Act;

(c) is dated and specifies the financial year in respect of which the accounts to which it relates have been prepared;

(d) specifies that it is a report in respect of an audit carried out under section 43 of the 1993 Act and in accordance with regulations made under section 44 of that Act;

(e) states whether in the auditor's opinion the statement of accounts complies with the requirements of regulation 3 or, as the case may be, 4, above and gives a true and fair view of the state of affairs of the charity at the end of the financial year in question and of the incoming resources and application of the resources of the charity in that year;

(f) where the auditor has formed the opinion –

(i) that accounting records have not been kept in respect of the charity in accordance with section 41 of the 1993 Act; or

(ii) that the statement of accounts does not accord with those records; or

(iii) that any information contained in the statement of accounts is inconsistent in any material respect with any report of the charity trustees prepared under section 45 of the 1993 Act in respect of the financial year in question; or

(iv) that any information or explanation to which he is entitled under regulation 8 below has not been afforded to him,

contains a statement of that opinion and of his grounds for forming it.

431

(3) Where a receipts and payments account and statement of assets and liabilities have been prepared under section 42(3) of the 1993 Act for the financial year in question the auditor shall make a report on that account and statement to the charity trustees which –

  (a) states the name and address of the auditor and the name of the charity concerned;

  (b) is signed by him or, where the office of auditor is held by a body corporate or partnership, in its name by a person authorised to sign on its behalf and states that the auditor is a person falling within paragraph (a) or, as the case may be, (b) of section 43(2) of the 1993 Act;

  (c) is dated and specifies the financial year in respect of which the accounts to which it relates have been prepared;

  (d) specifies that it is a report in respect of an audit carried out under section 43 of the 1993 Act and in accordance with regulations made under section 44 of that Act;

  (e) states whether in the auditor's opinion –

    (i) the account and statement properly present the receipts and payments of the charity for the financial year in question and its assets and liabilities as at the end of that year; and

    (ii) the account and statement adequately distinguish any material special trust or other restricted fund of the charity;

  (f) where the auditor has formed the opinion –

    (i) that accounting records have not been kept in respect of the charity in accordance with section 41 of the 1993 Act; or

    (ii) that the account and statement do not accord with those records; or

    (iii) that any information or explanation to which he is entitled under regulation 8 below has not been afforded to him,

  contains a statement of that opinion and of his grounds for forming it.

(4) The auditor shall, in preparing his report for the purposes of paragraph (2) or, as the case may be, (3) above, carry out such investigations as will enable him to form an opinion as to the matters specified in sub-paragraph (e) and (f) of that paragraph.

(5) The auditor shall communicate to the Commissioners, in writing, any matter of which the auditor becomes aware in his capacity as such which relates to the activities or affairs of the charity or of any institution or body corporate connected with the charity and which the auditor has reasonable cause to believe is, or is likely to be, of material significance for the exercise, in relation to the charity of the Commissioners' functions under section 8 (general power to institute inquiries) or 18 (power to act for protection of charities) of the 1993 Act.

(6) Where an auditor appointed by charity trustees ceases for any reason to hold office he shall send to the charity trustees a statement of any circumstances connected with his ceasing to hold office which he considers should be brought to their attention or, if he considers that there are no such circumstances, a statement that there are none; and the auditor shall send a copy of any statement sent to the charity trustees under this paragraph (except a statement that there are no such circumstances) to the Commissioners.

(7) In the case of an auditor appointed by the Commissioners, the report required by paragraph (2) or, as the case may be, (3) above shall be made to the Commissioners instead of to the charity trustees.

Independent examination of charity accounts

7. An independent examiner who has carried out an examination of the accounts of a charity under section 43 of the 1993 Act shall make a report to the charity trustees which –

(a) states his name and address and the name of the charity concerned;

(b) is signed by him and specifies any relevant professional qualifications or professional body of which he is a member;

(c) is dated and specifies the financial year in respect of which the accounts to which it relates have been prepared;

(d) specifies that it is a report in respect of an examination carried out under section 43 of the 1993 Act and in accordance with any directions given by the Commissioners under subsection (7)(b) of that section which are applicable;

(e) states whether or not any matter has come to the examiner's attention in connection with the examination which gives him reasonable cause to believe that in any material respect –

(i) accounting records have not been kept in respect of the charity in accordance with section 41 of the 1993 Act; or

(ii) the accounts do not accord with those records; or

(iii) in the case of an examination of accounts a statement of which has been prepared under section 42(1) of the 1993 Act, the statement of accounts does not comply with any of the requirements of regulation 3 or, as the case may be, 4 above except the requirements specified in paragraph 1 of Part III of Schedule 1 to these Regulations;

(f) states whether or not any matter has come to the examiner's attention in connection with the examination to which, in his opinion, attention should be drawn in the report in order to enable a proper understanding of the accounts to be reached;

(g) where any of the following matters has become apparent to the examiner during the course of the examination, namely, that

> (i) there has been any material expenditure or action which appears not to be in accordance with the trusts of the charity; or
>
> (ii) any information or explanation to which he is entitled under regulation 8 below has not been afforded to him; or
>
> (iii) in the case of an examination of accounts a statement of which has been prepared under section 42(1) of the 1993 Act, any information contained in the statement of accounts is inconsistent in any material respect with any report of the charity trustees prepared under section 45 of the 1993 Act in respect of the financial year in question,

contains a statement to that effect.

Audit and independent examination: supplementary provisions

8.- (1) An auditor or independent examiner carrying out an audit or examination of the accounts of a charity under section 43 of the 1993 Act shall have a right of access to any books, documents and other records (however kept) which relate to the charity concerned and which the auditor or examiner in question considers it necessary to inspect for the purposes of carrying out the audit, or as the case may be, examination.

(2) Such an auditor or independent examiner shall be entitled to require, in the case of the charity concerned, such information and explanations from past or present charity trustees or trustees for the charity, or from past or present officers or employees of the charity, as he considers it necessary to obtain for the purposes of carrying out the audit or, as the case may be, examination.

Dispensations from audit or examination requirements

9.- (1) The Commissioners may, in the circumstances specified in paragraph (2) below, dispense with the requirements of section 43(2) or (3) of the 1993 Act in the case of a particular charity or of a particular financial year of a charity.

(2) The circumstances referred to in paragraph (1) above are where the Commissioners:

(a) are satisfied that the accounts of the charity concerned are required to be audited in accordance with any statutory provision contained in or having effect under an Act of Parliament which, in the opinion of the Commissioners, imposes requirements which are sufficiently similar to the requirements of section 43(2) for those requirements to be dispensed with;

(b) are satisfied that the accounts of the charity concerned have been audited by the Comptroller and Auditor General;

(c) are satisfied that the accounts of the charity concerned for the financial year in question have been audited or, as the case may be, examined in accordance with requirements or arrangements which, in the opinion of the Commissioners, are sufficiently similar to the relevant requirements of section 43 of the 1993 Act applicable to that financial year of that charity for those requirements to be dispensed with;

(d) are satisfied that there has in the financial year in question been no transaction on the part of the charity concerned which would be required to be shown and explained in the accounting records kept in pursuance of section 41 of the 1993 Act;

(e) consider that, although the financial year in question of the charity concerned is one to which subsection (2) of section 43 of the 1993 Act applies, there are exceptional circumstances which justify the examination of the accounts by an independent examiner instead of their audit in accordance with that subsection, and the accounts have been so examined,

and where the charity trustees of the charity concerned have supplied to the Commissioners any report made to them with respect to the accounts of that charity for the financial year in question which the Commissioners have requested.

SCHEDULE 2   **Regulation 4**

FORM AND CONTENTS OF STATEMENTS OF ACCOUNTS:

COMMON INVESTMENT FUNDS AND COMMON DEPOSIT FUNDS

PART I

STATEMENT OF TOTAL RETURN

1. The statement of total return shall show the net gain or loss on investments, gross income, total expenditure and total return of the fund, and the total amount distributed or due, including interest paid or payable, to participating charities out of the fund, during the financial year in respect of which the statement of accounts is prepared.

2. The information required by paragraph 1 above shall be analysed by reference to –

(a) net gains or losses on investments, indicated by –

    (i) gains or losses on investments sold during the financial year in question, based on the historical cost of the investment sold;

    (ii) any net appreciation or depreciation of such investments recognised in earlier accounting periods;

      (iii) the gains or losses on such investments based on their value as shown in the accounts (that is to say, the difference between or, as the case may be, the sum of the amounts entered in pursuance of paragraphs (i) and (ii) above); and

      (iv) net unrealised appreciation or depreciation of investments during the financial year in question;

(b) gains or losses on other assets;

(c) gross income, divided into –

    (i) dividends in respect of shares;

    (ii) scrip dividends;

    (iii) interest on securities;

    (iv) interest on deposits at banks and building societies;

    (v) underwriting commission; and

    (vi) other income;

(d) expenditure incurred in the administration of the scheme under which the fund was established, divided into –

    (i) amounts payable directly or indirectly by way of remuneration, reimbursement of expenses or otherwise to any trustee appointed to manage the fund or person connected with such a trustee;

    (ii) amounts payable directly or indirectly by way of remuneration, reimbursement of expenses or otherwise to any person to whom the trustees have delegated their functions in relation to management of the fund or to any person connected with that person;

    (iii) fees payable in respect of any audit carried out by an auditor under section 43 of the 1993 Act;

    (iv) any fees payable to the person carrying out such an audit in respect of other services for the fund provided by him;

    (v) any fees payable in respect of the safe custody of assets; and

    (vi) other expenditure divided into such categories as reasonably enable the user to gain an appreciation of the expenditure incurred;

(e) tax borne by the fund in respect of income, profits or gains during the financial year in question, divided into –

    (i) income tax or capital gains tax to which the fund is liable in the United Kingdom; and

    (ii) overseas tax;

(f) net income (that is to say, the total amount entered in pursuance of sub-paragraph (c) above less the total of the amounts entered in pursuance of sub-paragraphs (d) and (e) above);

(g) total return (that is to say, the total of the amounts entered in pursuance of sub-paragraphs (a), (b) and (f) above);

(h) the amount distributed or due in respect of income and accumulation shares, and interest paid or payable to charities who have deposited sums, during the financial year in question; and

(i) net increase or decrease in the value of the fund resulting from its activities (that is to say, the difference between the amounts entered in pursuance of sub-paragraphs (g) and (h) above).

3. In the case of a common investment fund established by a scheme which, in pursuance of section 24(5) of the 1993 Act, includes provision for enabling sums to be deposited by or on behalf of a charity on the basis that (subject to the provisions of the scheme) the charity shall be entitled to repayment of the sums deposited and to interest thereon at a rate determined by or under the scheme, the analysis required by paragraph 2 above shall distinguish between the amount of capital and income to be shared between charities participating otherwise than by way of deposit and the amounts excluded from such amount under provision made in pursuance of section 24(5) of the 1993 Act (that is, such amounts as are from time to time reasonably required in respect of the liabilities of the fund for the repayment of deposits and for the interest on deposits, including amounts required by way of reserve).

4. In respect of any information required by a sub-paragraph of paragraph 2 above to be divided into separate categories denoted by paragraphs of that sub-paragraph, the division of that information into such separate categories may, if the trustees appointed to manage the fund so elect, be effected by means of a note to the accounts made in pursuance of Part V of this Schedule rather than by division in pursuance of that sub-paragraph.

PART II

STATEMENT OF MOVEMENT IN FUNDS

1. The statement of movement in funds shall provide a reconciliation between the net assets of the fund at the beginning of the financial year in respect of which the statement of accounts is prepared and the net assets of the fund at the end of that year.

2. The reconciliation referred to in paragraph 1 above shall show –
   (a) the value of the net assets at the beginning of the financial year in question;
   (b) in the case of a common investment fund, the amount or value of any property transferred to or withdrawn from the fund during that year by participating charities;
   (c) the net increase or decrease in the value of the fund resulting from its activities during that year (that is to say, the amount entered in pursuance of sub-paragraph (i) of paragraph 2 of Part I of this Schedule);
   (d) in the case of a common investment fund, the amount of any distribution of income due in respect of accumulation shares; and
   (e) the value of the net assets at the end of the financial year in question.

3. In the case of a common investment fund such as is described in paragraph 3 of Part I of this Schedule, the analysis required by paragraph 2 above shall distinguish between the amount of capital and income to be shared between charities participating otherwise than by way of deposit and the amounts excluded from such amount under provision made in pursuance of section 24(5) of the 1993 Act.

PART III

BALANCE SHEET

1. The balance sheet shall show, by reference to the information specified in paragraph 2 or, as the case may be, 3 below, the state of affairs of the fund as at the end of the financial year.

2. Subject to paragraph 4 below, in the case of a common investment fund, the information referred to in paragraph 1 above is as follows:
  (a) tangible fixed assets for use by the fund;
  (b) investments;
  (c) current assets, divided into
      (i)   debtors;
      (ii) deposits and loans;
      (iii) cash at bank and in hand; and
      (iv) others;
  (d) liabilities, divided into
      (i)   creditors;
      (ii) bank overdrafts;
      (iii) other loans; and
      (iv) distributions payable to participating charities;
  (e) net current assets less liabilities (that is to say, the difference between the total amount entered in pursuance of subparagraph (c) above and the total amount entered in pursuance of sub-paragraph (d) above); and
  (f) net assets (that is to say, the total of the amounts entered in pursuance of sub-paragraphs (a), (b) and (e) above); and
  (g) total funds of the common investment fund.

3. In the case of a common deposit fund, the information referred to in paragraph 1 above is as follows:
  (a) cash at bank and in hand;
  (b) debtors;
  (c) deposits and investments, divided into –
      (i)   deposits at building societies within the meaning of the Building Societies Act 1986[2];
      (ii) deposits at the Bank of England or any institution which is authorised by the Bank of England to operate a deposit taking business under Part I of the Banking Act 1987[3];

(iii) other bank deposits;

(iv) other deposits; and

(v) other investments;

(d) current assets not included in any of paragraphs (a) to (c) above;

(e) tangible fixed assets for use by the fund;

(f) gross assets (that is to say, the total of the amounts entered in pursuance of sub-paragraphs (a) to (e) above);

(g) sums deposited by participating charities;

(h) other liabilities, divided into –

(i) creditors;

(ii) bank overdrafts;

(iii) other loans; and

(iv) interest accrued or payable to participating charities;

(i) total liabilities (that is to say, the total of the amounts entered in pursuance of sub-paragraphs (g) and (h) above); and

(j) total funds of the common deposit fund (that is to say the amount entered in pursuance of sub-paragraph (f) above less the amount entered in pursuance of sub-paragraph (i) above).

4. In the case of a common investment fund such as is described in paragraph 3 of Part I of this Schedule, the information referred to in paragraph 1 above is –

(a) in relation to the amount of capital and income to be shared between charities participating otherwise than by way of deposit, the information specified in paragraph 2 above; and

(b) in relation to the amounts excluded from such amount under provision made in pursuance of section 24(5) of the 1993 Act, the information specified in paragraph 3 above.

5. In respect of any information required by sub-paragraph (c) of paragraph 3 above to be divided into separate categories denoted by paragraphs of that sub-paragraph, the division of that information into such separate categories may, if the trustees appointed to manage the fund so elect, be effected by means of a note to the accounts made in pursuance of Part V of this Schedule rather than by division in pursuance of that sub-paragraph.

PART IV

METHODS AND PRINCIPLES

1. The methods and principles specified and referred to in Part III of Schedule I to these Regulations shall apply for the purposes of the preparation of the statement of accounts of a common investment fund or common deposit fund as they do for the purposes of the preparation of the statement of accounts of a charity to which that Schedule applies, subject to the following modifications.

2.–(1) For any reference to 'the charity' or 'charity trustees' there is sub-stituted a reference to the fund or, as the case may be, the trustees appointed to manage the fund.

(2) In paragraph 1(1), for 'statement of financial activities' there is sub-stituted 'statement of total return'.

(3) After paragraph 1(1), there is inserted the following subparagraph:

'(lA) The statement of movement in funds shall give a true and fair view of the movements in the net assets of the fund between their position at the beginning of that year and their position at the end of that year.'

(4) In paragraph 1(2), for 'Part I or, as the case may be, Part II and Part IV of this Schedule' there is substituted 'Part I, II or, as the case may be, III and Part V of Schedule 2 to these Regulations'.

(5) For paragraph 2(1), there is substituted the following subparagraph:

'(1) In respect of every amount required by paragraph 2 of Part 1 of Schedule 2 to these Regulations to be shown in the state-ment of total return, or by paragraph 2 of Part II of that Sched-ule to be shown in the statement of movement in funds, or by paragraph 2 or, as the case may be, 3 of Part III of that Sched-ule to be shown in the balance sheet, the corresponding amount for the financial year immediately preceding that to which the statement or balance sheet relates shall also be shown.'

(6) In paragraph 2(2), for 'statement of financial activities' there is substituted 'statement of total return, statement of movement in funds'.

(7) In paragraph 3, for 'Statement of Recommended Practice for Accounting by Charities issued in October 1995' there is substituted 'Statement of Recommended Practice for Authorised Unit Trust Schemes issued in April 1991'.

PART V

NOTES TO THE ACCOUNTS

1. The information to be provided by way of notes to the accounts of a common investment fund or common deposit fund is the information specified in Part IV of Schedule 1 to these Regulations in relation to the accounts of charities to which that Schedule applies, modified in accord-ance with the following provisions of this Part.

2.–(1) For any reference to 'the charity' there is substituted a reference to the fund and for any reference to 'the charity trustees' or 'trustees for the charity' or to any of them there is substituted a reference to the trustees appointed to manage the fund or to any of them, as the case may require.

(2) For paragraph 1(a) and (b) there are substituted the following sub-paragraphs:

'(a) a description of the accounting policies of the trustees, particularly regarding the basis of valuation of investments, the recognition of dividend income or interest and the conversion of any amounts expressed in currency other than pounds sterling, and of the accounting assumptions made by them, including any material change in these, the reason for such change and its effect (if material) on the accounts;

(b) where the trustees appointed to manage the fund have during the financial year in question entered into any transaction, agreement or arrangement made for the purpose of minimising the risk of loss to the fund in consequence of fluctuations in interest rates or in the market value of securities or in the rates of foreign exchange, or entered into any other transaction in financial futures or options relating to shares, securities, foreign currency or other financial instrument which is a trading transaction in its own right, the nature of and reason for entering that transaction, agreement or arrangement and the total value of, and the maximum extent of financial exposure as at the date of the balance sheet resulting from, that transaction, agreement or arrangement;'.

(3) In paragraph 1(c), (d)(i) and (ii) and (e), after 'trustees appointed to manage the fund' there is inserted 'or any person to whom they have delegated their functions in relation to management of the fund'.

(4) For paragraph 1(f) and (g) there are substituted the following sub-paragraphs:

'(f) an analysis of the amount and date of any distribution in respect of income and accumulation shares or payment of interest to participating charities;

(g) a note of any adjustments made in the statement of total return to reflect the amount of income included in the creation or cancellation price of a unit or share in the fund;'

(5) For paragraph 1(j) to (n) there are substituted the following sub-paragraphs –

'(j) an explanation of any amount entered in pursuance of paragraph 2(e)(i) of Part I of this Schedule (United Kingdom tax);

(k) an analysis of any entry in the balance sheet relating to:
  (i)   tangible fixed assets for use by the fund, according to the following categories –
    (A) freehold interests in land and buildings;
    (B) any other interest in land or buildings;
    (C) payments on account and assets in course of construction; and
    (D) plant, machinery, fixtures, fittings and equipment;
  (ii) debtors, according to the following categories –
    (A) in the case of a common investment fund, amounts receivable in respect of property transferred to the fund;
    (B) amounts receivable in respect of securities sold;
    (C) accrued income; and
    (D) other debtors;
  (iii) creditors, according to the following categories –
    (A) in the case of a common investment fund, amounts payable in respect of property withdrawn from the fund;
    (B) amounts payable in respect of securities purchased;
    (C) accrued expenses; and
    (D) other creditors;
(1) in the case of a common investment fund, the following statements, made up to the date of the balance sheet, that is to say –
  (i)   a portfolio statement, specifying –
    (A) details of each investment held by or on behalf of the fund, including its market value at that date;
    (B) the category of each such investment according to its geographical area or industrial sector;
    (C) the percentage of net assets represented by each investment so held and by each category of investment specified under paragraph (B) above; and
    (D) whether or not the investment in question is listed on a recognised stock exchange;
  (ii) a statement of major changes in the portfolio, specifying –
    (A) where the aggregate value of purchases or sales of a particular investment during the financial year in question exceeds 2 per cent of net assets at the beginning of that year, that value;
    (B) unless disclosed in pursuance of paragraph (A) above, the value of the 20 largest purchases and sales of a particular investment during the financial year in question; and
    (C) the total cost of purchase and net proceeds from sales of investments during the financial year in question;

        (iii) a statement of the number of shares issued as at the beginning of the year and as at the date of the balance sheet and the value of each income or accumulation share as at each of those dates, calculated by reference to the net asset value of the fund; and

        (iv) a statement of the amount, if any, in the dividend equalisation reserve;

  (m) in the case of a common deposit fund, details of sums deposited by participating charities as at the date of the balance sheet, divided into –

        (i) sums repayable on demand; and

        (ii) deposits with agreed maturity dates or periods of notice, divided into –

           (A) those repayable in not more than three months;

           (B) those repayable in more than three months but not more than one year;

           (C) those repayable in more than one year but not more than five years; and

           (D) those repayable in more than five years;

  (n) in the case of a common deposit fund, details as at the date of the balance sheet of –

        (i) sums placed on deposit, divided into –

           (A) sums repayable on demand; and

           (B) other deposits, indicating whether they are repayable in not more than 3 months, more than 3 months but not more than 1 year, more than 1 year but not more than 5 years or more than 5 years; and

        (ii) investments other than deposits, analysed in accordance with sub-paragraph (m) above;'.

(6) For paragraph 1(q) there shall be substituted the following sub-paragraph:

'(q) in the case of any amount required by any of the preceding sub-paragraphs (other than sub-paragraph (1)(i) and (ii)) to be disclosed, or the percentage of net assets represented by each category of investment required by sub-paragraph (1)(i)(C) above to be disclosed, the corresponding amount or percentage for the financial year immediately preceding that to which the accounts relate;'

PART VI

INTERPRETATION

1. In this Schedule, 'dividend equalisation reserve' means income withheld from distribution with a view to avoiding fluctuations in the amounts distributed.

2. For the purposes of this Schedule, a person is connected with a trustee appointed to manage the fund or a person to whom the trustees appointed to manage the fund have delegated their functions in relation to management of the fund (in this paragraph referred to as 'the manager') if –

    (a) he is the child, parent, grandchild, grandparent, brother or sister of the manager;

    (b) he is the spouse of the manager or of any person connected with him by virtue of sub-paragraph (a) above;

    (c) he is the trustee of any trust, not being a charity, the beneficiaries or potential beneficiaries of which include the manager or any person connected with him by virtue of subparagraph (a) or (b) above and is acting in his capacity as such;

    (d) he is a partner of the manager or of any person connected with him by virtue of sub-paragraph (a), (b) or (c) above and is acting in his capacity as such; or

    (e) the person is a body corporate, not being a company which is connected with a charitable institution within the meaning of section 58(5) of the Charities Act 1992, in which the manager has, or the manager and any other manager or managers or person or persons connected with him by virtue of subparagraph (a), (b), (c) or (d) above, taken together, have, a substantial interest.

3. Any expression in paragraph 2 above which also appears in Schedule 5 to the 1993 Act shall be construed in accordance with paragraphs 2 to 4 of that Schedule.

[1] 1993 c.10; section 42 was amended by the Charities Act 1993 (Substitution of Sums) Order 1995 (S.I. 1995/2696) and section 45 was amended by section 29 of the Deregulation and Contracting Out Act 1994 (c.40) and by Part II of Schedule 1 to the Companies Act 1985 (Audit Exemption) Regulations 1994 (S.I. 1994/1935).

[2] 1986 c.53.

[3] 1987 c.22, as amended by the Banking Co-ordination (Second Council Directive) Regulations 1992 (S.I. 1992/3218).

Appendix 3 – The Charities Act 1993 (Substitution of Sums) Order 1995 (SI 1995 No 2696)

Made - - - -	*16th October 1995*
Laid before Parliament	*20th October 1995*
Coming into force:	
articles 1 and 2(1) and (2)	*1st December 1995*
remainder	*1st March 1996*

The Secretary of State, in pursuance of sections 5(6), 42(6) and 43(8) of the Charities Act 1993(**a**), hereby makes the following Order:

1. – (1) This Order may be cited as the Charities Act 1993 (Substitution of Sums) Order 1995.
   (2) This article and paragraphs (1) and (2) of article 2 of this Order shall come into force on 1st December 1995 and paragraphs (3) and (4) of article 2 of this Order shall come into force on 1st March 1996.

2. – (1) The Charities Act 1993 shall be amended in accordance with the following provisions of this article.
   (2) In subsection (1) of section 5 (status of registered charity (other than small charity) to appear on official publications etc.), for the sum of £5,000 there shall be substituted the sum of £10,000.
   (3) In subsection (3) of section 42 (annual statements of accounts), for the sum of £25,000 there shall be substituted the sum of £100,000.
   (4) In subsection (1) of section 43 (annual audit or examination of charity accounts), for the sum of £100,000 there shall be substituted the sum of £250,000.

Home Office	*Blatch*
16th October 1995	Minister of State

(**a**) 1993 c.10; section 43(8) was amended by section 28(3) of the Deregulation and Contracting Out Act 1994 (c.40).

Appendix 4 – Extract from the Charities Act 1993: Part VI Charity accounts, reports and returns*

PART VI

CHARITY ACCOUNTS, REPORTS AND RETURNS

Duty to keep accounting records

41.– (1) The charity trustees of a charity shall ensure that accounting records are kept in respect of the charity which are sufficient to show and explain all the charity's transactions, and which are such as to –

(a) disclose at any time, with reasonable accuracy, the financial position of the charity at that time, and

(b) enable the trustees to ensure that, where any statements of accounts are prepared by them under section 42(1) below, those statements of accounts comply with the requirements of regulations under that provision.

(2) The accounting records shall in particular contain –

(a) entries showing from day to day all sums of money received and expended by the charity, and the matters in respect of which the receipt and expenditure takes place; and

(b) a record of the assets and liabilities of the charity.

(3) The charity trustees of a charity shall preserve any accounting records made for the purposes of this section in respect of the charity for at least six years from the end of the financial year of the charity in which they are made.

(4) Where a charity ceases to exist within the period of six years mentioned in subsection (3) above as it applies to any accounting records, the obligation to preserve those records in accordance with that subsection shall continue to be discharged by the last charity trustees of the charity, unless the Commissioners consent in writing to the records being destroyed or otherwise disposed of.

(5) Nothing in this section applies to a charity which is a company.

---

* Where amendments have subsequently been made by statute a reference has been made in the text to the relevant appendix in this book, together with the section number of that appendix.

Annual statements of accounts

42. –(1) The charity trustees of a charity shall (subject to subsection (3) below) prepare in respect of each financial year of the charity a statement of accounts complying with such requirements as to its form and contents as may be prescribed by regulations made by the Secretary of State.

(2) Without prejudice to the generality of subsection (1) above, regulations under that subsection may make provision –

(a) for any such statement to be prepared in accordance with such methods and principles as are specified or referred to in the regulations;

(b) as to any information to be provided by way of notes to the accounts; and regulations under that subsection may also make provision for determining the financial years of a charity for the purposes of this Act and any regulations made under it.

(3) Where a charity's gross income in any financial year does not exceed £25,000, [see App. 3, s2(3)] the charity trustees may, in respect of that year, elect to prepare the following, namely –

(a) a receipts and payments account, and

(b) a statement of assets and liabilities, instead of a statement of accounts under subsection (1) above.

(4) The charity trustees of a charity shall preserve –

(a) any statement of accounts prepared by them under subsection (1) above, or

(b) any account and statement prepared by them under subsection (3) above, for at least six years from the end of the financial year to which any such statement relates or (as the case may be) to which any such account and statement relate.

(5) Subsection (4) of section 41 above shall apply in relation to the preservation of any such statement or account and statement as it applies in relation to the preservation of any accounting records (the references to subsection (3) of that section being read as references to subsection (4) above).

(6) The Secretary of State may by order amend subsection (3) above by substituting a different sum for the sum for the time being specified there.

(7) Nothing in this section applies to a charity which is a company.

Annual audit or examination of charity accounts

43.– (1) Subsection (2) below applies to a financial year of a charity ('the relevant year') if the charity's gross income or total expenditure in any of the following, namely –

(a)   the relevant year,

(b)   the financial year of the charity immediately preceding the relevant year (if any), and

(c)   the financial year of the charity immediately preceding the year specified in paragraph (b) above (if any), exceeds, £100,000. [see App. 3, s2(4).]

(2) If this subsection applies to a financial year of a charity, the accounts of the charity for that year shall be audited by a person who –

(a)   is, in accordance with section 25 of the Companies Act 1989 (eligibility for appointment), eligible for appointment as a company auditor, or

(b)   is a member of a body for the time being specified in regulations under section 44 below and is under the rules of that body eligible for appointment as auditor of the charity.

(3) If subsection (2) above does not apply to a financial year of a charity, [App. 6, s28(2)] then (subject to subsection (4) below) the accounts of the charity for that year shall, at the election of the charity trustees, either –

(a)   be examined by an independent examiner, that is to say an independent person who is reasonably believed by the trustees to have the requisite ability and practical experience to carry out a competent examination of the accounts, or

(b)   be audited by such a person as is mentioned in subsection (2) above.

(4) Where it appears to the Commissioners –

(a)   that subsection (2), or (as the case may be) subsection (3) above, has not been complied with in relation to a financial year of a charity within ten months from the end of that year, or

(b)   that, although subsection (2) above does not apply to a financial year of a charity, it would nevertheless be desirable for the accounts of the charity for that year to be audited by such a person as is mentioned in that subsection, the Commissioners may by order require the accounts of the charity for that year to be audited by such a person as is mentioned in that subsection.

(5) If the Commissioners make an order under subsection (4) above with respect to a charity, then unless –

(a)   the order is made by virtue of paragraph (b) of that subsection, and

(b)   the charity trustees themselves appoint an auditor in accordance with the order, the auditor shall be a person appointed by the Commissioners.

(6) The expenses of any audit carried out by an auditor appointed by the Commissioners under subsection (5) above, including the auditor's remuneration, shall be recoverable by the Commissioners –

    (a) from the charity trustees of the charity concerned, who shall be personally liable, jointly and severally, for those expenses; or

    (b) to the extent that it appears to the Commissioners not to be practical to seek recovery of those expenses in accordance with paragraph (a) above, from the funds of the charity.

(7) The Commissioners may –

    (a) give guidance to charity trustees in connection with the selection of a person for appointment as an independent examiner;

    (b) give such directions as they think. appropriate with respect to the carrying out of an examination in pursuance of subsection (3)(a) above; and any such guidance or directions may either be of general application or apply to a particular charity only.

(8) The Secretary of State may by order amend subsection (1) [see App. 6, s28(3)] above by substituting a different sum for the sum for the time being specified there.

(9) Nothing in this section applies to a charity which is a company.

Supplementary provisions relating to audits etc.

44. – (1) The Secretary of State may by regulations make provision –

    (a) specifying one or more bodies for the purposes of section 43(2)(b) above;

    (b) with respect to the duties of an auditor carrying out an audit under section 43 above, including provision with respect to the making by him of a report on –

        (i) the statement of accounts prepared for the financial year in question under section 42(1) above, or

        (ii) the account and statement so prepared under section 42(3) above, as the case may be;

    (c) with respect to the making by an independent examiner of a report in respect of an examination carried out by him under section 43 above;

    (d) conferring on such an auditor or on an independent examiner a right of access with respect to books, documents and other records (however kept) which relate to the charity concerned;

    (e) entitling such an auditor or an independent examiner to require, in the case of a charity, information and explanations from past or present charity trustees or

     trustees for the charity, or from past or present officers
     or employees of the charity;

  (f) enabling the Commissioners, in circumstances specified in
    the regulations, to dispense with the requirements of
    section 43(2) or (3) above in the case of a particular charity
    or in the case of any particular financial year of a charity.

 (2) If any person fails to afford an auditor or an independent examiner any facility to which he is entitled by virtue of subsection
   (1)(d) or (e) above, the Commissioners may by order give –

  (a) to that person, or

  (b) to the charity trustees for the time being of the charity
    concerned, such directions as the Commissioners think
    appropriate for securing that the default is made good.

 (3) Section 727 of the Companies Act 1985 (power of court to grant
   relief in certain cases) shall have effect in relation to an auditor
   or independent examiner appointed by a charity in pursuance of
   section 43 above as it has effect in relation to a person employed
   as auditor by a company within the meaning of that Act.

Annual reports

45. – (1) The charity trustees of a charity shall prepare in respect of each
   financial year of the charity an annual report containing –

  (a) such a report by the trustees on the activities of the charity
    during that year, and

  (b) such other information relating to the charity or to its trustees
    or officers, as may be prescribed by regulations made by the
    Secretary of State.

 (2) Without prejudice to the generality of subsection (1) above,
   regulations under that subsection may make provision –

  (a) for any such report as is mentioned in paragraph (a) of
    that subsection to be prepared in accordance with
    such principles as are specified or referred to in the
    regulations;

  (b) enabling the Commissioners to dispense with any require-
    ment prescribed by virtue of subsection (1)(b) above in
    the case of a particular charity or a particular class of char-
    ities, or in the case of a particular financial year of a charity
    or of any class of charities.

 (3) The annual report required to be prepared under this section in
   respect of any financial year of a charity [see App. 6, s29(1)] shall
   be transmitted to the Commissioners by the charity trustees –

  (a) within ten months from the end of that year, or

  (b) within such longer period as the Commissioners may for
    any special reason allow in the case of that report. [see
    App. 6, s29(2)]

(4)   Subject to subsection (5) below, any such annual report [see
        App. 6, s29(3)] shall have attached to it the statement of accounts
        prepared for the financial year in question under section 42(1)
        above or (as the case may be) the account and statement so pre-
        pared under section 42(3) above, together with –
        (a)   where the accounts of the charity for that year have been
                audited under section 43 above, a copy of the report made
                by the auditor on that statement of accounts or (as the case
                may be) on that account and statement;
        (b)   where the accounts of the charity for that year have been
                examined under section 43 above, a copy of the report
                made by the independent examiner in respect of the
                examination carried out by him under that section.

(5)   Subsection (4) above does not apply to a charity which is a
        company, and any annual report transmitted by the charity
        trustees of such a charity under subsection (3) [see App. 6,
        s29(4)] above shall instead have attached to it a copy of the
        charity's annual accounts prepared for the financial year in ques-
        tion under Part VII of the Companies Act 1985, together with a
        copy of the auditors' report [see App. 6, s6] on those accounts.

(6)   Any annual report transmitted to the Commissioners under
        subsection (3) above, [see App. 6, s29(5)] together with the
        documents attached to it, shall be kept by the Commissioners
        for such period as they think fit.

[see App. 6, s29(6)]

Special provision as respects accounts and annual reports of exempt and other excepted charities

46. –(1) Nothing in sections 41 to 45 above applies to any exempt charity;
        but the charity trustees of an exempt charity shall keep proper
        books of account with respect to the affairs of the charity, and if
        not required by or under the authority of any other Act to prepare
        periodical statements of account shall prepare consecutive state-
        ments of account consisting on each occasion of an income and
        expenditure account relating to a period of not more than fifteen
        months and a balance sheet relating to the end of that period.

    (2) The books of accounts and statements of account relating to an
        exempt charity shall be preserved for a period of six years at least
        unless the charity ceases to exist and the Commissioners consent
        in writing to their being destroyed or otherwise disposed of.

    (3) Nothing in sections 43 to 45 above applies to any charity
        which –
        (a)   falls within section 3(5)(c) above, and
        (b)   is not registered.

(4) Except in accordance with subsection (7) below, nothing in section 45 above applies to any charity (other than an exempt charity or a charity which falls within section 3(5)(c) above) which –

   (a) is excepted by section 3(5) above, and

   (b) is not registered.

(5) If requested to do so by the Commissioners, the charity trustees of any such charity as is mentioned in subsection (4) above shall prepare an annual report in respect of such financial year of the charity as is specified in the Commissioners' request.

(6) Any report prepared under subsection (5) above shall contain –

   (a) such a report by the charity trustees on the activities of the charity during the year in question, and

   (b) such other information relating to the charity or to its trustees or officers, as may be prescribed by regulations made under section 45(1) above in relation to annual reports prepared under that provision.

(7) Subsections (3) to (6) of section 45 above shall apply to any report required to be prepared under subsection (5) above as if it were an annual report required to be prepared under subsection (1) of that section.

(8) Any reference in this section to a charity which falls within section 3(5)(c) above includes a reference to a charity which falls within that provision but is also excepted from registration by section 3(5)(b) above.

Public inspection of annual reports etc.

47. – (1) Any annual report or other document kept by the Commissioners in pursuance of section 45(6) above shall be open to public inspection at all reasonable times –

   (a) during the period for which it is so kept; or

   (b) if the Commissioners so determine, during such lesser period as they may specify.

(2) Where any person –

   (a) requests the charity trustees of a charity in writing to provide him with a copy of the charity's most recent accounts, and

   (b) pays them such reasonable fee (if any) as they may require in respect of the costs of complying with the request, those trustees shall comply with the request within the period of two months beginning with the date on which it is made.

(3) In subsection (2) above the reference to a charity's most recent accounts is –

(a)   [see App. 6, Sch 12(a)] in the case of a charity other than one falling within any of paragraphs (b) to (d) below, a reference to the statement of accounts or account and statement prepared in pursuance of section 42(1) or (3) above in respect of the last financial year of the charity the accounts for which have been audited or examined under section 43 above;

(b)   in the case of [see App. 6, Sch 12(b)] such a charity as is mentioned in section 46(3) above, a reference to the statement of accounts or account and statement prepared in pursuance of section 42(1) or (3) above in respect of the last financial year of the charity in respect of which a statement of accounts or account and statement has or have been so prepared;

(c)   [see App. 5, s7] in the case of a charity which is a company, a reference to the annual accounts of the company most recently audited under Part VII of the Companies Act 1985; and

(d)   in the case of an exempt charity, a reference to the accounts of the charity most recently audited in pursuance of any statutory or other requirement or, if its accounts are not required to be audited, the accounts most recently prepared in respect of the charity.

Annual returns by registered charities

48. – (1) [see App. 3, s30(2)] Every registered charity shall prepare in respect of each of its financial years an annual return in such form, and containing such information, as may be prescribed by regulations made by the Commissioners. [see App. 3, s30(3)]

(2) Any such return shall be transmitted to the Commissioners by the date by which the charity trustees are, by virtue of section 45(3) above, required to transmit to them the annual report required to be prepared in respect of the financial year in question.

(3) The Commissioners may dispense with the requirements of subsection (1) above in the case of a particular charity or a particular class of charities, or in the case of a particular financial year of a charity or of any class of charities.

[see App. 3, s30(4)]

Offences

49. Any person who, without reasonable excuse, is persistently in default in relation to any requirement imposed –

(a) by section 45(3) [see App. 3, s29(8)] above (taken with section 45(4) or (5), as the case may require), or

(b) by section 47(2) or 48(2) above, shall be guilty of an offence and liable on summary conviction to a fine not exceeding level 4 on the standard scale.

Appendix 5 – Extract from The Companies Act 1985 (Audit Exemption) Regulations 1994 (SI 1994 No 1935)

SCHEDULE 1
CONSEQUENTIAL AMENDMENTS
OF ENACTMENTS

PART II
AMENDMENTS OF CHARITIES ACT 1993

6. In section 45 of the Charities Act 1993(**e**) (annual reports), in subsection (5), for the words 'the auditors' report' there shall be substituted the words 'any auditors' report or report made for the purposes of section 249A(2) of that Act'.

7. In section 47 of that Act (public inspection of annual reports etc.), in subsection (3) for paragraph (c) there shall be substituted the following paragraph –

'(c) in the case of a charity which is a company, a reference to the most recent annual accounts of the company prepared under Part VII of the Companies Act 1985 in relation to which any of the following conditions is satisfied –
(i)   they have been audited;
(ii) a report required for the purposes of section 249A(2) of that Act has been made in respect of them; or
(iii) they relate to a year in respect of which the company is exempt from audit by virtue of section 249A(1) of that Act; and'.

(**e**) 1993 c. 10.

Appendix 6 – Extracts from The Deregulation and Contracting Out Act 1994: sections 28 to 30 and from Schedules 11 and 17

Annual audit or examination of charity accounts

28. – (1) Section 43 of the Charities Act 1993 (annual audit or examination of charity accounts) shall be amended as follows.

(2) In subsection (3) (which requires a charity's accounts for a financial year to be audited or independently examined if its gross income and total expenditure in that year, and each of the two previous financial years, is £100,000 or less) after 'a charity' there shall be inserted 'and its gross income or total expenditure in that year exceeds £10,000'.

(3) In subsection (8) (power of Secretary of State to amend sum specified in subsection (I)) after '(1)' there shall be inserted 'or (3)'.

Annual reports of charities

29. – (1) In section 45 of the Charities Act 1993 (annual reports) in subsection (3) (automatic duty to transmit annual report to the Commissioners) for the words from the beginning to 'a charity' there shall be substituted 'Where in any financial year of a charity its gross income or total expenditure exceeds £10,000, the annual report required to be prepared under this section in respect of that year'.

(2) After that subsection there shall be inserted –

'(3A) Where in any financial year of a charity neither its gross income nor its total expenditure exceeds £10,000, the annual report required to be prepared under this section in respect of that year shall, if the Commissioners so request, be transmitted to them by the charity trustees –

(a) in the case of a request made before the end of seven months from the end of the financial year to which the report relates, within ten months from the end of that year, and

(b) in the case of a request not so made, within three months from the date of the request, or, in either case, within such longer period as the Commissioners may for any special reason allow in the case of that report.'

(3) In subsection (4) of that section, for 'any such annual report' there shall be substituted 'any annual report transmitted to the Commissioners under this section'.
(4) In subsection (5) of that section, for 'subsection (3) above' there shall be substituted 'this section'.
(5) In subsection (6) of that section, for 'subsection (3) above' there shall be substituted 'this section'.
(6) At the end of that section there shall be inserted –

'(7) The charity trustees of a charity shall preserve, for at least six years from the end of the financial year to which it relates, any annual report prepared by them under subsection (1) above which they have not been required to transmit to the Commissioners.
(8) Subsection (4) of section 41 above shall apply in relation to the preservation of any such annual report as it applies in relation to the preservation of any accounting records (the references in subsection (3) of that section being read as references to subsection (7) above).
(9) The Secretary of State may by order amend subsection (3) or (3A) above by substituting a different sum for the sum for the time being specified there'.

(7) In section 46(7) of that Act (application of section 45(3) to (6) to annual reports under section 46(5)) after 'section 45' there shall be inserted '(as originally enacted)'.
(8) In section 49 of that Act (penalty for persistent default in relation to certain requirements) in paragraph (a), after '45(3)' there shall be inserted 'or (3A)'.

Annual returns by charities

30. – (1) Section 48 of the Charities Act 1993 (annual returns by registered charities) shall be amended as follows.
(2) In subsection (1) (duty to prepare annual return) at the beginning there shall be inserted 'Subject to subsection (1A) below,'.
(3) After subsection (1) there shall be inserted –

'(1A) Subsection (1) above shall not apply in relation to any financial year of a charity in which neither the gross income nor the total expenditure of the charity exceeds £10,000.'

(4) At the end there shall be inserted –

'(4) The Secretary of State may by order amend subsection (lA) above by substituting a different sum for the sum for the time being specified there.'

SCHEDULE II

Charities Act 1993 (c. 10)

12. In section 47(3) of the Charities Act 1993 –

(a) paragraph (a) shall be omitted, and
(b) in paragraph (b), for the words from 'such' to '46(3) above' there shall be substituted 'a charity other than one falling within paragraph (c) or (d) below'.

SCHEDULE 17

Chapter or Number	Title	Extent of repeal
1992 c. 41.	The Charities Act 1992.	Section 67(3)(b) and the word 'but' immediately preceding it.
1993 c. 10.	The Charities Act 1993.	Section 47(3)(a).

Appendix 7 – section 505 ICTA 1988

505. Charities: general

(1) Subject to subsections (2) and (3) below, the following exemptions shall be granted on a claim in that behalf to the Board –

[(a) exemption from tax under Schedules A and D in respect of any profits or gains arising in respect of rents or other receipts from an estate, interest or right in or over any land (whether situated in the United Kingdom or elsewhere) to the extent that the profits or gains –

    (i) arise in respect of rents or receipts from an estate, interest or right vested in any person for charitable purposes; and

    (ii) are applied to charitable purposes only;][5]

(b)...[1]

(c) exemption –

    (i)...[6]

    [(ii) from tax under Case IV or V of Schedule D in respect of income eqivalent to income chargeable under Case III of that Schedule but arising from securities or other possessions outside the United Kingdom,

    [(iia) from tax under Case V of Schedule D in respect of income consisting in any such dividend or other distribution of a company not resident in the United Kingdom as would be chargeable to tax under Schedule F if the company were so resident, and][5]

    (iii) from tax under Schedule F in respect of any distribution,

where the income in question forms part of the income of a charity, or is, according to rules or regulations established by Act of Parliament, charter, decree, deed of trust or will, applicable to charitable purposes only, and so far as it is applied to charitable purposes only;

[(d) exemption from tax under Schedule D in respect of public revenue dividends on securities which are in the name of trustees, to the extent that the dividends are applicable and applied only for the repair of –

    (i) any cathedral, college, church of chapel, or

    (ii) any building used for the purposes of divine worship;][6]

(e) exemption from tax under Schedule D in respect of the profits of any trade carried on by a charity [(whether in the United Kingdom or elsewhere)][5], if the profits are applied solely to the purposes of the charity and either –

(i)   the trade is exercised in the course of the actual carrying out of a primary purpose of the charity; or

(ii)   the work in connection with the trade is mainly carried out by beneficiaries of the charity.

[(f)   exemption from tax under Schedule D in respect of profits accruing to a charity from a lottery if –

(i)   the lottery is promoted and conducted in accordance with section 3 or 5 of the Lotteries and Amusements (Northern Ireland) Order 1985; and

(ii)   the profits are applied solely to the charity's purposes.][3]

[(1A) In subsection (1)(d) above 'public revenue dividends' means –

(a)   income from securities which is payable out of the public revenue of the United Kingdom or Northern Ireland;

(b)   income from securities issued by or on behalf of a government or a public or local authority in a country outside the United Kingdom.][6]

(2) Any payment which –

(a)   is received by a charity from another charity; and

(b)   is not made for full consideration in money or money's worth; and

(c)   is not chargeable to tax apart from this subsection; and

(d)   is not, apart from this subsection, of a description which (on a claim) would be eligible for relief from tax by virtue of any provision of subsection (1) above;

shall be chargeable to tax under Case III of Schedule D but shall be eligible for relief from tax under subsection (1)(c) above as if it were an annual payment.

(3) If in any chargeable period of a charity –

(a)   its relevant income and gains are not less than £10,000; and

(b)   its relevant income and gains exceed the amount of its qualifying expenditure; and

(c)   the charity incurs, or is treated as incurring, non-qualifying expenditure;

relief shall not be available under either subsection (1) above or section [256 of the 1992 Act][2] for so much of the excess as does not exceed the non-qualifying expenditure incurred in that period.

(4) In relation to a chargeable period of less than 12 months, subsection (3) above shall have effect as if the amount specified in paragraph (a) of that subsection were proportionately reduced.

(5) In subsection (3) above 'relevant income and gains' means –

(a)   income which apart from subsection (1) above would not be exempt from tax together with any income which is taxable notwithstanding that subsection; and

(b) gains which apart from section [256 of the 1992 Act][2] would be chargeable gains together with any gains which are chargeable gains notwithstanding that section.

(6) Where by virtue of subsection (3) above there is an amount of a charity's relevant income and gains for which relief under subsection (1) above and section [256 of the 1992 Act][2] is not available, the charity may, by notice to the Board, specify which items of its relevant income and gains are, in whole or in part, to be attributed to that amount ...[7]; and if within 30 days of being required to do so by the Board, a charity does not give notice under this subsection, the items of its relevant income and gains which are to be attributed to the amount in question shall be such as the Board may determine.

(7) Where it appears to the Board that two or more charities acting in concert are engaged in transactions of which the main purpose or one of the main purposes is the avoidance of tax (whether by the charities or by any other person), the Board may by notice given to the charities provide that, for such chargeable periods as may be specified in the notice, subsection (3) above shall have effect in relation to them with the omission of paragraph (a).

(8) An appeal may be brought against a notice under subsection (7) above as if it were notice of the decision of the Board on a claim made by the charities concerned.

---

1. Subs(1)(b) repealed by FA 1988 Sch 14 Pt V.
2. Words in subss(3), (5)(b), (6) substituted by TCGA 1992 Sch 10 paras 14(1), (31).
3. Subs(1)(f) inserted by FA 1995 s138(1), (2) with effect for chargeable periods beginning, in the case of a company, after 31 March 1995, and in any other case, after 5 April 1995.
4. Words in subs(6) substituted by FA 1995 s74(2), Sch 17 Pt II, para 7, with effect from the year 1995–96 (and apply to every settlement, wherever and whenever made or entered into).
5. Subs(1)(a) and subs(1)(c)(ii), (iia), (iib) substituted (latter for subs(1)(c)(ii)) and words in subs(1)(e) inserted by FA 1996 s146 with effect for the purposes of income tax from the year 1996–97 and for the purposes of corporation tax for accounting periods after 31 March 1996.
6. Subs(1)(c)(I) repealed, subs(1)(d) is substituted and subs(1A) inserted by FA 1996 Sch 7 para 19, Sch 41 Pt V(2) with effect as respects income tax from the year 1996–97, and for the purposes of corporation tax, for accounting periods ending after 31 March 1996.
7. Words in subs(6) repealed by FA 2000 ss41(5), (9), 156, Sch 40 Pt II(1) with effect for covenanted payments falling to be made by individuals after 5 April 2000 or made by companies after 31 March 2000.

Appendix 8 – Extra-statutory concessions

C4 More charity fund-raising events exempted from tax – revised extra statutory concession

More charity fund-raising events than before will be exempt from income and corporation tax following a revised Extra Statutory Concession published by the Inland Revenue today.

The revised ESC C4 will exempt the profits of events run by a charity or voluntary organisation to raise funds for charity which fall within the VAT exemption for fund-raising events.

The VAT exemption is being extended from 1 April 2000 to include:

- up to fifteen events of the same kind at the same location in any financial year; and
- any number of events of the same type, where the gross weekly takings do not exceed £1,000.
- The text of the revised ESC C4 is attached.

Details

1. The revised ESC C4 is part of the Getting Britain Giving measures announced by the Chancellor, Gordon Brown, in his Pre-Budget Report of 9 November 1999 and his Budget Statement of 21 March 2000. It aligns the direct tax exemption with the new, extended VAT exemption for charity fund-raising events. As a result, exemption will in future be available for a wider range of events and charities will no longer have to operate two sets of rules and deal with two Government departments.
2. Details of the VAT exemption are contained in the VAT (Fund-raising by charities and other qualifying bodies) Order 2000 laid by HM Customs & Excise on Budget Day. Although the direct tax relief applies only to charities or voluntary organisations raising funds for charity, the VAT relief covers charities, their wholly owned trading companies, and certain other qualifying bodies specified in VAT law. Customs & Excise will be publishing a draft public notice on the exemption on their website (www.hmce.gov.uk). www.inlandrevenue.gov.uk

Appendix 9 – Statement of practice

SP 3/87 (26 March 1987) Repayment of tax to charities on covenanted and other income

1. FA 1986 contains provisions designed to deal with certain abuses of the tax reliefs for charities. These include a requirement that tax should in all cases be deducted at source from covenant payments by companies to charities FA 1986, s30(2) inserting ICTA 1970, s248(8a), now ICTA 1988, s339(7). Charities are entitled to claim repayment of the tax, provided that they meet the conditions for tax exemption on their income.

2. This statement describes the procedure which the Revenue are adopting in order to minimise any delay in making repayments of tax to charities. Paragraphs 3-8 deal with the particular case of 'profit-shedding' covenants. Paragraph 9 makes it clear that the same principles will be applied to other repayment claims by charities.

Profit-shedding covenants

3. Many charities set up subsidiary companies to carry on fund-raising activities. The profits of such a subsidiary are usually covenanted to the charity, relieving the subsidiary of its corporation tax liabilities. Prior to FA 1986, many of those companies were, under the group relief rules, able to make such covenant payments gross, so that it was unnecessary for the charity to claim repayment.

4. Under ICTA 1988, s505(2), however, such payments are now required to be made under deduction of tax at source. The charity will thus have received income under deduction of tax and will qualify for repayment of the tax if it is otherwise eligible for tax exemption under the normal rules.

5. In examining claims for repayment it is the Revenue's practice in appropriate cases to verify, by reference to the tax records of the person making the payment, that the amount claimed is correct and that the tax deducted from the payment has, where necessary, been accounted for. This can take some time.

6. In order to minimise any cash flow disadvantage for charities while awaiting repayment, the Revenue are prepared to repay provisionally the tax

apparently suffered without awaiting the results of the verification process described above, provided that –

(a) the identity of the charity and the subsidiary, and their relationship to each other, are all well known in advance of the claim; and

(b) the Revenue are satisfied that the affairs of the charity are otherwise in order, and

(c) the repayment claim is not otherwise likely materially to exceed the amount ultimately due.

7. In order to obtain corporation tax relief, the subsidiary company must make its payment during the accounting period in which the profits arise, even though the true profit for corporation tax purposes may not be known for some months after the end of that period. Most companies therefore make a payment which to some extent exceeds the likely profit, accounting for tax on the full amount and adjusting the payments later.

8. It follows that, when the verification referred to above is complete, the tax paid over by the subsidiary, and the tax repayment made to the charity, may prove to be excessive. The Revenue will in such cases have power, under the provisions of TMA 1970, s30 (as amended by FA 1982, s149) to recover the over-repayment from the charity by assessment. In practice, however, unless the amount over-repaid is significant in relation to the sum claimed, it will normally be collected from subsequent repayment claims. Similarly the excess paid over by the subsidiary will be repaid to it by the inspector or set against any other tax liabilities.

Other income

9. Similar procedures for provisional repayment of tax and verification of claims will be adopted, so far as appropriate, where charities receive other income under deduction of tax, for example from other covenanted donations or from investments.

Appendix 10 – Deeds of covenant model versions approved by the Inland Revenue

Version 'A'

[Form of covenant by an individual to a charity for use in England and Wales from 31 July 1990]

DEED OF COVENANT

	Notes
To	
[Name of Charity]	
I promise to pay you for ......years, or until I die if earlier,	1
such a sum as after deduction of income tax at the basic rate	
amounts to	
£	2
each [week] [month] [quarter] [year]	3
from [the date shown below] [....]	4
Signed and delivered	5
Date	
Full Name	
Address	

Witnessed by:
Signed ....

Full Name ....

Address ....

Notes
1 Enter the period of the covenant, which must be longer than *three* years.
2 Enter the amount you will be paying to the charity.
3 Delete as appropriate to show how often you will make the payment.
4 Delete as apropriate. If you choose to enter an actual date *it must not be earlier than the date you sign the deed.*
5 You must sign the form and enter the date you actually sign it in the presence of the witness, who should also sign where shown.

465

Appendix 11 – section 256 TCGA 1992

CHARITIES AND GIFTS OF NON-BUSINESS ASSETS ETC.

256 Charities

(1) Subject to section 505(3) of the Taxes Act and subsection (2) below, a gain shall not be a chargeable gain if it accrues to a charity and is applicable and applied for charitable purposes.

(2) If property held on charitable trusts ceases to be subject to charitable trusts –

    (a) the trustees shall be treated as if they had disposed of, and immediately reacquired, the property for a consideration equal to its market value, any gain on the disposal being treated as not accruing to a charity, and

    (b) if and so far as any of that property represents, directly or indirectly, the consideration for the disposal of assets by the trustees, any gain accruing on that disposal shall be treated as not having accrued to a charity,

and an assessment to capital gains tax chargeable by virtue of paragraph (b) above may be made at any time not more than 3 years after the end of the year of assessment in which the property ceases to be subject to charitable trusts.

Appendix 12 – Model Gift Aid Declaration

Gift Aid declaration

Name of Charity ....

Details of donor ....

Title .... Forename(s) .... Surname ....

Address ....

....

.... Post Code ....

I want the charity to treat

    * the enclosed donation of £ ....

    * the donation(s) of £ .... which I made on ..../..../........

    * all donations I make from the date of this declaration until
    I notify you otherwise

    *all donations I have made since 6 April 2000, and all
    donations I make from the date of this declaration until I
    notify you otherwise

as Gift Aid donations.

*NB. Charities do not have to include all these statements on their declarations,
but can choose whichever is appropriate.*

See overleaf for notes

Notes

1. **You must pay an amount of income tax and/or capital gains tax at least equal to the tax that the charity reclaims on your donations in the tax year (currently 28p for each £1 you give).**
2. You can cancel this declaration at any time by notifying the charity.
3. If in the future your circumstances change and you no longer pay tax on your income and capital gains equal to the tax that the charity reclaims, you can cancel your declaration (see note 1).
4. If you pay tax at the higher rate you can claim further tax relief in your Self-Assessment tax return.
5. If you are unsure whether your donations qualify for Gift Aid tax relief, ask the charity. Or ask your local tax office for leaflet IR 65.
6. Please notify the charity if you change your name or address.

CHARITY X: SPONSORSHIP AND GIFT AID DECLARATION FORM

We, who have given our names and addresses below, and who have ticked the box entitled '(??) Gift Aid?', want the above charity to reclaim tax on the donation detailed below, given on the date shown. We understand that each of us must pay income tax or capital gains tax equal to the tax reclaimed by the charity on the donation.

Full name	Address	Post code	Amount pledged	Amount given	Date given (dd/mm/yy)	Gift Aid? (??)

Total donations: £

To be completed by the charity:

Date sumes collected passed to charity:

Total income tax to be reclaimed on above donations: £.

Index

References are to paragraph number.
Abbreviations:
   Ann – Annex
   App – Appendix
Legal cases and titles of documents referred to in the text are indicated in italic.

471